W9-BKU-532

EXPLORE AMERICA

EXPLORE AMERICA

Tours of discovery through our magnificent country

© Avenues, Inc.

All rights reserved. Except for use in any review, the reproduction or utilization of this work in whole or in part in any form by any electronic, mechanical or other means, now known or hereafter invented including xerography, photocopying and recording, or in any information storage or retrieval system, is forbidden without the permission of the Publisher, Avenues, Inc., 300 East 42nd Street, New York, New York 10017.

All information in the text of this volume has been compiled by the Publisher and is, to the best of its knowledge, accurate. Notwithstanding the foregoing, neither the Publisher nor the American Automobile Association shall be liable for any errors or omissions inadvertently herein contained.

R: Trademark(s) used under license and registered in the United States Patent and Trademark Office and in other countries.

ISBN: 1-55001-140-5

Written by Richard Marshall

Designed and edited by Marshall Editions

Publisher:	**Bruce Marshall**
Editorial Director:	**Ruth Binney**
Editor:	**Maggi McCormick**
Assistant Editor:	**Lindsay McTeague**
Contributing Editors:	**Beverly LeBlanc**
	Barbara Newman
Contributors:	**Judith Beadle**
	Michael Crossman
	Frances Jones
	Kathleen M. Kiely
	Gwen Rigby
Art Director:	**John Bigg**
Art Editor:	**Eddie Poulton**
Design Assistant:	**Katherine Harkness**
Picture Editor:	**Zilda Tandy**
Picture Researchers:	**Pat Hodgson**
	Judy Lehane
	Elizabeth Loving
	Richard Philpott
Production:	**Barry Baker**
	Janice Storr
Avenues, Inc.:	**Stuart Campbell**
	Donna Hayes
	Bryan Weaver
	Mark Mailman
	Thomas Burnside
	Candy Lee
Avenues, Inc. Production:	**Angela Meredith**
American Automobile Association:	**Alex Gamble**

Maps by Oxford Cartographers

Printed in America

ILLUSTRATION CAPTIONS

Page 1: Queens Gardens, Bryce Canyon National Park, Utah

Previous page: Durant Lake and Blue Mountain, Adirondack Mountains, New York

This page: Independence Hall, Philadelphia, Pennsylvania

Overleaf: Fishing at dawn

FOREWORD

To travel is to be free, to seek special places that refresh and renew us.

America offers more special places than you could ever know. *Explore America* will bring them to you.

AAA's travel experts have picked 144 touring areas across the country, each with its own character and beauty. They have written of the areas, their people, and their traditions. And they have included maps and lists of things to see.

Open the pages of *Explore America* and dream of adventure. Open your imagination and witness the vastness of our land.

Marvel at lakes bigger than some countries, deserts filled with barren beauty, forests of unending green, and beaches that stretch for miles. Feel the wind-whipped coldness of Montana's Glacier National Park or the steamy mystery of the Florida Everglades.

Meet the people of America as well. Visit the hardworking Amish who tend their farms in Pennsylvania, the Cajuns of Louisiana, and the shipwrights of Connecticut who craft magnificent vessels in the style of their ancestors.

Find a special place of your own in *Explore America*. Let it fill you with appreciation for the country we share. Then let it help you begin your adventure.

DIRECTOR OF PUBLICATIONS

American Automobile Association

CONTENTS

HOW TO USE THIS BOOK

Explore America is designed to give modern-day explorers an inkling of some of the fascinating places to see in our great country. The author and editors agree that, wherever you go in the United States, there is probably something to see and do, some site to visit, some wild place to explore. Because of the limited space available, the following pages can give only a sample of the vast choice—no doubt travelers in all these areas will find other things to interest and excite them. *Explore America* will, we hope, point the way.

Explore America is divided into eleven chapters, each a different area of the country. Each chapter begins with a map of the region; the individual tours are highlighted in yellow.

Each individual touring region or city contains a number of features to help you in your travels. The **main introduction** is designed to set the scene and place you, geographically speaking, in the area, which is detailed on a specific **locator map** on the page. The maps show towns, cities, and places of interest mentioned in the text. They include major highways and interstates, plus state and local roads that you can use to find your way to the places

mentioned. To make the maps as easy to read as possible, some places which are not mentioned in the text are not included on the maps. The **map legend** explains the information on the maps.

The photographs have been chosen for their breath-taking beauty as well as the interest and importance of each place shown in the pictures. Every attempt has been made to include as much information as possible about each illustration in the captions.

The **Sites to See** listings highlight some of the more interesting or unusual places in the region which are open to the public, but for reasons of space, no specific information, such as opening hours, prices, etc., has been included.

Each chapter has been **color-coded** in the contents on pages 6 and 7; the strip of color on the top right-hand corner of each double-page spread is printed with the name of the state and will tell you at a glance the area of the country in which that place is located.

An index is located at the back of the book.

Happy Trails!

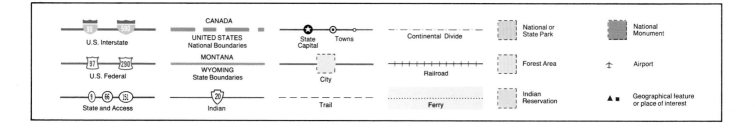

MAIN CHAPTERS

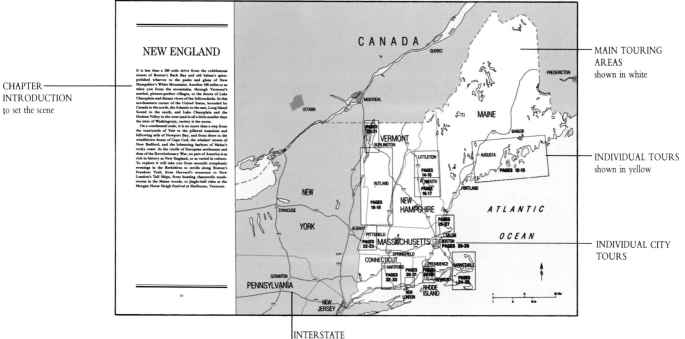

CHAPTER
INTRODUCTION
to set the scene

MAIN TOURING
AREAS
shown in white

INDIVIDUAL TOURS
shown in yellow

INDIVIDUAL CITY
TOURS

INTERSTATE
HIGHWAYS

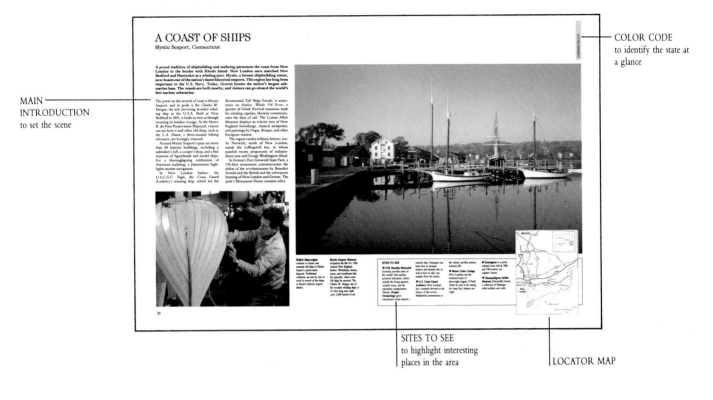

A COAST OF SHIPS
Mystic Seaport, Connecticut

MAIN INTRODUCTION to set the scene

COLOR CODE to identify the state at a glance

CONNECTICUT

SITES TO SEE to highlight interesting places in the area

LOCATOR MAP

CITIES

BOSTON

MAIN INTRODUCTION to set the scene

SITES TO SEE to highlight place of special interest

MAP

KEY to help locate the Sites to See

NEW ENGLAND

It is less than a 200 mile drive from the cobblestone streets of Boston's Back Bay and old Salem's spice-polished wharves to the peaks and glens of New Hampshire's White Mountains. Another 100 miles or so takes you from the mountains, through Vermont's nestled, picture-perfect villages, to the shores of Lake Champlain and distant views of the Adirondacks. In this northeastern corner of the United States, bounded by Canada to the north, the Atlantic to the east, Long Island Sound to the south, and Lake Champlain and the Hudson Valley to the west (and in all a little smaller than the state of Washington), variety is the norm.

On a continental scale, it is no more than a step from the courtyards of Yale to the pillared mansions and billowing sails of Newport Bay, and from there to the windblown dunes of Cape Cod, the whalers' streets of New Bedford, and the lobstering harbors of Maine's rocky coast. As the cradle of European settlement and then of the Revolutionary War, no part of America is as rich in history as New England, or as varied in culture. To explore it will take you from moonlit symphonic evenings in the Berkshires to strolls along Boston's Freedom Trail, from Harvard's museums to New London's Tall Ships, from hunting chanterelle mushrooms in the Maine woods, to jingle-bell rides at the Morgan Horse Sleigh Festival at Shelburne, Vermont.

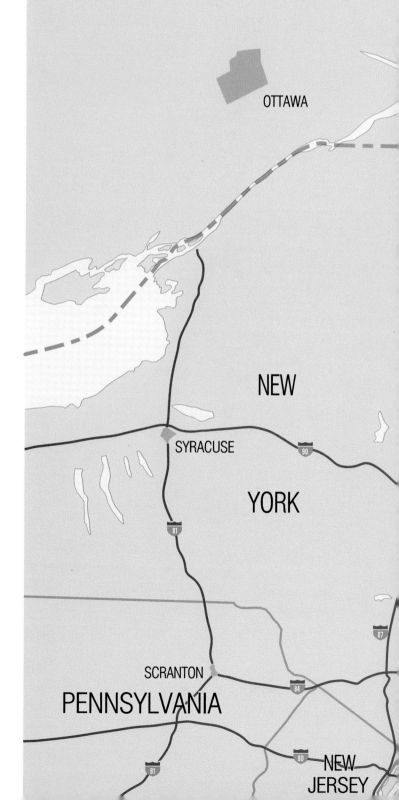

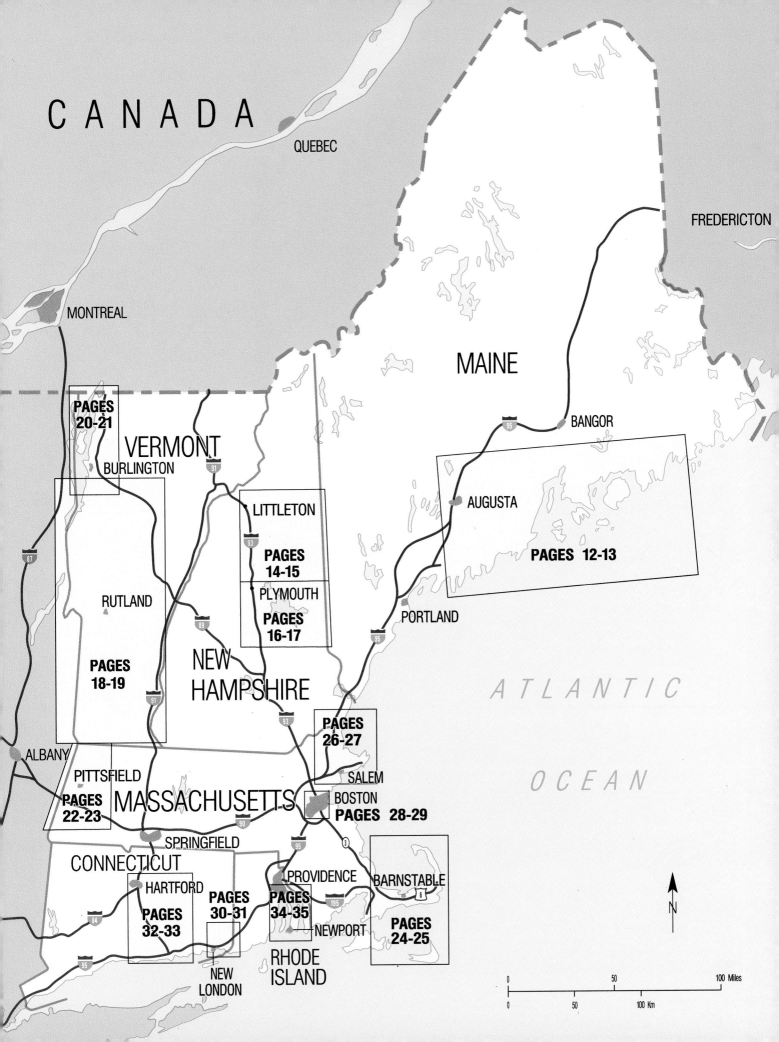

CANADA

QUEBEC

FREDERICTON

MONTREAL

MAINE

BANGOR

**PAGES
20-21**

VERMONT

BURLINGTON

AUGUSTA

LITTLETON

PAGES 12-13

**PAGES
14-15**

RUTLAND

PLYMOUTH

**PAGES
16-17**

PORTLAND

**PAGES
18-19**

NEW
HAMPSHIRE

ATLANTIC

ALBANY

**PAGES
26-27**

PITTSFIELD

SALEM

OCEAN

**PAGES
22-23**

MASSACHUSETTS

Boston

PAGES 28-29

SPRINGFIELD

CONNECTICUT

Providence

BARNSTABLE

HARTFORD

**PAGES
30-31**

**PAGES
34-35**

**PAGES
32-33**

NEWPORT

**PAGES
24-25**

NEW
LONDON

RHODE
ISLAND

N

0   50   100 Miles

0   50   100 Km

MAINE'S ROCKY SHORE

Maine Coast and Mount Desert Island

Some of the finest coastal scenery in the United States lies between Boothbay Harbor in southern Maine and Mount Desert Island to the north. Here Rte. One hugs the coast, skirting deep inlets carved by the glaciers that covered the area 10,000 years ago. In the region's cobbled, tree-shaded coastal towns, with their whitewashed homes and granite harbor walls polished by generations of Yankee elbows, the picturesque is commonplace.

Northerliness and the sea's cold tooth have etched the Maine coast with a fretwork of bays, inlets, and peninsulas. On a smaller scale, islands, rockpools, chasms, even the feathering spray and endless eddies of sand and water, repeat the enchanting filigree, the terms in the ancient debate between the land and sea.

The first European settlement here dates from the 17th century at Pemaquid Point, south of Damariscotta, where the Abnaki Indians once gathered freshwater clams. Colonial Pemaquid is now a State Historic Site. It has been excavated, and artifacts found here are displayed at the museum. At the Maine Maritime Museum in nearby Bath, you can see how the descendants of those hard-working first colonists made their living: summer visitors can tour the old Grand Banks schooner *Sherman Zwicker*, and see other evidence, lovingly preserved, of the area's shipbuilding and lobstering heritage. In the shipyard, traditional skills for building and repairing the old craft are taught. Boothbay Harbor, on the next inlet to the east, is still home to the 1822 Burnt Island Light Station, and to one of the coast's fishing fleets. Boats lie at anchor along wharves that follow the town's narrow, winding streets.

If you decide to make your own voyage on these blue-green waters, a ferry will take you from Port Clyde to the cliffs of Monhegan Island, the highest on the New England coast. Its harbor is busy with fishing and pleasure boats, its nature preserve aburst with spring and summer wildflowers. This wild beauty led to the establishment of an "artists' colony" in the late 1800s, and there are still many working studios. Or, from Rockland, one of the state's fishing ports, you can take a ferry across Penobscot Bay to Vinalhaven, formerly one of the nation's leading centers of granite quarrying. The abandoned quarries are now swimming holes and trout pools, and part of the island is now a wildlife refuge.

On Mount Desert Island, the site of Acadia National Park, some of the 19th century's most affluent citizens built summer homes that they insisted on calling "cottages," in spite of the fact that some of them had 100 rooms or more. The rare combination of coastal and mountain beauty that lured them to this wilderness, which the first settlers called Eden, is best enjoyed by taking the Park Loop Road. On its way to Cadillac Mountain (where dawn first touches the United States and arctic flowers grow), it passes Great Head, one of the mightiest cliffs on the Atlantic, and Thunder Hole, a chasm where the breaking sea can roar like a stormy sky.

Camden (*above*) Tree-lined streets, clapboard houses, and a picturesque harbor have made Camden one of Maine's most visited towns. The Old Conway House and Museum, an 18th-century farmstead, preserves a herb garden and antique farm equipment. Nearby Camden Hills State Park offers panoramic views across the town to Penobscot Bay and Vinalhaven.

Scallop Boat, Boothbay Harbor (*left*) Boat-building and fishing are Maine's ancient livelihood; Boothbay Harbor shelters one of the coast's larger fishing fleets.

SITES TO SEE

● **Southwest Harbor** is everyone's idea of what a charming Maine fishing village should look like; half the town is actually within Acadia National Park. **The Wendell Gilley Museum** has 200 bird carvings and a resident wood carver who gives demonstrations. **The Mount Desert Oceanarium** has live animals in touch tanks and interesting exhibits dealing with tides, whales, navigation, and other coastal topics.

● **Shore Village Museum** (Rockland) contains Coast Guard memorabilia, dolls with costumes from 1399, and a Civil War uniform and weapon collection.

● **Searsport**, a major port and shipbuilding center, is a popular stop for antique collectors. **The Penobscot Marine Museum** has a fine collection of model ships, nautical paintings, sailing memorabilia, and 7 buildings, including the first town hall and a sea captain's house.

● **Blue Hill** is a craft center with several potteries that welcome visitors. There are wonderful views of Mt. Desert Island from the top of 934-foot Blue Hill. Blue Hill Days, featuring a traditional lobster dinner, are held on a weekend in late July or early August. The Blue Hill Fair is held Labor Day weekend.

● **Vinalhaven Island** is reached by ferry from Rockland; the trip takes about 1 hour. Here, old quarries are now flooded and used as swimming pools and trout ponds.

● **Wiscasset** claims to be the home of American ice cream, first served to Gen. Lafayette in 1825. This is a picturesque town with 18th- and 19th-century mansions. The **Castle Tucker House Museum**, built 1807, includes Victorian furnishings and paintings. The **Nickles-Sortwell House**, built for a shipmaster, is noted for an elliptical staircase, illuminated by a third-floor skylight. The **Ft. Edgecomb State Historic Site** features an octagonal wooden blockhouse, built 1808–9.

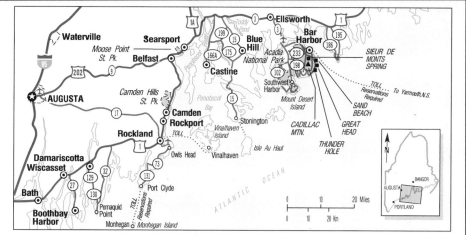

13

MOUNTAINS WITH A HUMAN FACE
The White Mountains and Presidential Range

Eight Presidents—Washington, Adams, Jefferson, Madison, Monroe, Pierce, John Quincy Adams and Eisenhower—are commemorated by peaks named after them in the White Mountains. This Presidential Range, running from Crawford Notch to Gorham, lies in the heart of a region whose natural grandeur has drawn tourists since the mid-19th century. Its white-capped peaks unfold into each other, and its valleys dissolve into mists and infinite shades of green, all softened to an astonishing beauty by the wear of time.

On a clear day, you can see the Atlantic from the top of Mount Washington. Unfortunately, clear days aren't common: the mountain has some of the most extreme weather in the United States, with an average annual temperature below freezing, and the world record for high wind— 231 mph, in April, 1934. The summit is smoothly weathered rock, but in summer the lower slopes are splashed with the colors of alpine flowers, the air is sweet and pure, and it is easy to imagine you're on top of the world.

But it isn't lonely at the top. Between mid-May and mid-October, weather permitting, drivers can reach the summit via a toll road completed in 1861 or take a three-hour round trip to the summit on America's oldest cog railway, built 1866–9. At the peak is a weather station, the Mount Washington Observatory, a cafe, and a small museum—and that colorful little red and green locomotive, panting smoke and steam.

Oddly, though, a steam engine on top of the Northeast's highest mountain doesn't seem entirely out of place. Because although there is as much wild grandeur here as you can find east of the Rockies,

history has given these mountains a human dimension. The presidential names are tokens of it, and so are local stories, like the tale of Timothy Nash, who crossed Crawford Notch in 1771 by hauling his horse up the cliffs on a rope.

The region's most famous storyteller is Nathaniel Hawthorne, whose story *The Ambitious Guest* recounts a deadly 1826 avalanche at Willey Mountain. Hawthorne was also one of the first to describe New Hampshire's emblem, the great stone face known as the Old Man of the Mountains, which peers from the cliffs at Franconia Notch. Occasionally, though, this human face of these mountains seems to wear a frown. If a fog comes down without warning on these trails, a sunny day can suddenly become a freezing one.

South of the Presidential Range, the Kancamagus Highway, the highest in the Northeast, runs east from Lincoln to North Conway, crossing Kancamagus Pass at 2,860 feet. There are wonderful views along the way, especially when the fall color peaks. Like the mountains to the north, the highway commemorates a patriot: Kancamagus was the last leader of the Penacook Indian Confederacy.

The White Mountains from Mount Washington (*above*) Even in summer, mists often hang in the valleys of the White Mountains, and sudden fogs and chilling storms can descend without warning from a blue sky, making the high elevations hazardous. The reward is the wildest wilderness east of the Rockies.

The Mount Washington Cog Railway (*left*) This is the oldest cog railway in America, built 1866–9. The engine's boiler is deliberately set at an angle to prevent the water from spilling out as the train climbs.

SITES TO SEE

● **Mt. Washington Hotel** (Bretton Woods) was the site of the 1944 World Monetary Fund Conference which set the world's gold price; the conference room has been preserved in this luxurious turn-of-the-century resort.

● **Bethlehem**, known as Crossroads of America, has a model railroad museum, as well as model cars and airplanes.

● **Arethusa Falls**, 1½ miles along a trail off the road near Crawford Notch, drops 200 feet, making it one of

the highest waterfalls in New Hampshire.

● **Silver Cascade** at the north of Crawford Notch tumbles 1,000 feet down Mt. Webster.

● **Franconia Notch State Park** is an exceptionally beautiful area. The Flume is an 800-foot-long gorge with walls 60 to 90 feet high and impressive waterfalls and pools. **The Basin**, a 20-foot wide glacial pothole, is reached via a trail from US3, north of The Flume. **The Cannon Mtn. Aerial Tramway II** takes passengers 2,022 feet to the

Summit Observation Platform.

● **The Old Man of the Mountains** is best viewed from the eastern side of Profile Lake. This rock formation, also known as the Profile, towers 1,200 feet above the lake and is 40 feet tall.

● **Wildcat Mtn. Gondola Tramway** (Pinkham Notch) and **Loon Mtn. Gondola Skyride** (Lincoln) both offer spectacular aerial rides.

● **Lincoln** hosts the New Hampshire Highland Games each mid September.

● **Grand Manor Antique Car Museum** (Glen) has more than 40 cars, dating from 1908. In summer, picnic on the landscaped grounds or hire a paddleboat to use on the pond. In the winter, Glen is a popular ski area with a nearby cross-country skiing center.

● **The Robert Frost Place** (Franconia) is the restored 1859 farmhouse the poet bought in 1915, where he lived and worked for 5 years. Personal belongings and signed first-editions of Frost's books are displayed in 2 rooms of the house.

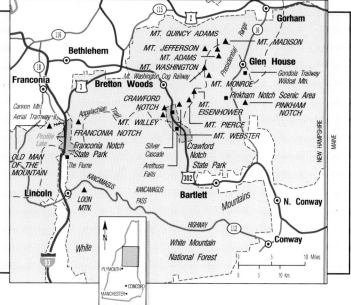

SMILE OF THE GREAT SPIRIT

Lake Winnipesaukee

Forty miles south of the granite uprearings of the Presidential Range is New Hampshire's lake country—a region as different in character and topography as a next-door neighbor could be. The heart of the district is Lake Winnipesaukee, 72 square miles of limpid water, wandering shorelines, and myriad islands. The state's largest lake, it has been a magnet for tourists since the first Harvard-Yale boat race was held on it in 1852.

The Algonquin Indians seem to have understood that the lands around Lake Winnipesaukee were a benevolent inversion of the mountains to the north. There, an irresistible force had thrust up the cloud-piercing peaks and carved high passes in them; to the south, it had dug into the land, made deep lake beds, and filled them with clear waters. Instead of piercing the clouds, the lakes reflected them. In any event, the Indians gave the biggest of the lakes a name meaning "The Smile of the Great Spirit"—and today most visitors find it apt.

To the northeast and northwest of Winnipesaukee, the Ossipee and Squam Mountains form a protective "V." The other lakes in the area—the litany of the names of the largest is Squam, Winnisquam, Ossipee, Wentworth, and Merrymeeting—circle Winnipesaukee like young apprentices, while a man-made lake, the Franklin Falls Flood Control Reservoir, lies to the west. Within this area people come to fish, boat, and swim. They can also explore small islands and large promontories, and climb into the hills for panoramic views that sweep northward from this beautiful land of lakes to the

rugged White Mountains.

One man who recognized the splendor of the area was Thomas Gustave Plant. In 1913, he completed his dream house, now known as the Castle in the Clouds, in the Ossipee Mountains below the peak of Mount Shaw, near Moultonborough. So he could always be surrounded by beauty, Plant spent $7 million to make his home and 6,000-acre estate New Hampshire's finest. There are trails for walking, horseback riding, and snowmobiling. Tours of the gardens and house, in which stained-glass windows repeat some of the vista seen outside, are also available.

The best way to get a close-up view of the big lake is to take one of the cruises from Weirs Beach or Wolfeboro. One of the boats, the *Mount Washington*, which began life in 1872 as a side-wheeler, was replaced after being destroyed by fire in 1939.

In the fall, the greatest sight is the countryside itself, as it bursts into glowing reds, golds, and oranges. With the white clapboard buildings set against such a spectacular backdrop, it is easy to believe the "Great Spirit" is, indeed, smiling on New Hampshire.

New England Churches (*above*) In keeping with the religious attitudes for which they were founded, these churches are plain and free of decoration both inside and out, the better to focus the mind and spirit on worship rather than worldly matters. Clapboard buildings like these are made of overlapping planks, attached horizontally to the wooden frame beneath.

Recreational Fishing (*left*) draws a steady stream of visitors to Lake Winnipesaukee, which contains 274 habitable islands, and to the thick sprinkling of surrounding lakes left behind by the continental ice sheet that once completely covered the state. Live bait—worms, insects, and minnows—produce the best results in these lakes, which are well stocked with salmon and bass.

SITES TO SEE

● **Wolfeboro**, sprawling picturesquely uphill beside Lake Winnipesaukee, is the site of the 1778 **Clark House**. Built in the Cape Cod-style, it has high beams and wide floorboards, and antique furnishings that include a good collection of pewter. The nearby **Hampshire Pewter Company** still makes

pewter by 16th-century methods and offers free factory tours.

● **Libby Museum** (Wolfeboro) displays 1,000 items covering the region's natural and social history. Exhibits include stuffed animals, as well as Indian artifacts and local memorabilia.

● **Daniel Webster Birthplace** (Franklin), a restored 2-room wing of a frame house, contains period furnishings. The statesman is also commemorated by a Daniel Chester French bust in front of the 1822 Congregational Church.

● **Weirs Beach** is a popular lakeside resort community with a boardwalk and amusement arcades.

WORTH A DETOUR

● **Shaker Village** (near Canterbury Center) was established in 1792. Today, the site is a museum of Shaker life with 22 of the original buildings remaining, including the 1792 **Meeting House**, the 1838 **Trustee's Building**, and a schoolhouse. The museum features Shaker crafts.

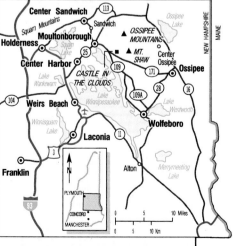

IN THE HEART OF THE COUNTRY

Vermont's Green Mountains

Much like the human heart, the Green Mountains are a bit off-center. In the north, they veer toward Lake Champlain, and in the south, they hurry down to join the Berkshires in western Massachusetts. And, like some human hearts, they have been softened by age. In the Cambrian period, the mountains were probably as high and jagged as the Rockies are today, but repeated glacial scourings have softened them, made knifelike ridges blunt, and formed gentle valleys that now shelter farms and villages so picturesque they serve as the country's touchstone of an ideal rurality.

When Norman Rockwell put his friends and neighbors on the cover of the *Saturday Evening Post*, he made the earnest Vermonter a symbol of all that was decent and familiar in the United States. Grandma Moses did the same for the Vermont landscape, making it—with its red barns and white-steepled churches, its hills, woods, and ponds—the evocation of an American innocence. First-time visitors to Vermont often think they already know it intimately and are surprised to find, especially in the Green Mountains, how little they really do know of its variety.

In Bennington, Grandma Moses' paintings and a fine collection of glass can be seen in the Bennington Museum. Once the world's tallest war memorial, the 306-foot-high Bennington Battle Monument is still the state's tallest structure. Bennington is also the site of Old First Church, considered by many to be Vermont's most beautiful church; poet Robert Frost is buried here.

At Proctor, more marble is quarried than anywhere else in North America. Its Marble Exhibit includes a view of a working marble factory; the town still uses the stone mundanely for sidewalks and windowsills.

Wilson Castle, a few miles away, is far from mundane with its turrets and parapets: it boasts French Renaissance furnishings and Indian peacocks. In nearby Manchester is Hildene, a 24-room mansion in the lee of Mt. Equinox, which was built in 1904 by Robert Todd Lincoln, the son of Abraham Lincoln. The house and gardens are open to the public during the summer months. The American Museum of Fly Fishing displays classic split-cane rods, and tackle belonging to such notable anglers as Bing Crosby and Dwight D. Eisenhower.

Villages that preserve the Vermont archetype intact are easy to find here: Dorset, with its marble streets; Weston, with its 1797 tavern; and Castleton, where the Green Mountain Boys planned their attack on Fort Ticonderoga. Covered bridges span winding, rushing streams on the way to these villages, and in late February visitors might spot sugar maples set with sap buckets.

In summer, the hills are cloaked in the green wood that gave Vermont its name; by September and October, the trees have turned to flame, orange, and Valentine red—the touchstone of fall color in the heart of the country.

Winter Wonderland (*left*) Ever since 1934, when Woodstock erected its first tow, Vermont has been an irresistible magnet for ski enthusiasts of all ages. Resorts have bloomed on the slopes like alpine flowers, along with cross-country ski centers, and snowmobiles can now crisscross the state on over 1,800 miles of "corridor" trails.

New England Sampler (*right*) Nestled in the shadow of Mt. Mansfield, Vermont's highest mountain, Stowe thrives on old-fashioned charm, glistening ski resorts, and a booming trade in antiques. Indians made maple syrup or sugar originally by dropping hot rocks into the sap drained from the surrounding maple forests. The candy produced here today is famous throughout the world.

SITES TO SEE

● **Hildene** (near Manchester) is a 24-room Georgian Revival mansion in the lee of Mt. Equinox. It contains the memorabilia of Abraham Lincoln's son Robert, whose family lived here until 1975.

● **Mt. Equinox** is the highest peak in the Taconic Range of the Green Mountains. The 5-mile Equinox Skyline Drive, a toll road with steep grades, goes to the 3,816-foot summit, with views of the rest of New Hampshire, New York, Maine, and Canada.

● **Park-McCullough House** (North Bennington), built 1865, features inlaid floors and Italian marble fireplaces. Nearby is a replica of the 1832 Burt-Hentry Covered Bridge over the Walloomsac River.

● **The Norman Rockwell Museum** (Rutland) has over 2,000 works by the artist on display.

● **Topping Tavern Museum** (Shaftsbury) is on the site of a 1777 stagecoach inn.

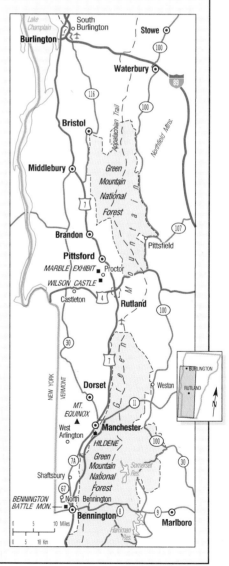

SHORES RICH IN HISTORY

Lake Champlain

Where Vermont's Green Mountains give way to the gentle terraces of orchards and farmland bordering Lake Champlain, history looms large. French explorer Samuel de Champlain became the first non-Indian to see the huge lake in 1609. He also claimed first sight of its horse-headed, barrel-thick, 20-foot-long water serpent. In 1814, Commodore Thomas MacDonough defeated the British Navy in the Battle of Lake Champlain, thwarting British plans to use the waterway as a back door into New York.

Burlington, Vermont's largest city, chartered in 1763, was all but abandoned during the Revolutionary War. From its lakefront Battery Park, the British fleet was bombarded during the Battle of Lake Champlain. Today, the *Spirit of Ethan Allen*, modeled on a Mississippi paddle steamer, cruises the waterfront.

North of Burlington, Ethan Allen Park includes part of the hero's farmstead. A tower provides good views of the lake Allen and his Green Mountain Boys crossed to capture Fort Ticonderoga during the Revolutionary War.

At Shelburne, south of Burlington, Shelburne Museum and Heritage Park offers a 45-acre village of 37 historic buildings assembled from throughout New England. On display are the Old Colchester Reef Lighthouse and the S.S. *Ticonderoga*, one of the last passenger steamers to travel on the lake.

The land around Lake Champlain is mostly arable. Near Charlotte, the Vermont Wildflower Farm has a self-guiding nature trail winding through 16 acres of woodland, marsh, and rough meadow; it glows with color in spring and summer.

At the lake's northern end are the Lake Champlain Islands. Grand Isle boasts the oldest log cabin in the U.S., Hyde Cabin, built in 1783.

Isle La Motte, named after pioneer Pierre La Motte, was the site of Vermont's first European settlement. In 1666, La Motte built Fort St. Anne, and Jesuit missionaries soon built Vermont's first chapel, St. Anne's Shrine, nearby. Today it contains crutches abandoned by those cured here. At the beach-front site of old Fort St. Anne, there is a Gethsemane garden, picnic area, and swimming beach.

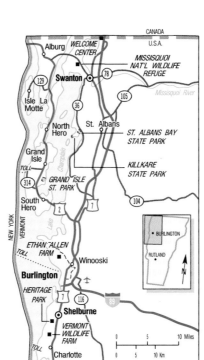

Sunset on Lake Champlain (*above*) The humped rock breaking the lake's surface might be the sea monster called "Champ," which is still sighted sporadically by imaginative visitors. For navigation purposes, the lake is connected to the Hudson by the Champlain Canal. It serves as a link in the Hudson-Saint Lawrence waterway that allows ships to sail from New York City to the Great Lakes and Montreal.

Near Shelburne Point (*left*) Shelburne Farms contains an elegant inn, built 1899 as a private estate, complete with restored formal gardens that overlook the lake.

SITES TO SEE

● **Shelburne Farms** (Shelburne) is the historic estate and dairy farm of railroad magnate William Seward Webb and Lila Vanderbilt Webb. Built as a summer estate in the 1880s, it contains many of the original furnishings. It is still a working farm; cheese is made on the site.

● **Shelburne Museum** (Shelburne) contains an outstanding collection of American art, including quilts, cigar-store Indians, dolls, and paintings.

● **Lake Champlain Discovery Festival** (Burlington) every June and July includes a fishing derby, Highland games, and jazz festival.

● **Missisquoi National Wildlife Refuge** (Swanton) lies in the flood plain of the Missisquoi River. This is a good place to see migrating water birds in May and June, and from late September to early October. Self-guiding trails follow the Black and Maquam creeks.

● **Charlotte** still contains many buildings built when it was founded in the late 18th century, and 3 covered bridges.

● **St. Albans** hosts the Vermont Maple Festival in early April.

WORTH A DETOUR

● **University of Vermont** (Burlington)

● **St. Albans Bay St. Pk.**

● **Kill Kare St. Pk.**

● **Sand Bar St. Pk.**

ART AND NATURE

The Berkshires

From atop Mount Greylock, Massachusetts' highest point, the peaks and ridges of the Berkshires lie below like an undulating green and blue counterpane. Far beyond them unfold the mountains and valleys of four more states: Vermont, New Hampshire, New York, and Connecticut. Those who drive the winding road to Greylock's summit see one of the loveliest parts of New England. Not so apparent is this region's longstanding partnership of natural beauty and the arts, from Hawthorne and Melville's time to Shakespeare festivals and the Berkshire Music Festival at Tanglewood.

On the Berkshires' southwestern edge, two towns epitomize the regional tradition of harmony between the arts of nature and nurture. Great Barrington, now a ski resort, was the world's first town with electric lights. William Stanley, who pioneered their development, was born there, as was Dr. W.E.B. Dubois, the first black man to receive a Ph.D. from Harvard. Another celebrated doctor, not a native, is honored at the town's Albert Schweitzer Center.

Stockbridge, set in wild and beautiful country to the north, was the home of illustrator Norman Rockwell and also of sculptor Daniel Chester French, whose statue of "Honest Abe" is the centerpiece of the Lincoln Memorial. French's estate, Chesterwood, is open to the public.

The homes of two very different "ambassadors" are here, too. Mission House was the home of John Sergeant, who preached Christianity to the local Indians; open to the public, it contains early American antiques. Naumkeag, the home of Joseph Choate, an ambassador to England, has landscaped gardens and a fine collection of Chinese porcelain and ceramics that belonged to Choate's daughter Mabel.

Near Pittsfield, Herman Melville wrote *Moby Dick*. His home, Arrowhead, and Pittsfield's public library, the Berkshire Athenaeum, contain memorabilia.

Nathaniel Hawthorne lived in nearby Lenox. His home has been re-created at Tanglewood, where each summer the Boston Symphony Orchestra gives celebrated open-air concerts.

Hancock Shaker Village, west of Pittsfield, celebrates the religious sect that survived there from 1790 to 1960. Eighteen of the 40 original buildings have been restored.

The Berkshires offer many out-of-the-way museums, galleries, and theaters. At Dalton, northeast of Pittsfield, is the Crane Museum of Papermaking. At Becket, the Jacob's Pillow Dance Festival books major international companies each summer. Williamstown is home for the Sterling and Francine Clark Art Institute's excellent collections of European and American paintings and of the Williamstown Theater Festival.

The Seed Room at Hancock Shaker Village (*right*) Although celebrated today chiefly for the elegance of their furniture (the chair here is a typical design), the Shakers were just as skilled in husbandry, and sales of their high-quality seeds helped support the community. Self-sufficient in every way, their religious communities were distinguished by celibacy, simplicity of life, joyful dances, and the tremulous emotional experiences that gave the sect its name.

Officially, the Shakers were members of the United Society of Believers in Christ's Second Appearing, a Quaker sect formed in England in 1747. In 1774, eight members of the sect followed the charismatic Ann Lee to America, and by 1826 Shaker communities had been established as far west as Indiana. In addition to celibacy, their members were committed to a belief in God's dual nature (the male aspect being incarnate in Christ, the female aspect in Mother Ann Lee). They also believed in the efficacy of public confession, in the communal ownership of property, and in the equality of the sexes.

Boston Symphony Orchestra at Tanglewood's Berkshire Music Festival (*left*) Open-air concerts at Tanglewood (named for Nathaniel Hawthorne's home at nearby Lenox) are major events in the Berkshire's cultural calendar, attracting world-famous orchestras and performers. The Festival dates from 1934, when the orchestra was mainly composed of members of the New York Philharmonic-Symphony. Two years later, the Boston Symphony Orchestra took their place, and the BSO has been orchestra-in-residence ever since. The 1938 "Music Shed," designed by Eliel Saarinen, seats 6,000, and thousands more hear concerts from Tanglewood's lawns.

SITES TO SEE

● **The Mount** (Lenox), home of novelist Edith Wharton, the first woman to win the Pulitzer Prize, was built 1901–2. Fifty acres of woodlands and formal gardens, designed by the author's niece, landscape architect Beatrix Ferrand, are open to the public, along with the restored house. Shakespeare & Company presents plays outdoors during the summer; matinee productions based on Wharton's life and works are held in the salon.

● **The Gingerbread House** (Tyringham) was designed by sculptor Henry Kitson and is now a gallery and store selling modern art. The house's roof is actually an 80-ton sculpture of a thatched roof. Kitson's "Pilgrim Maid" can be seen in Plymouth.

● **Merwin House** (Stockbridge) was built about 1825. It contains American and European period furnishings and Tiffany glass.

● **Cheshire** has a replica of the press used to make a 1,235-lb. cheese for President Jefferson.

● **Western Gateway Heritage State Park** (N. Adams) features the history of 19th-century railroads and construction of the nearby Hoosac Tunnel. This engineering marvel runs 5 miles under Hoosac Mtn.

● **The Berkshire Scenic Railway** visits Lee, Stockbridge, and Housatonic.

● **Mt. Everett State Reservation** (Great Barrington) has views of 3 states from the upper parking area.

WORTH A DETOUR

● Mohawk Trail State Forest

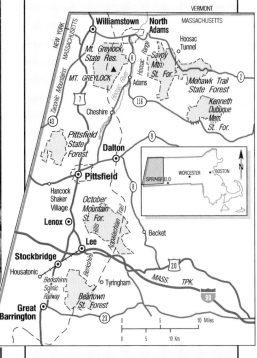

A WORLD APART

Cape Cod, Martha's Vineyard, and Nantucket

Cape Cod marks the eastern limit of glaciation in North America during the last Ice Age some 15,000 to 25,000 years ago. When the ice sheets melted here, their billions of tons of gravel, sand, and outwash called terminal moraines were left behind, forming the outcrop known as Cape Cod. Today, eroded by innumerable tides and storms, the Cape juts into the Atlantic like a beckoning world apart at the threshold of America.

South of Cape Cod, the jut of the continental shelf makes the Gulf Stream swing sharply east. To the north, the fish-teeming shallows of Georges Bank were known to fishermen even before the Pilgrims made landfall near Provincetown in 1620. The land that Henry David Thoreau called "the bared and bended arm of Massachusetts" had by then been home to the Wampanoag Indians for more than 3,500 years.

Just as the Pilgrims did, modern visitors to the Cape come upon a different world. Dunes and freshwater ponds echo miles of beach and pounding surf. Fine old mansions of the whaling captains stand preserved like bulwarks against shifting 20th-century tides. On Nantucket Island, a few cobbled streets remain as well. The Nantucket Whaling Museum displays model ships, elaborate scrimshaw, portraits of the captains, and the trophies that they brought back from exotic foreign ports.

Chatham is a good starting point for exploring Cape Cod National Seashore— 28,000 acres of beach, dunes, and heath, with swimming and picnic areas. The first transatlantic radio station was built near South Wellfleet between 1901 and 1903, and a trail leads to an unusual and picturesque swamp of white cedars. Whale-watching cruises sail from Provincetown, which has the only harbor on the Cape

deep enough for whaling ships, and where the fishing fleet unloads its catch between 4:00 and 6:00 p.m..

Native flora and marine fauna can be seen in Brewster, at Sealand of Cape Cod, and at the Cape Cod Museum of Natural History.

At Sandwich, on the sheltered waters of Cape Cod Bay, Heritage Plantation is devoted to American crafts, cars, and other theme exhibits. The 1637 Hoxie House has furnishings dating from 1680–90. Sandwich Glass Museum displays art glass by the Boston and Sandwich Glass Company which was founded in 1825, and the scenic old Cape Cod & Hyannis Railroad passes through Sandwich on its way to Buzzards Bay and Hyannis.

The renowned Woods Hole Oceanographic Institution and the National Fisheries Service Aquarium nearby are both open to the public.

Hyannis harbor cruises skirt the Kennedy family's summer compound, and ferries serve Nantucket Island and Martha's Vineyard.

On the Vineyard, tiny ornate cottages mark Oak Bluffs, the site of a Methodist summer camp first held here in the 1830s. Edgartown's Tisbury Museum depicts 19th-century island life. Vincent House, the oldest on the island, is open to the public.

Winter Dunes (*right*) Cape Cod's National Seashore is never more beautiful than when winter brings solitude to the dunes. Autumn, when the sandy heaths of the Seashore's Province Lands section glow with fall color like a miniature Vermont, is also a fine season for a visit.

Gingerbread Cottages, Martha's Vineyard (*left*) Numerous tiny but cheerfully ornate cottages at Oak Bluffs mark the site of a Methodist summer camp, first held here in the 1830s.

SITES TO SEE

● In **Mashpee**, descendants of Mashpee Indians still harvest cranberry bogs; the Old Indian Meetinghouse, built 1684, is located in the old burying ground just south of the town.

● **The Maria Mitchell Science Center** (Nantucket) is the restored 1818 home of the first U.S. woman astronomer and discoverer of Mitchell's Comet. The observatory is open Wednesday nights in summer.

● **Seth Nickerson House** (Provincetown) was built 1746 in Cape Cod style. The interior is made of articles scavenged from wrecks.

● **West Parish Meetinghouse** (West Barnstable) is the oldest Congregational church in the U.S. It was built 1717, and has a 1723 English weathercock and 1806 Revere bell.

● **Heritage Plantation** (Sandwich) covers 76 acres with theme exhibits that include American crafts, military firearms, and automobiles. The restored 1756 Eldred House is home of the **Thornton W. Burgess Museum**, with memorabilia of the naturalist and children's book author.

● **Wellfleet Historical Museum** (Wellfleet) contains fine examples of scrimshaw and Sandwich glass.

● **Abigail Adams' birthplace** (Yarmouth) was built 1685 and contains furnishings that belonged to the wife of the second U.S. president.

● In **Chatham**, the fishing fleets usually unload their day's catches in the late afternoon.

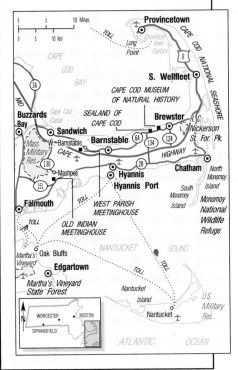

COLONIAL DAYS

The North Shore

The nation's formative years were spent along this cape- and harbor-studded coast, where history still seems very much alive. Between Lynn and Newburyport are many of the finest 17th-century buildings in the U.S.A., and evidence remains of 18th- and 19th-century prosperity—a fascinating heritage of great mansions and treasures imported from Europe and the Orient. The region's seafaring traditions still thrive at Gloucester, and on Plum Island, north of Cape Ann's rocky headlands, primeval nature holds sway among the birds and along the wide beaches of the Parker River National Wildlife Refuge.

From 1626–30, Salem was the Pilgrims' leading settlement. Its historic buildings recall both the religious zeal and the commercial enterprise of those early years. The Courthouse, where the witch trials of 1692 took place, is open to the public. So is the Witch House, Magistrate Corwin's home, where some 200 unfortunates were brought for pre-trial hearings. Some homes of the wealthy are preserved at the Essex Institute Museum Neighborhood, including the finely crafted Gardner-Pingree House and the Ropes Mansion. The Salem Maritime National Historic Site, a renovation of Salem's wharves and dock buildings, remains redolent of the romance of trade, and among the Peabody Museum's vast collections are many of the exotic goods that found their way here.

Across the harbor lies pretty and historic Marblehead, bought from the local Indians in 1684. The Jeremiah Lee Mansion contains curiosities gathered from around the world by seamen and traders. Beverly, north of Salem, preserves the 1781 house

of John Cabot, with relics of the Continental Navy. Nearby Ipswich is said to have more 17th-century homes than any other U.S. town.

Cape Ann is now a place for tourists, summer homes, harbors, lobsters, and antiques. Rockport's James Babson Cooperage Shop dates from 1658 and displays antique tools and furniture. The Sewall-Scripture House commemorates the local granite industry. Whale-watching trips depart from Gloucester, still a major fishing port. Exuberant Hammond Castle in Magnolia, built by the inventor of the Hammond organ, boasts an 8,000-pipe organ and a collection of medieval art.

At the old shipbuilding town of Newburyport, the U.S. Coast Guard was born at the mouth of the Merrimack River. The Custom House Maritime Museum displays Coast Guard memorabilia. Nearby Plum Island, named for its delicious wild beach plums which make equally delicious jam, attracts multitudes of birds and has the region's best beaches.

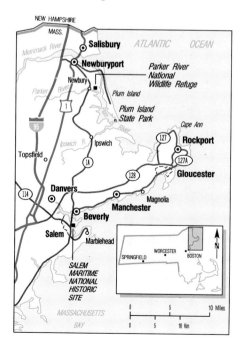

Salem Witch House (*left*) The witchcraft hysteria that shook Salem in the 1690s interpreted convulsions and incoherent babbling as the effects of a bewitching. In 1692, after derisory trials in rooms like this one, 19 people were hanged and one crushed to death before the mindless fury abated.

Salisbury Beach, North Shore (*above*) These modern residences enjoy the twin pleasures of pounding surf and crystalline light. In the old seaports, the historic buildings that have survived the effects of time and weather embody the rugged heritage of the fishermen and shipbuilders who occupied them.

SITES TO SEE

● **Balch House** (Beverly), built 1636 and one of the oldest frame houses in the country, contains period furnishings.

● **The John Hale House** (Beverly), built 1694 by the town's first minister, contains a collection of witchcraft materials.

● **Sedgewich Gardens at Long Hill Reservation** (Beverly) is a 1918 estate modeled after a Charleston, SC, home of the early 1800s. The grounds include fields, woods, wetlands, and a formal garden; the home is partially furnished and only open by appointment.

● **Heard House Museum** (Ipswich) is a 1795 sea captain's home with period furnishings and numerous mementoes of seafaring trade with China.

● **Our Lady of Good Voyage Church** (Gloucester) reflects the area's fishing heritage with ornate decorations and models of fishing vessels on the walls. Sailors use a statue between the church's 2 steeples to guide them into port.

● **Parson Capen House** (Topsfield), built 1683, is an outstanding example of early colonial architecture with period furnishings. Tea is occasionally served in the herb garden.

● **Sewall-Scripture House** (Rockport) contains a mixed collection that includes local memorabilia and Victorian furnishings.

BOSTON

One of America's oldest and most illustrious cities, Boston was a vital, exciting place 300 years ago, and it is just as vital and exciting today. Founded in 1630 by a group of settlers led by John Winthrop, it launched itself immediately into international trade and quickly grew rich on the cod that thickened its waters, shipping them as far as the West Indies and the Mediterranean. One hundred and fifty years after its founding, the city honored the source of its original wealth by hanging a Sacred Cod in its State House. America's oldest university, Harvard, was founded in 1631 just across the Charles River in Boston's sister city, Cambridge.

Independent thinking and intellectual activity flourished side by side during Boston's first century, so it is little wonder that the city became the cradle of American democracy. The citizens rocked the cradle in 1768, when they rioted against the iniquities of British rule, and they shook it even harder in 1773, when they organized the Boston Tea Party to protest British taxation without representation.

Although the Revolution began in and around Boston, the British evacuated the city in March, 1776, and never returned. But history still sailed its waters and walked its brick-lined streets. Having lost their British markets, the merchants discovered new ones in the Far East, and sleek clipper ships brought prosperity. Boston's social character and historical voice were freshly defined in the drawing rooms of the elegant houses on Beacon Hill, and the city's shape was redrawn when the waters of the Back Bay were filled to create new residential land. While poets, philosophers, and educators maintained Boston's fabled literary traditions, the great Irish immigration that began in the 1840s increased the population enormously and changed the social and political complexion of the city forever.

Boston is now home to over 50 colleges and universities and to roughly 700 companies exploring and developing technology for computers, science, and industry. Skyscrapers soar above the towers of 18th-century landmarks in the financial district, and medical research continues to advance at Massachusetts General Hospital. Within an area only a few miles square, the earliest days of America's history and its most modern manifestations meet in delightful combinations and mingle with unexpected ease.

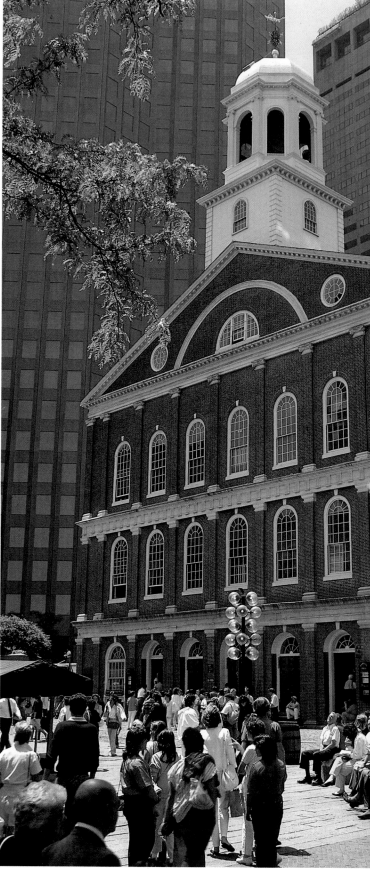

Faneuil Hall (*near left*) After serving the patriots as a market and meeting hall, the so-called "Cradle of Liberty" was used by the British during their occupation of Boston as a theater, despite a 1750 city law that forbade plays, and as a storehouse for confiscated weapons. In the 19th century, a group was formed here to assist runaway slaves. Beneath the famous copper weathervane, street theater now flourishes, and the market stalls are again packed with goods.

The swan boats (*far left*) in the Public Garden are also well-known landmarks, and no visit is complete without a gliding ride behind their gently curving prows.

MAP REFERENCE

1. Arthur M. Sackler Museum
2. Boston Tea Party Ship and Museum
3. Bunker Hill Monument
4. Faneuil Hall
5. Granary Burying Ground
6. Harrison Gray Otis House
7. Harvard University
8. John Hancock Observatory
9. Museum of Afro-American History
10. New England Aquarium
11. Old North Church
12. Old South Meeting House
13. Old State House
14. Paul Revere House
15. USS *Constitution*

HISTORIC SITES AND DISTRICTS

Beacon Hill Developed in the early 1880s, this area is beautifully preserved.

Bunker Hill Monument actually stands on Breed's Hill, where the Revolutionary War battle occurred. A spiral staircase climbs to the top.

MUSEUMS

Arthur M. Sackler Museum (Cambridge)

Isabella Stewart Gardner Museum Built to house Mrs. Gardner's private art collection.

Museum of Afro-American History traces the growth of the abolitionist movement.

Museum of Fine Arts

NOTABLE BUILDINGS

Harrison Gray Otis House A striking private mansion designed by Charles Bulfinch.

Old North Church The oldest Boston church.

Old South Meeting House Many of the plots and protests that ignited the Revolution were first expressed here.

Old State House Boston's oldest public building.

Paul Revere House Revere's home from 1770 to 1800, this is Boston's oldest building.

PARKS

Boston Common The site of the city's first settlement is the oldest park in America.

OTHER ATTRACTIONS

Black Heritage Trail and **Freedom Trail**

Boston Tea Party Ship and Museum

John Hancock Observatory

New England Aquarium

USS *Constitution*

Granary Burying Ground

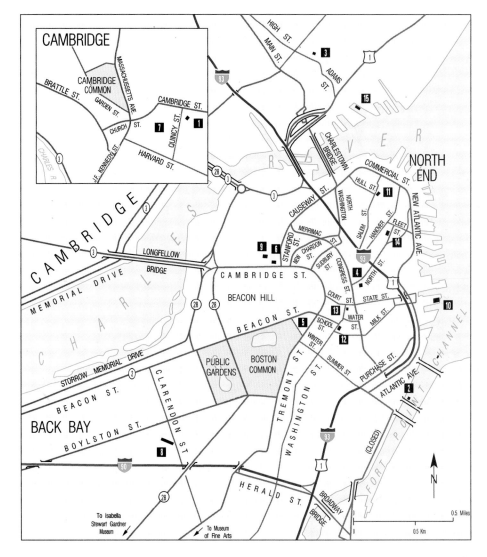

A COAST OF SHIPS

Mystic Seaport, Connecticut

A proud tradition of shipbuilding and seafaring permeates the coast from New London to the border with Rhode Island. New London once matched New Bedford and Nantucket as a whaling port. Mystic, a former shipbuilding center, now boasts one of the nation's finest historical seaports. This region has long been important to the U.S. Navy. Today, Groton houses the nation's largest submarine base. The vessels are built nearby, and visitors can go aboard the world's first nuclear submarine.

The jewel on this stretch of coast is Mystic Seaport, and its pride is the *Charles W. Morgan*, the sole surviving wooden whaling ship in the U.S.A. Built at New Bedford in 1841, it looks as trim as though awaiting its maiden voyage. At the Henry B. du Pont Preservation Shipyard, visitors can see how it and other old ships, such as the *L.A. Duton*, a three-masted fishing schooner, are lovingly restored.

Around Mystic Seaport's quay are more than 60 historic buildings, including a sailmaker's loft, a cooper's shop, and a fine museum of figureheads and model ships. For a thoroughgoing celebration of American seafaring, a planetarium highlights marine navigation.

In New London harbor, the U.S.C.G.C. *Eagle*, the Coast Guard Academy's training ship, which led the

Bicentennial Tall Ships Parade, is sometimes on display. Whale Oil Row, a quartet of Greek Revival mansions built for whaling captains, likewise commemorates the days of sail. The Lyman Allyn Museum displays an eclectic mix of New England furnishings, classical antiquities, and paintings by Degas, Braque, and other European masters.

The region exudes military history, too. At Norwich, north of New London, stands the Leffingwell Inn, in whose paneled rooms proponents of independence met and George Washington dined.

In Groton's Fort Griswold State Park, a 135-foot monument commemorates the defeat of the revolutionaries by Benedict Arnold and the British and the subsequent burning of New London and Groton. The park's Monument House contains relics.

Skilled Shipwrights continue to restore and maintain old ships in Mystic Seaport's preservation shipyard. Traditional craftsmen can also be seen at work in several of the shops in Mystic's historic seaport district.

Mystic Seaport Museum recaptures the life of a 19th-century New England harbor. Workshops, houses, stores, and warehouses line the quayside, where some 100 ships lie moored. The *Charles W. Morgan*, last of the wooden whaling ships, is 111 feet long and could carry 2,300 barrels of oil.

SITES TO SEE

● **USS *Nautilus* Memorial** (Groton) provides tours of the world's first nuclear-powered submarine, which include the living quarters, torpedo room, and the operations compartment. Nearby, **Project Oceanology** gives educational cruises aboard a research ship. Passengers can learn how to measure lobsters and identify fish, as well as how to take core samples from the seabed.

● **U.S. Coast Guard Academy** (New London) has a museum devoted to the history of this service. Multimedia presentations at the visitors' pavilion portray academy life.

● **Monte Cristo Cottage** (New London) was the boyhood home of playwright Eugene O'Neill, which he used as the setting for *Long Day's Journey into Night*.

● **Stonington** is a pretty colonial town rich in 18th- and 19th-century sea captains' homes.

● **Tantaquidgeon Indian Museum** (Uncasville) houses a collection of Mohegan tribal artifacts and crafts.

RIVER AND COAST
The Lower Connecticut River Valley

Largest of New England's rivers, the Connecticut flows more than 500 miles from its source—New Hampshire's Connecticut Lakes on the Canadian border—to its sea mouth at Old Saybrook. En route, it forms the Vermont-New Hampshire border and flows past Massachusetts and Connecticut tobacco fields. Widening as it approaches Long Island Sound, where so-called "sea meadows" of marsh grass supplied hay for the colonists' cattle without even being cultivated, the river lends civility and its own mellow beauty to an area whose charm and rich history have fascinated generations of travelers.

Rivers are best seen by boat, and at Essex and Haddam visitors can do just that. The Essex Steam Train and Riverboat offers rides to Deep River with the option of a river cruise. In the train yard is a railroad museum. Essex was once a major shipbuilding center and during the War of 1812, the British burned 26 ships at what is now Historic Landing and Steamboat Dock at the foot of Main Street. Exhibits in the Connecticut River Museum, an 1878 steamboat warehouse, portray the river's history and shipbuilding heritage. One of the many sea captains' homes, the 1732 Pratt House, is open to the public.

From Haddam, a nine-hour cruise on the Connecticut River steams out into Long Island Sound. Across the river, East Haddam's riverside Goodspeed Opera House is a splendid six-story structure, built in 1878, with interior decor derived from ornate old riverboat saloons. Plays are still staged here, and the theater has a particularly fine reputation for its revivals of long-lost musicals. Not far east of the old theater on a river bluff stands rustic Gillette Castle. It was built (1914–19) by actor William Gillette, famous for portraying Sherlock Holmes. He reputedly spent over $1 million on the eccentrically furnished house, which now stands in a

122-acre state park with river views.

Upstream at Middletown, the worlds of art and learning are served by Wesleyan University. Its Olin Memorial Library displays manuscripts by John and Charles Wesley, Albert Einstein, W.B. Yeats, and other notables. The Davison Arts Center in the elegant Alsop House contains an exceptionally fine print collection.

Near the mouth of the river, Old Lyme and Old Saybrook are towns rich in architecture and history. Many consider Old Lyme's Congregational Church the prettiest in New England; the original design is thought to have been done by Sir Christopher Wren. Down the coast at Guilford, where about 400 18th- and 19th-century buildings still stand, is perhaps the oldest stone house in New England, now the Henry Whitfield State Historical Museum. Built in 1839, it contains 17th- and 18th-century furniture and colonial artifacts. The house was the colony's meeting hall and fortress as well as Whitfield's home, but it was never attacked. The Hyland House is a fine example of an early New England salt-box house. It was built in 1660 and restored to its original state early this century. Exhibits in the Florence Griswold House relate to 300 years of history in this region of coast and river.

Hartford State Capitol (*right*) Opened in 1879 at a cost of $2·5 million, this ornate landmark of Gothic spires, stained glass, ringing marble floors, and local granite commemorates the people and events that shaped the state's colorful history. Outside, the tributes are carved in bas-reliefs and ornate medallions. Inside, evocative relics of the past include the Civil War battle standards of various Connecticut regiments and the figurehead from Admiral Farragut's celebrated flagship, *Hartford*. It is said to owe its gilded dome, not to architect Richard Upjohn, but to Hartford's insistent citizens, who demanded one whether it suited the original designs or not.

Gillette Castle (*right*) This rustic pile, splendidly situated above the Connecticut River, might have been designed for the Flintstones. But it was actually modeled on a castle on the Rhine at the express request of its owner, actor-playwright William Gillette. It took five years to build, 1914–1919, and is said to have cost $1 million, a princely fortune in those days. Gillette made his acting debut and wrote two successful plays about the Civil War before he hit the jackpot in 1899 as both actor and author of a theatrical version of *Sherlock Holmes*. His castle, with its bare stone walls, is as odd inside as out, and contains one-way mirrors that allowed Gillette to observe his guests in secret.

Tobacco Plant in Flower (*left*) The fields of the Connecticut River Valley are fertile, lush, and free of the glacial boulders that often made farming difficult for the Colonial settlers. A coarse perennial with large leaves, tobacco needs such rich, well-drained soil if it is to thrive. The leaves of this flowering crop will be used as the outer wrapping for cigars.

SITES TO SEE

● **General William Hart House** (Old Saybrook), built about 1767, shows how the wealthy lived before the Revolution.

● **St. Stephen's Church** (East Haddam) claims to have the world's oldest church bell, cast in 815.

● **The Moodus Noises** (Moodus) is the site of mysterious underground rumblings. Indians claimed it was the noise of demons, early non-Indian settlers though it was the noise of witches in the mountains, and modern scientists say it is the noise of crystal fractures grating against each other.

● **Harriet Beecher Stowe House** (Hartford) contains personal belongings of the author of *Uncle Tom's Cabin*. **The Mark Twain House**, a 19-room Victorian Gothic black brick home, is next door.

● **Wadsworth Atheneum** (Hartford) contains excellent collections of American and European art, including paintings, glass, silver, and porcelain. Ship models are on display in a glass-covered courtyard in the Avery Memorial.

WORTH A DETOUR

● **Yale University** (New Haven) has been at its present location since 1716. The oldest building on campus is Connecticut Hall, built in 1752, where Nathan Hale lived as a student. The Yale University Art Gallery is the oldest university art museum in the United States. Its collection includes outstanding examples of American decorative arts. Free campus tours are offered from the Phelps Archway.

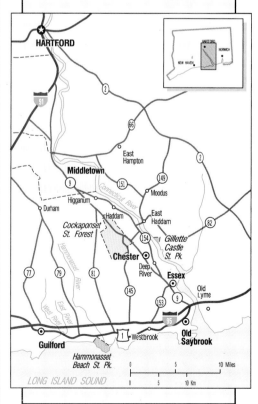

FREEDOM AND WEALTH
Newport and Narragansett Bay

Rhode Island was settled by Roger Williams, a religious exile from Massachusetts, who founded Providence in 1636. He advocated religious tolerance and democratic government. King Charles II chartered the colony in 1663 as Rhode Island and Providence Plantations. Blessed with fish-rich waters and many sheltered harbors, the colony prospered. People of all religious beliefs were welcomed. By the late 18th century, Newport rivaled Boston and New York as a port, and in 1852, a merchant grown wealthy in China trade built the first of the great mansions, Chateau-Sur-Mer, for which the region is now famous.

For the best commoner's-eye-view of America's Age of Wealth, stroll along Newport's Cliff Walk from Easton's Beach to Bailey's Beach. On one side are rugged cliffs and the deep blue waters of Rhode Island Sound, and on the other some of the world's most extravagant mansions. Even the wrought-iron fence around Cornelius Vanderbilt's Renaissance-style mini-palace, The Breakers, built in 1895 and furnished with rare antiques, tapestries, and marble mosaics, is a work of art. Rosecliff, modeled on the Grand Trianon palace at Versailles, is hardly more modest. Its furnishings include Louis XV and XVI antiques, and garden sculpture is by Augustus Saint-Gaudens.

Newport, and the rest of the Narragansett Bay area, boasts much besides the homes of the 19th century's rich and famous, however. A wealth of 17th- and 18th-century architecture stands here. Newport's Wanton-Lyman-Hazard House, once home to colonial governors, is an outstanding example of the Jacobean style. The 1699 Friends Meeting House, with 18th- and 19th-century additions, is one of the nation's oldest Quaker assemblies. Trinity Church, built in 1726 in the style of Sir Christopher Wren, features Tiffany glass, an organ once played by Handel, and chandeliers on their original ropes. The 1763 Touro Synagogue, the United States' oldest, has a Georgian interior. At Wickford, Smith's Castle, a plantation and trading post, dates from about 1678.

The bay area is also notable for its gardens. Newport's Hammersmith Farm has 50 acres of pasture and gardens designed by Frederick Law Olmstead. John and Jacqueline Kennedy had their wedding reception in the house here. Among mansion gardens, those of The Elms are exceptional. Green Animals in Portsmouth is one of the most unusual gardens in America, with topiary dating from 1880.

Fort Adams State Park, in Newport, preserves the fort that guarded these waters until 1945 and showcases a replica of the *Providence*, the first ship commanded by John Paul Jones. The Naval War College Museum, in Founders Hall on Coaster's Harbor Island, gives outstanding coverage of the area's naval history.

Chateau-Sur-Mer (*right*) One of the first of nearly 60 Newport mansions that their owners blithely dubbed "cottages," this one established a breathtaking standard for opulence with its three-story hall, massive mirrored ballroom, and ornately carved library.

Single-Handed-Around-the-World Race (*left*) A shipbuilding town by 1646 and the former home of the Naval Academy, Newport has an impressive maritime tradition. To this day, wealthy residents amuse themselves by yachting, and international competitors navigate Narragansett Bay in thrilling races.

SITES TO SEE

● **Marble House** (Newport) was a Vanderbilt mansion, built in 1892. It is noted for the grand staircase of Siena marble and the Gold Saloon, modeled after Versailles. Other notable mansions include The Astors' Beechwood Mansion, Belcourt Castle, and The Elms. The Newport Mansions sell tickets that offer discounts for multiple admissions; details are available at houses.

● **East Greenwich**, a yachting center, has 18th-century homes. The **General James Mitchell Varnum House Museum**, a 2-story frame house built 1773, was visited by George Washington and Lafayette. The nearby **Varnum Military Museum** has a collection of period weapons and military memorabilia.

● **Jamestown**, on Conanicut Island at the mouth of Narragansett Bay, is reached by a bridge from Newport. **Watson Farm** consists of 280 acres with orchards, cattle, and sheep. The Jamestown Windmill was built 1787, and the town's **Quaker Meetinghouse** was built 1786.

● **Prescott Farm** (Middletown) has a working 19th-century windmill, country store, and museum with Pilgrim furnishings. The nearby **Norman Bird Sanctuary** has 15 miles of trails in 450 acres.

● **Museum of Yachting** (Fort Adams State Park) highlights the region's sailing history, including the classic international races.

● **International Tennis Hall of Fame and Museum** (Newport) is in the Newport Casino, site of the United States National Tennis Championships from 1881 through 1919.

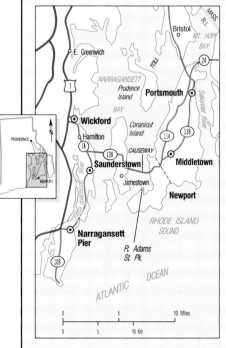

THE MID-ATLANTIC STATES

Along the great rivers of the mid-Atlantic states—the Hudson, Delaware, Potomac, and Susquehanna—the settlements of colonial America first began to reach for the continent's interior, and it was at their mouths that the great cities of the region grew: New York, the great port; Philadelphia, the cradle of independence; and Washington, the nation's capital. Baltimore and Wilmington lie at the heads of the Chesapeake and Delaware bays, where yachting, crabbing, and fine beaches now draw visitors. The Brandywine Valley was the home of the Dupont dynasty and its great mansions and gardens. Pittsburgh presides over the triple confluence of the Allegheny, Ohio, and Monongahela rivers, the nexus of trade between the Mississippi and the Great Lakes. These cities, rich in history, are the nation's treasure house.

But there is wildness here, too: the Adirondack wilderness is bigger than Yosemite, Grand Canyon, Glacier, and Olympic National Parks combined. Wild ponies roam Chincoteague Island, off the Delmarva Peninsula. Whales spout off Long Island Sound, New Jersey's Pine Barrens are the home of rare orchids, and black bears roam the upland woods of the Delaware Water Gap. In the north of the region, Lake Erie and the great St. Lawrence form America's "Fourth Coast." Where the land is nurtured, there are special pleasures, too: the Finger Lakes are a place of vineyards, automobiles, and innovation, and in Pennsylvania's Amish country, where horse-drawn buggies clip-clop through landscapes of head-high corn and hex signs decorate the barn doors, the peace is tangible.

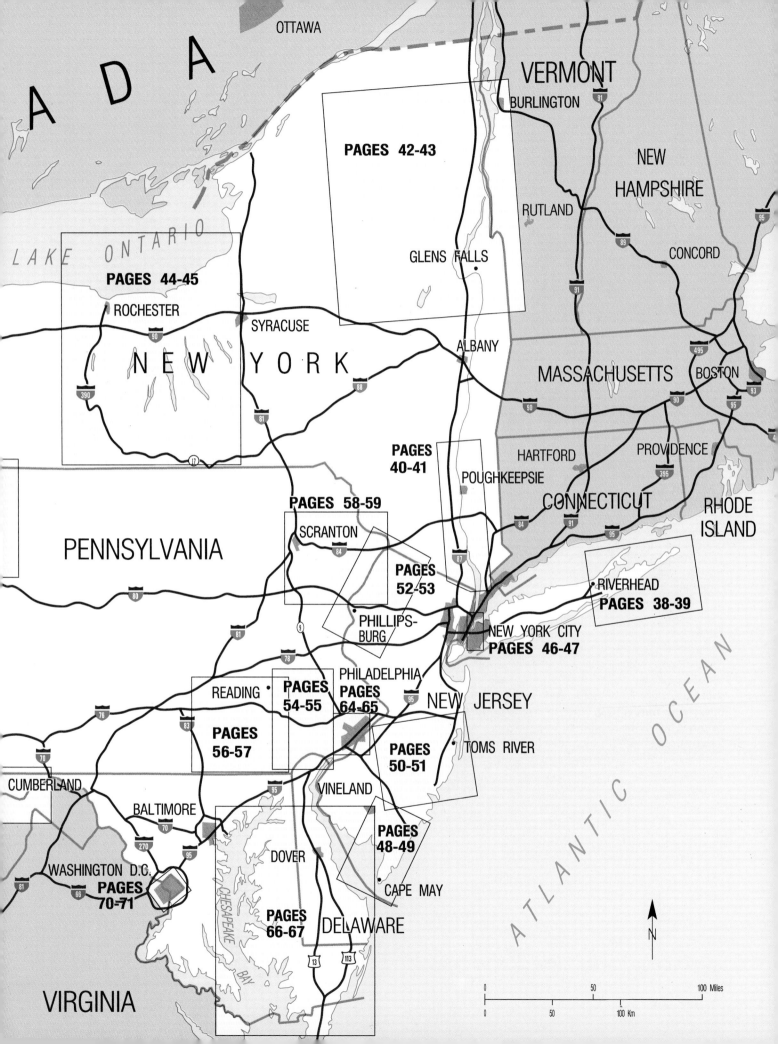

ADA

OTTAWA

VERMONT

BURLINGTON

NEW
HAMPSHIRE

PAGES 42-43

RUTLAND

CONCORD

LAKE ONTARIO

PAGES 44-45

ROCHESTER

SYRACUSE

GLENS FALLS

ALBANY

MASSACHUSETTS

BOSTON

N E W   Y O R K

HARTFORD

PROVIDENCE

POUGHKEEPSIE

**PAGES
40-41**

CONNECTICUT

RHODE
ISLAND

PAGES 58-59

SCRANTON

PENNSYLVANIA

**PAGES
52-53**

PHILLIPS-
BURG

RIVERHEAD

PAGES 38-39

NEW YORK CITY
PAGES 46-47

PHILADELPHIA

READING

**PAGES
54-55**

**PAGES
64-65**

NEW JERSEY

**PAGES
56-57**

**PAGES
50-51**

TOMS RIVER

CUMBERLAND

VINELAND

BALTIMORE

DOVER

**PAGES
48-49**

WASHINGTON D.C.
**PAGES
70-71**

CHESAPEAKE BAY

**PAGES
66-67**

CAPE MAY

DELAWARE

A T L A N T I C   O C E A N

N

VIRGINIA

0   50   100 Miles

0   50   100 Km

NORTH AND SOUTH FORKS
Long Island's Eastern Reaches

Long Island lies east-west in the Atlantic like a slender whale. Its jaws point at Staten Island; its flukes, the North and South Forks, trail 100 miles away into the eastern sea. When summer comes, the island swallows New Yorkers like plankton, but in spring and fall—before Memorial Day and after Labor Day—its eastern reaches are quiet. The beaches, dunes, and scrubby headlands become solitary places, where keening winds mourn times gone by.

Wine is the newest business on the North and South Forks. If you take SR 25 from Riverhead to Cutchogue, you will be in the grape-growing region, home of the Hargrave Vineyard, Long Island's first "estate-grown-and-bottled" winery.

Cutchogue's village green preserves buildings that recall earlier ways of life on the North Fork. The Old House, with period furniture, huge fireplaces, and the original 1649 mullioned windows, was built when the settlers were whalers, sea captains, and fisherfolk. Nearby is Wickham Farmhouse, built in the early 1700s during the first phase of the area's agricultural development. The third building, the Old Schoolhouse, dates from 1840, just before vacationers discovered the region.

The spirit of the past is also captured at Greenport's Museum of Childhood with its antique doll collection. Ferries depart from this charming seaport community for Shelter Island between the North and South Forks.

At Orient, near the North Fork's tip, old lifestyles are preserved at the Museums of the Oysterponds Historical Society, a collection of historic buildings. They include a 19th-century house with maritime exhibits and a 19th-century inn with period rooms. Beyond the village lies Orient Beach State Park, a five-mile peninsula with wide beaches. Across Gardiners Bay is Shelter Island, once a haven for persecuted Quakers.

The South Fork of Long Island, a fashionable resort area in the 19th century, is now a haven for harassed Manhattanites. Southampton, founded in 1640, has a fine museum of local history housed in an 1843 whaling captain's home. The Parrish Art Museum and Arboretum provides a glimpse of the wealth that came here.

Beyond Southampton lies Bridgehampton, a pretty village surrounded by potato fields and country lanes. To the north is Sag Harbor, once a major whaling and smuggling village. The Sag Harbor Whaling Museum displays whaling relics; Morton National Wildlife Refuge has

birdwatching on the Atlantic flyway.

East Hampton, settled in 1648, is a place of elegant summer residences. "Home Sweet Home," the childhood home of actor, playwright, and diplomat John Howard Payne, who wrote the song "Home Sweet Home," has a collection of English pottery, 17th- and 18th-century furniture, and a 1774 windmill. The Mulford Farmhouse, built in 1689, was a family home for eight generations, and today displays an elegant collection of 18th-century furniture and decorative arts.

Amagansett was a whaling village despite not having a harbor. Montauk, the setting for the movie *Jaws*, is still the haunt of big-game fishermen, and on Montauk Point, the Atlantic winds still blow clean and fresh. Somehow, on the North and South Forks, things change, and yet they stay the same.

Sail Away (*above*) The Long Island shore has long been a playground for the city dwellers of New York. The sports and dress may change, but the appeal remains the same.

Sag Harbor Whaling and Historical Museum (*top left*) in Sag Harbor, built in 1845 in Greek Revival style, was originally the home of whaling Captain Benjamin Huntting. Today, as the facade proclaims, the upper floor has become a masonic temple, while the ground floor houses a huge collection of whaling artifacts and memorabilia, including a full-size whaling ship, as well as model ships, fishing and whaling equipment, scrimshaw, logbooks, paintings, and collections of antique guns and dolls.

Sag Harbor's sheltered position gave it importance as a port from early times, and in 1789, Congress designated it one of the first two Ports of Entry.

Home Sweet Home (*bottom left*) in East Hampton was the childhood home of actor and diplomat John Howard Payne. It contains a fine collection of English pottery and early furniture. But perhaps the greatest attractions are the mid-eighteenth-century windmill on the museum's grounds and the well-tended, aromatic herb garden, which, on a warm, sunny day, delights both the eye and the nose.

SITES TO SEE

● **The Old Hook Mill** (East Hampton), an 1806 windmill on the town's Memorial Green, is open to visitors. It incorporates the center post of an older mill that was on this site, and is still in working order.

● **Montauk Lighthouse** (Montauk Point) was built in 1796 and is 85 feet tall. Ferries for Block Island, RI, depart from Montauk each day during the summer.

● **Riverhead** hosts an annual Polish festival in August with traditional foods, crafts, music, and dancing. The festivities are a celebration of the town's Polish heritage.

WORTH A DETOUR

● **Old Westbury Gardens** (Old Westbury) are the beautiful English-style gardens on the grounds of Westbury House; off I-497, this is an ideal stopping-off point on the way to the North and South Forks of Long Island from New York City. An oasis of color from May through October, the garden features an elegant formal rose garden, a walled garden, and a charming children's cottage. The house, build 1906 in the manner of a grand English manor house, features an outstanding art collection and antique furniture. Costumed mannequins are occasionally displayed in the summer as if attending a lavish social event.

● **Old Bethpage Village Restoration** (Old Bethpage) is a lovingly restored Long Island farm depicting life before the Civil War with costumed guides explaining each site. Self-guiding tours are along paths made of crushed oyster shells.

● **Fire Island National Seashore** reaches 32 miles eastward from Democrat Point. Popular with Manhattanites as a summer retreat, the island is also home to a variety of wildlife year round; 1,400 acres have been set aside as a national wilderness area. Car access is only available from the eastern and western entrances; other access is via ferries, which require reservations in the summer.

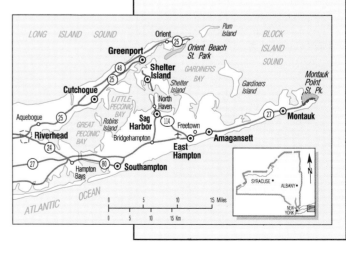

VALLEY OF MEETINGS

New York's Hudson River Valley

Along the Hudson and in the haunted, ancient mountains to the west, Iroquois warriors confronted the peaceful woodland Mohicans. French fur trappers, Dutch farmers, and English traders met in the rivalry of commerce here, and the valley's comfortable old towns still boast their successes. Later, the English and upstart Americans would meet here in war and, eventually, in friendship. Indeed, in this narrow strip of land along the Hudson, New England meets the rest of America—in towns that recall Vermont, but bear Dutch names. Proud of its trees and old stone fences, its little colleges, and its beautiful river, this is a civilized and honest burgher land.

From New York City to Albany, the Hudson has been plied by summer yachts and steamers and by huge tankers all year round. From the magnificent cliffs of the Palisades that guard the west just past New York City, to where the icy Mohawk joins the river far upstream, the Hudson is the chief inhabitant of every town along its banks. It offers, under curious opalescent skies seen nowhere else in the world, ever-changing vistas that 19th-century painters such as Cole and Church made famous.

Past dark Tarrytown, of Sleepy Hollow fame, a thriving community with some historic places restored for visitors, the river skirts old mill towns, like Newburgh and Poughkeepsie, whose rose brick warehouses are being converted to artists' studios. Inland to the east are vineyards and small family wineries that welcome visitors.

Along the river's eastern bank, Commodore Vanderbilt laid out the railroad that eventually opened the West. Trim

Amtrak trains offer choice commuting to New York, the big city at its mouth. They run past sculpted hillsides and the lawns of the patrician homes of the Astors, Mills, Vanderbilts, Roosevelts, Delanos, Aldriches, and Livingstones—and past little towns that served them, Hyde Park and Rhinebeck, themselves full of grand old houses. The 1826 house and 200-acre estate of Franklin D. Roosevelt at Hyde Park has been preserved just as it was at the time of his death.

Upstream, the Vanderbilt Mansion National Historic Site preserves the opulent lifestyle of one of the nation's wealthiest families in 1891. Highlights include the dining room with a table for 30, and Mrs. Vanderbilt's bedroom, decorated as if for a French queen, in the Louis XV style.

In Clermont, where, in 1807, the first commercially successful steamboat got its fuel—and its name—the cool summer breezes blow through from the notch in the wild Catskills across the water.

Day's Catch of Hudson River Sturgeon (*left*) Any fisherman would be delighted with a catch like this, but even bigger species can be found in landlocked waters. A common sturgeon might reach a length of 10 feet and could weigh more than 1,000 pounds. The flesh of the fish is considered quite coarse, but smoked sturgeon is eaten as a delicacy and the finest grades of caviar are made from sturgeon eggs.

United States Military Academy (*above*) Commonly called West Point, the Academy occupies the site of a Revolutionary War fort built to guard the river. For added safety, the Americans stretched a chain across the river from the fort to Constitution Island, but the attack never came. Its graduates include Ulysses S. Grant, Robert E. Lee, and Dwight D. Eisenhower.

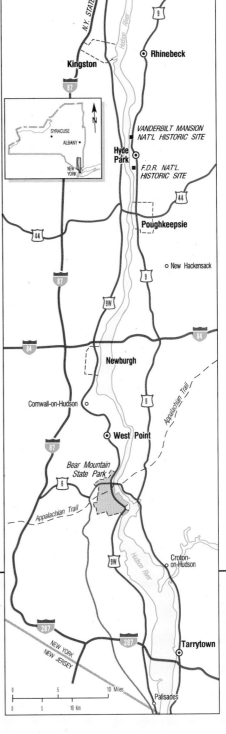

SITES TO SEE

● **The United States Military Academy** (West Point) was established along the shores of the Hudson in 1802. Among the campus buildings open to visitors are the museum with its excellent collection of military artifacts, the Cadet Chapel, built 1910, and the Old Cadet Chapel, a Greek Revival building from 1836.

Check with the visitor center for the dates and times of cadet parades.

● **Sunnyside** (Tarrytown) was described by its one-time owner, Rip Van Winkle's creator Washington Irving, as "all made up of gable ends and as full of angles as an old cocked hat." Furnishings include some of Irving's possessions; guided tours are conducted.

● **Lyndhurst** (Tarrytown) is an outstanding 1838 Gothic Revival mansion, once owned by railroad magnate Jay Gould, with sumptuous period furnishings.

● **Eleanor Roosevelt National Historic Site** (Hyde Park) preserves the 1925 cottage the First Lady and her friends built as a retreat.

● **Washington's Headquarters State Historic Site** (Newburgh), also known as the Jonathan Hasbrouck House, is where Washington had his headquarters April 1782 to August 1783.

● **The Vassar College Art Gallery** (Poughkeepsie) includes 75 works by Rembrandt.

PLENTIFUL WILDERNESS
The Adirondacks

In the Adirondack forests, which occupy six million acres of upstate New York, is a wild region bigger than Yosemite, Grand Canyon, Glacier, and Olympic National Parks combined. It encompasses nearly 90 towns, but from the High Peaks Wilderness to Silver Lake, it is overwhelmingly a region of unspoiled natural beauty. More than 30,000 miles of streams and rivers and 1,000 miles of footpaths crisscross the park, where rare lynx and marten now prowl.

Iroquois Indians called this region Ha-De-Ron-Dah, meaning "bark eaters," a sneer at its indigenous Algonquins, who did, in fact, eat tree barks.

Only 15 years before the state deemed the area a wild forest, fashion reigned in Saratoga Springs at Morrissey's Elegant Hell, a stylish casino built by heavyweight champion John Morrissey. The casino still boasts its Tiffany window and Italian gardens, and the town now welcomes the New York City Ballet and Philadelphia Orchestra in the summer. The National Museum of Thoroughbred Racing stands opposite the famous racetrack, but the brooding mountains and forests remain much as they were when the Algonquins knew them.

History surrounds this wilderness. Fort Ticonderoga, immaculately restored according to the original 1755 French blueprints, contains memorabilia of Ethan Allen and his Green Mountain Boys, who crossed Lake Champlain in the dead of night to take the fort without firing a single shot. The Six Nations Indian Museum at Onchiota preserves costumes, artifacts, and other relics of the Iroquois Confederation—including a remarkable 75-foot beadwork record belt. The John Brown State Historic Site, home and grave of the controversial abolitionist, is at Lake Placid. The grave is near those of his sons and followers who died at Harpers Ferry, West Virginia, following their ill-fated armory raid.

The visitor can enjoy winter sports at Lake Placid, international dogsled races at Saranac Lake in late January, the Eastern States Speed Skating Championships at Saratoga Springs, also in January, paintings by Da Vinci and Picasso at Glens Falls, or the Adirondack Hot Air Balloon Festival at Lake George in late September.

Or, the visitor can leave civilization behind and wander on isolated winding trails from rock peaks to the peaceful shores of plenteous mountain lakes.

Fort Ticonderoga (*left*), originally called Fort Carillon by the French who built it in 1755, stands on a thin strip of land between Lake George and Lake Champlain. Captured for England by Jeffrey Amherst in 1759 during the French and Indian Wars, and given its present name, it was taken by Ethan Allen in 1775 and abandoned to the British again two years later, during the Saratoga campaign of the Revolutionary War.

Whiteface Mountain Winterscape (*above*) The first forest preserve in the United States, a large portion of the Adirondack Mountains was deemed "forever wild" by state decree. The wilderness had already been damaged by lumbering activity, and forest fires in 1899, 1903, and 1908 scarred it further. But its pine-scented peaks and clear, still lakes gradually drew a host of wealthy visitors, whose presence turned the area into an all-year resort. The beauties of the landscape, known to every skier on the sparkling, frosty slopes, are just as alluring today.

SITES TO SEE

● **Lake Luzerne** offers whitewater rafting trips along the Sacandaga River. The White Water Derby is in early September, and the Adirondack Championship Rodeos are held here July to September.

● **Great Camp Sagamore** (Raquette Lake) was a Vanderbilt family retreat built 1897. Its 25 buildings include a Tyrolean lodge and a bowling alley.

● **High Falls Gorge** (Wilmington) is a deep and picturesque ravine cut by the Ausable River. It is crisscrossed by paths and bridges.

● **Tupper Lake**, a booming lumber and sawmill town at the end of the 19th century, is a popular year-round resort. In summer, it provides boating, fishing, and swimming; in winter, the Big Tupper Ski Area has slopes suitable for all skill levels.

● **Robert Louis Stevenson Cottage** (Saranac Lake) was the author's home for the winter of 1887–8, and is furnished with his belongings. Stevenson called this the "little Switzerland in the Adirondacks."

● **Prospect Mountain Veterans Memorial Highway** (Lake George) takes motorists almost to the mountain's peak, with spectacular views over Lake George and the surrounding countryside. Viewmobiles transport visitors to the summit from a parking lot near the peak.

● **Fort William Henry Museum** (Lake George) is a reproduction of a 1755 British log fort, with stockades and dungeons. James Fenimore Cooper featured this fort in *The Last of the Mohicans*.

● **Kent-Delord House** (Plattsburgh) is a Federal-style home built 1791–1811 and commandeered by the British in 1814. Furnishings include an oak silver chest left behind by the British.

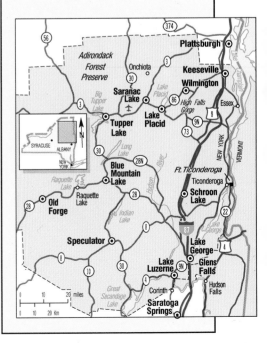

THE LAND WHERE GOD LAID HIS HAND

The Finger Lakes

Orchards and vineyards have prospered in this relatively warm part of northern New York. So have radical and reformist causes: abolitionism, Mormonism, and women's rights were all fostered here. Science, technology, and the arts have done well, too. The first public demonstration of heavier-than-air flight was given at Hammondsport. The art of soaring was developed at Elmira, where Mark Twain wrote *The Adventures of Huckleberry Finn*. Corning is world famous for its glass, and Cornell University, at Ithaca, for its gardens and agricultural and veterinary scholarship. All this, and great houses, too, abound, with landscapes of lakes, rolling hills, spectacular gorges, and waterfalls.

The vineyards that hem these lakes and valleys signify Earth's bounty. Near Palmyra, Joseph Smith found another sign. In 1827, he was directed by an angel to discover in the ground the golden tablets that became the writ of a new religion, Mormonism. A golden statue of the Angel crowns the hill he called "Cumorah," and every year a colorful pageant commemorates the revelation.

To the Indian nations who inhabited their shores, the Finger Lakes—Seneca, Cayuga, Canandaigua, Keuka, Owasco, and Skaneateles—were miraculous. Some said they were formed when the Great Spirit laid his hand on the earth here. Others say they were pools between the ridges on a great turtle's shell.

For slaves making their way north on the Underground Railroad, the Finger Lakes were a place of freedom. Harriet Tubman, escaped slave turned "conductress," lived at Auburn after the Civil War.

At Seneca Falls, another kind of freedom was pursued. Elizabeth Cady Stanton organized the first Women's Rights Convention here in 1848. Both homes are open to the public, as is the Rochester home of Susan B. Anthony, another great champion of women's suffrage.

A fine Victorian estate, Sonnenberg Gardens in Canandaigua, boasts fountains, streams, "theme" gardens—Japanese, Italian, Colonial, Rose, Rock, and Moonlight—and elegant furnishings.

At Hammondsport, there are wineries, including Bully Hill Vineyards, home of refreshing vintages and readable labels, and the picturesque Taylor Wineries. At Branchport, Finger Lakes Wine Cellars give tastings and hay-wagon tours.

Some of the region's wildest scenery can be found in Letchworth State Park, where the Genesee River Gorge—"the Grand Canyon of the East"—runs for 17 miles between cliffs as high as 600 feet, with spectacular overlooks, waterfalls, and the Letchworth Pioneer and Indian Museum. Other spectacular falls and gorges include those at Watkins Glen State Park.

From Vine to Table (*left*) Most of the vineyards in the Finger Lakes are relatively small farm wineries with a capacity of under 50,000 gallons a year. Tending the vineyards requires a great deal of personal attention throughout the season. Although many grape varieties have been introduced, the original wineries were based on the Lambrusca grape. This thriving industry's principal products are a range of white wines.

Finger Tip (*above*) The beautiful town of Watkins Glen is nestled on the southern tip of Seneca Lake. The adjoining state park which shares its name is cut by a deep ravine, with walls up to 200 feet high. A riverside path climbs 700 feet over a distance of two miles. There are waterfalls, caves, grottos, and countless other rock formations to reward the hiker. A bridge 165 feet above the water provides beautiful views of the picturesque gorge.

SITES TO SEE

● **Corning Glass Center** (Corning) is a fascinating 3-part complex devoted to glass worldwide, with one of the world's most comprehensive historical collections. Visitors can watch renowned Steuben glass being made and engraved, and learn how fiber optics work.

● **Rockwell Museum** (Corning) houses a collection of Steuben glass by designer Frederick Carder, as well as American paintings, Indian artifacts, and a doll collection begun in the early 1900s.

● **Elmira College** (Elmira) has preserved Mark Twain's octagonal study, where he wrote many of the Tom Sawyer stories. The auth' and his family are buried in a nearby cemetery.

● **Rose Hill** (Geneva), on Seneca Lake, is a 21-room mansion built 1839 with Empire-style furnishings, perhaps the finest Greek Revival home in the U.S.

● **Taughannock Falls,** north of Ithaca, plummets 215 feet in a glen in Taughannock Falls State Park.

● **Watkins Glen** is home of the 3.377-mile former Grand Prix racetrack.

● **Montour Falls,** named for Queen Catharine Montour of the Iroquois Nation, has Greek Revival buildings against the stunning backdrop of the 156-feet Che-qua-ga Falls. The Schuyler County Historical Society Museum has memorabilia depicting life in rural upstate New York in the 19th century. The collection includes fashion, antique toys, implements and tools, and Indian artifacts.

NEW YORK CITY

New York is a city of superlatives. At its heart, it is a tiny rocky island with limited space; but it is the nation's biggest city and its busiest, with 40 percent of the country's foreign trade passing through its port. From Wall Street's stock exchanges to the galleries of SoHo, the blooms of the flower market, and the glittering wares in the diamond district, the range and scale of business make New York the nation's commercial center. In cultural affairs, the city sets America's standards for both variety and excellence. It boasts the world's largest natural history museum, the largest botanical library housed in a single U.S. collection, and the world's largest collections of American Indian artifacts and 20th-century American art. Radio City Music Hall, home of the Rockettes, is the largest theater in the country, and the art in the Guggenheim Museum lines a spectacular spiral ramp. The Metropolitan Opera House and Broadway's theaters lure the finest talent in the nation, and three-quarters of America's books are produced here. The outer boroughs of Brooklyn, the Bronx, Queens, and Staten Island united with Manhattan in 1898, but that borough alone contains unparalleled resources for visitors. Intriguing ethnic neighborhoods jostle with commerce, finance, and fashion. And despite their reputation, busy New Yorkers are as friendly as any people in the United States.

Rockefeller Center at Christmas (*right*) The luminous tree over the skating rink is the central focus for the holiday decorations along Fifth Avenue. A lacy star hangs in front of Tiffany's, and clockwork dolls, dancing animals, and miniature scenes of old New York light the department store windows.

The Thanksgiving Day Parade (*below*) snakes through the city for four miles. In between marching bands and decorated floats, the giant helium balloons are anchored by dozens of Macy's employees. The store produces the annual parade, and members of the staff walk cartoon characters between the skyscrapers to Herald Square. People still talk about the one that got away.

SITES AND DISTRICTS

Chinatown and Little Italy Colorful adjoining neighborhoods packed with some of New York's best restaurants.

South Street Seaport Museum The Fulton Fish Market, full-rigged museum ships, and historic buildings.

Times Square Once "the crossroads of the world," the heart of the theater district blazes with lights.

Wall Street Visit the bustling trading room of the N.Y. Stock Exchange.

MUSEUMS

American Museum of Natural History Over 36 million items. Highlights are the dinosaurs and dioramas of wild animals. Don't miss the Hayden Planetarium.

Cloisters A collection of medieval treasures including the Unicorn Tapestries, made in 1499, perched on a bluff overlooking the Hudson River.

MAP REFERENCE

1. American Museum of Natural History
2. Children's Zoo
3. Chinatown
4. Circle Line
5. Cloisters
6. Empire State Building
7. Hayden Planetarium
8. Little Italy
9. Metropolitan Museum of Art
10. Metropolitan Opera House
11. Museum of Modern Art
12. New York Stock Exchange
13. Radio City Music Hall
14. Rockefeller Center
15. SoHo
16. Solomon R. Guggenheim Museum
17. South Street Seaport Museum
18. Staten Island Ferry
19. Times Square
20. United Nations Headquarters
21. Wall Street

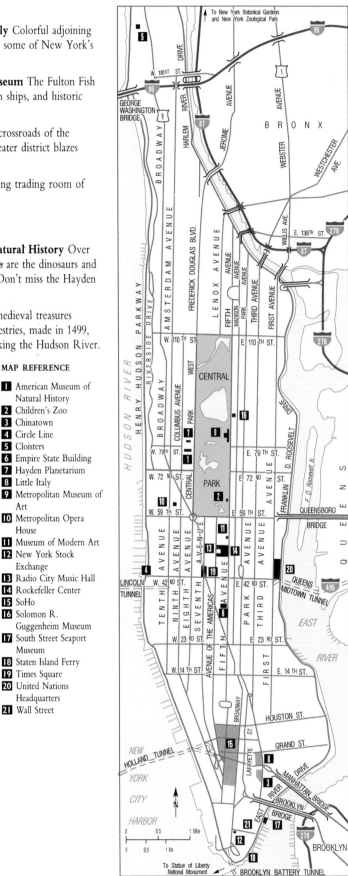

Metropolitan Museum of Art One of the world's greatest museums, with everything from Egyptian mummies to European paintings and Tiffany glass.

Museum of Modern Art Comprehensive survey from the Impressionists to the present. One-third of the collection is by American artists and produced since 1945.

BUILDINGS

Empire State Building A cherished landmark gives the best overall view of Manhattan from observatories on the 86th and 102nd floors.

Rockefeller Center The Art Deco splendor of Radio City Music Hall and NBC television studio tours are both part of this 14-building 1930s complex.

Statue of Liberty National Monument A French gift of 1886 that has welcomed millions of immigrants to New York. A museum in the base commemorates them, and visitors can climb into the statue.

United Nations Headquarters Tour these famous buildings, symbols of world peace, and attend the General Assembly when it is in session.

PARKS

Central Park The city's largest open space contains a carousel, a zoo and separate Children's Zoo, and free concerts and theater performances.

New York Botanical Garden (Bronx) Landscaped grounds and gardens feature a restored 1902 conservatory with a Hanging Garden, Fern Forest, and Palm Court.

New York Zoological Park Called the Bronx Zoo, the biggest city zoo in America contains over 4,000 animals.

ATTRACTIONS

Circle Line A three-hour boat tour that circles Manhattan Island offers a guided tour of its rivers and historic sites.

Staten Island Ferry At 25 cents, still the best entertainment in New York.

CAPE MAY DIAMONDS

New Jersey's Southern Shore

New Jersey's southern shore, Cape May, was one of the nation's first resort areas. Finding it more temperate than coastal regions to the north, but still convenient to metropolitan New York and New Jersey, well-to-do families built summer homes here and de-camped from the sweltering cities. Hotels and private clubs were built, and an elegant beach society developed, nurtured by miles of broad beaches, sparkling waves, and the unique inland terrain of the Pine Barrens.

The first European settlement on Cape May was a small colony established by the Dutch West India Company in 1623. Its leader, Captain Cornelius Mey, provided the name of the region, but the local Indians were not impressed with his generosity. The Lenni Lenapes themselves liked to summer on the coast, and they burned the settlement to the ground.

Before long, however, the Cape was permanently settled by New England whaling folk; memorabilia can be seen in the Historical Museum at Cape May Court House. At Leamings Run Gardens and Colonial Farm stands a replica of an old whaler's cottage and 25 gardens arranged along a one-mile walk.

The city of Cape May was the nation's first planned resort. A disastrous fire in 1887 destroyed many buildings, but some, such as the Abbey and the Mainstay Inn (built in 1872 as Jackson's Clubhouse), survived. The town, rebuilt in a gloriously ornamented gingerbread style with ornate fretwork and columned verandas, is today a pink-and-white showplace of exuberant Victorian resort architecture.

Cape May Point State Park offers 190 acres of beach, dunes, freshwater marshes, ponds, and woodland. Quartz crystals,

known as "Cape May Diamonds," can sometimes be found along the beach. Near Cape May Point, the Cape May-Lewes Ferry crosses the bay to Delaware and offers moonlight cruises in July and August.

North of Cape May City on the Atlantic shore is Wildwood, with a 2½-mile boardwalk and seven amusement piers. Its beaches are the widest, and probably the safest, on the East Coast.

Farther north, Ocean City was established as a Christian resort in 1879, the year after Cape May City's Great Fire. Alcohol was, and still is, banned, but an eight-mile beach and good fishing guarantees its popularity. In late July, the Night in Venice Boat Parade is held, and October sees the town's Indian Summer Weekend.

Between the coast and the Cape's offshore islands, the Intracoastal Waterway threads its intricate way. Stone Harbor Bird Sanctuary is the nation's only heronry inside a town. In addition to herons, ibis, loons, and grebes, cattle egrets can be seen riding on the backs of local livestock. The Wetlands Institute, dedicated to the study and preservation of coastal ecology, celebrates a Wings 'n' Water Festival in the fall.

Colorful Concoction
(*right*) The variety of architectural treats in Cape May makes it unique as a town. Although Cape May has been designated a national historic landmark, the liveliness of the community provides a considerable contrast to other, quieter parts of this shore.

Summer Pleasures (*left*) In the harbor, vibrant sails jostle with each other as they billow in the breeze. Pleasure craft of all kinds take to the sea, while land-loving tourists sample the pleasures of the boardwalk and the beach.

SITES TO SEE

● **Pink House** (Cape May) is one of the splendid Victorian gingerbread homes in this popular seafront resort town. Although many of the ornate houses are private, walking tours and trolley rides give visitors plenty of opportunities to admire the charming architecture. **Wilbraham Mansion** is another attractive building with Victorian period furnishings. The 1840 farmhouse is open on Wednesday evenings in the summer. A gaslight tour held each week in the summer takes in Physick House, Mainstay Inn, the Abbey, and Humphrey Hughes House.

● **Congress Hall** (Cape May) was former President Benjamin Harrison's retreat to escape from the sweltering summer heat of Washington.

● **Cape May** celebrates the town's Victorian heritage each October with a festival featuring live music, food, and numerous crafts.

● **Ocean City Historical Museum** (Ocean City) recalls 19th-century life along the southern New Jersey coast, with an emphasis on maritime exhibits. Other maritime displays, such as whaling equipment and ship models, can be seen at the nearby Historical Museum at Cape May Court House.

● **The Lighthouse at North Wildwood**, built 1873, is open to visitors during the summer.

● **Historic Cold Spring Village** (Cape May) re-creates local 19th-century farm life with a working farm and children's petting zoo.

● **Enjoy afternoon outdoor band concerts** in the summer at Cape May Country Park.

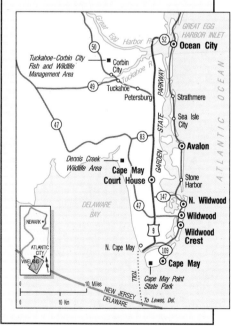

ORCHIDS AND IRON
The Pine Barrens

Within 25 miles of Atlantic City—and less than 40 miles from Philadelphia—is the last vast wilderness in the metropolitan corridor connecting Washington and Boston. The Pine Barrens, 3,000 square miles of sandy forests, streams, and marshes, are far from barren. Wild orchids abound with more than 400 other flowering plants. The tiny curly grass fern, *Schizaea pusilla*, occurs nowhere else in the world. The tiny Pine Barrens tree frog, bright green with a lavender stripe, lives here and in small colonies in Georgia and North Carolina. Once a center for iron-smelting, the woods house the ruins of old furnaces. Blueberries, tomatoes, peaches, and apples are cultivated, and to the south are historic vineyards.

Although the Pine Barrens once lay beneath the sea, they owe their dune-marked character to sediment carried here by the last melting of Ice Age glaciers. The land is dry, but the water table is close to the surface, creating numerous streams and the marshes whose bog iron was once the foundation of a thriving iron industry.

In Atsion State Park, the iron master's mansion survives from the old iron-making community. Mount Holly was established as a Quaker town in 1676. Its Smithville Mansion was the Victorian home of Hezekiah B. Smith, foundry owner and inventor of the bicycle railroad.

The best preserved of the old iron-making centers is Batsto Historic Village, where Batsto Ironworks was founded in 1766. At its height, the community had a population of 1,000; the restored village includes the iron master's mansion, the gristmill, sawmill, and furnaces. Stagecoach tours are given in summer. Batsto Nature Area is a 150-acre preserve nearby.

Surrounding Batsto, Wharton State Forest has 500 miles of sandy roads, including Batsto Wilderness Trail. The Barrens mark the southern limit for 60 species of plants native to Canada and the northern limit for some southern plants.

Some 150 species of birds frequent the Pine Barrens. Twice that number can be seen at the Edwin B. Forsythe National Wildlife Refuge, 2,000 acres near Oceanville. The town's Noyes Museum has a large display of decoys and gives demonstrations of decoy-carving.

The southern Pine Barrens is good grape country. German settlers planted vineyards around Egg Harbor City in 1858 and were followed later by Italian vintners.

Iron Master's Mansion, Batsto (*right*) Some portions of this 36-room house date from 1766, others from the 1870s.

Pine Barrens Tree Frogs (*left*).

Moving the Floating Cranberry Harvest, Haines Bogs (*below*) The native cranberry has been cultivated here since about 1840.

SITES TO SEE

● **Batona Wilderness Trail** winds 40 miles through Wharton State Forest. Canoes can be hired at Atsion Lake off US 206.

● **Mount Holly** was named after a nearby 183-foot "mountain," and still contains many 18th- and 19th-century buildings. Abolitionist John Woolman may have taught in the **John Brainerd School**; **Burlington County Historic Prison Museum** was built 1810; **Smithville Mansion** features Christmas tours in December.

● **Historic Renault Winery** (Egg Harbor City), established 1864, gives tours and tastings.

WORTH A DETOUR

● **Cooper House** (Burlington), 1780, was the birthplace of author James Fenimore Cooper in 1789. Cooper memorabilia is displayed along with furniture that belonged to Napoleon's brother, who settled nearby after the Battle of Waterloo. The **Capt. James Lawrence House**, next door, was where the War of 1812 naval hero was born; Lawrence is best remembered for his rallying cry "Don't give up the ship." The house is furnished in 1812 style.

● **Clara Barton School** (Bordentown) preserves the memory of the founder of the American Red Cross. She opened the school in 1852 as part of a crusade for free public education.

● **Huddy Park** (Toms River) re-creates the spirit of the Revolutionary War with a replica of a blockhouse burned down by the British in 1782.

● **Museum of American Glass** (Millville) highlights the history of American glassmaking from 1837 with 7,000 items. Millville grew into the nation's second largest glass-producing community by the end of the last century after silica sand was discovered here. Today, the tradition continues at the Wheaton Glass Co. **Wheaton Village** re-creates an 1888 glassmaking town, with daily demonstrations. The site includes an 1876 one-room schoolhouse and period general store, and picnic facilities.

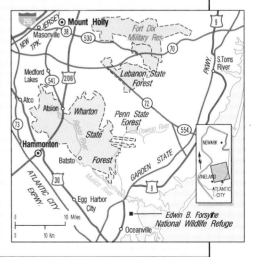

THOROUGHFARES AND WILD SCENERY

The New Jersey Highlands

New Jersey's wildest country straddles the Kittatinny Ridge where the Delaware River cuts its famous Delaware Water Gap. Bears roam these Appalachian hills, whose spring and summer woods are delicately colored with the flowers of mountain laurel and rhododendron. The heart of the region is the Delaware Water Gap National Recreation Area. Not so long ago, the attractions were copper, zinc, and iron. Some of the nation's earliest wagon roads crossed the region, and the Morris Canal formed a major thoroughfare between the Delaware and Hudson rivers. The old trades still color the area, which today combines breathtaking scenery with industrial history.

One of the nation's oldest roads—some say the oldest maintained road—crosses I–80 at the New Jersey entrance to the Delaware Water Gap National Recreation Area. Popular as a resort since the early 1900s, the recreation area still has much to offer those interested in natural and cultural history, as well as outdoor activities.

The Old Mine Road once ran from the Water Gap's copper mines to Esopus, as Kingston, New York, was then called, on the Hudson River. It winds northeast along the Delaware's east bank, past the old Dutch copper mines to restored Millbrook Village. Here blacksmiths, carpenters, and weavers ply their trades in period dress; Millbrook Village Days are celebrated each October with lots of old-fashioned fun and craft demonstrations. Beyond Millbrook, an unmaintained stretch of the road leads to the restored Van Campen Inn, built around 1745.

Northeast of the Water Gap, the 14,000-acre High Point State Park extends to the New York state line, with a road to the state's highest point, a 1,803-foot peak on the Kittatinny Ridge. A 220-foot obelisk, Memorial Tower, surmounts the ridge. From the top of the tower, visitors can sometimes see New York City. Several trails, including the Appalachian Trail, cross the park, and the beach at Lake Marcia provides good swimming. In the winter, cross-country skiing, ice fishing, and snowmobiling are popular pastimes.

East of the Water Gap at Allamuchy Mountain State Park, the rapid Musconetcong River meets the Morris Canal. An old lock can be seen near picturesque Saxton Falls. The canal's course leads to Waterloo Village near Stanhope, a restored ironmaking community dating from the 1760s, now restored to its mid-19th-century appearance, with craft shops, stores, and homes open to visitors. In the summer, daily concerts and craft demonstrations take place here, with guides in period dress to explain each exhibit.

At Franklin, 300 different kinds of minerals, including fluorescent Franklinite, are found, making the area prime ground for rock hounds. Zinc mining was foremost here, and until the 1950s, 500,000 tons of zinc ore were mined annually. The Franklin Mineral Museum offers a replica of a zinc mine and large mineral collections.

Farther north, at Vernon, is one of the world's largest adventure theme parks, Vernon Valley Action Park. Its 1,200 acres include facilities for speedboats and Lola formula race cars. Vernon Valley–Great Gorge ski area has four chairlifts and extensive snow-making equipment.

Wick House (*right*) This comfortable home and farm became the headquarters of Gen. Arthur St. Clair during the brutal winter of 1779–1780. The fact that Henry Wick and his wife were products of New England is reflected in the style of their home, which was built around a central chimney.

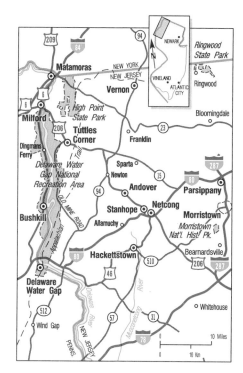

SITES TO SEE

● **Dingmans Falls** (*above*), near Dingmans Ferry, PA, is one of the scenic sites in Delaware Water Gap National Recreation Area. The visitor center is open daily May through October.

● **Morristown National Historical Park** (Morristown) preserves the Continental Army's 1779–80 encampment at Jockey Hollow, as well as Gen. George Washington's headquarters, and Wick House, Gen. Arthur St. Clair's headquarters. About 6 miles south of Morristown, troops survived in Jockey Hollow, near starvation and in freezing conditions. Washington ordered a fort to be built, which became known as Ft. Nonsense when the legend grew that the only purpose of the structure was to keep troops occupied; the site is marked, although none of the foundations remain.

● **Ringwood Manor** (Ringwood State Park) is an ironmaster's home started about 1807, which eventually grew to contain 51 rooms. Half of the rooms are restored with period furniture and contain interesting exhibits about the local iron mining industry. **Skylands Manor**, also in the park, is a 1924 summer home built for a millionaire. Although unfurnished, the house is notable for its lovely interior and beautiful European stained glass windows; open for Christmas tours.

WORTH A DETOUR

● **Edison National Historic Site** (West Orange) lets visitors see Thomas Edison's laboratory complex and Glenmont, his 23-room house.

THE DU PONT DYNASTY
The Brandywine Valley

Rich in history and culture, the Brandywine Valley boasts historic mills, the great mansions of the du Pont dynasty, and, in Wilmington, Delaware, an early cosmopolitan city. The region saw events of great military importance during the Revolutionary War: the Battle of Brandywine in 1777 was a prelude to the British occupation of Philadelphia and Washington's winter encampment at Valley Forge.

On its way from Pennsylvania's southeastern hills to Delaware Bay, the Brandywine River offered early settlers abundant water power and access to the sea. Within easy reach of the markets of Washington, Baltimore, and Philadelphia, the region naturally became a center of the milling industry. Its gristmills set the national price of wheat and shipped their products as far as Calcutta and Java. Its paper mills saw the invention of the first machines to produce paper in rolls, thereby promoting the local development of publishing. Its iron foundries supplied metal ware. All these activities made the region rich.

The greatest wealth, however, came with the du Ponts. Pierre Samuel du Pont fled to America from the French Revolution, and his son Eleuthère Irénée built the Brandywine gunpowder mills that founded the family's wealth. Hagley Museum, north of Wilmington, is on the original works site, now restored, overlooked by Eleutherian Mills, the family's "modest" 1803 Georgian resid-

ence. At Longwood, the former estate of Pierre du Pont, is one of the world's greatest gardens, with $3\frac{1}{2}$ acres of greenhouses and conservatories.

Even before the du Ponts arrived, Wilmington had been a substantial and cosmopolitan town on the Delaware side of the river. Named Fort Christina by its Swedish founders, it was swollen late in the 18th century by a diverse crowd of emigrés: French nobles escaping the Revolution, planters escaping the 1791 insurrection in Santo Domingo, Irish fleeing their troubled country. They all poured into Wilmington.

The city remains cosmopolitan beyond its size. Its Swedish heritage is preserved at Fort Christina. Nemours Mansion, former estate of Alfred du Pont, is modeled on a Louis XVI chateau and has a fine formal French garden. The Delaware Art Museum has the best collection of English pre-Raphaelite paintings in America, and Rockwood Museum, in a 70-acre Gothic estate, has outstanding exhibits.

Nemours Mansion and Gardens in Wilmington, DE, (*left*) is named for the ancestral hometown of the du Pont family in north-central France. The splendid centerpiece of the 300-acre estate is the 77-room mansion, which was completed in 1910 and filled with the finest antique rugs, tapestries, art, and furniture. The magnificent formal gardens extend one-third of a mile. The vast grounds also contain a hospital, the Alfred I. du Pont Institute, which opened in 1940. Loath to leave the estate he had so lovingly created, du Pont is buried beneath a bell tower on the grounds. Tour reservations are recommended for individual visitors and required for groups.

Hopewell Furnace National Historic Site (*right*) Near Birdsboro, this restored iron-making community gives visitors an amazingly detailed view of the work carried out in such 19th-century foundries. Built by Mark Bird in 1771, initially to make raw pig iron and cast stove plates, the furnace quickly became a source of ammunition and armaments for the Revolutionary War. After the war, Hopewell produced a variety of iron items including the "Franklin fireplace"; stoves of all kinds were its greatest success. Rendered obsolete by the advance of technology, the furnace closed in 1883. Its restoration in the 1930s was aided by photographs, archaeological discoveries, and interviews with former employees.

SITES TO SEE

● **Winterthur Museum and Gardens** (Wilmington, DE) was the magnificent home of Henry F. du Pont. Nearly two hundred rooms, furnished in styles from 1640 to 1860, house the U.S.'s richest collection of American decorative arts, with more than 89,000 items. Selected tours take in different rooms; reservations are recommended. The huge estate features gardens landscaped in naturalist style.

● **Valley Forge National Historical Park** (Valley Forge, PA) preserves the 1777–78 winter encampment of George Washington's Continental Army. The park can be explored on a self-guiding tour or on fee-charging bus tours which run throughout the summer.

● **West Chester** is a charming town with numerous preserved Greek Revival and Victorian homes. Brinton House, south of town, is a restored Quaker farmhouse. Gourmets will want to visit in mid-September when Brandywine Valley restaurants present the one-day Chester County Restaurant Festival.

● **Brandywine River Museum** (Chadds Ford), housed in an 1857 gristmill, displays works by noted American illustrators and painters, with a gallery of works by Andrew Wyeth and members of his family.

● **Brandywine Battlefield State Park** (Chadds Ford) is near the site of the historic 1777 battle, which is re-enacted each September. Visit a replica of Gen. Washington's headquarters and the restored house where Gen. Lafayette stayed.

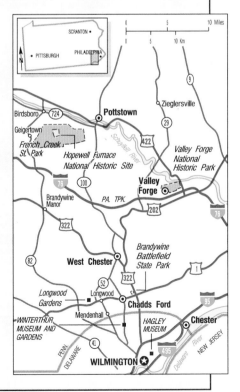

GENTLE PEOPLE OF THE GOOD EARTH
Pennsylvania's Amish Country

Less than two hours' drive from Philadelphia, peace can be found in the timeless serenity of Lancaster, York, Chester, Lebanon, and Berkshire counties. Here is the heart of the immaculately tended Pennsylvania Dutch country and home of the Plain People, the abidingly peaceful Amish and Mennonites. Even before visiting the region, it is easy to feel affection for these self-sufficient farm folk. Unique in our melting-pot society, they never melted. Celebrated on stage and screen, from the vintage Broadway musical *Plain and Fancy* to the powerful film *Witness*, the Amish represent an unbroken continuity of appearance, attitude, and practice, not a costumed re-creation of the past.

Two of colonial America's greatest lures to immigrants were freedom of worship and rich land to cultivate, and they attracted several religious sects. Mainly Germans (the *Deutsch* misleadingly blurred into "Dutch"), they settled and stayed. Their few still-faithful descendants perpetuate their customs and beliefs in all aspects of daily life. From dress to work to leisure, simplicity and modesty characterize them.

The sects vary, but they are alike in their distinctive speech, sound farming methods, strong visual traditions, and abundant provisions based on old-country favorites, like shoo-fly pie, schnitz, and schmiercase. A strong tradition of design is evident in the radial hex signs painted on barns to ward off the evil eye and in the stenciled and stitched geometric motifs used on furniture, tiles, and quilts.

The little towns of Intercourse and Bird-In-Hand on SR 340 leading to Lancaster are now commercialized. In other communities, however, such as Ephrata, Lititz, Manheim, Mount Joy, and Strasburg, the Plain People's way of life is clearly seen.

Pennsylvania Dutch country has no official boundaries. It is roughly defined by the Schuykill and Susquehanna rivers and SR 10 to the east and west, and I–78 and the Maryland state line to the north and south. Throughout the region, superbly presented features of the region's industrial past lend a satisfying balance to the homespun attractions of the Amish. Hopewell Furnace National Historic Site in Berks County is a magnificent example of an early iron-smelting village. Its original millrace and waterwheel, bridge house and cooling shed, and tenants' cottages have been faithfully restored. At Cornwall, the 1742–1883 iron furnace has been restored along with the ironmaster's house and an open-pit mine. Donegal Mills Plantation at Mount Joy offers guided tours of the mansion and garden, the mill, and the miller's house.

Contemplating the labors of the past can provoke an appetite. In Lebanon, opportunities abound to sample the town's famed bologna and to see how it is ground and cured. With its historic coexistence of German agricultural and English industrial communities, the town is a microcosm of this intriguing region.

SITES TO SEE

● **Hershey** is home of the chocolate of the same name. **Hershey's Chocolate World Visitor's Center** explains the production process from tropical plantations to the factory. The **Hershey Museum of American Life** houses a wide-ranging collection of Pennsylvania Dutch antiques and other Americana.

● **Wheatland** (Lancaster) is the restored 1828 Federal-style home of James Buchanan, the only Pennsylvanian U.S. president. The house contains period furnishings; highlights are the Empire-style dining room and Buchanan's study.

● **Ephrata Cloister** (Ephrata) consists of 10 medieval-looking buildings of an unusually successful semi-monastic German religious community that flourished here 1732–1834. The Saal (chapel) with its gabled roof and narrow windows typifies the buildings' medieval style.

● **Sturgis Pretzel House** (Lititz) lets visitors help twist soft pretzels before baking.

● **Strasburg Rail Road Co.** (Strasburg) gives round trips to Paradise on a steam locomotive. Next to the Strasburg depot, the **Railroad Museum of Pennsylvania** houses antique rolling stock.

● **Daniel Boone Homestead** (Baumstown) is the frontiersman's restored birthplace and childhood home. The site also includes a blacksmith shop, sawmill, and early regional memorabilia.

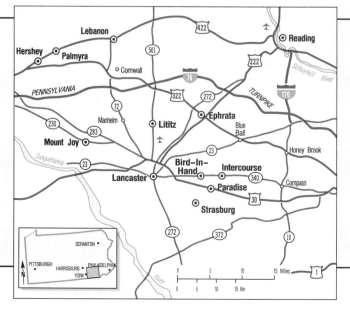

● **Landis Valley Museum** (near Lancaster) interprets rural Pennsylvania life before 1900. The 100-acre site displays items in 20 buildings.

● **The People's Place** (Intercourse) is the county center for Amish and Mennonite arts and crafts.

● **Tulpehocken Manor Inn and Plantation** (Lebanon) is a 150-acre working farm with a 1769 farmhouse remodeled in 1883.

WORTH A DETOUR

● **Reading** was founded 1748 and still has many 18th- and 19th-century buildings. In **York**, visit the **Golden Plough Tavern**, built in the 1740s of timber and brick, the **Bobb Log House**, typical of the county's early log homes, and the **Gen. Gates House**, where Lafayette blocked moves to oust Washington as commander of the Continental Army. The city is also a center for farmers' markets.

Pennsylvania Farmland (*above*) Although the Amish eschew modern farming methods, their fields are models of good husbandry, and their immaculate white farmsteads reflect their traditional family values.

Amish Farmers (*left*) The Amish work their fields with horses and travel in horse-drawn buggies. A strict Amish home can be recognized by the absence of electrical wires and motorized vehicles, and often by the presence of a yard rack for drying Mason jars.

57

HONEYMOON COUNTRY
The Poconos

Northeastern Pennsylvania's Allegheny Mountains have attracted vacationers from Philadelphia, New Jersey, and New York since 1815. Visitors were drawn to the marvel of the Delaware Water Gap, and then beyond it to the miles of gently wooded hills and lakes where tributaries of the Delaware and Susquehanna rise—the Poconos. Although many large resorts now specialize in the honeymoon trade, even the unromantic will find the Poconos idyllic, rich in quiet landscapes.

Farmers reached this Appalachian area in the 18th century. Tanners were drawn by the great hemlock forests rich with natural tannin. Early 19th-century settlers came to work rich deposits of iron, slate, and coal. Hot on their heels came the builders of roads, canals, and railroads.

At Scranton, once the richest coal mining town, the region's industrial history can be read like a book. In the first chapter are the four remaining smokestacks of the stone blast furnaces, built like medieval castles, that served the first iron foundry. The 250-foot-deep Lackawanna coal mine in McDade Park and the excellent anthracite museum next door make up the second chapter. Third, visitors can see the iron horses that hauled the wealth to market at the Steamtown railroad museum. The final chapter contains the culture that wealth brought to Scranton at the Everhart Museum, where paintings, sculpture, and fine glass, a beehive and small planetarium are on display.

At Eckley Miners' Village near Hazleton, an earthier episode in the industrial saga unfolds. This real mining village (where scenes from the movie *The Molly Maguires* were shot) breathes the atmosphere of bygone days.

Thick forests in the mountains and along the Delaware still shelter a few virgin stands of hemlock. At Bushkill Falls, north of the water gap, bridges and catwalks provide intimate views of eight falls, the highest with a drop of 100 feet.

At Dingmans Ferry, trails lead through woods to 100-foot Silver Thread Falls and Dingmans Falls, a silvery staircase on Dingmans Creek.

Upriver at Lackawaxen stands the engineering marvel that put Dingman and his ferry out of business, the Delaware Aqueduct. Built by John Roebling, designer of New York's Brooklyn Bridge, it was the first cable suspension bridge in the U.S., carrying the Delaware and Hudson canals across the Delaware River. Honesdale was the terminal for New York-bound coal barges on the canal. On August 29, 1829, it saw the first journey of a steam locomotive in the U.S.A. Today, a replica of that engine is displayed near West Park Street.

Eckley Miners' Village, Hazleton (*left*) Some of the houses in this 19th-century town of 50 buildings are still inhabited by local miners who once worked the rich anthracite seams that web the ground around Hazleton. Mining activity boomed here from the 1830s until well after the Civil War. Preserved today amid open-strip mines, a restored 1850 miner's house, two restored churches, and various exhibits give a detailed picture of the difficult life the miners endured.

Dingmans Creek, Pocono Mountains (*above*) Only a few hours from the crowded streets of Manhattan and the busy pavements of Philadelphia, the deeply wooded hills and clear mountain streams of the Poconos seem like an oasis of rural calm. Bright with mountain laurel and wildflowers in spring, cool and shady in summer, flaming with colorful foliage in the fall, they provide an endlessly changing display of nature's wonders.

SITES TO SEE

● **Colony Village**
(Canadensis) is a spacious recreation of a 19th-century
village, set in meadows
around a pond, with a small
museum, a blacksmith's
shop, a carriage house, and a
white clapboard chapel. A
gem-and-mineral store sells
examples of Pocono coal
carving.

● **Steamtown National
Historic Site** (Scranton)
preserves an outstanding
collection of locomotives and
rolling stock. Among the
displays is the Union
Pacific's "Big Boy," one of
the largest locomotives built
in the U.S. It is 130 feet
long and weighs about 1.2
million pounds.

● **Pennsylvania
Anthracite Heritage
Museum** (Scranton) is
located at the site of a
former strip mine, now
McDade Park. Exhibits
cover regional history,
highlighting coal mining, the
canals, and the role women
played in local silk milling.

WORTH A DETOUR

● **Jim Thorpe** was
incorporated in the mid-
1950s to honor the 1912
Olympic gold medalist;
formerly it was the towns of
Mauch Chunk and East
Mauch Chunk. A memorial
to the athlete is just east of
town on SR 903. The **Asa
Packer Mansion** is the
lavish 1860 Victorian home
of a local philanthropist and
industrialist. **St. Mark's
Episcopal Cathedral**, paid
for by Mrs. Packer, has a
Tiffany window.

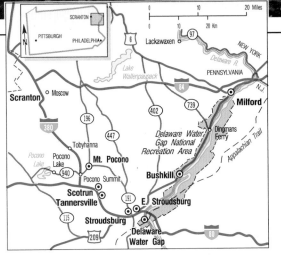

A WORLD ADRIFT FROM TIME

Allegheny National Forest

Forest County, in the heart of the almost virgin wilderness of Pennsylvania's Allegheny National Forest, is the least populated part of the state. There are no multi-lane highways here, no traffic lights, no county newspaper to tally comings and goings, and no local radio station. Instead, there is an abundance of solitude and fresh air, of woods, hills, winding rivers and clear lakes. Among the immense old hemlocks of the forest, some of which were young when Shakespeare was a boy, there is also an abundance of time.

From its source, the Allegheny River flows north into New York, turns south, and is dammed to form the mighty Allegheny Reservoir, which two states, New York and Pennsylvania, share. Pennsylvania's 12,000 acres contain marinas, campgrounds, and spectacular mountain laurel. From the reservoir, the river flows south to Tidioute, a village settled in 1800 by members of the New Harmony religious community. East of the town is Tidioute Overlook, with fine views of the village and the river.

Continuing northeast to a fork, the eastbound road, SR 666, is a primitive one, but it leads through some of the most beautiful country in the forest to Heart's Content Recreation Area. Hemlock trees in these acres of primeval wilderness are 400 years old.

Beyond Heart's Content, the road continues east to Sheffield. The ranger station provides information about this area. At Kinzua Bridge State Park north of Mt. Jewett, the 2,053-foot-long bridge that carried the Erie Railroad 301 feet above Kinzua Creek was, in its heyday, the world's highest railroad bridge. Excursions came from as far as Buffalo to see it. Now it provides fine views of the valley.

At Bradford, the Penn-Brad Historical Oil Museum commemorates the discovery of oil here in 1875.

The southern gateways to the National Forest are Tionesta (whose Indian name means "Home of the Wolves") and Marienville. The approach to Marienville passes close to Clear Creek State Park. In late June or July, the white rhododendrons flower in spectacular profusion. From Marienville, the Kinzua Railroad runs excursions to Kane and across the bridge.

Near Tionesta is one of the largest tracts of primeval hardwood forest in the eastern U.S.A., the Tionesta Scenic Area. The town's late-August Indian Festival celebrates the region's native heritage. The Allegheny Mountain Championship Rodeo is held in July at the Flying "W" Ranch in nearby Kellettville.

Bridging the Gap (*right*) The Alleghenies proved to be the first great challenge to the railroad builders pushing their way westward. Their engineering skill is legendary, and one of the many feats they performed was crossing the Kinzua Valley. Today, a Chinese steam locomotive pulls trains along the line from Marienville to just beyond the Kinzua Bridge and back again.

Allegheny River (*left*) The melodious chorus of the resident Pennsylvania songbirds and their migratory visitors enhances the peaceful aura that the landscape of the Allegheny River valley inspires.

SITES TO SEE

● **SRs 66 and 666**, scenic drives through Allegheny National Forest, are particularly enjoyable when the woods are ablaze with spectacular fall colors. Almost 170 miles of hiking trails wind through the forest, and there are 17 campgrounds.

● **Crook Farm** (Bradford) is a village of reconstructed buildings, including a one-room schoolhouse.

WORTH A DETOUR

● **Drake Well Museum** (Titusville) commemorates where oil was struck in 1859. The museum displays antique equipment and photographs of the region's early oil boom days. Nearby **Oil Creek State Park** is popular for snowmobiling. In summer, the park offers camping, picnicking, and fishing facilities.

● **Pennsylvania Lumber Museum** (Galeton) recalls the days when lumbering was king in this heavily wooded section of the state. Visitors can wander through a reconstructed 19th-century logging village with a restored blacksmith shop and bunkhouse. An 1890 steam-powered circular sawmill is on display, along with felling equipment and a locomotive that was especially designed to work on the steep grades of Pennsylvania's vast pine forests.

● **Chautauqua, NY**, on the shores of Chautauqua Lake, is a resort community with many Victorian summer cottages. The community became known in the mid-1870s when the Chautauqua Institution was founded to teach Methodist Sunday school teachers in a retreat surrounding. The still-popular program has evolved into a non-demoninational summer school with wide-ranging topics. **SR 430** from Bemus Point to Mayville is a scenic drive along the lake.

● **Conneaut Lake Park** is an amusement park that has been attracting families since the beginning of the century. Sightseeing cruises take passengers around the state's largest natural lake, and the local winery offers tastings.

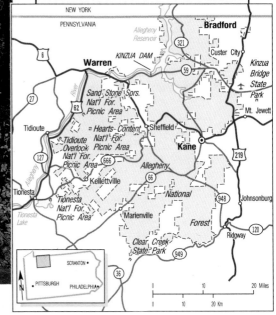

ROADS WEST, RIVERS NORTH

The Laurel Highlands

The last great obstacles along the National Road before it reached the Ohio River in 1818 were the ridges and valleys of the Laurel Highlands in Pennsylvania's southern Alleghenies. This is an area rich in water, wood, coal, iron, and natural beauty. Its major rivers, the Monongahela and Youghiogheny, flow north from the mountains to meet the Allegheny at Pittsburgh. There they form the Ohio River, which flows northwest before turning south to become, via the Mississippi, the great river road to the Gulf of Mexico. With natural resources and a crossroads location, this beautiful land prospered and was strategically vital in both the French and Indian Wars and the Civil War.

Before the National Road—now US 40—became the major axis of east-west travel, the nation's main thoroughfare was the river route connecting the Gulf of Mexico with the Great Lakes. Brownsville, an unassuming town on the Monongahela whose position and local walnut and oak forests made it an early boat-building center, was the easternmost junction of these north-south and east-west routes. Many of the keelboats that plied the Ohio and Mississippi were made here.

Today, Brownsville's Nemacolin Castle, a red brick, Tudor-style mansion, looks down from steep bluffs on the river and the bridge that carries the National Road across. Named for the Indian who first established a trade route between Maryland and Ohio, the mansion began life as a trading post. As its owner prospered, it acquired distinctive crenellations, an octagonal tower, a walled garden, and splendid furnishings.

The same forests used to build keelboats—and later the rich deposits of anthracite beneath them—also fueled the region's foundries. Uniontown, on the old road, was an early iron-and-steel town whose most famous son was General George C. Marshall, 1953 Nobel Peace Prize winner for his Marshall Plan to aid Europe after World War II.

Still farther southeast down the road is Fort Necessity National Battlefield, where George Washington and a small company of Virginians fought combined French and Indian troops at the beginning of the French and Indian Wars. The battle marked Washington's first major military command, and the only time he surrendered. A replica of the fort has been constructed, and Mount Washington Tavern, nearby, is a restored 19th-century stagecoach inn. The original fort was destroyed by the French as the Colonial troops marched away after surrender.

Northeast are the folded ridges and valleys of the Alleghenies. The Laurel Highlands Hiking Trail runs 70 miles over wild ridgetops from Conemaugh Gorge near Johnstown to Ohiopyle State Park, a place of rugged beauty and rafting.

North of Ohiopyle, near Mill Run, is Fallingwater, a weekend home designed by Frank Lloyd Wright in 1936. Its revolutionary plan, cantilevered over a waterfall, set new standards for the integration of buildings with their environment. Many consider it one of the 20th century's most important buildings. The house, which was the subject of an exhibition at the Museum of Modern Art, has been photographed endlessly. Even decades after its construction, it retains the modernity which made it striking when first built. The refinement of the line and the daring nature of the cantilevers are characteristic of the architect's work. The inspired choice of Wright as architect for the difficult site at Bear Run resulted in one of the milestones of modern architecture.

Stately Towers (*left*) Picturesque church steeples are a reminder of the centers of community life. The variety and craftsmanship of the local churches are a reflection of the skills and inspiration of local builders and artisans. These striking spires dotted across the tree-covered landscape mark the settlement of these highlands.

Fallingwater (*above*) This contemporary architectural masterpiece by Frank Lloyd Wright was donated to the Western Pennsylvania Conservancy in 1963 by Edgar Kaufmann, Jr., son of the Pittsburgh department store owner who commissioned it. The harmony of the structure with its surroundings, and the appropriateness of its scale, make it truly unique.

SITES TO SEE

● **Laurel Caverns** (south of Uniontown) along Summit Mtn. differ from chamber-style caves in that these are more like catacombs with numerous passageways off each. Guided tours cover about three-quarters of a mile of dry limestone passages.

● **Johnstown Flood National Memorial** (northeast of Johnstown) recalls the 1889 flood that left 2,209 dead and $17 million worth of property damage in its wake. Exhibits near the site of the old South Fork Dam explain the background of the tragic event and remember the $3.7 million in donations from around the world.

Grandview Cemetery, in the town, has graves of 777 unknown victims.

● **Somerset Historical Center** (Somerset) has a restored log house, smokehouse, and covered bridge as part of its tribute to rural life of 1750–1950. A Mountain Craft Days festival is held each September.

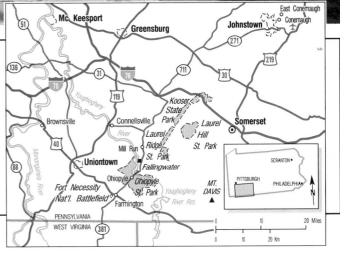

PHILADELPHIA

It was here in Philadelphia that Thomas Jefferson drafted the Declaration of Independence. On July 4, 1776, it was signed in the State House, now called Independence Hall, where the Continental Congress had previously voted to resist British rule and George Washington had been named commander of the Continental Army. Four days later, the Declaration was read in public in the State House grounds. While the British occupied Philadelphia in 1777, the Continental Congress was in exile in York, Pennsylvania, only returning a year later after the British had withdrawn. Congress Hall, built 1787–89, was the seat of the U.S. Government from 1790 to 1800, and the scene of John Adams' inauguration.

Most of these momentous events took place in the few square blocks now preserved in Philadelphia'a Independence National Historical Park. Here, visitors can see the Liberty Bell, Independence Hall, and Carpenters' Hall, distinguished by an octagonal cupola, where the First Continental Congress met in 1774. One of the most unusual structures is Franklin Court, where history and the present meet. Steel beams outline the three-story home Benjamin Franklin built here. An underground museum contains memorabilia of Franklin's life as a scientist, diplomat, printer, and politician.

Outside the historic area, however, Philadelphia is perhaps the least explored and most under-appreciated of America's great cities. It offers an extraordinary wealth of museums and galleries, a great many fine and historic buildings, and, along the Schuylkill River, one of the largest and most magnificent urban parks in America. All things considered, no American city is more interesting or more important to the nation's history.

Independence Square (*right*) In the heart of the historic city, America's struggle for liberty breathes life into the roughened bricks and worn cobblestones. Built as Pennsylvania's State House, Independence Hall embraced the framing and signing of the Declaration of Independence and the momentous meetings of the Second Continental Congress, which created the Continental Army. The Liberty Bell, now displayed in its own pavilion, hung here for nearly 100 years. Nearby stands Old City Hall, which was briefly the home of the U.S. Supreme Court.

Assembly Room, Independence Hall (*far right*) Restored to its post-Revolutionary War appearance, this room contains the actual inkstand used for the signing of the Declaration of Independence and the "rising sun" chair from which Washington presided over the Constitutional Convention.

HISTORIC SITES AND DISTRICTS

Independence National Historical Park Attractions include Liberty Bell Pavilion where visitors can touch the bell, and B. Free Franklin Post Office and Museum commemorating the nation's first postmaster, who franked letters by hand; visitors' letters are still hand franked.

MUSEUMS

Afro-American Historical and Cultural Museum Black culture in the Americas is described with art, artifacts, and documents.

Franklin Institute contains a science museum, planetarium, and the Benjamin Franklin National Memorial, with personal memorabilia.

Norman Rockwell Museum On display are all the illustrator's *Saturday Evening Post* covers, paintings, and a replica of his studio.

Philadelphia Museum of Art The world's third largest art collection features Oriental art, Renaissance paintings, and modern masterpieces.

Rodin Museum Located in Fairmount Park, this is the largest collection of Rodin's works outside Paris; his *Gates of Hell* is at the entrance.

The Rosenbach Museum and Library A mid-19th-century home with American, English, and French furnishings, and rare books and manuscripts, including *The Canterbury Tales* and *Ulysses*.

NOTABLE BUILDINGS

Betsy Ross House The first U.S. flag was sewn here in 1776.

Philadelphia City Hall When completed in 1900, this was the world's largest occupied building.

PARKS

Fairmount Park The world's largest metropolitan park with scenic drives, walking trails, and bridle paths, as well as historic buildings. Outstanding houses include Lemon Hill, built around 1800 in the Federal style, with an oval salon, and Mount Pleasant (1763), known for Chippendale-style furnishings and ornate woodwork.

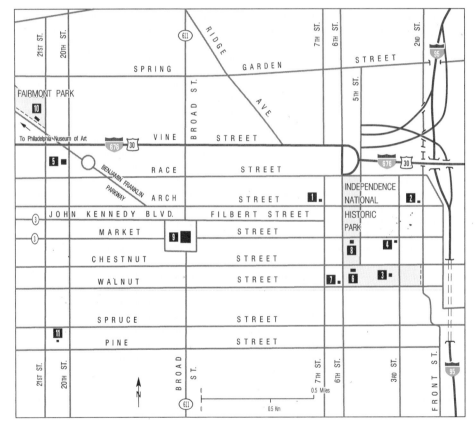

MAP REFERENCE

1 Afro-American Historical and Cultural Museum
2 Betsy Ross House
3 Carpenters' Hall

4 Franklin Court
5 Franklin Institute
6 Independence Hall and Congress Hall
7 Norman Rockwell Museum

8 Liberty Bell Pavilion
9 Philadelphia City Hall
10 Rodin Museum
11 Rosenbach Museum and Library

WHERE LAND AND SEA INTERTWINE
The Delmarva Peninsula

No American place so neatly encapsulates the maritime and the agricultural—sea and land—as the 175-mile-long Delmarva (DELaware/MARyland/VirginiA) Peninsula, bounded by Chesapeake Bay to the west and Delaware Bay and the Atlantic to the east. Barrier islands with wide, sandy beaches, stretch south from Cape Henlopen, while the western shore is deeply indented by bays and estuaries. Inland, the landscapes range from rolling hills and woods to level fields of corn and soybeans—and myriad chicken ranches.

Just south of the Chesapeake and Delaware Canal, Odessa, Delaware, is the Delmarva's northern gateway. Once a major grain-shipping port, its wealth can still be seen in its fine old homes—many open to the public the last Sunday in April.

There are more vintage houses in Dover, Delaware's capital since 1777, and excellent collections at the Delaware Agricultural and State museums. West of Dover there are Amish farms, and to the northeast Bombay Hook National Wildlife Refuge. To the south, Assateague Island National Seashore fronts the ocean for miles, a place of dunes, quiet beaches, and snow geese. Farther south on the island is Chincoteague National Wildlife Refuge, a magical place of marshes and pine woods, host to flocks of migrant water birds and deer and wild ponies.

Across the peninsula is Crisfield, Maryland, the so-called "Crab Capital of the World." Ferries go to Tangier Island,

Virginia, settled in 1686. The islanders make a living from fishing and crab-farming, and practice a still-archaic lifestyle.

Smith Island, Maryland, settled in 1657 and still populated by descendants of Lord Baltimore's colony, is even more archaic, especially in its speech.

At Crisfield, visitors can see decoy carvers at work at the Ward Museum. At Salisbury, the Atlantic Flyway Wildfowl Carving and Arts Exhibition is held in October, and the North American Wildfowl Art Museum houses excellent collections of decoys. Blackwater National Wildlife Refuge on the Nanticoke River is another haven for migrating birds.

At Cambridge, Maryland, sailboats race in summer on the Choptank River. The High Street Historic District preserves 18th- and 19th-century houses. Another popular yachting center is St. Michaels, an unspoiled port from the 17th century.

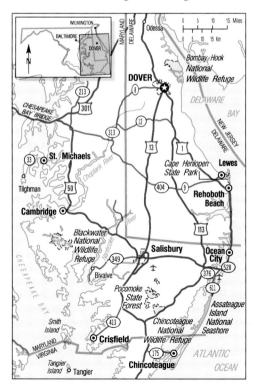

Hooper Strait Lighthouse, St. Michaels, MD (*left*) Once called Shipping Creek, St. Michaels was an active port before the Revolution and enjoyed great success as a shipbuilding center until about 1830. A museum complex of 16 buildings contains many of the region's oystering boats and commercial schooners.

Snow Geese Over Bombay Hook, Delaware Bay (*above*) A longstanding favorite of birdwatchers for the variety of migrating waterfowl it attracts, this wildlife refuge has been visited by 300 different species of birds since it opened in the 1930s. Sharp eyes will spot hawks, owls, and hummingbirds.

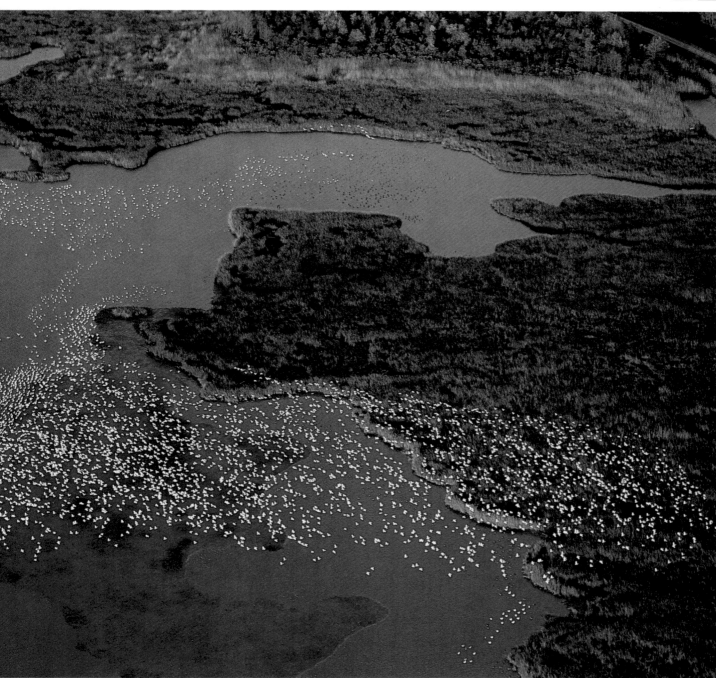

SITES TO SEE

● **Rehoboth Beach** is one of the popular resorts along Delaware's Atlantic coast that Washington DC, residents flock to every weekend during the summer. The annual Sand Castle Building Contest is held in August.

● **Zwaanendael Museum** (Lewes, DE) preserves the community's Dutch heritage. The building was modeled on a town hall in the Netherlands, and displays include local memorabilia as well as Indian and maritime artifacts.

● **Cambridge, MD**, is the site of the National Muskrat Skinning Championship each February. The town's **Old Trinity Episcopal Church** was built in 1765.

● **Corbie-Sharp House** (Odessa, DE), built 1774, is a Georgian-style home with a

collection of Chippendale furniture and other period furnishings. Nearby **Brick Hotel Gallery** displays Rococo-style furniture made by John H. Belter, a New York cabinetmaker.

● **Life Saving Station Museum** (Ocean City,

MD), built 1891, covers local history and the role of the station. Models and dioramas show how this popular resort community has developed.

● **Oxford, MD**, was the colony's official port of entry in 1683. **The Custom House** is a replica of the

first federal customs point. The **Oxford Museum** highlights local maritime traditions with wide-ranging displays.

APPALACHIAN CORNER
Maryland's Western Highlands

Maryland's wandering southern border is formed by the Potomac River flowing north to Cumberland and then east out of the Appalachian highlands to Washington, D.C. Before it reaches Hancock, the river swoops north toward Pennsylvania, nipping the state to a span of less than three miles. At Hancock, I-70 turns north, but US 40, the old National Road, runs west, cutting its way through the scenic mountains and Green Ridge State Forest. Then Maryland takes a deep breath again and broadens out into the western highlands—a region thoroughly distinct from any other part of the Free State.

Near Maryland's western border, a curious microclimate has formed the Cranesville Subarctic Swamp near the Youghiogheny River. Whooping cranes live here in vegetation normally found only hundreds of miles north. Finzel Swamp, north of Frostburg, is another area of strange transposed northerliness.

At Swallow Falls State Park, Henry Ford, Harvey Firestone, and Thomas Edison camped on wilderness expeditions in 1918 and 1921. Here, the Youghiogheny flows over Muddy Creek Falls, the state's highest waterfall, and through virgin hemlock forest. Henry Ford and friends were not the first to recognize the appeal of this region. St. Matthew's Episcopal Church in Oakland is known as the church of the Presidents: Grant, Harrison, and Cleveland worshiped here while vacationing nearby. Mountain Lake Park was a resort community for wealthy participants in the Chautauqua program of self-help education. The community flourished from 1881 to 1942, and many of the outstanding Victorian homes have been

lovingly preserved.

Victorian tourists came to the region on the railroads. Oakland's Queen Anne-style Baltimore and Ohio Railroad station, built in 1884 with incised brickwork and a conical tower, is one of the nation's earliest. At Cumberland, visitors can enjoy old-style rail travel on the Allegany Central Railroad on scenic steam train rides to Frostburg. The old Western Maryland Railway Station houses a visitor center for the C & O Canal National Historical Park; and five miles south is the C & O Canal Boat Replica, with quarters for the captain and mules.

At Paw Paw, West Virginia, on the state line, the Paw Paw Tunnel, a major accomplishment of 19th-century engineering, carried the canal through 3,118 feet of solid rock. Other mementoes of the days when roads, rails, and canals were penetrating this part of the Appalachians can be seen in and near Grantsville. Casselman Bridge, once the longest (80 feet) single-span stone arch bridge in the nation, was built in 1813 as part of the National Road.

Paw Paw Tunnel, Chesapeake and Ohio Canal (*above*) Bikers on the towpath will have a smooth journey, but the canal rises from sea level to an elevation of 605 feet at Cumberland. Built at the same time as the Baltimore and Ohio Railroad, which by 1842 reached as far as the **Western Maryland Railway Station** (built 1913) in Cumberland (*left*), the canal was nearly obsolete by the time it was completed in 1850.

SITES TO SEE

● **Penn Alps** (Grantsville) is an Allegheny craft center and restaurant occupying a remodeled log stagecoach inn from about 1818. Visitors can watch once-everyday colonial crafts, such as woodcarving, spinning, and weaving, demonstrated daily from Memorial Day through October. A Quilt Festival is held here each July.

● **Stanton's Mill**
(Grantsville), which claims to be the nation's oldest gristmill, was built in 1795, rebuilt in 1856, and is still in operation.

● **Casselman Hotel**
(Grantsville) first opened its doors in 1824 as an inn for coach drivers along the old National Road, and is still functioning today as a hotel.

● **History House**
(Cumberland) portrays life in

1867 with period furniture and antiques in 18 restored rooms. During the Christmas holidays, the house is decorated with traditional ornaments, and evening candlelight tours are offered.

● **Appalachian Collection**
(Cumberland), on the campus of Allegheny Community College, records the regional lifestyle through local history and various memorabilia.

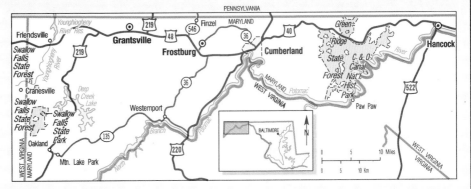

WASHINGTON, D.C.

When Congress first moved to Washington, D.C., in 1800, few of Pierre L'Enfant's elegant designs for the city were yet realized. Only one wing of the Capitol had been built, and muddy roads recalled the marshes that distinguished the city's original plots, chosen by George Washington nine years earlier. During the War of 1812, when the British occupied the city, most of it was burned to the ground. Postwar building was rapid, with the smoke-blackened walls of the President's House painted white, transforming it into the White House. Railroads and the Chesapeake and Ohio Canal came into the city. As the Civil War broke out, Washington had a population of about 75,000.

Today, the nation's capital has a population of just under one million, and the metropolitan area more than three million. The city is a place of parks and shade trees, with buildings in every known style of architectural revival. The splendid vistas envisioned by Pierre L'Enfant at its heart stretch from the Capitol to the Potomac River. Superb museums, libraries, archives, monuments, and festivals reflect the city's status among the world's capitals.

In addition to the Smithsonian Institution's 13 galleries and museums in Washington, the city has dozens of other smaller, equally top-notch museums. The Phillips Collection houses fine 19th- and 20th-century American and European paintings in what was once a wealthy family's home. Rare Renaissance books and manuscripts, including early editions of Shakespeare classics, are on display at the Folger Shakespeare Library, where there is also a model of London's Globe Theatre. The National Zoological Park, set in 163 acres, is home to 4,400 animals.

One of the best ways to see the numerous attractions is via sightseeing tourmobiles operated by the National Park Service: tickets include unlimited stops, and the routes cover all the major sites. During summer, White House tours require tickets; these are free on a first-come, first-served basis from booths on The Ellipse. The rest of the year, tours start from the East Gate from 10 a.m. until noon, and include the East Room and the Green, Red, and Blue Rooms.

Georgetown is a fashionable residential district in northwest Washington with quiet streets of restored elegant townhouses and stores. Georgetown University is here.

MUSEUMS

Freer Gallery of Art American and Eastern art, including more Whistler paintings than any other collection.

National Archives The original Bill of Rights, Constitution, and Declaration of Independence are on display here.

National Gallery of Art Masterpieces by Raphael, Rembrandt, El Greco, and the French Impressionists.

National Museum of American History Inaugural gowns worn by First Ladies and the flag that inspired the "Star-Spangled Banner" are among the highlights of this collection.

National Museum of Natural History The $44\frac{1}{2}$-carat Hope Diamond is among the more than 500,000 items displayed, including specimens of prehistoric animals, and an insect zoo.

NOTABLE BUILDINGS

Lincoln Memorial Words from the Gettysburg and Lincoln's Second Inaugural addresses are carved on the marble walls.

Thomas Jefferson Memorial The nation's third president and Declaration of Independence author is commemorated with a 19-foot bronze statue in a simple circular domed building.

U.S. Capitol The seat of U.S. government since 1800, where all presidents since Thomas Jefferson in 1801 have been inaugurated. Tours start frequently from under the Rotunda.

Washington Monument One of the world's tallest masonry structures, this obelisk is almost 556 feet tall. Visitors are taken to the 500-foot level and back by elevator; advance arrangements can be made to walk down.

White House Home of American presidents.

National Air and Space Museum (*above*) The history of aviation and space technology soars through 23 exhibition areas. Aircraft of all ages and sizes hang in the air, and the displays and films focus on every aspect of their use. The black granite wings of the **Vietnam Veterans Memorial** bear the names of every soldier who died in that conflict or is still missing.

MAP REFERENCE

1. Folger Shakespeare Library
2. Freer Gallery of Art
3. Lincoln Memorial
4. National Air and Space Museum
5. National Archives
6. National Gallery of Art
7. National Museum of American History
8. National Museum of Natural History
9. Phillips Collection
10. Thomas Jefferson Memorial
11. U.S. Capitol
12. Vietnam Veterans Memorial
13. Washington Monument
14. White House

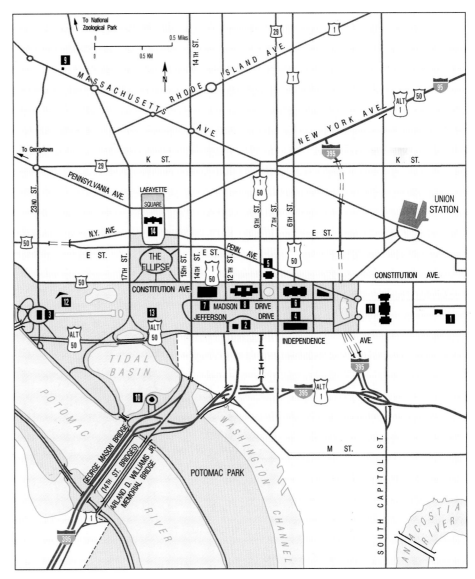

THE
APPALACHIAN
SOUTH

South of the great tidewater rivers of the mid-Atlantic, the rough spine of the Appalachians divides the coastal plains of Virginia and the Carolinas from what was once America's western frontier. It was not until 1775 that Daniel Boone blazed his trail through the wilderness into Kentucky, and the settlers who followed him were no less adventurous than those who later struggled across the Rockies. Today, the traveler who criss-crosses the Appalachian Mountains will find back roads that lose themselves or become hazardous in the deep woods, and may briefly recall the region's one-time wildness. For most, though, these gentle states blend their momentous pasts into 20th-century settings of hospitality.

On Roanoke Island, for instance, where Sir Walter Raleigh founded the eastern seaboard's first English colony in 1585, the neat plots of an Elizabethan garden commemorate the pioneers who disappeared from the colony, leaving only an enigmatic word, "Croatoan," as their epitaph. A few miles north at Kill Devil Hills, the Wright Brothers made the world's first heavier-than-air flight. Nothing commemorates their achievement as well as the stiff breezes. These winds that still stir the dunes, poised at the margin between the land and sea, remind us that their flight marked the boundary between the Age of Flight and all previous history.

In Kentucky, only 34 years after the Wilderness Road was blazed, Abraham Lincoln was born in a shaky cabin that is now enshrined in a mausoleum of granite and marble. At Yorktown, Virginia, an afternoon's walk from the Jamestown Colony and Williamsburg's neat streets, Lord Cornwallis surrendered his British troops, effectively ending the Revolutionary War. The tatters of George Washington's campaign tent are among the memorabilia of the victory, but in this region of heroes, only the Civil War sites seem fully eloquent: Antietam, for example, whose tall markers distinguish the square mile where 18,000 men died, and Appomattox, where Confederate soldiers laid down their arms.

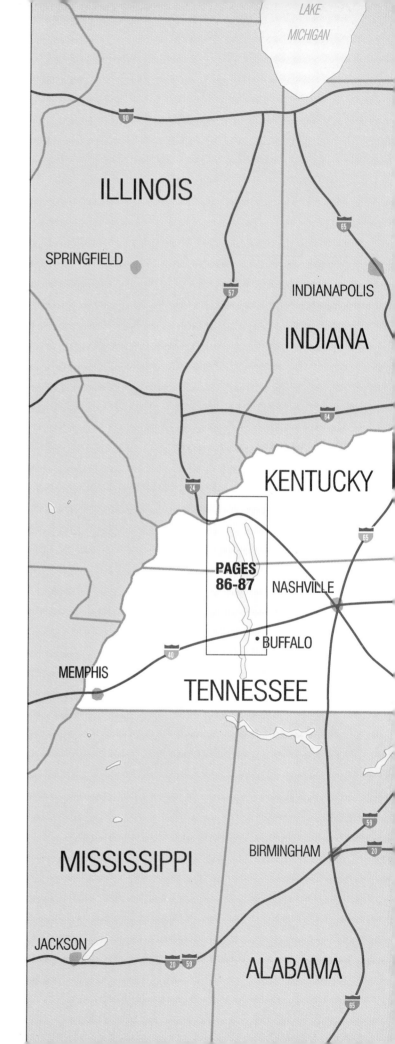

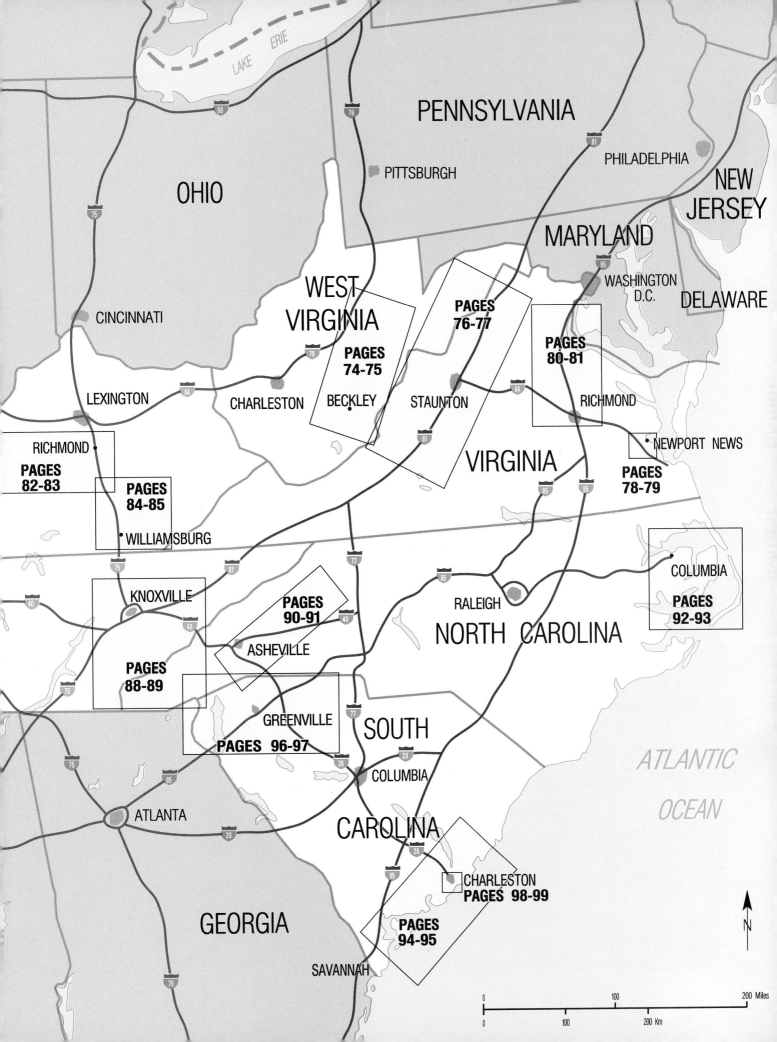

LAKE ERIE

PENNSYLVANIA

OHIO

PITTSBURGH

PHILADELPHIA

NEW JERSEY

MARYLAND

WASHINGTON D.C.

DELAWARE

WEST VIRGINIA

PAGES 76-77

PAGES 80-81

CINCINNATI

PAGES 74-75

LEXINGTON

CHARLESTON

BECKLEY

STAUNTON

RICHMOND

VIRGINIA

NEWPORT NEWS

RICHMOND

PAGES 78-79

PAGES 82-83

PAGES 84-85

WILLIAMSBURG

COLUMBIA

PAGES 92-93

KNOXVILLE

PAGES 90-91

RALEIGH

PAGES 88-89

ASHEVILLE

NORTH CAROLINA

GREENVILLE

SOUTH

PAGES 96-97

COLUMBIA

ATLANTIC

OCEAN

ATLANTA

CAROLINA

CHARLESTON
PAGES 98-99

GEORGIA

PAGES 94-95

SAVANNAH

N

0   100   200 Miles

0   100   200 Km

APPALACHIAN HIGHLANDS
West Virginia's Reluctant Hills

A branch of the mightier Appalachians, the Alleghenies form a demarcation line between Virginia and West Virginia more profound than a mere geographical barrier. While Virginia radiates landed opulence, her sister state, still dressed in homespun, hews and delves for her living in ravishing but reluctant valleys. The nation's great folk hymn to arduous labor, the hundreds of verses of the "Ballad of John Henry," sprang spontaneously from workers in the mines that scar these forested hills. Virginia, it is said, looks eastward toward Washington, D.C. and the coast, while West Virginia looks to the west. Nevertheless, in these hills and valleys, her gaze seems mostly inward.

The issues that polarized the nation during the Civil War also split Virginia's 25 western counties away from their mother state. In 1863, the bitter Battle of Droop Mountain (commemorated by an interesting museum) confirmed the creation of West Virginia as a new Union state.

Most opportunities for work and play in West Virginia are associated in one way or another with the coal lying under her hills, or the forests that cloak them. Coal mining has long been one of the state's most vital—and volatile—industries. Vast unexploited deposits of coal still remain in the region. Exhibition galleries and tunnels at Beckley show how coal is mined.

Above ground, in the Monongahela National Forest, 850,000 acres of mountains and remote valleys are preserved for wilderness exploration or for more leisurely enjoyment in several well-appointed state recreation areas. At French Creek State Game Farm, see the animals that once roamed all over this part of the Allegheny Mountains.

Although the overwhelming impression of these highlands is of trees enrobing steep and difficult terrain, the area has other perspectives and dimensions. Lost World Caverns, near Lewisburg, complete with stalactites and stalagmites, provide a troglodyte's view of the region. For an eagle's view, Cass Scenic Railroad conveys travelers at the leisurely pace of the steam era to the summit of Bald Knob, West Virginia's second highest mountain. For a descending view, take the aerial ride down from Hawk's Nest, near Ansted, to the gorge of the New River.

Two other curiosities are a must for visitors to these mountains. At the Cranberry Glades Botanical Area, view northerly terrain and vegetation that would not exist so far south but for some freakish eddy in a distant Ice Age. At Beartown State Park near Droop, explore a wooded hillside of fascinating miniature canyons, crevasses, and sandstone cliffs.

Quilts Handmade by Cooperative of Mountain Women (*left*) In the Appalachian hilltowns, the handicrafts of the last century are a vibrant part of the present. Designs for quilts seem endlessly varied and produce breathtaking, intricate effects. Cherished old patterns include the Friendship Star, Puss in the Corner, Log Cabin, Grandmother's Flower Garden, and Drunkard's Path. Originally assembled on a frame or large hoop in a cooperative effort, quilts are often made today on a sewing machine.

Spruce Knob (*right*) The rugged mountain scenery of this area climbs to 4,862 feet at the top of Spruce Knob, the highest point in the state.

SITES TO SEE

● **Halliehurst** (Elkins) is the mansion built by a senator with presidential aspirations in 1890 for $300,000. The house, with a ballroom, has more than 60 rooms.

● **Lewisburg**, named after Gen. Andrew Lewis, who defeated Shawnee Indians at the Battle of Point Pleasant in 1774, contains more than 60 18th- and 19th-century buildings. The **Old Stone Church**, built 1796, contains hand-hewn woodwork and the original gallery used by slaves. Self-guiding walking tours of the downtown national historic center are available.

● **New River Gorge National River** winds 52 miles along the New River from Hinton to the New River Gorge Bridge; a 1,700-foot single-arch spare makes the bridge the world's longest. The New River also has several distinctions: it is one of the world's few rivers to flow northward, and may be North America's oldest river.

● **Fayetteville** is a center for rafting trips along the Gauley, New, and Cheat rivers.

● **Pearl S. Buck Birthplace Museum** (Hillsboro) preserves the farmhouse where the Pulitzer Prize-winning author was born in 1892.

WORTH A DETOUR

● **Blackwater Falls State Park** (Davis) is best known for its 63-foot waterfalls with a 500-foot-deep gorge underneath and an observation deck at the rim.

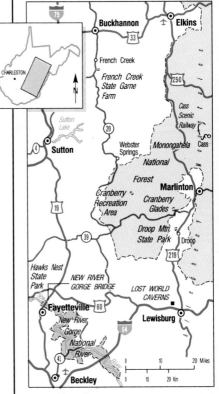

BLUE RIDGE JOURNEYS
Virginia's Mountain Backlane

In the mountains and valleys of the Blue Ridge and beyond, where landscapes unfold like blue-green waves, or greet the traveler with roadside flowers and zigzag fences, neat meadows and orchards, wilderness and settlement seem in perfect harmony. This balance between human and natural frontiers, as delicate as the merging of distant ridges with the sky, echoes the region's past (which is also about frontiers) and makes a Blue Ridge journey strangely reassuring, as if you were traveling through lands that had reached a profound agreement with all of human history.

Some of the first pioneers paused in the Blue Ridge Mountains, settled the valleys, and turned them into a stable frontier between the old east and the new west. When the frontier moved to Ohio and Kentucky, the Blue Ridge retained its character; today the Blue Ridge is still a frontier, preserved beyond its time.

During the Civil War, the mountains divided Confederate Virginia from the breakaway counties that formed West Virginia. To the east, between the Potomac and Richmond, the Civil War surged north and then south. When the end was near, the South's great general, Robert E. Lee, dispatched Jubal Early into the Shenandoah Valley to divert Union forces from the state capital; General Sheridan's Union HQ during the Battle of Cedar Creek is preserved at Middletown's Belle Grove Plantation. When the war was over, Lee put his mind to reconciliation and national unity. He found a quiet haven as president of the college now called Washington and Lee University in Lexington, which is also the home of the famed Virginia Military Institute. Lee's grave is in Lee Chapel on the university's campus.

In the northern part of the Blue Ridge range, the Shenandoah Valley covers a network of caverns, (several of which are open to the public), where underground streams flow and calcite flowers bloom as delicately as the real flowers in the fields above. The way these fields were first cultivated can be seen at the Museum of American Frontier Culture in Staunton. The town, undamaged by the Civil War, preserves fine 19th-century buildings.

Northwest of Staunton, at Green Bank in West Virginia, the great mushroom-shaped dishes of the National Radio Astronomy Observatory probe the frontiers of space, gathering ancient radio transmissions from stars and galaxies. At White Sulphur Springs, the fine old Greenbrier Hotel was used to confine foreign diplomats during World War II. It is a survivor through miles of time, like Green Bank's radio signals, Shenandoah's stone cave-flowers, or the mountain farms, or like the mountain ridges themselves, worn smooth by their survival from the Cambrian era.

Luray Caverns (*left*) Magnificent rock formations here include a "Stalacpipe" Organ; on the grounds is a collection of antique autos.

Mabry Mill (*right*) At mile marker 176.1 on the Parkway, this working gristmill sells cornmeal ground on the premises.

SITES TO SEE

● **Natural Bridge of Virginia** (near Bridgewater) is a limestone arch over Cedar Creek 215 feet high and up to 150 feet wide. The Monocan Indians knew it as the "Bridge of God" before it was purchased by Thomas Jefferson from King George III for 20 shillings. Look closely and you will be able to see where George Washington carved his initials on the rock face.

During the Revolutionary War, the bridge was used as a shot tower.

● **New Market Battlefield Park** commemorates one of the most unusual incidents in the Civil War. Cadets from Virginia Military Institute marched 90 miles to the site and held the line against seasoned Union troops long enough to allow for a Confederate victory; the battle is re-enacted on the second Sunday in May.

Bushong House is a restored 19th-century farmhouse on the site with period furnishings. The cadets' courage is recalled at the **Hall of Valor**. The museum here gives an overview of the war and Stonewall Jackson's Valley Campaign in particular.

● **Shenandoah Caverns** (near New Market) are among the most impressive of the Shenandoah Valley's limestone caves. Nearby

Endless Caverns have fine stalactites and stalagmites, flowstones, and other formations.

● **Natural Chimneys Regional Park** (Mt. Solon) is named for intricately weathered limestone pillars here. Since 1821 an annual jousting tournament has been held in the meadows below the pillars. The visitor center is home of the National Jousting Hall of Fame.

The Appalachian Trail (*above*) America's most famous footpath, the 2,000-mile Appalachian Trail, follows the Blue Ridge Parkway on its way from Georgia to northern Maine.

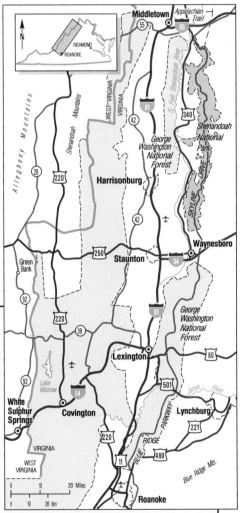

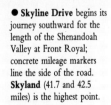

● **Skyline Drive** begins its journey southward for the length of the Shenandoah Valley at Front Royal; concrete mileage markers line the side of the road. **Skyland** (41.7 and 42.5 miles) is the highest point.

● **Belle Grove** (Middletown) is a plantation with details added by Thomas Jefferson in 1794. Gen. Sheridan used it as his HQ during the Battle of Cedar Creek. Today, the estate is a farm and celebrates Shenandoah Valley Farm Craft Days the first weekend in June.

● **Tri-Mountain Winery and Vineyards** (Middleton) offers tours and tastings.

● **Roanoke** is an attractive Virginia town with a rich history. **Center in the Square** is the site of the **Roanoke Valley History Museum**; it also has the **Science Museum of Western Virginia** with a planetarium, a transportation museum, and the **Roanoke Museum of Fine Arts**. Its collection includes Old Masters and contemporary and local artists.

● **Stonewall Jackson House** (Lexington) is where the Confederate general lived before the Civil War from 1859–63, and is furnished with his personal belongings. Jackson's grave is also in Lexington.

● **Staunton** was laid out in 1749 and, because it was undamaged by the Civil War, has outstanding 19th-century buildings; Trinity Episcopal Church was built in 1855. Former U.S. President Woodrow Wilson was born in the 1846 manse of the First Presbyterian Church, which has been restored to look as it did in 1856, the year of his birth. Among the memorabilia is a Pierce Arrow automobile.

COLONIAL NATIONAL HISTORICAL PARK

Where England's Rule Flowered and Faded

From Jamestown to Yorktown is a drive of about 20 miles and almost 175 years. From the once dismal, disease- and starvation-ridden peninsula where the English established their first permanent colony in 1607, the road leads over the neck of land that separates the James and York rivers to Williamsburg, once the crown jewel of colonial society. This road, the Colonial Parkway, continues to Yorktown, where the colonists laid siege to Lord Cornwallis's army and brought the Revolutionary War to an end.

Only the tower of the 1639 brick church at Jamestown, the first permanent English settlement in the New World, still stands; the ruins of the glass furnace and some excavated foundations and streets are preserved. In fact, the absence of relics here is an apt and melancholy memorial to Jamestown's tribulations. These troubled times peaked in 1609, a year of starvation and Indian attacks, when numerous colonists died.

Jamestown Settlement, built in 1957 to celebrate the colony's 350th anniversary, puts flesh on the remarkable story of the colony. Full-scale reproductions of the three ships that carried the first settlers here are anchored; they look far too small to have crossed the Atlantic. There are also re-creations of James Fort, the settlers' palisaded, wattle-and-daub village, and of a 17th-century Powhatan Indian village.

By 1633, Middle Plantation had been set up on healthier, higher ground between the two rivers. It prospered, was renamed Williamsburg, and became the state capital until 1780. The restoration of colonial Williamsburg, funded by John D. Rockefeller, Jr., began in 1926, and today it is the nation's preeminent monument to its colonial past. The greatest buildings—the Governor's Palace, the Capitol, the College of William and Mary—are essential

viewing, but it is the detail that gives the area its unique charm and intimacy.

Among the restored Williamsburg homes, the Brush-Everard House, built 1717, re-creates the lifestyle of an 18th-century middle-class family. Period furnishings include library furniture and books from a list compiled by Thomas Jefferson of those a gentleman should own.

Popular Williamsburg events include Junior Fife and Drum Corps parades on Duke of Gloucester Street at mid day on Saturdays from April through mid-November.

The neighboring College of William and Mary campus contains the 1695 Wren Building. The oldest college building still in use in the U.S., its design is attributed to Sir Christopher Wren; student guides give tours during the academic year.

At Yorktown, on the other side of the peninsula, is the Yorktown Battlefield National Historic Site. Here, on October 19, 1781, the British Army succumbed to a siege by American and French troops and artillery, effectively ending the Revolutionary War. Each October, Yorktown Day is a celebration of victory which commemorates the event, and exhibits at the Visitor Center include fragments of Washington's campaign tents and naval exhibits.

Williamsburg, Fourth of July (*above right*) The last shots of the Revolutionary War were fired at Yorktown. These musketeers commemorate the fight for independence.

Living History (*left*) Colonial Williamsburg is perhaps the nation's most ambitious restoration. The fabric and furnishings of every major building have been made new, gardens and grounds have been restored to their period, and on the streets, the colonial ambiance is re-created.

SITES TO SEE

● **Duke of Gloucester Street** (Williamsburg) is almost a mile long with the Capitol at one end and William and Mary College at the other. Notable buildings are the **Red Lion Tavern** with the clipped gables typical of this part of Virginia, and the elegant **Bruton Parish Church**, built 1711–15. Virginia's "Liberty Bell," rung when the 1783 peace treaty was signed, hangs in the wooden

tower. Other buildings to visit include **Pasteur-Galt Apothecary shop, Raleigh Tavern Bakery**, the **Magazine** and **Guardhouse**, the **Courthouse**, and **Boot and Shoemaker's Shop**, which includes craftsmen using 18th-century tools.

● **Abby Aldrich Rockefeller Folk Art Center** (Williamsburg), one of the top collections in the U.S., is displayed in rooms designed to resemble 19th-century interiors.

● **Busch Gardens** is an amusement park designed to represent 17th-century England, France, Germany, and Italy. Visit includes free brewery tours and tastings.

● **Moore House** (Yorktown Battlefield), built 1725, is where the terms of British surrender were drafted. Nearby **Nelson House**, built 1711, is an excellent example of Georgian architecture. The cannonballs lodged in one wall were supposedly fired during the Battle of Yorktown. **Encampment Drive** is a 12-mile car tour with stops at Washington's HQ, the French cemetery, and the French Artillery Park.

WORTH A DETOUR

● **Chippokes Plantation State Park** Named for an Indian chief who was a great friend of the early English settlers, this plantation was a working farm for more than 350 years. It was given to the state in 1967. The 1854 mansion and 1750 kitchen are open to the public. Other buildings include tenants' houses, barns and a second large house. A picnic area overlooks the James River.

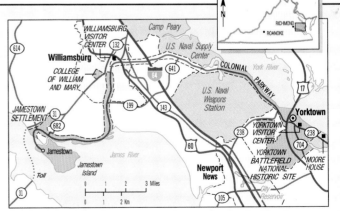

THE CIVIL WAR'S BLOODY CORRIDOR

From Manassas to Appomattox

From Washington to Richmond is a little less than 100 miles as the crow flies, and not much more by I-95. During the Civil War, though, those miles between the Federal capital and the capital of Virginia separated cultures and aspirations that seemed to belong to different continents. The bloody struggles enacted along this narrow corridor are commemorated in battlefields and military parks that form a unique monument to some of the most formative years in U.S. history.

On July 21, 1861, a hot day for a battle, 35,000 Union troops under the command of General McDowell clashed with 23,000 Confederate troops led by Generals Beauregard and Johnston. The two sides met at Manassas Junction alongside Bull Run Creek, now preserved as the Manassas National Battlefield Park. On the low hills surrounding the site, ladies and gentlemen had come from Washington in their carriages to picnic and see the Union Army—a motley brigade of rag-tag militiamen, Zouaves in baggy red trousers, and regular troops in Union blue—administer a sound thrashing to the upstart Southerners. By the end of the day, however, the Union Army had been convincingly beaten.

For a year, the Confederacy was too disorganized, and too harried by Union successes in the South, to press home its advantage. Then, in August, 1862, the two sides met at the Battle of Second Manassas (also known as Second Bull Run), and again the Confederacy, now led by Robert E. Lee, triumphed. Dioramas of both battles can be seen at the Visitor Center.

From the fall of 1862, the Union's major efforts in the northern Confederacy would be to capture Richmond: the Fredericksburg and Spotsylvania National Military Park preserves some of the principal sites of those campaigns.

On December 13, 1862, General Burnside led a Union Army of 142,551 against 91,760 Confederate troops commanded by Lee at Fredericksburg. Lee could not be shifted, and Burnside, with 12,653 men dead or wounded, had to retreat. The following May, some 60,000 Southerners turned General Hooker's 130,000-strong army back across the Rappahannock at the Battle of Chancellorsville.

In 1864, Ulysses S. Grant launched his Army of the Potomac against Lee's Army of Northern Virginia in the area known as the Wilderness, now part of the Fredericksburg and Spotsylvania National Military Park. At the Battle of Spotsylvania Court House, Lee resisted a five-day onslaught and then withdrew to Cold Harbor, ten miles from Richmond. Grant pursued him, lost 6,000 men in a one-hour assault, but again failed to break the line. At last, on April 2–3, 1865, Lee's greatly reduced ranks were broken. Grant captured Richmond, and on April 9, Lee surrendered at Appomattox Court House.

Henry House, Henry Hill, Manassas (*right*) The Battle of First Manassas, during which Gen. Thomas Jackson earned his celebrated nickname, "Stonewall," was the first major field battle of the Civil War. At the time, many believed it would be the only battle. But though the Union Army was routed, the war continued for four bloody years. Mrs. Judith Henry, who lived in the original structure this house replaces, was the only civilian killed in the battle.

The Wilderness, Fredericksburg and Spotsylvania (*left*) saw the first pitched encounter between Gen. Grant and Gen. Lee.

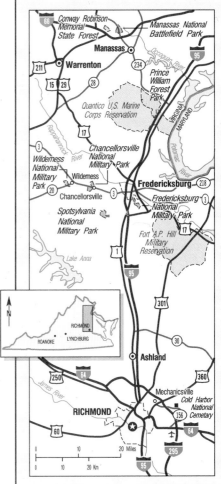

MR. LINCOLN'S HOME

A Kentucky Birthplace

"Mr. Lincoln," as the great man is called in these parts, was never very popular in Kentucky. During his campaign for the presidency, they say he received one vote from his native state—and that was from a cousin. Only the efforts of Mark Twain and a few others assured the preservation of the little log cabin where Lincoln was born, now enclosed in a grand memorial. The Abraham Lincoln Birthplace National Historic Site, and others in the area commemorating his birth and childhood, mark the beginning of Lincoln's long journey, through times of flux and violence, to Illinois, the presidency, and immortal fame.

The countryside where Lincoln was born is now a workaday landscape of wood lots, fields, and farms. Compared to the horse-farm country farther east, where the fences are pure white and the pastures appear to be hand-clipped daily, it looks ungroomed. The marble and granite temple erected at the great president's birthplace seems ill at ease in such a setting; inside it, the diminutive log cabin almost cowers beneath the stone blocks of its protective shrine. In contrast, Lincoln's boyhood home, located in Knob Creek near Hodgenville, would now be considered inferior accommodation in a children's summer camp.

In a letter written shortly after the end of the Civil War, Lincoln said that he would be pleased to revisit the fondly remembered scenes of his childhood if only the local population could guarantee he would not be lynched. Today, it is difficult to imagine those politically passionate times when visiting Bardstown, where the Oscar Getz Museum of Whiskey History documents the influence of whiskey in Kentucky.

But passions did run high in the land of Lincoln's birth. The vehement Cassius Marcellus Clay was obliged to defend the office of his anti-slavery newspaper, the *True American*, with a pair of cannon. In his embittered old age, he also fortified the sober opulence of his home, White Hall. The traveler here inevitably encounters worlds at odds with each other. The world of thoroughbred horses and fine old bourbon exists side by side with traditions of pioneering hardiness recalled in the exhibits at the Old Fort Harrod State Park.

Lincoln's Birthplace (*right*) Housed in a marble and granite building designed by John Russell Pope and completed in 1911, the log cabin thought to be Abraham Lincoln's birthplace evokes the simplicity of the early life of one of our nation's greatest presidents. The 48-acre homestead bought by Thomas and Nancy Hanks Lincoln in 1808 was named Sinking Spring Farm. The spring, which still produces water, provided for the needs of the young Lincoln family when they lived here between 1808 and 1811. In 1860, the cabin was moved from this site to a nearby farm where it was used as a residence and schoolhouse until 1894. Above the entrance of the memorial building itself, marked by six impressive granite columns, are carved Lincoln's words, "With malice toward none, with charity for all."

My Old Kentucky Home (*left*) Federal Hill, home of Judge John Rowan, is said to have been the inspiration for Stephen Foster's ever-popular ballad. The house was completed in 1818. Rowan, a U.S. senator and state chief justice, wanted to represent symbolically the original states in the union. The number 13 crops up time and again. There are 13 windows on the front of the house, 13 treads in each flight of stairs, and 13-foot ceilings.

SITES TO SEE

● **Shakertown at Pleasant Hill** takes visitors back to 1805–1910 when the religious sect known for its refined designs maintained a community here. All 30 original buildings have been restored; they display a comprehensive collection of domestic and farming memorabilia. Centre Family House, a stone dwelling, contains outstanding examples of Shaker-style furniture. Crafts are demonstrated, and handicrafts are sold.

● **Old Fort Harrod State Park** (Harrodsburg) includes the **Lincoln Marriage Temple**, the log cabin where Abraham Lincoln's parents were married. The **Mansion Museum** has items illustrating life for the region's early settlers.

WORTH A DETOUR

● **Lexington**, the state's second largest city, is in the heart of famed Bluegrass horse-breeding country. The local passion for horses and horse racing is captured at **Kentucky Horse Park**. Tours take in all aspects of the training facilities, as well as equine demonstrations. **The Man O'War Monument** marks the legendary horse's burial site.

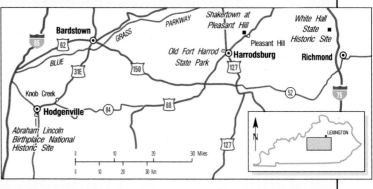

THE WILDERNESS ROAD
Boone Country

When Daniel Boone, then employed by a land development agency, blazed the 200-mile Wilderness Road into Kentucky in 1775, he and his troop of axmen opened an important frontier for the great surge of western migration. In this southeastern part of Kentucky, the wild country he first explored still carries his name at many sites, and his fame as a backwoodsman—which drew many settlers to the American wilderness—is commemorated everywhere.

Daniel Boone is best remembered as a man of the wilderness, and his most impressive memorial is the 664,000 acres of the Daniel Boone National Forest, containing much of Kentucky's wildest and most beautiful scenery. From the Cumberland Gap, the boundless forested ridges still look as they must have when Boone first saw them.

Cumberland Gap, the great notch in the Allegheny Mountains that gave pioneers on the Wilderness Road access to the grasslands of Kentucky, was first explored by Dr. Thomas Walker in 1750. In 1769, Daniel Boone passed through the Gap with a hunting party, and he marked the Road six years later. During the Civil War, the Gap was strategically important; the remains of military earthworks are still visible today.

Within the Cumberland Gap National Historical Park's 20,274 acres are 50 miles of hiking trails and a preserved half-mile section of the Wilderness Road. A four-mile paved road leads to Pinnacle Overlook, which, from a height of 2,440 feet, commands the best view of the famous pass and the scenic panoramas beyond. In this wilderness, you'll find upland lakes in mountain valleys and dramatic riverscapes; at Cumberland Falls, rainbows and "moonbows" lend irides-cence to the translucent jade-colored waters of the cascade.

From Cumberland Gap, the Road went north through Pineville. In 1797, the state legislature authorized 500 pounds sterling to be spent maintaining the Road and constructing a tollgate at what was then called the Narrows. The annual Mountain Laurel Festival is held every May in Pineville.

Barbourville was one of the first settlements set up on the Wilderness Road; it celebrates its Daniel Boone Festival in early October. Dr. Thomas Walker State Historic Site honors the first European to cross the Cumberland Gap. Walker also named the Cumberland River, and a replica of his cabin can be seen here.

The Levi Jackson Wilderness Road State Park near London preserves a section of Boone's Trace, a trail blazed by Daniel Boone from the Cumberland Gap to the Kentucky River, and commemorates the 200,000 pioneers who passed along the Wilderness Trail between 1775 and 1796. The park also marks the site where some of these travelers were massacred by Indians. The Mountain Life Museum includes a log manor house, barn, settlers' church, and some early domestic utensils and various Indian artifacts.

Cumberland Falls (*right*) This breathtaking crescent of rushing water, 125 feet wide, falls 68 feet into the gorge of the Cumberland River near Corbin. It hits the rock-strewn riverbed with a continuous roar, spraying such a fine mist over the surrounding valley that a full moon will cast "moonbows" in the mist just as the sun will produce rainbows. The shady paths of the historic **Wilderness Road, Cumberland Gap National Historical Park** (*left*) echo with the ghosts of the Indians, hunters, and frontiersmen who followed this route to the west.

SITES TO SEE

● **Cumberland Gap National Historical Park Visitor Center** (near Middlesboro) has a small museum recalling the region's varied history, with pioneer and Civil War weapons and tools. The park's interpretive programs include campfire talks and craft demonstrations; events are held daily during summer, and on weekends in spring and fall.

● **Hensley Settlement** (Cumberland Gap National Park) was an isolated family farming community started by Sherman Hensley about 1904. In the mid-1930s, almost 100 people lived here, but in the early 1950s, the community was abandoned and it quickly deteriorated. Today, 3 farms, along with their outbuildings, the school, and the cemetery, have been restored, and farmers demonstrate the techniques the Hensleys advocated. Situated along the Ridge Trail, the settlement is reached by a day-long hike; during summer a minibus runs from the visitor center (reservations required). **Ridge Trail** crosses the park for 17 miles with outstanding views along the way.

● **Corbin, KY**, was the site of Col. Harland Sanders' first restaurant, before he went on to introduce the world to "Kentucky Fried Chicken." A plaque marks the site of the former restaurant.

● **Abraham Lincoln Museum** (Harrogate, TN) honors its neighboring state's most famous son with exhibits of 25,000 items. Among the former president's personal possessions on display are the walking stick Lincoln had with him at Ford's Theater, several of his watches, and numerous items of clothing. Civil War memorabilia is also exhibited.

WORTH A DETOUR

● **Big South Fork National River and Recreation Area** crosses the Kentucky/Tennessee state line, and contains an abundance of scenic gorges and valleys in its more than 100,000 acres.

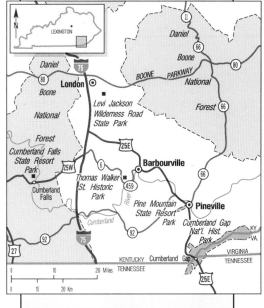

PARADISE RECLAIMED

Land Between the Lakes

Today's visitors to this lakeland region shared by Kentucky and Tennessee enjoy a landscape that seems ideally southern: a view of lake, meadow, and woodland, of small, tree-shaded farms with white-fenced pastures, of homesteads well maintained by honest husbandry. Today this is a picture-book scene, but it was not always so. This was a ravaged land: first by repeated flooding of the Tennessee River, then by the Civil War, and finally by the Great Depression. Then, in the 1930s, the newly formed Tennessee Valley Authority built dams to tame the region's great rivers and make them productive. Here, where Tennessee jogs north into Kentucky, the land between the Tennessee and Cumberland rivers was flooded. The lush forest and wetland full of birds, lakeshores, and trails is now protected and managed. It has become a southern idyll.

Enclosed to the north by great dams on the Tennessee and Cumberland rivers, the reclaimed, almost re-created, Land Between the Lakes is a prime example of what the T.V.A. has done to provide access to some of the lovelier parts of Tennessee and Kentucky.

This lush peninsula is laced with hundreds of miles of trails throughout its more than 170,000 acres. There are all types of camping facilities and numerous attractions: a farm with demonstrations of self-sufficient agricultural and energy techniques and a "living history" settlement. There is even a buffalo herd. The surrounding region includes magnificent public golf courses, and elaborate marinas that help boats exploit the vast new expanses of navigable water created by the dams.

Just south of the Land Between the Lakes lies the site of a crucial battle in the war between the states, commemorated by Fort Donelson National Battlefield. It was here, in 1862, that Brigadier General Ulysses S. Grant outmaneuvered a Confederate force under Brigadier General Simon B. Buckner into the famous unconditional surrender which delivered control of the Tennessee and Cumberland rivers, Kentucky, and much of Tennessee to the Union.

Southwest, hundreds of thousands of birds travel the Tennessee Valley's ancient flyway. Extensive acres have been set aside for wildlife refuges in the area, and the Tennessee National Migratory Wildlife Refuge is home for numerous species of waterfowl.

To round out the variety available in this region are two little corners of America, within striking distance, which demonstrate its past and present charm. Murray, Kentucky, is home of the National Museum of the Boy Scouts of America on the campus of Murray State University. Fifty-four of Norman Rockwell's "World of Scouting" paintings are displayed here. At Mayfield, Kentucky, the half life-size Wooldridge Monuments stand, 18 marble and sandstone figures, a touching expression of warmly eccentric Kentucky sentiment in the late 19th century. Created by Henry G. Wooldridge, the eroding statues represent Wooldridge's family as well as two figures of himself.

Taking It Easy (*left*) The stresses of modern life make relaxation a national sport, and a family picnic is just one of the ways to take advantage of the idyllic scenery. Fishing and boating also attract visitors hoping to while away some lazy days.

Sporting Life (*right*) For the more energetic, a round of golf on one of the many courses is a perfect way to relax while improving your game. For the more adventurous, skin diving, water-skiing, and rafting can be enjoyed.

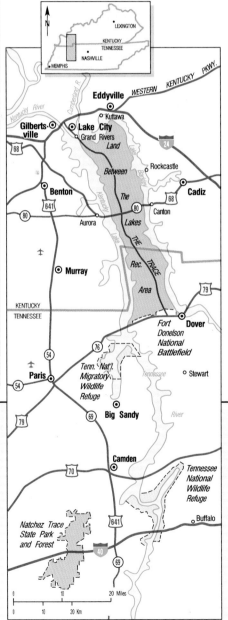

The Homeplace-1850 (*left*) This fascinating living history farm re-creates life in the fields and at home during the mid-nineteenth century. Sixteen restored log buildings have been moved to the 60-acre site, where members of a two-generation farm family reenact life as it would have been before mechanization changed the pace forever. Dressed as farm workers of the period, these men work their ox-and-plow through the ritual process of preparing the soil. The farm, situated 12 miles south of US 68, has an interpretive center with an audiovisual presentation on this traditional way of life.

SITES TO SEE

● **Duncan Tavern** (Paris, KY), built in 1788 from local limestone, was a favorite meeting place for Daniel Boone and other frontiersmen. John Fox, Jr's. manuscript of *The Little Shepherd of Kingdom Come*, chronicling Appalachian life, is in the tavern library's collection. The adjoining **Anne Duncan House**, built at the beginning of the 19th century, has also been restored.

● **Cane Ridge Meetinghouse** (Paris) is a one-room log church built in 1791. The Disciples of Christ church was founded here in 1804.

● **Dover Hotel** (Dover, TN), built 1851–53, was Gen. Buckner's headquarters for the Battle of Fort Donelson, and where Buckner surrendered to Grant; more than 14,000 Confederate soldiers were transported from here to northern prisoner-of-war camps. After the surrender, the hotel was converted to a hospital for Union soldiers. The restored building, with a re-created hotel lobby of the 1860s, is the only surviving original building where a major Civil War surrender took place. The building is reached via a short drive from the National Battlefield along US 79.

WORTH A DETOUR

● **Fulton, TN**, once the major distribution point for bananas for the U.S., hosts the International Banana Festival each September. Festivities include a 1-ton banana pudding along with regional and Latin American crafts and free bananas.

● **House of Cash** (Hendersonville, TN) charts country singer Johnny Cash's career. The Georgian-style mansion is furnished with Cash's personal belongings, including high school memorabilia.

SKYWAYS AND BYWAYS

The Great Smoky Mountains

The way into the Smokies from the crowded east travels along high ridges that unveil waves of haze-blue mountains. Through trees on the ridge slopes, slumbering farmscapes appear like vignettes of secure traditional values. Soon after the first trails were blazed through these mountains, America's frontiers began their westward push, making pioneers like Davy Crockett and Daniel Boone legendary. Today the hills and small communities still breathe the old spirit of ornery, hillbilly independence and still echo with the wild and tumbling bluegrass music that was born in these "hills an' hollers."

Rising from the gentle mountains of Virginia are the imposing heights of the Great Smokies, once the preserve and hunting ground of the Cherokees. The grandeur of this wildlands sanctuary, along with the splendid variety of trees, wildflowers, and birds in its vast forests, make Great Smoky Mountains National Park the most popular in the land. Evenly divided between Tennessee and North Carolina, it offers opportunities for all kinds of outdoor recreation, ambitious hiking, and skiing. The adjoining Nantahala National Forest in North Carolina, offers particularly scenic facilities for whitewater canoeing and river rafting.

Here and there are the vestiges of earlier attempts to wrest a living from the rocky slopes. The poignant charm and brave prettiness of the first pioneering farms and homesteads are preserved at Cades Cove. Demonstrations of mountain skills are presented during the summer months. At Ducktown, TN, red, man-made moonscapes are all that remain of enormous tracts of land that were once mined for copper. Relics of the mines, old buildings, and a museum explain the history of the Copper Basin and of the procedures in the manufacture of sulfuric acid that caused its soil erosion and devastating defoliation.

Oak Ridge, built near Knoxville during World War II, is the birthplace of the nuclear reactor that made possible the first atomic bombs; the Graphite Reactor, the world's oldest nuclear reactor, is a National Historic Landmark open to the public. Extensive and detailed displays about energy in every form—from wood-burning to nuclear fission—crowd the American Museum of Science and Energy.

The focal point of Pigeon Forge, near Gatlinburg on the north side of the national park, is Dollywood, a shrine to the stardom of Dolly Parton and to the pioneer traditions, culture, and music that formed her. The park plays host to the National Mountain Music Festival in June and the National Crafts and Harvest Festival every October. Two other items of interest are the Old Mill and the Smoky Mountain Auto Museum. The former is an early 19th-century flour mill, still running and prospering, that is completely in keeping with the spirit of the region. The other is more incongruous: an exhibition of famous autos, from Al Capone's Cadillac to James Bond's Aston Martin.

The Great Smoky Mountains (*above right*) A persistent, softening haze gives the peaks and lush hollows of the Smokies their name. The Park's half-million acres include 16 mountains higher than 6,000 feet, and 180,000 acres of virgin forest. Wildflowers cover stream banks; bear and deer are the natural residents.

Shooting the Flume at Dollywood (*left*) Family fun and lively recreations of 19th-century life in the Smokies are key elements in Dolly Parton's tribute to her down-home heritage.

SITES TO SEE

- **Tuckaleechee Caverns** (Townsend) have hour-long tours of the massive underground hall, waterfalls, and onyx formations. The caves still have unexplored tunnels.

- **Cades Cove** has restored log cabins and barns, among other buildings. Scenic views are available from an 11-mile loop road circling the cove.

- **Lost Sea** (Sweetwater), covering $4\frac{1}{2}$ acres, is reputedly the world's largest underground lake. The subterranean chambers are explored in glass-bottomed boats; see trout and pretty cave flowers. Tours also include a visit to Civil War saltpeter mines.

- **Clingmans Dome** is the highest point in Tennessee at 6,643 feet. A trail leads to a spectacular overlook.

- **Scenic US 41** becomes the Newfound Gap Road from Cherokee, N.C., to Gatlinburg. It crosses the North Carolina–Tennessee line at over 5,000 feet. In many towns near Great

Smoky Mountains National Park special tours are available through the park for a relaxed view of the high and winding mountain roads.

● **Gatlinburg**, at the entrance to the park, is a popular resort. Among the town's numerous tourist attractions are craft shops with skilled crafters. The Great Smoky Arts and Craft Community is 3 miles east, and craft fairs are held regularly in the Civic Auditorium throughout the summer. Popular annual events include the Wildflower Pilgrimage in late April, the Gatlinburg Scottish Festival and Games in mid-May, and the Smoky Mountain Christmas Festival for all of December.

WORTH A DETOUR

● **Chickamauga and Chattanooga National Military Park** consists of 8,113 acres in Tennessee and Georgia. The **Chickamauga Battlefield**, south of Chattanooga, is one of the nation's most visited Civil War sites. Each regiment in the 1863 confrontation which left 18,000 killed, wounded, or missing is commemorated. The outcome of the battle was to leave Union troops in control of Chattanooga. A car tour of the site gives an impression of the battle's scale. violence, and tragedy.

● **Carl Sandburg Home National Historic Site** (Flat Rock, NC) is where the Pulitzer Prize-winning author lived from 1945 for the last 22 years of his life. House tours include Sandburg's cluttered work room and 10,000-volume library. Sandburg wrote his novel *Remembrance Rock* while living here.

● **Flat Rock**, one of the oldest resorts in this part of North Carolina, has many attractive 19th-century buildings, including many of the large summer homes. St. John's in the Wilderness, one of the state's oldest churches, was built in 1836 in the Romanesque Revival style.

BLUE RIDGE PARKWAY
North Carolina's Blue Ridge Mountains

After the Blue Ridge Parkway leaves Virginia for North Carolina, the mountains get higher and the character of the land changes. Here, the northern ruggedness of the high ground meets the beginnings of southern opulence. The rhododendrons, which flower in luscious shades of magenta and cerise in June, are unforgettable at these altitudes (6,000 feet at Craggy Gardens); gorges and waterfalls are more precipitous here than in the northern section of the Blue Ridge, and are clad in more luxuriant vegetation. There are frescoed churches in these highlands and at Asheville, which lies at the same latitude as Tangier in Morocco, is the most splendid achievement of this north-south nexus: Biltmore House, a 250-room chateau built with the great Vanderbilt fortune that flowed from the northern railroads.

The 6,684-foot summit of Mount Mitchell is the highest point east of the Mississippi River. It lies just north of the Blue Ridge Parkway; from the observation tower atop the mountain, overlooking miles of dense hardwood forest and the peak's own wind-stunted spruce and fir, you can sometimes see the Great Smokies, some 40 miles to the west.

Between these two massifs is Asheville's high plateau. Here George Washington Vanderbilt placed his 7,500-acre Biltmore Estate, with its Italian and English gardens, a rose garden with 3,000 bushes, and the magnificent Biltmore House; a winery now stands in the grounds as well. Self-guiding tours take visitors through the Vanderbilt family's living quarters, as well as the kitchen and servants' quarters. On the other side of town, Biltmore Industries and Museum commemorates Mrs. George W. Vanderbilt's efforts to preserve wool manufacturing methods brought here by the first Scottish settlers.

A wider variety of traditional crafts is on show at the Folk Art Center on the Blue Ridge Parkway. Run by the Southern Highland Handicraft Guild, it has excellent displays celebrating the area's crafting tradition and interesting accounts of the area's cultural history. In Moses H. Cone Memorial Park, north of Blowing Rock, old-time mountain crafts are demonstrated at the Parkway Craft Center in the old Flat Top Manor House; visitors can explore the ground's bridle trails, gaze at fine old trees, and visit the deer park.

Another, more modest, example of a north-south connection is Thomas Wolfe's boyhood home in Asheville. It served as the novelist's model for the Dixieland boarding house in *Look Homeward, Angel*, which he wrote while living in New York City.

The Zebulon B. Vance Birthplace State Historic Site in Weaverville includes the reconstructed two-story log house where North Carolina's Civil War Governor was born in 1830. There are reconstructed 19th-century farm buildings, as well as memorabilia of the man who guided North Carolina's fortunes throughout the war and was elected for four terms as U.S. Senator in the post-Civil War era.

Rhododendrons in bloom at Craggy Gardens (*left*) Spring and early summer are the best times to see the Blue Ridge mountains in their robe of wildflowers and canopies of cream dogwood and white and magenta rhododendrons.

Grandfather Mountain (*above right*) The southern parts of the Blue Ridge mountains offer warm meadows for picnicking and shady woods for pleasant strolling; for those who need to breathe a keener air, there are also mountain crags and bald peaks in the region.

SITES TO SEE

● **Blowing Rock** is a resort town named for a rock formation where a strong upcurrent of air flows from the John's River Gorge. It is claimed this is the only place in the world where snow falls up instead of down. **The Tweetsie Railroad**, a narrow-gauge steam train, gives scenic tours through the mountain passes. It was named by local residents because of its shrill whistle. Along the way, expect to encounter "robbers" and attacking "Indians". The railroad complex also includes frontier and mining towns, where children can pan for gold; there is also an animal petting area. Craft demonstrations and variety shows are held regularly.

● **Mast General Store** (Vale Crucis) has changed little since 1883. Listed with

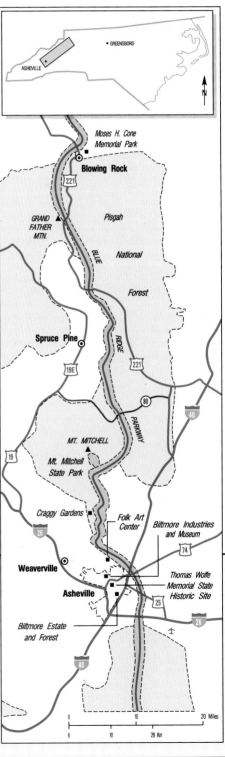

the National Register of Historic Places, it contains the original potbellied stove and counters.

● **Linville Falls** takes a spectacular two-level plunge into Linville Gorge. Lying below the falls is the **Linville Gorge Wilderness Area** with 10,975 acres that include Carolina hemlocks, black gum trees, birches, and rhododendrons. Permits are required.

● **Western North Carolina Nature Center** (Asheville) is home to bears, cougars, deer, foxes, turtles, and waterfowl among other animals. It also offers a nature trail, aviary, and petting zoo.

● **Singing on the Mountain** is a celebration of gospel music on Grandfather Mtn. on the fourth Sunday in June.

● **Museum of North Carolina Minerals** (Spruce Pine) has displays of the state's rich mineral reserves.

WORTH A DETOUR

● **Winston-Salem** was settled by Moravians from Pennsylvania. **Old Salem** preserves and re-creates many of the attractive 18th-century buildings, including **Fourth House**, built 1768, the oldest remaining original

building. **The Museum of Early Southern Decorative Arts** features displays from 1690 to 1820. **Reynolda House and Gardens**, built by the tobacco baron R. J. Reynolds, houses a museum of American art. Mary Cassatt, Andrew Wyeth, and Frederick Chase are among the artists displayed.

THE GOODLIEST LAND UNDER THE CAPE OF HEAVEN

Cape Hatteras National Seashore

Romance and mystery, aeronautics and piracy, maritime forests, and the East Coast's biggest sand dune share this golden coastline with flamingos, wild ponies, and tundra swans. America's tallest lighthouse can also be found along the coast, and along the alluvial plain protected by narrow barrier islands, the famous Outer Banks. The first English explorers called it "the goodliest land under the cape of heaven," and anyone who tires of its history, wildlife, and landscapes can enjoy the fishing, sailing, wild fowling, or hang gliding here—or simply relax on the miles of peaceful beaches.

At Fort Raleigh National Historic Site on Roanoke Island is the restored earthen fort of the first English colony in the Americas: the mysterious Lost Colony. Founded by Sir Walter Raleigh in 1585, it was briefly abandoned and then re-established in 1587. When its governor, John White, returned here from England in 1591, he found the site desolate and uninhabited. The only clue to the fate of its 118 settlers was the word "Croatoan" carved on a tree.

Some think the colonists were murdered by a Spanish expedition from Florida, others that they were killed or captured by Indians. The theories are elaborated at The Lindsay Warren Visitor Center, but the fate of the colonists remains an enigma. They are commemorated at Elizabethan Gardens, and at Manteo the Elizabeth II State Historic Site (with guides in Elizabethan dress) displays a full-scale reproduction of the type of ship used in the first voyage to Roanoke.

At Kill Devil Hills, north of Roanoke Island, is a national memorial to equally momentous pioneers; the Wright Brothers achieved the first powered flight here in 1903. A few miles south, at Jockey's Ridge State Park, hang-gliding fans launch themselves from two of the highest sand dunes in the world, taking advantage of the same winds that helped make that first powered flight of 12 seconds possible.

At the southern end of the national seashore, in Ocracoke Inlet, the famous pirate, Blackbeard, met his death in battle with a British warship in 1718. Local legend says his treasure still lies buried along the coast. At Edenton, the first colonial capital, there are also fine old buildings, and a picturesque waterfront.

Across the sound in Pettigrew State Park, near Creswell, is Somerset Place, a 14-room plantation house built in the 1830s on Lake Phelps. Farther south, Lake Mattamuskeet is the home of thousands of tundra swans in the winter, and of golden eagles in summer.

Cape Hatteras Lighthouse (*left*), built in 1870, at 208 feet is one of the tallest in the United States. It is one of a string of distinctive lighthouses on the Outer Banks, which stretch for 125 miles along the North Carolina coast. Despite warnings beamed out by the lighthouses, the waters off the Outer Banks, with their treacherous shoals and swift currents, have claimed more than 600 ships.

Kill Devil Hills (*above right*), four miles south of Kitty Hawk, is where Wilbur and Orville Wright conducted their gliding experiments and, on December 17, 1903, first took to the air in their flying machine. Today, the dunes are a paradise for hang gliders, who revel in the strong, steady winds.

At the Visitor Center, exhibits tell the Wright brothers' story, and there are full-scale replicas of their glider and of the 1903 flying machine.

Ocracoke Island (*below right*) can be reached only by a toll ferry ride from Cedar Island (2¼ hours) or Swan Quarter (2½ hours), for which reservations are necessary, or by a 40-minute free ferry trip from Hatteras. The island has long been noted for its excellent fishing and wildfowling, and the little port, with its shady, sandy streets, retains much of its early attraction and atmosphere.

SITES TO SEE

● **Elizabeth II State Historic Site** (Manteo) contains a reproduction sailing vessel like the one used by Sir Walter Raleigh. Guides in Tudor-style costumes describe life during the voyage.

● **Elizabethan Gardens** (Fort Raleigh National Historic Site) commemorates the first English settlers in America. The formal and informal gardens contain rose and herb gardens and antique garden statuary.

● **Cupola House** (Edenton), built 1725, is a charming Jacobean-style house with a Georgian interior. Numerous historic houses have been preserved in Edenton and are open to visitors; self-guiding 1½-mile walking tours are available from the Barker House Visitor Center.

● **Bath**, incorporated in 1705, is the state's oldest town. Historic buildings include **Palmer-Marsh House** (1744), one of the oldest remaining houses in North Carolina, and the **Van Der Veer House** (1795) with exhibits reflecting 300 years of Bath life. Blackbeard, the notorious pirate, lived here around 1717 after marrying a local woman.

● **Pea Island National Wildlife Refuge** (Hatteras Island) has observation platforms and trails for watching waterfowl and birds that fly through on their annual migrations.

● **Shipwreck life-saving drills** from the 19th century are re-enacted weekly during the summer at the U.S. Life Saving Service Station at Chicamacomico on Hatteras Island. Storms off the Outer Banks, known as the "Graveyard of the Atlantic," have claimed more than 600 ships.

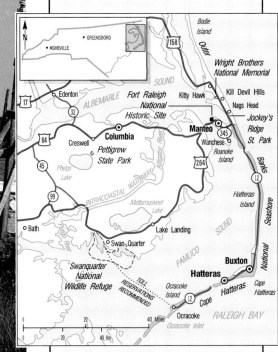

COASTAL TREASURES
South Carolina's Filigreed Shoreline

South Carolina's coast has more than its fair share of treasures. Between May and September, the sea temperature is commonly 80°, and the numerous islands and bays make its waters a delight for boating. The coast is a haven for wildlife, too, including rare sea turtles and the water birds that follow the Atlantic flyway. The area was once a prime producer of rice, indigo, and long-fibered cotton, and the well-preserved mansions and subtropical gardens of its old plantations are almost without equal. The hurricane of '89 did enormous damage to the area, but in spite of that, the air is full of brine or the scent of pines and flowers, and the world still seems blessed.

Spanish sailors first visited the islands, rivers, and marshes of this coast in the early 16th century. The Spanish chose Beaufort, now a charming, historic resort, as capital of the territory they called Florida. French Huguenots arrived next; then the English, represented by Captain William Hilton, laid their claim to the coast in 1663. The fine natural harbor aided the growth of the town. After a setback in 1715, when the Yemasee Indians burned down the town in retaliation for the advance of the white settlement, the town prospered during the 18th century.

Hilton Head Island, named in the captain's honor, was settled by the English in the early 1700s. During the Civil War, the island was the Union army's fueling station for ships blockading Confederate ports. Today, the U.S. Marine Corps Recruit Depot, with an interesting museum, is just a short trip across Port Royal Sound on Parris Island.

Hilton Head Island, as close to paradise as golfers and tennis players are likely to come, also has fine wildlife refuges. At Hunting Island State Park, southeast of Beaufort, once a site for deer, raccoon, and waterfowl hunting, there are miles of peaceful beach, a maritime forest, palmettos, and fine views from the top of a 140-foot-tall lighthouse. Still farther north, the Cape Romain National Wildlife Refuge offers 60,000 acres of barrier islands and saltwater marshes between the ocean and the Intracoastal Waterway.

Just west of Charleston are some of the finest examples of how plantation owners tamed this lush country. Middleton Place claims the oldest formal gardens in America, laid out in 1741. They have terraces, an octagonal sunken garden, camellia walks, and twin "butterfly" lakes. Magnolia Plantation and Gardens is a 500-acre estate with a 50-acre garden that was begun in the 1680s. It is outstanding for the abundance of camellias (900 varieties) and azaleas (250 varieties). The grounds also include a 125-acre waterfowl refuge, a miniature horse ranch, a biblical garden, a horticultural maze, and a petting zoo for children.

Magnolia Gardens, Charleston (*right*) Heady with the fragrance of trailing yellow jasmine and of the several varieties of camellia that are scented—*Camellia sasanqua* is Japanese and *Camellia sinensis* a native of India and Ceylon—these gardens seem to thrill all the senses at once. Some magnolias smell of aniseed, others of lemon, and the Japanese commonly burn the bark of several members of the magnolia family as incense. Although the perfume is undetectable in the evergreen species of azalea, all azaleas depend on their scent to attract the insects that pollinate them. Brighter azaleas need less scent than their paler sisters; the most fragrant blooms are pink, white, and yellow. The palette of color for camellias is relatively limited, from creamy white through shades of pink to ruby red. But magnolias cover an amazing spectrum ranging from pure white to nearly black. Blossoms can also be two-toned, with one tone shading into another or different hues on the outside and inside surface of one flower.

Harbor Town, Hilton Head Island (*left*) Thanks in large part to the bridge connecting it to the mainland, which was completed in 1956, Hilton Head is now a year-round resort. But it has a checkered historical past. Inhabited by Indians nearly 4,000 years ago, the island supported the English planters who helped colonize it and introduced an indigo crop. After the Revolution, Sea Island cotton became a popular crop. The large plantations were abandoned after the Civil War, and recently freed slaves, the "Gullak" people, established small farms in their stead.

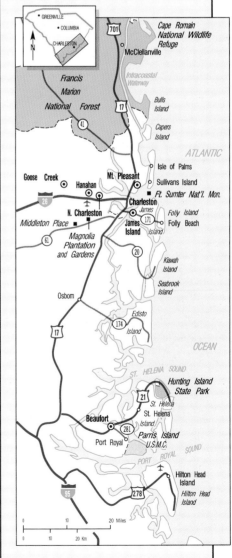

SITES TO SEE

● **Kiawah Island**, named for the Kiawah Indians who once lived here, is the site of the pre-Civil War **Vanderhorst Mansion**; the island also has a **straw market**.

● **SpringFest** is an annual March celebration on Hilton Head Island with musical events, sporting competitions, and plenty of local foods.

● **The John Mark Verdier House** (Beaufort), a Federal-style home built toward the end of the 18th century, is furnished as it might have been by a merchant planter in the period 1790–1825. During the Civil War, Union army officers used this house as their headquarters.

● **Saint Helena's Episcopal Church** (Beaufort), built 1724, was a hospital during the Civil War. Gravestones from the cemetery were supposedly used as operating tables.

UPCOUNTRY
South Carolina's Blue Ridge

The hills and valleys of South Carolina's Blue Ridge Mountains were home to the Cherokee until they were forced to cede their lands to the state late in the 18th century. Pushed west to Georgia, in 1838 they were deported by military force to the Indian Territory, which later became Oklahoma. In the west of the state, the Chattooga National Wild and Scenic River plunges through dramatic rocky gorges. The Blue Ridge Mountains loom to the north, while a string of important battlefields stretches to the east. The state's southern region is a patchwork of peach orchards and cotton mills, universities and art galleries, fine gardens, and elegant preserved antebellum plantations.

The Cherokee Foothills Scenic Highway begins near the Georgia state line and cuts an arc through South Carolina's Piedmont Plateau to Gaffney. The western end of the road passes Walhalla, a picturesque city settled by Germans in the mid-19th century and named after Valhalla, the mythical paradise of Norse legend. The road then swings east near Oconee State Park, which lies in the wild and beautiful Sumter National Forest. Keowee-Toxaway State Park sprawls alongside Lake Jocassee in the heart of what was once Cherokee country. Not far off is the highest point in the state, Sassafras Mountain, whose peak towers 3,560 feet above the rolling countryside.

Following the scenic road eastward, visitors will arrive at Caesars Head State Park, where a 2.2-mile trail leads to Raven Cliff Falls. An overlook at the park's entrance offers panoramic views of the Blue Ridge. Farther east is Cowpens National Battlefield, where on January 17, 1781, British troops fell foul of Gen. Daniel Morgan's backwoods militia of patriots, who trounced them soundly. At Kings Mountain National Military Park, a determined band of frontiersmen defeated a battalion of loyalists and helped turn the tide of the Revolutionary War.

The splendid Peachoid, a million-gallon water tank in the shape of a peach, stands proudly on the highway near Spartanburg, one of the largest centers for peach-shipping in the world and a textile center as well. At Greenville, which bills itself as "the textile center of the world," the Bob Jones University Art Gallery and Biblical Museum displays a large collection of religious paintings.

Clemson University's fine Botanical Garden is one of the largest collections of shrubs in the eastern U.S. It includes a pagoda, tea house, gristmill, arboretum, and separate wildflower, fern, and bog sections. The campus is also the site of two interesting homes. Fort Hill was the home of John C. Calhoun, Andrew Jackson's Vice President. Hanover House, built in 1716 by a French Huguenot, was both a residence and a frontier fortress against Indian raids.

Hiking (*left*) is a favorite pastime in South Carolina's Blue Ridge Mountains. In addition to providing splendid opportunities for camping, several state parks in the upcountry near the Blue Ridge offer special programs of walks conducted by naturalists, including wildflower walks in April and, in October, walks to view the brilliant colors of the fall foliage. Advance registration is required for these walks; contact the South Carolina State Park office.

Hagood Mill, Pickens (*above*) This gristmill drew such a steady stream of farmers that Benjamin Hagood, the miller who built it in 1825, opened a general store and a tannery on the same site, the better to benefit his customers. A sturdy clapboard structure, whose beams were joined with wooden pegs, the mill was in continuous operation for over 100 years. Now totally restored, it is still occasionally powered by spring water.

SITES TO SEE

● **Long Creek** is the starting point for thrilling whitewater raft trips along the Chattooga River. Some trips include Five Falls, a drop of 75 feet in less than half a mile. The chilling movie *Deliverance* was filmed along the Chattooga.

● **Hollywild Animal Park** (Inman) has more than 200 animals on display, including elephants.

● **World of Energy** (Clemson) explains different sources of power, as well as the history of electricity.

● **Old Hunter's Store** (Pendleton), built in the mid-19th-century, is the place to get taped tours of the town's historic district. The whole town and part of neighboring Pickens County are registered as a National Historic District, one of the largest in the U.S. **Woodburn**, west of town,

is a restored plantation, built about 1830 in the Greek Revival style. **Ashtabula** is another outstanding plantation.

● **Greenville County Museum of Art** (Greenville) contains an outstanding collection of Andrew Wyeth paintings as well as those of other American artists, specializing in southern art.

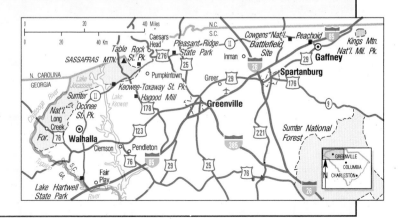

CHARLESTON

In this colonial port, history is as fresh as the sea air, as vivid as the flowers that spill over garden gates, and as resonant as the church bells' chimes. Eased and mellowed by time, the elegance of the past still lines the local streets. The old Colonial and Greek Revival buildings—formerly homes of proud and wealthy merchants—are softened by vine-clad walls and pastel doors and by the tracery of delicate wrought iron. The streets seem to hold the quietness of another era, as do the lavish residences like the Calhoun Mansion, with its 35 rooms and magnificent woodwork, and the Thomas Elfe Workshop, a scaled-down "single" house—one room wide by definition—built by one of Charleston's master cabinetmakers.

Named for King Charles II by the English settlers who founded it in 1670, Charleston was once called the Holy City. Because it was not subjected to the rule of the Church of England, Huguenots (French Protestants), Catholics, Lutherans, Unitarians, Baptists, and Jews joined the Anglicans (Episcopalians) here. Many houses of worship stand today on the sites of their original churches. Charleston occupied an important strategic location, so the military came here, too. At Fort Moultrie, situated on Sullivan's Island, Colonel Moultrie achieved one of the first colonial victories of the Revolutionary War when he successfully repelled nine British warships.

Not quite a century later, the first shots of the Civil War were fired against Fort Sumter in Charleston Harbor. The history of Charleston as a fighting city is alive in its military monuments and museums, just as its history as a port and vital center of trade—bolstered by the slaves imported from Africa and the West Indies—lives in its streets.

Colonial House Overlooking Charleston Harbor (*above*) A distinctive feature of local architecture was a porch, called a piazza, where visitors were often entertained. The bright, airy enclosure offered a more informal setting for guests than the formally decorated drawing room and provided the ground floor of such houses with welcome ventilation. **St. Philip's Episcopal Church** (*below left*) First established in 1670, this is the Mother Church of the Province. Originally sited where St. Michael's stands today, the present building is the third St. Philip's to be situated on this site in Church Street. It was built between 1835 and 1838, when it was known as the lighthouse church because a government-maintained light in the tall steeple was used to guide ships at sea. **Sculpture at Charles Towne Landing** (*below right*) The English settlers chose this site, then called Albemarle Point, hoping its seclusion would shield them from pirate raids.

HISTORIC SITES AND DISTRICTS

Downtown Charleston contains over 2,000 historic buildings, 200 of which pre-date 1800. Meeting Street marks the approximate western edge of the original walled city.

Four Corners of Law The intersection where the county courthouse stands bears this name since the buildings at each corner represent a different form of government: municipal, county, federal, and religious.

MUSEUMS

Charleston Museum The oldest museum in the U.S., founded in 1773. Its exhibits focus on state and city history, architecture, agriculture, and the Civil War.

Patriots Point Naval and Maritime Museum The aircraft carrier USS *Yorktown* can be toured, as can a nuclear-powered merchant ship.

NOTABLE BUILDINGS AND STRUCTURES

Beth Elohim Synagogue is the second oldest in the country, first established here in 1794, and the oldest in continuous use.

Circular Congregational Church housed the first religious dissenters in the state. This is the fourth church to stand here.

Dock Street Theatre One of America's first theaters opened here in 1763. Performances are staged today in a replica of the original playhouse.

Fort Sumter National Monument On the man-made island accessible only by boat, the fort's colorful history is recounted by tour guides and in a museum. Fort Moultrie was a vital military stronghold for over 170 years.

Nathaniel Russell House A lavishly furnished merchant's house with a celebrated "flying" staircase that spirals up three floors without touching a wall.

Old Exchange and Provost Dungeon The 18th-century center of the city's economic and political activity. The U.S. Constitution was ratified in the Great Hall.

St. Michael's Episcopal Church The city's oldest surviving church, completed in 1761. Its steeple served as a ships' beacon and, in the 19th century, as the local fire tower.

GARDENS AND PARKS

Boone Hall Plantation A working plantation since 1681. Nine original slave cabins, built from bricks produced here, still stand in one of the few extant "slave streets" in the South. Brick paths crisscross the extensive formal gardens.

Charles Towne Landing A 663-acre park on the original site of the city's settlement, whose reconstructed palisades can be visited. Explore the fortifications, the replica of a 17th-century trading ship, the Animal Forest, and the interpretive center, which offers films and exhibits.

ATTRACTIONS

Festival of Houses includes walking tours of historic houses, some of them more than 250 years old, oyster roasts at Drayton Hall, and a "glorious garden" tour of four spectacular old gardens. Mid-March to mid-April.

Spoleto Festival U.S.A. Since 1977, the American portion of Gian-Carlo Menotti's celebrated Festival of Two Worlds in Spoleto, Italy, has been held here. An important gathering of world-famous artists offers a varied program of music, theater, dance, and opera. Late May.

The Taste of Charleston An international food festival organized by the city's finest restaurants, allows the visitor to sample the cuisines of many nations in a single day in September.

Wildlife Month features the Southeastern Wildlife Exposition with its crafts and educational exhibitions. February.

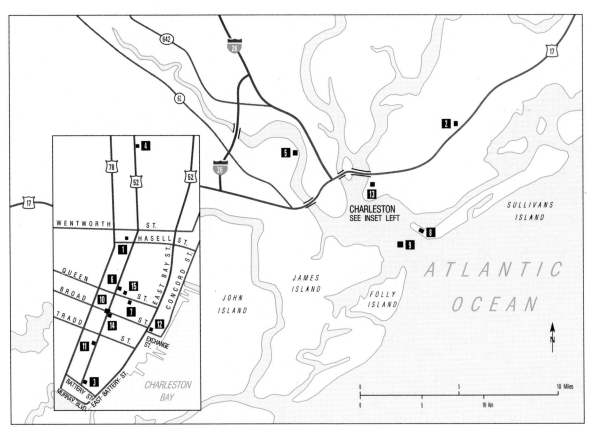

THE DEEP SOUTH

It isn't that the Deep South has more history than other parts of the United States, but it often seems that way. The reason, perhaps, is that these southernmost states of the old Confederacy preserve a deep-rooted sense of otherness, making the present more remote and the past more vivid. And the landscapes here contribute to the visitor's sense of being somewhere set apart from the rest of the country. The climate, uniquely, takes its weather from two coasts, the Atlantic and the Gulf; the vegetation is lush, and the wildlife exotic; the architecture still resonates with a French, Caribbean, and Plantation heritage, and the fields, even where catfish farms and soybeans have replaced the cotton, still unavoidably recall the slave years. Hills and valleys are still marked by traces of de Soto's El Dorado quest and the swath cut by Sherman marching to the sea.

Even where the South is most modern, an out-of-this-world quality remains: New Orleans and Baton Rouge hover like uncertain acrobats between an abundance of old-world charm and their role as world-class ports and leaders in a fading petrochemical boom. Central Florida celebrates the other-worldly theme with Disney's techno-fantasies—and leads the nation in attracting visitors from Europe and the Orient. Atlanta, a city of history and glass towers, is the flourishing and unquestioned hub of the New South; while at Huntsville, Alabama, NASA technicians strive literally to reach brave new worlds.

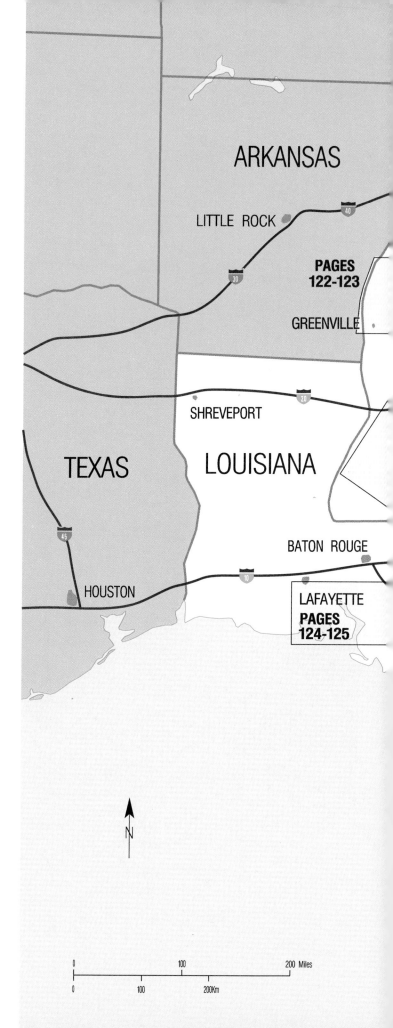

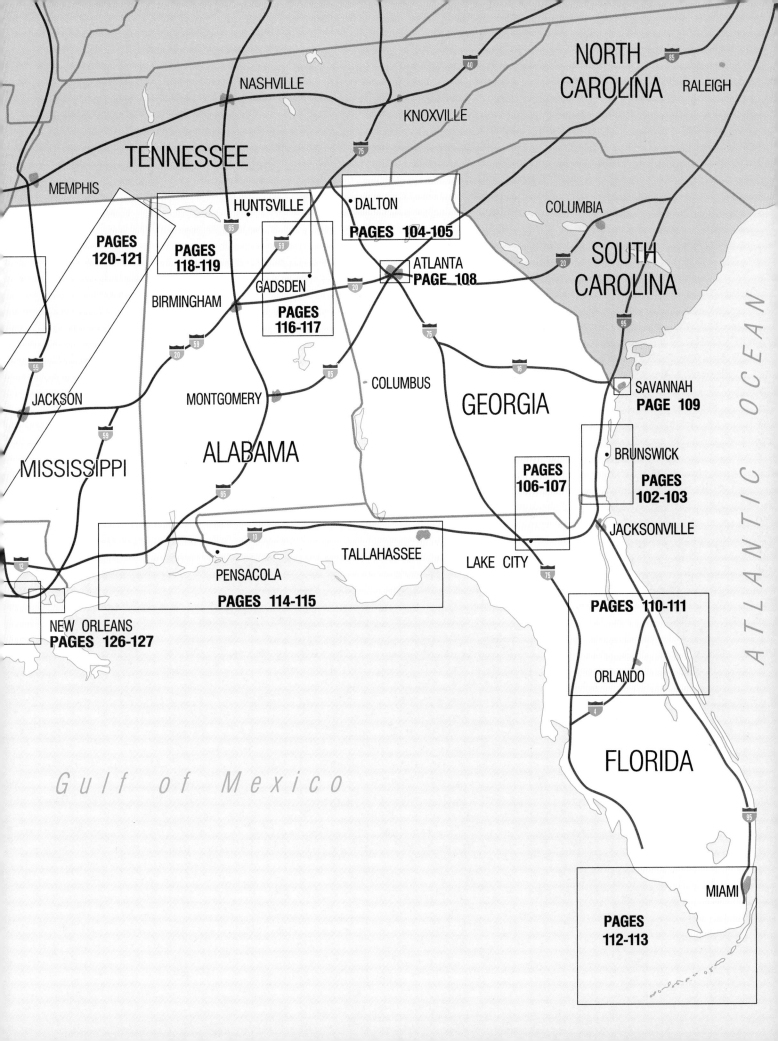

NORTH
CAROLINA

RALEIGH

TENNESSEE

NASHVILLE

KNOXVILLE

MEMPHIS

HUNTSVILLE

DALTON

PAGES 104-105

COLUMBIA

SOUTH
CAROLINA

PAGES 120-121

PAGES 118-119

GADSDEN

ATLANTA
PAGE 108

BIRMINGHAM

PAGES 116-117

COLUMBUS

GEORGIA

SAVANNAH
PAGE 109

JACKSON

MONTGOMERY

ALABAMA

BRUNSWICK

PAGES 106-107

PAGES 102-103

MISSISSIPPI

JACKSONVILLE

TALLAHASSEE

PENSACOLA

LAKE CITY

PENSACOLA
PAGES 114-115

PAGES 110-111

NEW ORLEANS
PAGES 126-127

ORLANDO

Gulf of Mexico

FLORIDA

MIAMI

PAGES 112-113

ATLANTIC OCEAN

GOLDEN ISLES
Georgia's Eastern Seaboard

Georgia's subtropical sea islands—the Golden Islands of Guale, as the Spanish called them—stretch from South Carolina to Florida. Separated from the mainland by marshes, sounds, and estuaries, their sparkling beaches rise to sand dunes and maritime woodlands of oak, pine, palmetto, and magnolia. The coastal plain once supported wealthy rice and indigo plantations. Now it is filled with pine forests, live oaks, and green marshes where egrets stalk. Among the fine old coastal towns is one of the most beautiful in America, Savannah.

The gateway to the Golden Isles is Brunswick, named for the German homeland of the royal House of Hanover and well worth seeing in its own right. The Glynn County Courthouse, surrounded by moss-draped oaks, swamp holly, and such exotic plants as Chinese pistachio, is especially fine, and the Shrimp Docks are picturesque when the fleet is in. The town prides itself on being the "Shrimp Capital of the World."

From Brunswick, causeways lead to Jekyll Island, St. Simons Island, and Sea Island. Jekyll was once owned by a consortium of millionaires whose members, early this century, were thought to control one-sixth of the world's wealth.

East of Brunswick is St. Simons Island. Fort Frederica National Monument, built in 1736 on the western edge of the island, was an important English bastion during the conflict with Spain known as the War of Jenkins' Ear (1739–42), which ended in a British victory at nearby Bloody Marsh. The Museum of Coastal History, housed in a restored lighthouse-keeper's home, preserves a fascinating record of the island's civil and military history. Aaron Burr fled here after his duel with Alexander Hamilton; John and Charles Wesley, the founders of Methodism, once preached near an ancient stand of live oaks outside Frederica; timber from St. Simons was used in the U.S. Navy's first ships and in the building of the Brooklyn Navy Yard.

A causeway from St. Simons leads to Sea Island, where Sea Island Drive, also known as Millionaires' Row, gives a new meaning to the name "Golden Isles." Some islands can only be reached by boat or ferry, including Blackbeard Island—where people say the legendary pirate buried his treasure—and Cumberland Island, which boasts a protected National Seashore. Once cultivated with fruit and long-fibered Sea Island cotton, Cumberland is now a preserve for more than 300 species of birds. It also harbors picturesque ruins of estates built by Revolutionary War General Nathanael Greene.

Spanish Moss (*left*) This plant is not a true moss, but a member of the pineapple family. It is shown here growing in an oak grove at the saltmarsh edge of the Cumberland Island National Seashore. The plant has no roots, but lives off moisture in the atmosphere and mineral-rich cells that wash off the host tree.

Christ Church, St. Simons Island (*right*) This white-painted frame church was established here in 1736, and John and Charles Wesley would come down from Fort Frederica to preach under the oak trees. The church was desecrated during the Civil War, and the present edifice was erected in 1885 by Anson Green Phelps Dodge, Jr., as a memorial to his first wife Ellen.

SITES TO SEE

● **Jekyll Island Club Historic District** preserves 33 buildings in 240 acres of the former playground for America's wealthiest families. Tram tours, about 1½ hours long, take in the major sites, including the Rockefeller and DuBignon cottages. **Faith Chapel**, built 1904, contains Tiffany stained-glass windows. **Mistletoe Cottage**, built 1901 for Henry K. Porter, a U.S. congressman from Pennsylvania, now features changing exhibits. **Goodyear Cottage**, built 1907, is also an art gallery with changing exhibits. **Crane Cottage**, modeled on an Italian villa, has 3 restored rooms open to the public.

● **Horton House ruins** (Jekyll Island) are the remains of a house built in the 1700s from "tabby," a combination of sand, water, lime, and crushed shells. Additions were made to the house in the early 1800s, when it was a Sea Island cotton plantation.

● **Mary Miller Doll Museum** (Brunswick) is home for more than 3,000 dolls of all sizes and shapes from around the world, including many antique dolls. Dollhouses and miniature vehicles are also on display.

● **Hofwyl-Broadfield Plantation** (Brunswick) was one of the coast's major rice producers before the Civil War. The house, built 1851–60, contains 19th-century furnishings and family possessions from the 1790s. A 1,268-acre wildlife preserve contains native animals such as deer, raccoons, and numerous birds.

● **Cumberland Island National Seashore** can be reached via a passenger ferry service from St. Marys; cars are not permitted on the island. **Plum Orchard Mansion**, built 1898, is only open one day a month and Sundays from April through August.

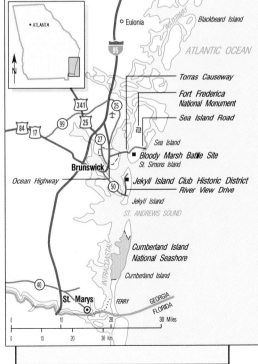

GOLD IN THE HILLS
Chattahoochee National Forest

In 1540, when Spanish explorer Hernando de Soto and his troops made their way into present-day Georgia, they were looking for gold; they found Cherokee Indians. It was not until 1828 that the first American gold rush brought prospectors to Dahlonega, named for the Cherokee word meaning "golden," at the western end of the Appalachians. Although many of the mines were abandoned at the beginning of the Civil War, specially panned gold was later used to gild the dome of the State Capitol. The real treasures of this area, however, are its mountains and gorges, its deep forests, and its wild rivers.

One of the places romantically linked with the Spanish exploration of Georgia is Fort Mountain on the western side of Chattahoochee National Forest. Named for the ruins of an 855-foot serpentine stone wall, it encloses some eight acres near the summit of the mountain. Although the origin of the wall is unknown, it may have been made by the same mound builders whose earthworks can be seen at other locations in Georgia.

From this mysteriously enclosed mountain top, there are wonderful views of peaks, forests, fields, and farms. Rocky Face Ridge, which General Johnston successfully defended against Sherman, lies to the west; to the east are the distant Cohutta Mountains.

All of this was once Cherokee land, and just west of Fort Mountain, at Spring Place, is the 1804 showplace mansion of Chief James Vann. At that time, the Cherokee capital was at New Echota, now a state historic site, northeast of Calhoun on SR 225. Most of the buildings on the site are accurate reconstructions and include the Supreme Court House and the *Cherokee Phoenix* printing office. The newspaper was the first to use the Cherokee alphabet originated by Sequoyah.

In the eastern section of the forest, near Blairsville, is the Brasstown Bald Visitor Center, which is the highest point in the state, 4,784 feet above sea level. From the observation deck at its peak, visitors have a panoramic view of four states.

Southeast of the visitor center on US 75 lies the once-deserted lumbermill town of Helen. In 1969, it was reconstructed to resemble an alpine village and now boasts an 18-bell glockenspiel, whose daily chimes add to the European atmosphere. Helen's Oktoberfest features Bavarian-style hospitality and the sound of alpine brass bands.

Nature's own festival, a year-round affair, is celebrated with whitewater rafting on the Chattooga River, boating on Lake Burton, and skiing on the most southerly ski slopes in the United States.

Old Dahlonega Mine (*left*) It is still possible to experience the thrill of anticipation while panning for gold in the stream here with the same basic equipment used by prospectors in the heady days of the country's first gold rush. Visitors can also see how mining was developed at the Dahlonega Courthouse Gold Museum, a Greek Revival building where a film about the Gold Rush and displays of old mining equipment, gold nuggets, and coins set the scene for this period of American history.

Amicalola Falls State Park (*above*) One of the seven wonders of Georgia, Amicalola Falls is the highest waterfall east of the Mississippi River. Amicalola is the Cherokee word for "tumbling waters," and these magnificent falls plunge 729 feet in seven separate cascades. The 700-acre State Park is situated between Ellijay and Dahlonega and offers facilities for camping, fishing, and hiking around its spectacular and varied trails.

SITES TO SEE

● **Traveler's Rest State Historic Site** (Toccoa), built 1825, was developed into a stagecoach inn about 1833. Once a thriving plantation, the inn and plantation house have been restored in pre-Civil War style with original furnishings.

● **Toccoa Falls** (near Toccoa) tumble 186 feet, making them higher than Niagara Falls.

● **Museum of the Hills** (Helen) re-creates the legends of hill country life using wax figures, as well as fairytale and nursery rhyme settings.

● **Chatsworth** is the center of Georgia's talc-mining region. Annual festivals held here include the Appalachian Wagon Train over the Fourth of July and the Georgia State Mule Draft Horse Frolic in the fall. The Fort Mountain Craft Village Fair is a popular event each September.

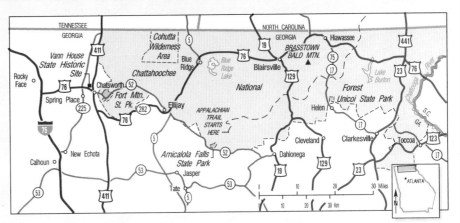

WHERE THE EARTH TREMBLES
Okefenokee National Wildlife Refuge

This primitive wilderness, which fills a shallow bowl roughly 40 miles long and 30 miles wide, resists human interference as surely as the most icy mountains. A corruption of the Indian word *Owaquaphenoga*, its name means "trembling earth" and refers to the swamp's curious floating islands. These hammocks begin as mats of decaying vegetation. Seeds germinate on them and sprout new roots which anchor the hammocks to the swamp bed. When all the surface vegetation dies, the islands sink, rot, and release gases that float them to the surface, where the entire process begins again. Thus the swamp is constantly renewed, and its quaking landscape is always changing.

In 1937, after persistent efforts to build a railroad through it had failed, the greater part of the Okefenokee was declared a National Wildlife Refuge. Today, the railroads gather at Waycross, a major marshaling center, where Rice Yard organizes freight cars into trains for nationwide shipping. The Okefenokee Heritage Center provides an introduction to the old life around the swamp with an 1840s farmhouse and a 100-ton steam locomotive. At the adjacent Southern Forest World, huge models of a loblolly pine and a giant cypress help tell the story of southern forestry, and visitors can sit in the cab of a 1905 logging locomotive.

Okefenokee Swamp Park lies south of Waycross. The northern entrance to the Okefenokee Swamp, it is a 1,600-acre wildlife sanctuary on Cowhouse Island, with flower gardens and animal exhibits. The Living Swamp Ecological Center displays insectivorous plants and also houses a serpentarium and a bear observatory.

Explore this strange environment, whose dark waters empty into the Suwanee River and then the Gulf of Mexico, in a flat-bottomed swamp boat, or follow a self-guiding wilderness canoe trail. Insect repellent is vital from April to November.

The swamp sustains an extraordinary range of animals: alligators, black bears, bobcats, opossums, otters, turtles, 40 kinds of fish, and 230 varieties of native birds. Among the plants are multicolored irises and carnivorous pitcher plants. The brown water reflects them all, along with the reeds and the bald cypresses, like a mirror.

South of the park in White Springs, Florida—a former health resort on the Suwanee River with sulfur springs the Indians believed made them invulnerable—the Stephen Foster State Folk Culture Center celebrates the life and work of the author of "Old Folks at Home."

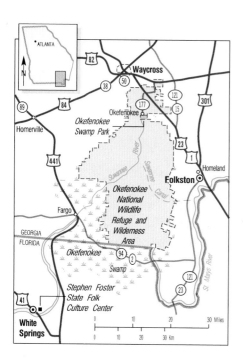

Common Egret (*left*) One of the many species of waterbirds that haunt the Okefenokee Swamp, the common egret is distinguished from the smaller snowy egret by the straightness of the plumes on its back. In snowy egrets, the plumes curl, which made them a popular trimming for Edwardian ladies' hats.

Bald Cypress and Water Lily Swamp, Okefenokee (*above*) Called "bald" because it is deciduous (but here clad in a wig of Spanish moss), *Taxodium distichum* is a water-loving conifer common to southern swamp lands. Its water-resistant wood and the "knees" that grow above the water from the roots are prized.

SITES TO SEE

● **Pioneer Island Museum** (Okefenokee Swamp Park) has displays describing the life of the area's early non-Indian settlers. The park's **Swamp Creation Center** explains the swamp's evolution with dioramas,

charts, and animated exhibitions.

● **Stephen C. Foster State Park** (near Fargo) has a small museum along with campsites and boat rentals.

● **Olustee Battlefield State Historic Site** (Olustee, FL) is where Florida's major Civil War battle took place in 1864; the Confederates won handily. Nearby **Lake City** hosts an annual 3-day festival and battle reenactment in late February.

WORTH A DETOUR

● **Georgia Agrirama** (Tifton) is a 92-acre outdoor museum devoted to life in the 1890s. It includes farms and a forest industries complex, along with numerous period buildings and guides dressed in

costumes. Bluegrass, country, and western and gospel music are performed in an outdoor setting nearby.

● **Jacksonville** is one of the major cultural cities of Florida. The **Cummer Gallery of Art** is an impressive center for fine

and decorative arts. In addition to the collection from pre-Christian times, there is an Italian-style formal garden along the St. John's River.

ATLANTA

When the windows of Atlanta's skyscrapers catch the last rays of afternoon sun, this phoenix-city of the South seems to blaze again with General Sherman's fires. In 1864, he destroyed 90 percent of the city by fire. But, thanks to carpetbagger money and the city's role as a major railroad junction, the city rose again to become, in spirit and in commerce, the leading city of the New South.

Where the Hyatt Regency Hotel now stands with its 21-story "lobby," Peachtree Street was once a woodland trail between Terminus (Atlanta's first name) and an Indian trading post called Standing Peachtree. Today, the street is a commercial district with many hotels, restaurants, and stores.

Although the Civil War destroyed antebellum Atlanta, the city remembers its past with vigor. In Grant Park is the Atlanta Cyclorama, a 400-foot circular painting of the Battle of Atlanta. Nearby, Georgia's Stone Mountain Park contains an 825-foot-high dome of granite with equestrian carvings and a reconstructed plantation with buildings from all over Georgia.

MUSEUMS

Carter Presidential Center In addition to archives and memorabilia of the Carter administration, the center also contains the former president's library and presents a multimedia history of the first 39 presidents.

High Museum of Art One of the major museums of the South, this collection is based on paintings by American artists, but also features European paintings and decorative arts. A children's gallery has participatory exhibits.

PARKS AND GARDENS

Atlanta Botanical Garden Visit a Japanese garden, rose garden, and 15-acre hardwood forest.

NOTABLE BUILDINGS

Swan House A 1928 Palladian-style home, the house gets its name from the swan motif used in the interior and exterior decorations; it contains an elegant spiral staircase.

Tullie Smith House A restored 2-story farmhouse of the 1840s with outbuildings.

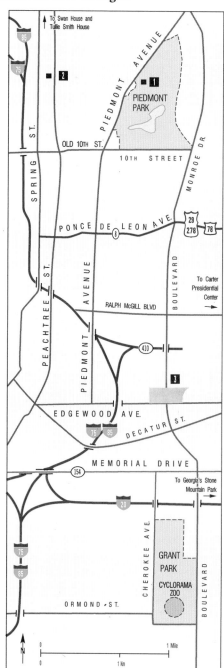

MAP REFERENCE

1 Atlanta Botanical Garden
2 High Museum of Art
3 Martin Luther King Jr. Nat. Hist. Site

Birthplace of Martin Luther King, Jr. (*above*) Between his birth here in 1929 and his assassination in Memphis in 1968, Dr. King became a unique leader in the American fight for racial equality and an eloquent spokesman for non-violent civil disobedience. Ordained at 19 and later pastor of Atlanta's Ebenezer Baptist Church, a position he held jointly with his father, King led historic marches in support of freedom, jobs, and voting rights for people of every race. He was awarded the Nobel Prize for Peace in 1964.

SAVANNAH

On December 21, 1864, General Sherman entered Savannah, his troops fresh from the burning of Atlanta. He stabled his horses in Colonial Park, chose the Green-Meldrim House as his headquarters, and, declaring the town too beautiful to burn, offered it as a Christmas present to President Lincoln. Today, many still believe Savannah is one of the most beautiful cities in the United States.

When the city was laid out in 1733, it consisted of 24 wards, each centered on a public square. Today, 20 of the wards are still intact, lined with oak trees and azaleas and elegant townhouses. Although one of the fastest-growing port cities on the Atlantic coast, Savannah still retains much of its elegant charm. Davenport House, built 1815–20 in the Federal style, has been restored and furnished with period pieces by the Historic Savannah Foundation. The Juliet Gordon Low Birthplace is a Regency-style home built about 1810 and furnished with family items. Low was the founder of the Girl Scouts, and the house is maintained as her memorial. King-Tisdell Cottage, with an ornate gingerbread porch, is furnished like a typical black family's coastal home of the 1890s.

MUSEUMS

Savannah History Museum Multimedia displays recount the city's history; exhibits include an 1890 locomotive and a cotton gin.

Ships of the Sea Maritime Museum occupies an 1898 warehouse. A re-created ship's carpenter's shop and collections of scrimshaw and figureheads help explain the city's maritime history.

Telfair Academy of Arts and Sciences A Regency mansion, built 1818, on the site of Government House, residence of Georgia's former royal governors. The Octagon Room is one of the finest period rooms in the U.S. The museum displays silver, furniture, and American and European Impressionist paintings.

NOTABLE BUILDINGS

Independent Presbyterian Church This 1890 church is a copy of the original that was built 1817–19; notable for its tall steeple, Georgian interior, and domed ceiling.

Mikve Israel Temple Built in the 1870s, this is the home of one of the oldest Torahs in the country and belongs to the third-oldest U.S. Jewish congregation.

PARKS AND GARDENS

Colonial Park Cemetery Site of the town's cemetery from 1752 to 1853, where Gen. Sherman's troops stabled their horses during the town's occupation.

Forsyth Park Laid out in 1851 with azaleas and a fountain based on the one in Paris's *Place de la Concorde*.

MAP REFERENCE

1. Davenport House
2. Green-Meldrim House
3. Independent Presbyterian Church
4. J.G. Low Birthplace
5. Mikve Israel Temple
6. Savannah History Museum
7. Ships of the Sea Maritime Museum
8. Telfair Academy of Arts and Science
9. U.S. Customs House

Savannah River Waterfront (*above*) Lined with buildings rich in military and maritime history, the waterfront offers a capsule version of the city's past. Ballast from European sailing ships became the cobblestone for the streets of Factors Walk, where 19th-century cotton merchants met to transact business. The buildings in which they traded still stand, linked to the bluff by iron bridges.

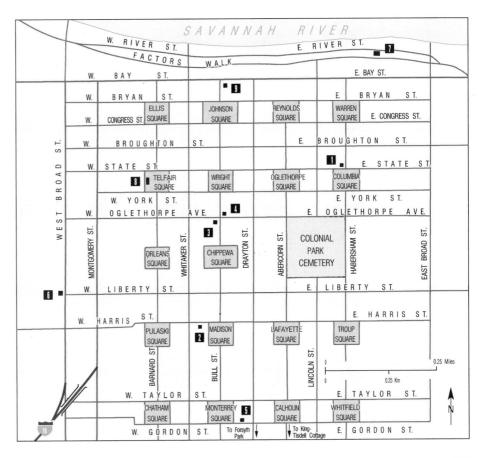

STRANGE WORLDS, GREAT ESCAPES

Central Florida

Central Florida was a magical, mysterious land long before Walt Disney carved his Magic Kingdom out of the swamplands south of Orlando. There are no bears in pink tutus, ticking alligators, or re-creations of Marrakesh's Koutoubia Minaret outside Walt Disney World. But this region of natural spectacles and man-made wonders encompasses a space-launch center, a house built on snail shells, wild pigs, crystalline silver springs, orange groves, and miles and miles of ocean coastline with golden beaches.

In 1513, Ponce de León launched the European exploration of the New World when he sailed to Florida in search of the Fountain of Youth, and landed near St. Augustine. He returned in 1521 to establish a permanent settlement, but was wounded by hostile local Indians and died before the colony's future was guaranteed. Lured by the same fables of riches that had seduced Ponce de León into his initial exploration, other brave Spaniards led their followers into the lush interior. Panfilo de Narvaez, Hernando de Soto, and Tristan de Luna left their names to history, but their settlements disappeared without a trace and their search for vast wealth did not meet with any success.

About 400 years later and 100 miles south of Ponce de León's landing point, Cape Canaveral became the principal launching point for the U.S. space program.

Adjacent to the John F. Kennedy Space Center, Merritt Island National Wildlife Refuge is a staging point for migratory water birds on their seasonal voyages to new worlds. They have adjusted to the rockets' roar, and to the visitors at Spaceport U.S.A.

The renowned Walt Disney World, home of singing mice and Audio-Animatronic presidents, is divided into three realms. Magic Kingdom concentrates on nostalgia and fantasy, while EPCOT (Experimental Prototype Community of Tomorrow) Center focuses on high-tech previews of the future and colorful portrayals of the cultures of many nations. The newest addition is Disney-MGM Studios, offering guided tours of a real movie back lot. The scale, scope, and execution are stunning, and so too are the crowds. To see performing water life, head for Sea World of Florida or the Gator Jumparoo Show at Kissimmee's Gatorland Zoo.

Speed demons will want to visit Daytona Beach, on whose 23 miles of hard sand numerous speed records have been set. Speed Weeks, a series of races preceding the Daytona 500 every February, celebrate the town's heritage. Visitors can drive on the famous sands, but racing is now banned there.

For a panoramic view of the area's lakes and hills from Florida's highest observation point (226 feet tall), climb the Florida Citrus Tower near Clermont. Beyond the orange groves, near Orange City, is Blue Spring State Park, where the first permanent home in the area (about 1872) stands on a shell mound left by centuries of snail-eating Timucuan Indians.

Future World at EPCOT Center, Walt Disney World *(below)* The huge silver geosphere, called Spaceship Earth, marks the start of Future World. Inside the 17-story dome, visitors travel through a history of communications that spans everything from cave paintings to futuristic technology.

John F. Kennedy Space Center *(right)* All U.S. manned space flights have begun here since Alan Shepard's historic launch in 1961. Seven years later, space vehicles from these launch pads landed on the moon, and more recently, the space shuttles *Discovery* and *Columbia* started their journeys here.

SITES TO SEE

● **Ft. Christmas Museum** (Christmas) is a reconstructed fort built for action during the Second Seminole War in 1837; construction began on Christmas Day.

● **Big Tree** (Sanford) is a giant cypress, thought to be the world's largest. Known locally as "The Senator," the tree is 17½ feet across, 138 feet tall, and has a circumference of 47 feet.

● **Tupperware Exhibit and Museum** (Kissimmee) is located at the international headquarters of this all-American product. In addition to explaining modern production techniques, the museum displays containers from as long as 5,000 years ago.

● **Florida's Silver Springs** (Silver Springs) claims to be the world's largest clear artesian springs. Tours in glass-bottomed boats let visitors see a large variety of fish and underwater animals. The **Antique Car Collection** shows off glistening restored antique and classic cars in period settings, with Americana memorabilia adding atmosphere.

● **Ponce de León Inlet Lighthouse**, 175 feet tall, operated 1887–1970 and was brought back into service in 1982. The adjoining lighthouse keepers' cottages present local nautical history and recall the numerous shipwrecks along the coast.

● **Ocala** is the center of Florida's thoroughbred breeding country, with about 400 horse farms, some of which welcome visitors. During the last century, the citrus industry blossomed here, resulting in ornate Victorian homes being built by the prosperous growers. A historic district preserves some of these houses, reflecting the wealth of the time.

● **Ocala National Forest** covers 366,000 subtropical acres in north-central Florida. Juniper Springs, a recreational area, contains an old-fashioned water wheel.

● **The Minnesota Twins** baseball team has its spring training camp in Orlando.

WETLANDS AND CORAL ISLANDS
Everglades National Park and the Florida Keys

Two of the nation's most exotic environments lie along the coast of southern Florida. The Everglades are the nation's largest subtropical wilderness, and the Florida Keys are a chain of coral and limestone islands whose southern tip lies closer to Havana than to Miami. The Everglades contain mangrove swamps where manatees graze, labyrinths of overhung waterways, and vast prairies of snag-toothed saw grass. On the Florida Keys, everything is light, dazzle, and reflection. Sunsets smear the sky with a jeweler's palette of gold, amethyst, turquoise, jacinth, and pearl.

Essentially a slow-moving river 50 miles wide and a few inches deep, Everglades National Park is the nation's largest subtropical wilderness. It flows over a bed of limestone which here and there supports islands of vegetation called hammocks.

Each entrance to the park offers its distinct perspective on this great wilderness. From the main entrance west of Florida City, SR 9336 becomes the Main Park Road and continues to Flamingo, with trails branching from the highway into areas of scrub palmetto, mahogany forests, and vast saw grass prairie.

At Flamingo, a tram runs through the hardwood forest, which flickers with a great variety of butterflies – dingy purple wings, mimics, and Florida skippers.

Along the Anhinga Trail from the Royal Palm Interpretive Center, the visitor can often see surprising congregations of alligators, garfish, egrets, gallinules, and water turkeys.

At Shark Valley, water from Lake Okeechobee, north of the park, flows into the Everglades via Shark River. The river and valley are so named because of the sharks sometimes feeding at the river's mouth. Bicycles can be rented and self-guiding trails provide a leisurely way to observe the valley's plants and wildlife. Here mangroves grow 75 feet tall.

From Everglades City, cruises set out for the maze of shifting islets, oyster bars, shallows, and shell beaches known as the Ten Thousand Islands. Such cruises make an intriguing prelude to the nearly 1,000 islands of the Keys.

Key West, the U.S.A.'s southernmost city, is New England with palm trees and hibiscus. People come out to watch the sunsets and be entertained by jugglers. Among the town's historic sites are the Audubon House and Gardens, where painter John James Audubon stayed in 1832, and the Ernest Hemingway Home and Museum, the mansion in which Hemingway wrote *A Farewell to Arms* and *For Whom the Bell Tolls*.

A Japanese submarine captured at Pearl Harbor stands in the garden of the Key West Lighthouse Museum. The view from atop the 1897 lighthouse provides a scenic overview of the city and out to sea. At Mel Fisher's Treasure Exhibit, booty from wrecked Spanish galleons is on display.

New England Poet
Robert Frost was one of a long line of artists and writers who lived temporarily in Key West. His house (*left*), set in subtropical gardens, has been preserved. Others who retreated to Key West include painter John James Audubon, writer Ernest Hemingway, and playwright Tennessee Williams.

SITES TO SEE

● **Boardwalks and nature trails** in Everglades National Park include Anhinga, Gumbo Limbo, Long Pine Key, Pinelands, Mahogany Hammock, and Pa-hay-okee Overlook. The **Royal Palm Interpretive Center** provides park information.

● **Shark Valley Tram Tour** (US 41) is a 15-mile, 2-hour round trip through the valley's saw grass wilderness. A half-hour stop at an observation tower offers views of alligators and white-tailed deer; there are also self-guiding bicycle tours.

● **Coral Castle of Florida** (Homestead) is a surreal maze of structures hewn by hand from local coral.

● **Orchid Jungle** (Homestead) contains orchids from around the world in a rain forest setting. Visitors can watch the laboratory cloning of plants.

● **John Pennekamp Coral Reef State Park** (Key Largo) boasts over 150 square miles of protected ocean. Travel in glass-bottomed boats and view a 9-foot-tall underwater statue called "Christ of the Deep." A boardwalk with observation platforms lets visitors walk through a mangrove area.

● **Theater of the Sea** (Islamorada) has marine life performances with dolphins and sea lions. Some animals can be petted, and trainers supervise swims with the dolphins.

● **Wrecker's Museum** (Key West) is in the home of former state senator and Key West wrecker Capt. Francis

Watlington. "Wrecking" is the local name for the marine salvage industry, which provided prosperity for the town during the last century. The museum contains intriguing period pieces and wrecking business memorabilia.

● **Pelican Path** (Key West) is a self-guiding tour through the town's historic district, marked with pelican signs. The Chamber of Commerce at Mallory Square provides a brochure describing the sites along the way.

● **Key West Aquarium**, opened in 1934, was one of the nation's first open-air aquariums. Tours include feedings.

● **Conch Tour Train** (Key West) gives 1½-hour trips through the Old Town in open-air tram trains. Sites along the way include **Sloppy Joe's,** Hemingway's favorite watering hole.

● **Museum of Old Key West** preserves a collection of island buildings.

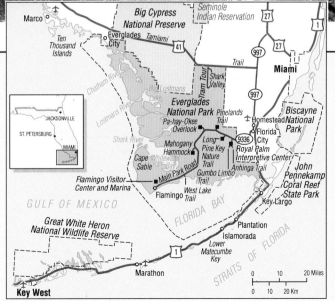

The Everglades National Park covers 1,400,533 acres and is a priceless breeding ground for such rare animals as the American crocodile. Numerous alligators, snakes, and sea turtles live here, as well as over 300 kinds of birds, 600 species of fish, and 100 varieties of grasses. Insect repellent is essential for visitors who venture into the park between May and November.

113

PROTECTED SHORES

The Gulf Coast

Behind the barrier islands that shelter the coasts of Mississippi, Alabama, and northwestern Florida are barriers of another kind: a system of coastal forts whose history begins with the Spanish, continues through the War of 1812 and the Civil War, and ends with active military bases. The region's cities and towns preserve historic districts and buildings redolent of a colorful and fast-changing past. The natural world is protected, too, with 135,000 acres of Gulf Islands National Seashore, in subtropical parks, gardens, and forests.

When Hollywood made Tarzan movies in the late 1930s, it cast the subtropical surrounds of one of Florida's largest springs in the role of darkest Africa. Today, visitors can sometimes cruise Tarzan's "lagoon," actually a spring, in glass-bottomed boats at the Edward Ball Wakulla Springs State Park. Alligators and otters swim in the great pool, and there are trails through the cypress-tupelo-magnolia forest, where exotic native birds flit and cry.

Across the state line in Alabama's Gulf State Park, a more open landscape of pine and palmetto forests, heath, marsh, and alligator-patroled canals is preserved, all fronted by fine beaches. Still farther west is the chain of island preserves that make up Gulf Islands National Seashore.

The Old Spanish Fort, one of the oldest forts on the Gulf, was built in 1717 at Pascagoula, Mississippi. A museum on the site contains relics of the early Spanish period. Alabama's Fort Morgan and Fort Gaines, two splendid brick forts, once guarded the entrance to Mobile Bay, and the Gulf's modern naval and Air Force bases are equally impressive. Eglin Air Force Base, near Fort Walton Beach, Florida, is a giant, and hosts the Air Force

Armament Museum. At Pensacola, the U.S. Naval Air Station has museums devoted to survival training and naval aviation.

In Mobile, the U.S.S. *Alabama* Battleship Park features the submarine U.S.S. *Drum*, a B-52 bomber, and World War II fighter planes, as well as the *Alabama*.

Among the many streets, squares, and historic houses preserved along this section of the Gulf Coast, none is more nostalgic than Biloxi's Beauvoir-Jefferson Davis Shrine, the last home of the only President of the Confederacy. The complex includes a Confederate museum and the Library Pavilion, where Davis wrote *The Rise and Fall of the Confederate Government*. Family heirlooms are on display, as well as the 1978 Congressional declaration restoring Davis's U.S. citizenship.

In Mobile, several districts preserve antebellum homes. They include De Tonti Square, Oakleigh Garden District, and Spring Hill, dating from the 1820s and including Greek Revival homes built as summer retreats. Pensacola also preserves interesting 18th- and 19th-century buildings including the 1810 Charles Lavallé House in Gulf Coast Creole style.

Biloxi Boats (*right*) The heritage of the seafood industry is celebrated early each June with the Blessing of the Fleet Festival. Decorated shrimp and oyster boats provide colorful floats. The local Seafood Industry Museum has equipment used in crabbing and shrimping, and exhibits demonstrate the growth of the area.

Gulf Islands National Seashore (*left*) This 150-mile stretch of seashore is a haven for the great blue heron and brown pelican. The sea oats that grow along the coast are a protected species and are not to be picked.

Oakleigh Garden District
(*above*) This tree-lined street
in one of Mobile's grandest
neighborhoods reveals some
fine 19th-century homes.
The originality of the
architecture reflects the
influence of individual styles.
One of the most impressive
houses is Oakleigh Mansion,
an antebellum home built by
slaves in 1833. Now restored,
guided tours allow visitors to
marvel at past grandeur.

SITES TO SEE

● **Fort Massachusetts** (Ship Island, MS)
was one of the many 19th-century forts
along the Gulf Coast. The island was used
as a staging post in the War of 1812. Ship
Island, part of the Gulf Island National
Seashore, is reached by boat from Biloxi
and Gulfport.

● **Conde-Charlotte Museum House**
(Mobile, AL), built about 1822, contains
rooms in the style of specific periods of
the 18th and 19th centuries and has a
Spanish-style garden. The Richards
D.A.R. House, in the De Tonti Square
Historic District, was a steamboat captain's
townhouse from the mid-19th century.

● **Bellingrath Gardens and Home**
(Theodore, AL) was the home of a
pioneering Coca-Cola bottler. The 65
acres of semitropical gardens surrounding
the house were designed after French,
English, and Italian gardens, so there is a
year-round spectacle of color. The house
displays an excellent china collection.

● **Mississippi Deep Sea Fishing Rodeo**
is held annually in Gulfport around July 4th.

● **Julee Cottage** (Pensacola, FL), built
1804, was the cottage belonging to Julee
Panton, a free black woman. Today, it is a
museum of regional black history.

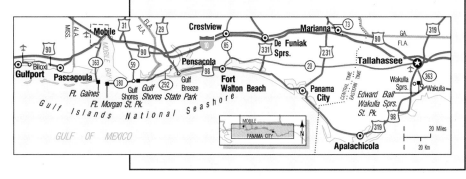

GLACIAL PATH
The Talladega Skyway

The Appalachians spill southward over the Tennessee border, fading softly through Alabama, until they spread to near-delta flatness near Montgomery. This northern part of the state, has lush, dramatic mountains and gorges and fine caverns. Old Indian place names add dimension to the landscape, recalling ancient geographic—and sometimes tragic—perspectives. Princess Noccalula's sad legend of love is commemorated in the name of a waterfall, and the word "Talladega," from the Creek words meaning "border town," is famously preserved in the names of a speedway and a skyline drive.

The glacial folds running northeast to southwest through Alabama have been the region's travel routes since time immemorial. In 1540, Spanish explorer Hernando de Soto recorded the 100-foot waterfalls that bear his name in today's DeSoto State Park.

Later, Southerners made the trip from the lowlands to the mountains, often to escape the summer heat. At Mentone, musical gatherings, mountaintop cottages, and a village of craft centers attest to the popularity of this summer retreat. South of the village lies Little River Canyon, one of the deepest gorges east of the Rockies, lush with lowland mountain greenery.

To the south, parallelling the canyon, is the Coosa River valley, where legend mingles with history and commerce. The falls named for Princess Noccalula, who, according to legend, leaped to her death rather than abandon her true love for an arranged marriage, are near Gadsden. At Childersburg, the DeSoto Caverns were occupied and have been an Indian burial

ground for 2,000 years. The cave is longer than a football field and more than 12 stories deep. Confederate soldiers mined saltpeter to make gunpowder here, and during Prohibition, it concealed a popular speakeasy.

Anniston's remarkable Museum of Natural History includes an authentic replica of an Alabama cavern and a life-size model of a prehistoric pteranodon, the largest animal to fly, with a 30-foot wing span. The museum's Lagarde African Hall re-creates life on the African plain in the shelter of a huge baobab tree. North of town, Fort McClellan remembers the contributions of the Women's Army Corps, which existed from 1942 to 1978, with a museum.

Talladega National Forest, served by the Talladega Scenic Drive, has deer, wild turkey, and red-tailed hawks that ride the updrafts off the ridges. Near the center of this long strip of forest is Cheaha Mountain, which at 2,407 feet is the state's highest point.

Cash Lake (*right*), with its calm beauty, shows only one aspect of the varied scenery around DeSoto State Park, which lies 11 miles northeast of Fort Payne. Fort Payne itself boasts the oldest active theater in Alabama, the Opera House, now a cultural arts center.

The park—named for Spanish explorer Hernando DeSoto—covers 5,067 acres along the Little River, which here plunges 110 feet down the DeSoto Falls and flows into a 600-foot canyon, 16 miles long and the deepest east of the Rockies. There is a scenic drive along the canyon rim, and hikers can follow nature trails to its floor and to the surrounding wooded ridges. Needle Eye Rock, named for the split all the way down its middle, is a popular site. Camping, fishing, and swimming are also available in the park, and there is boating on a small lake above the falls.

The Turkey (*left*) is believed to be indigenous to the Americas, and plump wild birds, along with deer, are plentiful in the woodlands of northern Alabama. Hunting (with a special license) is permitted in Alabama state parks at certain times of the year. Outdoor enthusiasts will also enjoy excellent freshwater fishing, with no closed season (but a license is needed), in the numerous streams and lakes.

SITES TO SEE

● **Talladega Superspeedway** (Talladega) is one of the world's major race tracks with a 2.66-mile course. The Winston 500 NASCAR Cup Race takes place the first Sunday in May, and the Talladega 500 Diehard NASCAR Winston Cup Stock Car Race is held the last Sunday in July. The adjoining International Motorsports Hall of Fame recalls the history of the sport and its outstanding drivers; track tours depart from here.

● **Emma Sansom Monument** (Gadsden) commemorates the 15-year-old girl who guided Confederate troops across Black Creek to defeat 2,000 Federal soldiers.

● **Noccalula Falls Park** (Gadsden) includes a botanical garden and pioneer village with 18th-century split-log buildings. Visitors can reach the village by train, passing Noccalula Falls along the way.

● **St. Michael and All Angels Episcopal Church** (Anniston), built 1890 in the Norman Gothic style, features a 95-foot-tall bell tower.

● **Women's Army Corps Museum** (Fort McClellan, Anniston) recalls the role of women soldiers since 1942; guest passes to the base are available at the entrance gate.

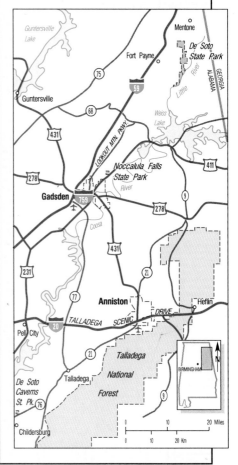

PRIMITIVE SETTLEMENTS TO SPACE FRONTIERS

The Tennessee River Valley

In a line as slack as an empty hammock hung across the top of Alabama's map, the Tennessee River valley cradles a pioneering tradition that began 10,000 years ago with paleolithic hunters and continues with space research. Huntsville, once famous only as the world's watercress capital, joined the Space Age when Dr. Wernher von Braun and his rocketeers came here to beat the Russians to the moon. Today, NASA scientists at the Marshall Space Flight Center plan space exploration in the next millennium. Like the valley's Stone Age hunters, they are ballistics experts, wielding rockets instead of spears.

A handful of chipped flint spearheads are the surviving possessions of the Tennessee River valley's earliest inhabitants, the hunter-gatherers who wintered more than 8,000 years ago under the overhang known as Russell Cave. For thousands of years, the cave was home to successive Indian cultures, and today at the Russell Cave National Monument, park rangers demonstrate the Indians' techniques of flint napping and corn grinding.

During the Civil War, the Tennessee River and the railroad were both a curse and a blessing to towns like Decatur. It was occupied several times by Confederate and Union forces and in 1864 was burned to the ground by northern soldiers. It was later rebuilt, but true revitalization only came late in the 1880s with an influx of Yankee industrialists from Albany, New York. Their influence can be seen in the town's Albany Heritage District, which preserves Victorian buildings built before a yellow fever epidemic in 1888.

In the 1930s, the Tennessee Valley Authority brought hydroelectric power, flood control, and electrification to the region, and with them relative prosperity. Life had been hard here, and local heroes are those who overcame adversity. Ivy Green, the birthplace and early home of Helen Keller, international symbol of hope for the deaf and blind, is near Tuscumbia. Visitors can see the pump, where Keller said "water," her first word. The home of W. C. Handy, "Father of the Blues," another regional hero, is preserved at Florence. His memory is also honored with the town's annual W. C. Hardy Festival in August.

Wilson Dam, with one of the world's highest single-lift navigation locks, is also in Florence. An observation area is open.

This is a region of remarkable, even bizarre, places and achievements. They range from the strange canyon at Dismals Gardens, to the folk-baroque curiosities of Cullman's Ave Maria Grotto, to the extra-terrestrial activities at Huntsville's Space and Rocket Center, where titanic booster rockets crowd the grounds, and lessons in zero-gravity movement are considered down to earth.

At the **Space and Rocket Center** in Huntsville (*left*), visitors can experience some aspects of space travel, by enjoying more than 60 hands-on exhibits in the museum. In the adjoining Spacedome Theater, with its wrap-around, 67-foot dome screen, space and science films are shown every hour. Regular bus tours from the Center to NASA's Marshall Spaceflight Center nearby also take in the Spacelab training facilities. The complex is open every day except Christmas.

SITES TO SEE

● **Twickenham Historic District** (Huntsville) has one of the state's largest collections of antebellum homes. The **Huntsville Pilgrimage** each April visits some of the city's most beautiful and architecturally interesting houses.

● **Burritt Museum and Park** (Huntsville) is an 11-room house, set in 167 acres, that displays local memorabilia, Indian artifacts,

The Impressive Natural Bridge (*left*) is one of the more spectacular sights of Bankhead National Forest. Throughout the 180,000 acres of this splendid natural forest, with its scatterings of virgin timberland, there are deep limestone canyons in which crystal-clear streams with dramatic waterfalls run. In the 26,000-acre Sipsey Wilderness Area, the tracks of deer and raccoons can be seen—and, if you are quiet, sometimes the animals themselves. Here and there, the great stands of oak and pine give way to wild magnolia trees, which in May open their white dinner-plate-size blossoms.

and antique furniture. Reconstructed pioneer village buildings are on the grounds.

● **Ceremonial Indian Mound** (Florence) is 145 feet long and 43 feet high, making it one of the largest mounds in the Tennessee River valley. Indian artifacts from the Mississippian period are on display.

● **Albany Heritage District** (Decatur) preserves homes in a variety of styles

from lavish late Victorian to more contemporary. The town's **Old Decatur District** also contains many 19th-century buildings. The **Old State Bank**, built in 1833, is one of the few buildings to have survived the Civil War. Self-guiding walking tours of the neighborhoods are available.

● **Huntsville Museum of Art** (Huntsville) displays contemporary and historical collections.

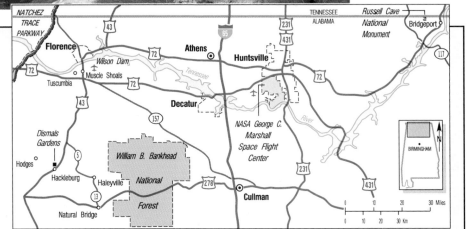

THROUGH THE HARDWOOD FOREST
The Natchez Trace Parkway

The Natchez Trace Parkway, the ancient trail of the Natchez Indians and early settlers, follows a diagonal course from Mississippi's northeast corner to the Mississippi River at Natchez. It preserves a strip of wild country as the first pioneers saw it. It also presents visitors with a topographical and cultural cross-section of the state, stretching from the mansions of antebellum Natchez through Tupelo, a town with a modern legend.

There is something aristocratic in the air at Natchez, the oldest non-Indian settlement on the Mississippi. Until the French planted their flag here in 1716, it was the home of the Natchez Indians, a people governed by an aristrocracy that regarded human sacrifice as its due. In 1729, the warriors of the Great Sun, as the Natchez leader was known, massacred many French settlers here, provoking a prompt and massive retaliation. Two sites preserve the memory of the Natchez: Emerald Mound, a ceremonial site built around 1300 by their forefathers, and the Grand Village of the Natchez Indians, with its museum, archaeological displays, and nature trails through the woods.

Between 1729 and 1797, Natchez was the booty of the French, English, and then the Spanish. In 1797, Andrew Ellicott, acting on President Washington's orders, raised the American flag over the town, and the following year the Spanish quit their holding without a struggle. On the 200-foot bluffs above the river are the town's antebellum mansions, which were mostly out of range of Union gunboats during the Civil War. Many are open to the public year round, and tours can be arranged to see many of the others. A sizeable area of the town is included in the Natchez National Historic Park, and the Spring and Fall Pilgrimages, featuring house and garden tours and southern belles in hoop skirts, are a Natchez must.

At Lorman, The Old Country Store, which first opened its doors to customers in 1875, bills itself as the nation's oldest, continuously operating general store.

Jackson, the state capital since 1821, is a bustling town whose fine museums include the Mississippi State Historical Museum in the Old Capitol, and the Smith Robertson Museum and Cultural Center, the state's first museum devoted to black history. General Sherman's headquarters for his 1863 siege of the city are preserved in The Oaks, an 1848 Greek Revival "cottage."

Tupelo was the 1935 birthplace of Elvis Presley, and his home, a two-room house without indoor plumbing, is preserved. Although it gives no clue that Elvis would become the King of Rock 'n' Roll, his subsequent career proves, perhaps, that something aristocratic still lingers in the air.

Taking a Bit of Elvis (*left*) Many tourists and hero-worshippers want to return home from the birthplace of the rock 'n' roll legend with some precious memento of their pilgrimage. The accommodating merchants of Tupelo are happy to oblige with a wide range of souvenirs. The quality of the craftsmanship may vary, but what is most important is the treasured image of "the King" himself.

SITES TO SEE

● **Port Gibson**, a small town rich in Civil War history, retains many of its pre-war buildings because Gen. Ulysses S. Grant declared them "too beautiful to burn." The atmospheric old **Grand Gulf Cemetery** is near the **Spanish House** in Grand Gulf Military Park.

● **Casey Jones Museum** (Vaughan), housed in a 1900 railroad station, is devoted to the folk hero who died in

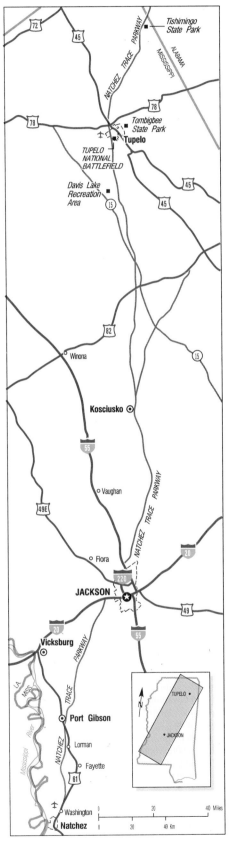

the legendary train crash less than a mile down the track. Numerous items of train memorabilia are on display.

● **Tishmingo State Park** (near the MS/AL state line) has 13 miles of nature trails and float trips on Bear Creek past thick woods.

● **Mississippi Petrified Forest** (Flora) has signposts guiding visitors along a woodland path that takes about 40 minutes to walk. A

small museum devoted to petrified wood is on the site.

● **Windsor Ruins** (Port Gibson) are the ghostly Corinthian columns of a once great Greek Revival mansion destroyed by fire in 1890. Located on the side of the road, these columns are all that remain of the house.

● **Longwood** (Natchez) is the octagonal shell of a splendid mansion started by Dr. Haller Nutt just before

the Civil War. When the war stopped its construction, some downstairs rooms were the only ones completed, and the Nutt family took refuge in the ground-floor rooms during the war. These rooms, open to the public, contain family heirlooms and period furnishings.

● **Auburn** (Natchez) is a beautiful mansion noted for its elegant freestanding spiral staircase.

Antebellum Grandeur

(*above*) Stanton Hall, named after its owner, Frederick Stanton, is one of the finest examples of an antebellum mansion in the Greek Revival style. Stanton allowed only the best materials to be used, many of which came from overseas. The columns, pediments, and restrained details create an impressive statement of wealth and refinement. Unfortunately, Stanton died only a few months after its completion.

HOME OF THE BLUES

The Mississippi Delta

The pancake-flat fields of the Mississippi Delta have become some of the nation's richest farmland. The repeated flooding of the Mississippi River brought the rich, black soil here, and slaves were brought from Africa to tend the cotton it produced. They also cultivated their own culture, and early this century it produced its own fruit in the music called the Delta Blues. Bittersweet and sharply rhythmic, it expressed the soul of the people here and of the landscape, where the seasons spring from a clear, steady background with unexpected piquancy.

In the Delta, an isolated shack with a refrigerator on the porch can loom over the flat fields as dramatically as a castle would elsewhere. The region's own castle, a great complex of Indian mounds at Winterville Mounds State Park, is about 1,000 years old. From the top of the largest mound, the visitor sees a striking circular panorama of fields and woodlands. At the Museum, there are artifacts found at this site that include a collection of tiny carved hands, the universal symbol of labor and creativity.

Cotton is still the region's most important crop—what was once the largest cotton plantation in the world is at Scott, north of the Winterville Mounds—but farmers also tend vast fields of soybeans and the recently ubiquitous farms for catfish. For a glimpse of the old world of cotton, visit Greenwood, the self-proclaimed "Cotton Capital of the World." The town's 19th-century Cotton Row, now listed in the National Register of Historic Places, is the second largest cotton exchange in the U.S. Cottonlandia Museum gives a comprehensive overview of cotton's history and of the Delta's archaeological and social heritage. Outside the town, on the banks of the Yazoo River, Florewood River Plantation recreates an 1850s cotton plantation. Exhibits range from the fine plantation house to a rare 1860s steam-powered engine for a cotton gin, still in working order.

A summer drive along US 82 between Greenville and Greenwood provides the ideal opportunity to view the major cash crops of the area. Flooded rice fields, and acres of cotton and soybean nourished by huge irrigation systems, provide a counterpoint to the ever-increasing number of catfish farms.

Since paddle steamers were the prime movers of Delta cotton in the 19th century, the Washington County Welcome Center at Greenville honors the past by looking like one. The building, called the "River Road Queen," was built to resemble a 19th-century sternwheeler.

The Great River Road, designated SR 1 here, follows the river to St. Louis and even farther north. From the stockade-like observation tower at Great River Road State Park near Rosedale stretch splendid views of the all-nourishing Mississippi. Northeast at Clarksdale, the Delta Blues Museum commemorates the music that has also nourished the region.

Armor-plated (*left*) The nine-banded armadillo is the only member of the species native to North America. Most females give birth to four identical offspring.

Pickin' Cotton (*above right*) Even with modern machinery, harvest season is the busiest time of year in cotton country.

Winterville Mounds (*right*) The Lower Mississippi Valley Indians built temple mounds at their ceremonial gathering sites. The remaining mounds conjure up a culture distanced by time.

SITES TO SEE

● **Cottonlandia Museum** (Greenwood) explains the history and impact of cotton in the Delta, as well as featuring an extensive and important collection of Indian artifacts. A collection of dolls from around the world was started more than 100 years ago. A garden on the grounds displays native wildflowers. The art gallery has permanent collections, as well as changing exhibits. Tours of some of the Delta's 80,000 acres of catfish ponds and processing plants can be arranged through the museum.

● **Greenville** comes alive with the sounds of the blues each September when it hosts the Delta Blues Festival.

● **Mississippi River Flood Museum** (Greenville) commemorates the great flood of 1927 with photographic exhibits and artifacts.

● **Greenwood's Cotton Row** goes on parade the first Saturday in August with a bustling street fair called CROP Day, featuring local crafts, food stalls, and plenty of toe-tapping music.

● **Great River Road State Park** (Rosedale) has a signposted nature trail winding through heavy woodland with mulberry and Virginia creeper. Perry Martin Lake offers boating and fishing facilities.

WORTH A DETOUR

● **Rowan Oak** (Oxford) is the home where novelist William Faulkner wrote his 1954 Pulitzer Prize-winning novel, *A Fable*. The 1840 house, set in a cedar grove, is now owned and maintained by the University of Mississippi; Faulkner's office remains as it was when he died in 1962. His 1949 Nobel Prize citation, along with personal papers, are on display at the university's library.

● **"Ole Miss,"** as the university is nicknamed, houses the **Center for the Study of Southern Culture** in its Barnard Observatory and the **Ole Miss Blues Archive**, where the blues are sung all day, in Farley Hall.

ACADIANA

Cajun Country

The Acadians, or Cajuns as they are known, are the descendants of the original settlers of L'Acadie, a French colony located in eastern Canada and Nova Scotia. Expelled from their colony by the British in the 18th century, many of them drifted down the eastern seaboard, finally establishing themselves in New Orleans and the delta of the Mississippi, especially in the region known as Acadiana, a region of 22 parishes centered around Lafayette. Their unique patois, cooking, music, and *savoir vivre* give the area its spicy cultural flavor.

Before Morgan City discovered offshore oil, it boasted of being "The Jumbo Shrimp Capital of the World." Today, with the cheerful resilience typical of the settlers in this part of the Gulf, the town proudly celebrates a Shrimp and Petroleum Festival.

The French and Spanish explorers and traders who first settled this bayou country were later joined by the Acadians and by aristocratic refugees from the French Revolution. More refugees arrived when planters and merchants fled from the West Indian slave rebellions, and the slave trade brought even more. Life was either very easy or very hard, but regardless of their economic condition, the new Acadians were tough survivors, whose essential vigor overcame the difficult transition to this steamy, exotic coast.

Their bold vitality can still be seen in Acadiana today. The stateliness of a mansion like Nottoway Plantation in White Castle breathes the perfect breeding of the Old South. In Lafayette's Acadian Village, all the dwellings are raised on pilings to keep them from being flooded. Together with hot boudin sausage and astringent fiddle and accordion music, they represent a European, peasant way of life that has adapted to its new habitat without imposing on it.

All sorts of ghosts haunt Acadiana. The magnificent live oaks, some 300 years old and draped with spanish moss that was once used as furniture stuffing, inspire passion in the local people, whose heritage includes so much uprooting. Those whose ancestors were bullied into coming here particularly relish the memory of the French-born smuggler, Jean Lafitte, who led his band of buccaneers against the British to help Andrew Jackson defend New Orleans from them. And the ghost of former deprivations may fuel the whole-hearted gusto with which Cajuns celebrate the carnival of Mardi Gras each spring, when parades, lavish feasts, and masked balls highlight the festivities.

As if compensating for those old deprivations, the natural environment lends lush vitality to the region. As Avery Island's Jungle Gardens demonstrate, Acadiana is as botanically exuberant as anywhere in the U.S.A. Wildlife is abundant here, too: white cattle egrets attend the dairy cows and horses. In the Barataria unit of Jean Lafitte National Historical Park, alligators torpidly rest in the dark waters of the shady, moss-draped bayous.

Atchafalaya (*above*) A dreamy route to the Gulf of Mexico, the Atchafalaya River flows through a complex system of floodways and guide levees which provides vital flood control for the lower end of the Mississippi.

Alligators (*left*), which are often 9 feet long and can weigh 250 pounds, float just below the water's surface to keep cool. Once hunted for their hide, they are now protected by law in the U.S.

SITES TO SEE

● **McIlhenny Company** (Avery Island) produces Tabasco, the world-famous hot-pepper sauce. Visit the factory and see how this essential ingredient in Cajun cooking has been made since 1868.

● **Oaklawn Manor** (Franklin) is a Greek Revival mansion with gardens modeled after those at Versailles in France. The 3-

story house's 20-inch walls are made of clay and dirt that came from the estate.

● **Shadows-on-the-Teche** (New Iberia) is a splendid restored 1834 mansion, originally built for a local planter in the French colonial style. Celebrities who have visited include novelist Henry Miller.

● **Delcambre Harbor** (New Iberia) hosts a fall Shrimp Festival and Fair.

● **Turn-of-the-Century House** (Morgan City), built 1906, captures the comfortable lifestyle of a wealthy family at the start of the 20th century. Exhibits include Mardi Gras costumes from 1928 to the present, and a screening of the 1917 silent movie *Tarzan of the Apes*, made near the city.

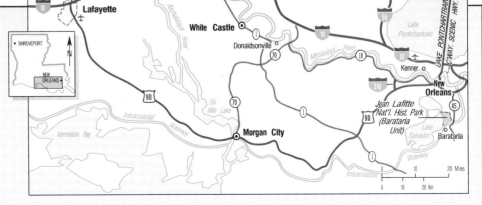

NEW ORLEANS

New Orleans is a town accustomed to the ebb and flow of change. Familiar with the vagaries of the ocean and shifting bayous, as well as with the varied character of the cultures and nations that have claimed it, this most foreign of American cities has matured to show the world a blend of high style and easy living, occasionally spiced with a dash of cynicism. Where modern high-rise buildings tower above the old city, they do so as gracefully as anywhere in America, for the town still owes as much to France, Spain, and Africa as it does to the New World.

The French Quarter, or Vieux Carré, formed the original 1718 settlement of New Orleans and in many ways is still the distinctive heart of the city. Now more Spanish than French, since disastrous fires at the end of the 18th century destroyed the original buildings, the narrow streets, quaint dwellings with beautiful ironwork, cafes, and bars provide the color. Visitors can still hear the cool, sweet pitch of clarinets on Bourbon Street, and the air is redolent with the seductive aroma of Creole cuisine. Be sure to enjoy a hearty gumbo. This Creole classic has thousands of variations, but will include seafood, chicken, or okra.

The French Market offers five blocks of food and music where you can sample New Orleans favorites such as pralines and beignets, or visit the farmers' market and centuries-old shopping arcades. The intimately graceful homes, the fine old churches, and the crescent bend of Ol' Man River, all deny the sharp verticalities of modern business.

The city's parks also have much to offer visitors. Audubon Park, named for the artist John James Audubon, has a children's village and the Louisiana Swamp Exhibit, with safe viewing of rare white alligators as well as shaded lagoons. In City Park, enjoy an original merry-go-round from 1906.

The highlight of the New Orlean year is the Mardi Gras carnival during the two weeks before Ash Wednesday. The two biggest parades—Rex, King of Carnival and Monarch of Merriment, and the torchlight Comus, God of Revelry— take place on Shrove Tuesday, winding their merry way through crowds of brightly costumed and jovial spectators. Singing and dancing are enjoyed by both the marchers and the swirling crowds.

In spirit, New Orleans still prefers the thick cool walls of its Spanish courtyards, and the delicate wrought-iron balconies in its French Quarter, to the 20th century's air-conditioned geometry. When the town dreams, it remembers, not mergers and takeover battles, but a time when fortunes were made or ruined by the turn of a card, and honor was only satisfied by a duel beneath the oaks in City Park.

HISTORIC SITES AND DISTRICTS

Chalmette The site of General Jackson's historic victory over the British at the Battle of New Orleans.

Garden District Famous for its houses and the splendor of its parks and gardens. Old ceramic tiles spell out street names.

Jackson Square The center of the French Quarter, and the site of a bronze equestrian statue of the hero of the Battle of New Orleans. Also the unofficial "Left Bank," where artists hang their work on the railings daily.

Metairie Cemetery Grandest of all the city's cemeteries, whose landscaped gardens contain extraordinary architecture and statues.

MUSEUMS

Gallier House Museum National historic monument, once the home of New Orleans architect James Gallier, Jr., and now restored as an authentic French Quarter residence of the 1860s.

Musée Conti: the Wax Museum of Louisiana Legends Life-size wax figures in accurate settings tell the story of New Orleans.

New Orleans Museum of Art (City Park) Extensive collection of European art, together with works from the Orient, Africa, and pre-Columbian America.

New Orleans Pharmacy Museum An early 19th-century pharmacy complete with antique instruments and bottles of voodoo potions, together with a medicinal herb garden.

The Historic New Orleans Collection A group of typical 18th- and 19th-century French Quarter houses. The centerpiece is Williams Residence, furnished throughout in an eclectic manner with styles from the 1700s to the 1940s. In the Merieult House are the documents relating to the Louisiana Purchase of 1803.

NOTABLE BUILDINGS

Beauregard-Keyes House Home from 1866–68 of Confederate General P. G. T. Beauregard and later of novelist Frances Parkinson Keyes.

Hermann-Grima House This lavish 1831 mansion is restored with original slave quarters, stable, and courtyards, as well as the oldest functioning Creole-era kitchen in New Orleans.

Pontalba Buildings Built as luxury apartments and shops in 1849–50.

Preservation Hall Famous jazz club and purist's paradise with traditional New Orleans jazz.

St. Louis Cathedral One of the oldest churches in the country, it was completed in 1794.

U.S. Customs House Built in 1849, this imposing Egyptian Revival building still serves as government offices.

U.S. Mint Home of the Jazz and Carnival Museum.

World Trade Center Known as a buyers' crossroad serving the hemisphere. The 31st floor observation deck offers panoramic views.

MAP REFERENCE

1. Beauregard-Keyes House
2. Hermann-Grima Historic House
3. Gallier House Museum
4. Jackson Square
5. Lower Pontalba Building
6. Musée Conti
7. New Orleans Pharmacy Museum
8. Preservation Hall
9. St. Louis Cathedral
10. The Historic New Orleans Collection
11. Upper Pontalba Building
12. U.S. Customs House
13. U.S. Mint
14. World Trade Center

The Stern-wheeler *Natchez* (*far left*) River and bayou cruises on a Mississippi paddleboat are part of the New Orleans experience. So is the city's extravagantly-costumed **Mardi Gras** carnival (*left*), designed to dispel the coming rigors of Lent.

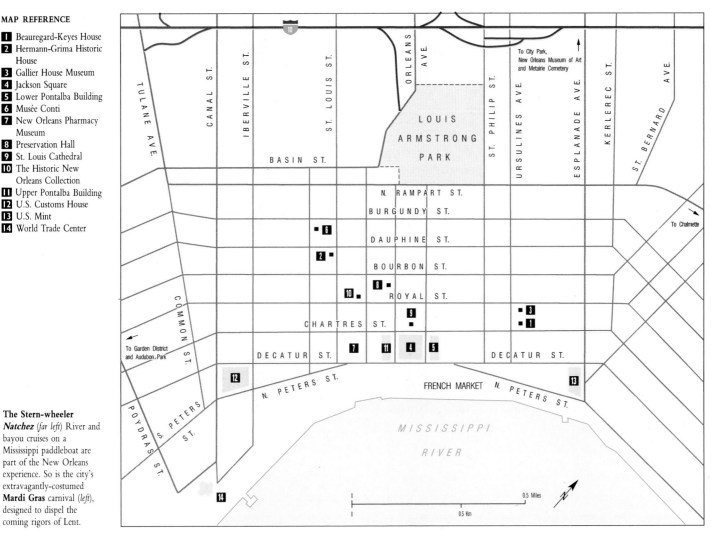

THE SOUTHERN PLAINS

If the Northern Plains seem a place of equipoise, the Plains states to the south are quickened by southern heat. As far north as Missouri, where a tongue of the ancient Gulf of Mexico once reached to form the Mississippi Embayment, the cultural echoes of the south are still heard. Neighboring Kansas felt a southern influx, too, when the Chisholm Trail brought thundering herds of Texas longhorns to the railhead at Abilene. Oklahoma, host to the National Cowboy Hall of Fame, was the destination for waves of Indians driven from their southeastern homelands, and in Arkansas, where visitors can search in the nation's only diamond mine, an area of abundant hot springs became the first forerunner of our National Park system.

By the time the southern plains have become Texas, the transformation is complete, and the nation faces squarely south. Here a Spanish heritage and the memory of those who threw off Spanish rule—the heroes of the Alamo, the men who fought shoulder to shoulder with Sam Houston—are adjacent planks in the platform of state pride, along with a Tex-Mex musical tradition whose roots are south of the border. Equal with these are the Texan's delight in the state's great cities—San Antonio, Austin, Houston, Dallas, Fort Worth—in the incomparable beaches and islands of the Gulf, in the rolling hills in the west of the state, and in the sheer bravado of its size.

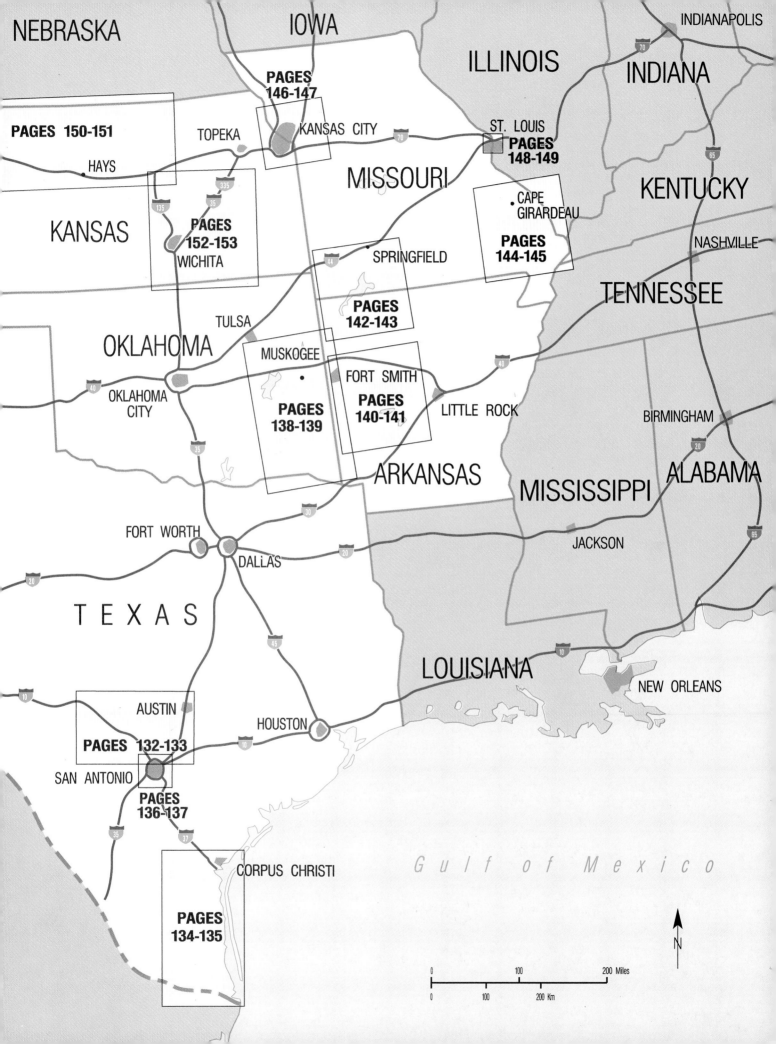

NEBRASKA

IOWA

ILLINOIS

INDIANAPOLIS

INDIANA

PAGES 146-147

PAGES 150-151

TOPEKA

KANSAS CITY

ST. LOUIS

PAGES 148-149

HAYS

MISSOURI

KENTUCKY

KANSAS

PAGES 152-153

CAPE GIRARDEAU

NASHVILLE

WICHITA

SPRINGFIELD

PAGES 144-145

TENNESSEE

PAGES 142-143

TULSA

OKLAHOMA

MUSKOGEE

FORT SMITH

PAGES 140-141

OKLAHOMA CITY

PAGES 138-139

LITTLE ROCK

BIRMINGHAM

ARKANSAS

ALABAMA

MISSISSIPPI

FORT WORTH

DALLAS

JACKSON

T E X A S

LOUISIANA

NEW ORLEANS

AUSTIN

HOUSTON

PAGES 132-133

SAN ANTONIO

PAGES 136-137

CORPUS CHRISTI

Gulf of Mexico

PAGES 134-135

N

0   100   200 Miles

0   100   200 Km

BIG BEND IN THE RIO GRANDE

Texas's Forgotten Corner

The Chihuahuan desert stretches across southwest Texas like a Mexican blanket, striped by colorful badlands, and wrinkled along its southern edge where the Rio Grande twists through deep canyons to mark the border between the United States and Mexico. Big Bend National Park preserves this great wilderness area, where the desert floor can heat up to 180° in midsummer, and the spectacular Chisos Mountains rise to a cool 5,000 feet.

Not many people have ever chosen to live in the Chihuahuan desert, or along the Big Bend in the Rio Grande. The terrain, where in Indian legend the Great Spirit dumped stones left over from the creation of the Earth, is hot, dry, rugged and remote, and few came here without a compelling reason. In the 1850s, soldiers built Fort Davis to protect the southern trail to the California gold fields from raiding Comanche Indians; and in the 1870s, miners flocked to Shafter, then to Terlingua, lured by rich veins of silver and mercury. After the mines were abandoned, the great emptiness of the Big Bend region flowed into the ghost towns, and now they seem an almost natural part of the desert.

For many years, the 107-mile course of the Rio Grande in Big Bend National Park lay hidden behind a rocky fortress. Not until 1852, when Major William H. Emory and his party arrived for a boundary survey, were the three spectacular canyons—Santa Elena, Boquillas, and Mariscal—discovered.

On the way to Santa Elena, the most impressive of the canyons, visitors pass through a unique environment. The road skirts the green floodplain along the river's edge before ending at an overlook from which you can peer up at the wall of the Santa Elena Canyon. At Rio Grande Villate near Boquillas Canyon, in the east of the park, there are facilities for camping, and from the lofty heights at the canyon's rim is an expanse that seems like the edge of the world. The third of Big Bend's canyons, Mariscal, can be reached only by boat or trail.

Relief from the desert's heat can be found at The Basin, an immense bowl-shaped rock amphitheater high in the Chisos Mountains in the center of the park. Here the desert plants, such as sotol and button cactus, give way with the elevation to stands of juniper, pinyon, and scrub oak. Trails meander into the highlands, home to the Colima warbler and the Sierra del Carmen whitetail deer, and where ponderosa pine and bigtooth maple reach the southern limit of their growth in the United States, the remains of forests which once covered the area.

Park visitors can learn more about the natural wonders along the Rio Grande from summer talks given frequently at the visitor centers.

The Great U-turn (*right*)
As the Rio Grande cut into the landscape, the resistance of the rock forced the river to backtrack on itself and in the process created the dramatic canyons of Big Bend. Spring rains feed the river and bring the surrounding desert to life in a carpet of color.

Cautious Spectator (*left*)
The desert mule deer, like all the wildlife in the park, is part of a fragile and complex ecosystem. The wildlife ranges from the soaring peregrine falcon to a mosquito fish whose whole world is restricted to the confines of one pond.

SITES TO SEE

● **Ft. Davis National Historic Site** (Ft. Davis) has about 25 restored original buildings to be explored via a self-guiding tour. Five buildings, including the commanding officer's quarters, have been refurbished with period pieces. The fort is significant in U.S. military history because it was one of the first with black soldiers; black units fought in the Indian wars. As a sign of respect, the Indians called their black enemies "Buffalo soldiers."

● **W. J. McDonald Observatory** (north of Ft. Davis) sits atop Mount Locke at 6,802 feet, taking advantage of the desert emptiness to probe the bright night sky with a 107-inch telescope. Visitors can take self-guiding tours of the complex. On Tuesday, Friday, and Saturday nights, the public can look at stars through 24- and 14-inch telescopes; reservations are required for the one night each month when the giant telescope is used.

● **Museum of the Big Bend** (Alpine) presents the region's history from the first visits by Spanish explorers, through the Civil War and Indian wars, and on to present days. **Burgess Water Hole**, downtown, was a popular watering spot for early pioneers and stagecoach passengers crossing the desert.

● **Terlingua** is a virtual ghost town, except for one week in early November when thousands of cooks and chili fans flock here for the World Championship Chili Cook-Off, a chance to sample some of the best of one of Texas's favorite foods.

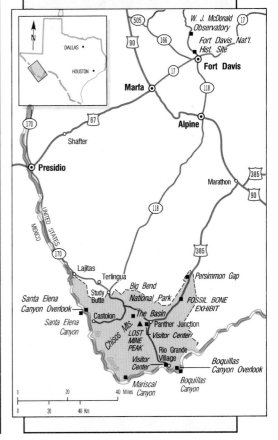

IN THE HEART OF THE HEART OF TEXAS

The Hill Country

In the heart of Texas, west of Austin, the plains break and fold into the steep limestone ridges and rugged valleys of the hill country. Colorful plateaus dotted with cedar and oak shelter white-tail deer, while clear streams tumble into the scrubby lands below—a country of vast cattle ranches, where cowboys still ride ranges bristling with prickly pear. North of Austin, the Colorado River forms a long series of scenic lakes, a popular playground for the people of a sophisticated city that was once a dusty way station for cattle drovers on the Chisholm Trail.

The residents of Austin protectively regard their town (named for Stephen F. Austin, founder of the state's first American settlement), as the Heart of the Heart of Texas. The pink granite dome of the Capitol towers 300 feet over Austin's busy streets and sprawling suburbs; in the evenings, the clubs along 6th Street sway to music from country-and-western to jazz, while open-air beer gardens nearby sometimes bounce to the lively sound of German polka bands.

In Fredericksburg, west of Austin, a more sedate atmosphere prevails. Germans settled the area in 1846 and later negotiated a peace treaty with the Comanches. Each spring, the Easter Fires Pageant commemorates the time hilltop fires were lit around the town by the Indians. Children frightened by the flames were told that Easter bunnies had lit fires to boil and dye Easter eggs. Now a tradition, hillside fires glow each year on Easter eve.

Many of the area's German settlers were farmers and merchants, but it was the pioneering ranchers who gave the region

its character when Texas was "a paradise for men and dogs, but hell on women and oxen." Ranching is still big business here, as it was when Lyndon B. Johnson, the nation's 36th president, grew up in Johnson City in the early 1900s. At the LBJ National Historical Park, visitors can trace the history of ranching and tour the LBJ Ranch, still a working cattle spread.

Dude ranches, wild hillside parks, and cowboy lore are still the order of the day around Kerrville, set on the banks of the Guadalupe River. At the Cowboy Artists of America Museum, you can view paintings depicting the romantic life of the cowboy—and see similar cattle and cowboy scenes through the museum windows. Beneath these rugged landscapes, where javelinas (collared peccaries) nibble the tips of the ubiquitous prickly pear, there are streams which surface at San Marcos to make natural spring-fed swimming holes. At Cascade Caverns, southeast of Boerne, subterranean rivers took years to carve some of the nation's most beautiful caverns.

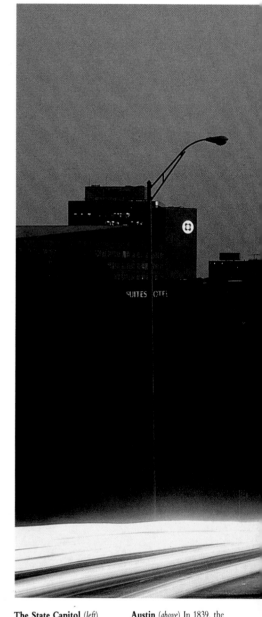

The State Capitol (*left*) Taking its inspiration from the Capitol in Washington D.C., this impressive neo-classical structure was built between 1882 and 1889. Although the original specification called for limestone, the type found in Texas was not considered suitable. Rather than use limestone from Indiana, Texan pink granite, quarried at a ranch near Marble Falls in Barnet County, was substituted.

Austin (*above*) In 1839, the frontier town of Waterloo on the north bank of the Colorado River was chosen as the best location for the capital of the Republic of Texas and renamed Austin. Attempts were made to change the capital, mainly at the instigation of Sam Houston, but in 1850, after much to-ing and fro-ing, Austin's status was reconfirmed. From those difficult beginnings grew the dynamic capital city of today.

SITES TO SEE

● **Lyndon B. Johnson National Historical Park** (Johnson City) consists of **Johnson City Unit** and the **LBJ Ranch Unit**. The ranch is only accessible by a free bus tour from the visitor center. Highlights are a stop outside the ranch house, a tour of a reconstruction of the house the former president was born in, and a visit to the family cemetery.

● **Admiral Nimitz State Historical Park** (Fredericksburg) honors native son Adm. C.W. Nimitz, WW II commander of the Pacific Fleet, and the service personnel who served under him. The **Garden of Peace** was presented by Japan, **Memorial Wall** remembers all who died in the war, and **History Walk of the Pacific** displays artifacts of Pacific battles, including airplanes and tanks.

● **Wonder World** (San Marcos) offers tours through a 35-million-year-old cave formed by an earthquake, and an antigravity house.

● **O. Henry Museum** (Austin), where short-story writer William Porter, known as O. Henry, lived from 1885–95, is furnished with his personal possessions. The museum sponsors the O. Henry Pun-off every May.

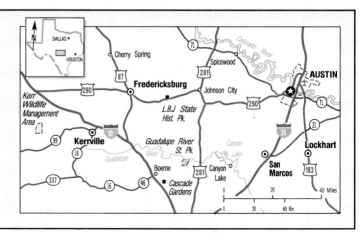

FROM CORPUS CHRISTI TO THE MOUTH OF THE RIO GRANDE

The Texas Gulf Coast

The western end of the Texas Gulf Coast is an intriguing mix of narrow islands, broad beaches, and swaying palm trees, of ports, ranches, and seaside resorts. From Corpus Christi Bay to the citrus orchards that line the Rio Grande Valley on the Tex-Mex border, subtropical weather and warm seas attract enthusiastic visitors. On Padre Island National Seashore, where whooping cranes fly and beachcombers wander along wind-sculpted dunes, Spanish galleons once washed ashore, and smugglers with their contraband were the only tourists.

In 1519, when the Spanish explorer Alonzo de Pineda first sailed along this shore, he saw islands rising from the blue waters of the Gulf of Mexico like slivers of a crescent moon, and named them Las Islas Blancas, the White Islands.

Around 1800, the missionary Padre Nicholas Balli came ashore here to convert the local Narankawa Indians; Padre Island, now a national seashore, is named in his honor. More than 70 miles of undisturbed white beaches and dunes fringe the subtropical barrier island, and for those who prefer a tent on the beach and the company of great blue herons and diving pelicans to the high-rise hotels of South Padre and Mustang Island, the national seashore offers primitive camping. The seashore's beaches, dunes, grasslands, and tidal flats are natural sculptures, changing daily. Wild sea oats take root, anchoring sands in place; then once the sands are secure, dunes up to 40 feet tall form.

Corpus Christi (named by Pineda for the Catholic feast day) was a town favored by smugglers and pirates when entrepreneur Henry Kinney established his trading post there in 1839. Much trade was in contraband, but today the ships that ply the deep waters of Corpus Christi Bay carry legitimate cargoes of oil and cotton. From the yacht basin and wide city beach, to the fishing boats that pass the town's bayfront park, life in Corpus Christi is geared to the water.

Farther south, toward the Tex-Mex border, ruby-red Texas grapefruit and orange orchards follow the Rio Grande Valley. Brownsville, twinned historically with Matamoros just over the border, has been an important city since it prospered as the Confederacy's chief cotton port during the Civil War. A subtropical climate, and streets that are lined with palm trees and bougainvillea, lend the seaport of Brownsville a relaxing southern air, but there is plenty to see here, too, of a more muscular kind.

At nearby Harlingen, air shows are staged by the remarkable Confederate Air Force Flying Museum, which has one of the nation's finest collections of vintage war planes, all lovingly maintained in excellent working order.

Endangered Turtles (*left*)
Kemp's ridley sea turtles were at a point of virtual extinction when the U.S. and Mexican governments began a campaign to save the species. Eggs are collected and incubated on Padre Island in the hope that the turtles will return there as nesting adults.

Coastal Paradise (*above*)
Sections of the long white sand and shell beaches have become home to many high-rise dwellers. However, development has been limited so that much of the island can be enjoyed in its natural windswept state as a refuge for people and countless varieties of wildlife.

SITES TO SEE

● **Port Isabel** is a popular site for deep-sea fishing. The lighthouse here was a beacon for ships along the Gulf Coast from before the Civil War until 1905. The Queen Isabella Causeway links the mainland with Padre Island.

● **Grasslands Nature Trail** (Padre Island National Seashore) is a ¾-mile hiking path through sand dunes and grasslands. The beach, about 5 miles south, preserves 55 miles of Gulf-front beach for 4-wheel-drive vehicles and primitive camping.

● **Museum of Oriental Culture** (Corpus Christi) provides a unique insight into life in the Far East. A highlight is a 1766 bronze statue of Buddha.

● **Stillman House Museum** (Brownsville), the town founder's home, is furnished with antiques.

● **Corpus Christi Naval Station** (Corpus Christi) offers free tours. The training facility is also a base for Marine and Coast Guard.

SAN ANTONIO

San Antonio remembers the Alamo, which stands like an old-world oasis at the city's center. Founded by Spanish missionaries in 1718, Mission San Antonio de Valero, later known as El Alamo, was the first of five missions built along a stretch of the San Antonio River during the early 1700s.

In the battle of 1836, the Alamo's four-foot-thick adobe walls shielded Texas freedom fighters against the Mexican army of General Santa Anna. Davy Crockett and Jim Bowie were among those who died in that fight for Texan independence, which was finally won on April 21 of that year at San Jacinto. Today, though, the colorful atmosphere of Alamo Plaza, shaded by giant oaks, seems to celebrate the Spanish heritage from which the town once fought so hard to be free.

This is very much a walker's city, and just a few blocks from the Alamo, visitors can stroll along the Paseo del Rio, or River Walk, a tree-lined path that follows the winding course of the San Antonio River through a charming district of landscaped riverbanks, waterside cafes, and floating river restaurants. Romantically lit at night, and alive with the sound of mariachi bands and flamenco music, the Paseo is the festive heart of the city.

A short walk up some grassy steps leads to the elegant adobe houses of La Villita. Now a district of galleries, craft studios, and boutiques, this area was first settled by Spanish soldiers associated with the Mission San Antonio, but later developed by local aristocratic families, and the bright stalls that line the open-air market are still full of south-of-the-border goods. For a more European atmosphere, The King William District, lined with the elaborate Victorian homes of the city's early German immigrants, stands in sharp contrast to the skyscrapers of the modern city.

To view the best panorama of the old and new worlds, take the glass-fronted elevator to the top of the Tower of the Americas, 750 feet above the HemisFair Plaza. Here you will understand why San Antonio—multicultural, warm and hearty as Texas chili—is the star of the Lone Star State.

Mission San José (*above*) Built in 1768–82, this "Queen of the Missions" is famous for its ornate facade, dome, rose window, and restored granary and workshops. Other missions in the San Antonio Missions National Historical Park include the massive, twin-towered Mission Nuestra Señora de la Purísima Concepción de Acuña, Mission San Francisco de la Espada, with a lookout tower and a 1740 aqueduct, and the Mission San Juan Capistrano. Most famous of all is the Alamo (Mission San Antonio de Valero), used as a fortress during the Texas Revolution.

Paseo del Rio (*left*) The River Walk follows the winding San Antonio River through the town's old center.

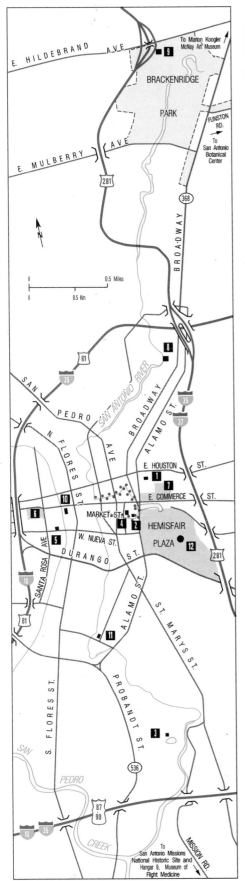

HISTORIC SITES AND DISTRICTS

HemisFair Plaza The original site of San Antonio's World Fair in 1968, this 92-acre area contains the San Antonio Convention Center, the start of the Paseo del Rio, where the river flows through the Atrium.

Market Square More than 100 years old, this area includes El Mercado, an enclosed emporium selling clothes, blankets, pottery, and leather crafts from Mexico; the open-air Farmers' Market offers fresh produce and flowers from surrounding farms.

José Antonio Navarro State Historic Site Eclectic buildings of adobe and limestone, built for the eminent statesman between 1830 and 1850. The buildings are beautifully restored with original furnishings.

San Antonio Missions National Historical Park Four of the fine 18th-century missions set up by the Franciscans include Mission Nuestra Señora de la Purisima Concepción de Acuña; Mission San Francisco de la Espada; Mission San Juan Capistrano; and Mission San José.

MUSEUMS

Buckhorn Hall of Horns Museum An unusual collection of horns and animal trophies, as well as the bar from the famous Buckhorn Saloon.

Hangar 9, Museum of Flight Medicine On Brooks Air Force Base, this is the USAF's oldest aircraft hangar. The museum houses exhibits relating to the history of the base, manned flight, and aerospace medicine.

Hertzberg Circus Collection The history of the big top, with Tom Thumb memorabilia, paintings, and a miniature circus.

Marion Koogler McNay Art Museum The collection includes paintings by Van Gogh, Picasso, El Greco, and Cézanne, all housed in a sprawling Spanish mansion with landscaped grounds.

NOTABLE BUILDINGS

Arneson River Theater A Spanish-style structure, located beside the San Antonio River; the tiered grass seats overlook the stage on the opposite bank.

Spanish Governor's Palace Used by the Spanish governor when Texas was a Spanish colony. Built in 1749, it served as a restaurant, tailor's shop, and school before being restored to its former glory.

The Steves Homestead One of the finest houses in the city, this yellow limestone Gothic Revival mansion was built by Edward Steves in 1876. It now operates as a museum.

PARKS

San Antonio Botanical Center features the Halsell Conservatory, a glass structure built onto the side of a hill, that makes use of the earth's insulating properties. A variety of ecosystems and native Texas areas are included among the formal gardens, ponds, and fountains.

San Antonio Zoological Gardens and Aquarium shows animals in their natural habitats, plus a Barrier Reef Aquarium display with sharks and eels. It also has the only whooping cranes on exhibit in a U.S. zoo.

OTHER ATTRACTIONS

Cinco de Mayo The May 5 festival commemorates Mexico's independence from France with Mexican food, dancing, and craft displays in Market Square.

Market Street Bridge and River Center Mall Embarkation point for a boat tour or a water taxi along the river.

CHANGING LANDSCAPES

Oklahoma's Eastern Quarter

When the Indians of the Five Civilized Tribes—Cherokee, Chickasaw, Choctaw, Creek, and Seminole—reached this part of eastern Oklahoma in the 1830s, they were in designated Indian Territory. Behind them lay what is known as the Trail of Tears, and beyond it their former homes in the Georgia and South Carolina mountains. Along the trail, they had left the bodies of wives, husbands, children, and companions—more than 4,000 died on the march, compelled by Andrew Jackson's Removal Act of 1830. Although no one knew it then, the territory had been a prehistoric center of the Mississippian civilization and had, just possibly, been visited by Viking explorers in the 11th century. Before long, it would be prowled by desperadoes. In the 20th century, the state would gush with oil, be ravaged by the winds of the Great Dust Bowl, and, at length, be green and serenely beautiful once again.

In 1871, when "Hanging Judge" Parker was keeping the peace, this area was a notorious haven for criminals. Jesse James and the Younger Brothers were among the many who kept a hideout at what is now Robbers Cave State Park near Wilburton.

By the 1870s, the Indians had established their own government and their own police force. The Creek Council House Museum at Okmulgee preserves the House of Kings and the House of Warriors chambers.

At Muskogee, the Five Civilized Tribes Museum, housed in the 1875 Union Indian Agency, contains a trading post and artifacts of each of the tribes. But their greatest artifact was the work of just one man, Sequoyah, whose 86-character Cherokee syllabary is the only written language known to have been invented by a single person. His 1829 home is at Sallisaw.

At the Heavener–Runestone State Park, visitors can hike over hill and dale to see what may be a more ancient language: a 12-foot-high slab carved with what some claim are eight Nordic runes, indicating Viking explorers had reached this far west by the early part of the 11th century.

Fort Smith National Historic Site (*right*) Guarding the border from Arkansas across to Oklahoma, the original wooden fort of 1817 was built to oversee Indian territory, but was replaced with a large stone fort when settlers needed reassurance of safety from Indians following the Trail of Tears. The fort was later used by the U.S. District Court, and justice was served on those who tried to live outside the law by "Hanging Judge" Isaac Parker, who sent no fewer than 79 men to the gallows during his term of office. This photo shows the reconstruction of the gallows and courtroom where original furniture and exhibits, along with an audiovisual program, tell the history of the fort.

Ouachita National Forest (*left*) A far cry from the frontier days, the cowboy's trusted companion takes a more sophisticated kind of equestrian through her paces.

138

SITES TO SEE

● **Fort Gibson Military Park** (Fort Gibson) contains a museum and the reconstructed log stockade of the 1824 fort that was abandoned in 1890. Nearby **Fort Gibson National Cemetery** includes the grave of Sam Houston's Cherokee wife.

● **Tahlequah**, capital city of the Cherokee Indian Nation, is rich in Cherokee history. **Tsa-La-Gi Ancient Village** is a reconstruction of a 17th-century Cherokee settlement, with demonstrations of pottery and basketmaking. During the summer, *"Trail of Tears,"* a musical drama about the long forced march from the southeast, is presented in an open-air amphitheater. The **Cherokee National Museum** explains the tribe's ancient history.

● **War Memorial Park** (Muskogee) displays the USS *Batfish*, a World War II submarine open to visitors.

● **Thomas-Foreman Home** (Muskogee), where historians Grant and Carolyn Foreman wrote about the Five Civilized Tribes, is furnished with many of their possessions. Nearby **Honor Heights Park** has the nation's second largest azalea park, with about 70,000 azaleas; the Azalea Festival is every April.

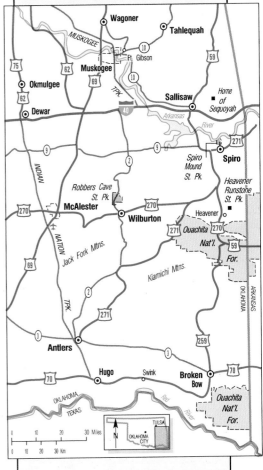

THE STEAMING VALLEY
Arkansas' Hot Springs

Soon after the Louisiana Purchase in 1803, scientists were sent to investigate a mysterious steaming valley at the edge of the Ouachita Mountains. By 1832, when the Valley of Vapors, as the Indians called it, was made a Federal Reserve, Hot Springs was already a popular spa. Sumptuous pavilions, built late last century, have been splendidly refurbished and are now national treasures that give the town the cheerful air of another age.

The same volcanic heat that set the local hot springs bubbling also endowed the Ouachitas with precious and semi-precious stones: with diamonds, with quartz of unsurpassed brilliance, and with ruby-red cinnabar. Crater of Diamonds State Park near Murfreesboro, an eroded volcanic pipe that yields agates, jasper, garnets, and amethysts as well as diamonds, is the only sizable diamond field in the U.S. The field is plowed regularly to bring new stones to the surface, and visitors can keep their finds. To the west of Lake Ouachita, Mount Ida is the region's quartz crystal headquarters.

For those who come to the Ouachitas without a geologist's hammer, the mountains themselves are the reward. Talimena Scenic Drive (SR 88), which runs for more than 50 ridge-top miles between Talihina, Oklahoma, and Mena, Arkansas, is one good way to see them. If you do make the drive, be sure to stop at Janssen Park in Mera, with spring-fed lakes, a deer herd, and an 1851 log cabin. There are also splendid mountain views from Queen Wilhelmina State Park, on one of Arkansas' highest peaks.

With almost 1,000 miles of wandering shoreline, man-made Lake Ouachita is one of the gems of these mountains. From the state park at the northeast end of the lake, you can take the Geo-Float Trail to caves and earthquake sites. The Ouachita River flows into Lake Hamilton at Hot Springs, where the riverboat *Belle of Hot Springs* gives cruises.

Arkadelphia, at the junction of the Caddo and Ouachita rivers, was once a steamboat port. It celebrates its heritage during April's Festival of Two Rivers. But the region's major thoroughfare was always the Arkansas River valley. Explorers, pioneers, and soldiers came along it, followed by steamboats and stagecoaches heading west.

Van Buren was settled as steamboat landing in 1818 and preserves a ten-block historic district with 19th-century homes and stores, as well as a church and schoolhouse. Neighboring Fort Smith was founded a year earlier. The Fort Smith National Historic Site preserves remains of the two forts that once stood here. It includes "Hanging Judge" Isaac C. Parker's notorious courtroom.

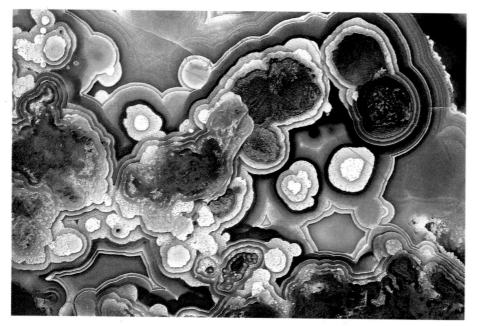

Special Strata (*left*) Quartz agate is the result of silica solutions seeping into the crevices of older rock. The resulting banded patterns make it an extremely beautiful semi-precious gemstone. The structure is said to be crypto-crystalline because the crystal structure is not evident unless magnified.

Slow Drip (*above*) Over a period of 4,000 years, rainfall becomes the naturally pure water flowing into the hot springs. As the water is absorbed into the earth, it journeys 4,000–8,000 feet underground, where it is warmed by the earth's interior heat before it returns to the surface through pores and cracks in the rock.

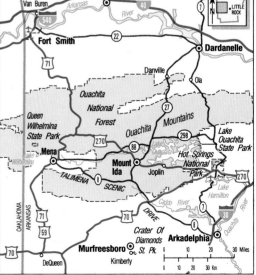

SITES TO SEE

● **Take a Hot-springs Bath at Buckstaff Bathhouse along Bathhouse Row** (Hot Springs National Park), in operation since 1911, or at bathhouses in local hotels. The **Fordyce Bathhouse**, also on Bathhouse Row, has been restored.

● **Hot Springs Mountain Observation Tower** (Hot Springs National Park) provides visitors with 360° panoramic views across the park and city from 216 feet above ground.

● **Mid-America Museum** (Hot Springs) has hands-on energy-related exhibits that allow visitors to launch a

hot-air balloon and generate electricity. Other interesting features include several Arkansas natural history displays.

● **Ka-Do-Ha Indian Village** (Murfreesboro) is a prehistoric archaeological site, still inhabited about 1,000 years ago.

● **Ouachita National Recreation Trail** provides hikers with 186 scenic miles through the Ouachita National Forest from near Little Rock to Talimera State Park, OK.

MOUNTAIN FOLK AND COUNTRY
The Southern Ozarks

The southern Ozarks, scrambling across the Missouri–Arkansas line in a region of peaks, glades, gorges, and rushing streams, are the only mountains between the Appalachians and the Rockies. Except in a few valleys where fruit and vines grow, the soil is poor. The old methods of subsistence farming still survive, and with them the crafts and folkways of Ozark mountain people.

America first paid nostalgic attention to the Ozarks in 1907 when Harold Bell Wright published his novel *The Shepherd of the Hills*, about Ozark country folk. Today, the area, enhanced by man-made lakes, is a major tourist center, known for country music and folk festivals. Silver Dollar City, near Branson, Missouri, is an outstanding re-creation of a pioneer community and amusement park, popular for its craft and music festivals. Wright and his Ozark characters are remembered at Shepherd of the Hills Homestead.

Agronomist George Washington Carver, the best-known Ozark pioneer, who was orphaned by the Civil War, is remembered at George Washington Carver National Monument near Joplin.

Pea Ridge National Military Park in northwestern Arkansas commemorates the biggest Civil War battle west of the Mississippi River, which secured Missouri for the Union.

Eureka Springs, Arkansas, is a mountain town famous for the 63 springs within its city limits, and for tourist attractions with a Christian theme. These include the Great Passion Play, performed in a hillside amphitheater, the 50-acre New Holy Land, and the Christ of the Ozarks statue, weighing more than 1 million pounds, on Magnetic Mountain.

If your time for exploration is brief, the ravines and bluffs of the War Eagle Creek in Withrow Spring State Park near Huntsville, Arkansas, offer a ravishing encapsulation of Ozark scenery. If you have more time and are inclined to adventure, the Buffalo National River offers canoeing, 500-foot-high bluffs, and one of the highest waterfalls in mid-America. Leave the river at Ponca and drive north to Dogpatch. At Dogpatch U.S.A., a "L'il Abner" theme park, Ozarks nostalgia is drawn with a cartoonist's pen, a vaudeville Shepherd of the Hills.

Whitaker Point (*right*) in Ozark National Forest provides a grand lookout over the wild headwaters of the Buffalo River. A paradise for canoeists and anglers the upper reaches of this turbulent stream flow between 500-foot cliffs over daunting rapids. They gradually give way to tranquil pools in open valleys as the river nears its confluence with the White River near Buffalo City.

Quilting (*left*) and other traditional crafts, such as glassblowing and gunsmithing, are a part of the heritage of the Ozark region. Demonstrations of these skills are held at several centers, notably at Silver Dollar City, a replica of an Ozark pioneer settlement 9 miles from Branson, MO, where the National Quilt Festival is held each year.

SITES TO SEE

● **Marvel Cave** (Branson, MO), located beneath Silver Dollar City, is one of the world's largest caves with a chamber 20 stories high, as well as a 505-foot waterfall. Visitors walk into the cave along a path and are later brought back to the surface in tram cars.

● **Eureka Springs** was a popular 19th-century resort that grew up around the spas with their hot-water springs. The historic district preserves the lavish Victorian homes; many houses are open for tours in April and December. The **Queen Anne Mansion**, built 1891 in Missouri, was dismantled and moved here in 1984. Its exquisite interior includes 7 fireplaces and carved woodwork. Worshipers at **St. Elizabeth Church** enter through the bell tower and walk down to the sanctuary. A major arts-and-crafts fair is held in the town each May.

● **Onyx Cave** (east of Eureka Springs) is known for its unusual formations.

● **University of Arkansas** (Fayetteville) grew out of the Arkansas Industrial University, established in 1871. The **University Museum** displays quartz crystal, pressed glass, pioneer memorabilia, and anthropological artifacts.

● **Headquarters House** (Fayetteville) is a Greek Revival building, built 1853, with the distinction of having been used by both Union and Confederate forces during the Civil War. It contains a small museum and Civil War-era furniture and memorabilia.

● **Elkhorn Tavern** (Pea Ridge National Military Park) was the center of the historic Civil War battle; a roadside exhibit and recording explain the course of the fighting. The tavern burned during the battle and was rebuilt soon after on the original foundations on Telegraph Road, named in 1860 for the telegraph line strung the length of the road. In the late 1850s, the tavern was a stagecoach stop on the journey to Fort Smith.

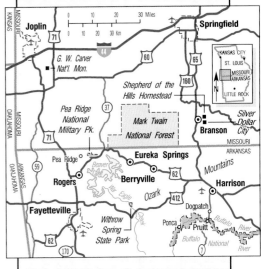

BOOTHEEL AND LITTLE FRANCE

Southeastern Missouri

The riverlands of southeastern Missouri are a quilt of preservations: the needlework Spanish and French, the colors from a palette of canebrake green and corn yellow, of Mississippi River brown, and in the south, of peach gold and cotton white. To the west, the deep-valleyed Ozarks rise abruptly from the alluvial plain, clad in the most westerly extension of the eastern hardwood forest but patched with glades—sunlit openings where bluestem grass and flowers carpet the thin soil, relics of the glacial ice front that once pushed their ancestors south into these mountains.

It is difficult to wander through Missouri's Bootheel region without the feeling of having stepped into the past. The Mississippi embayment here, which long ago was an arm of the Gulf of Mexico, has since filled with 3,000 feet of Mississippi slit: the land itself here a relic of ancient floods. There are other relics, too. Big Oak Tree State Park near East Prairie was named for a massive bur oak that was there when the first settlers arrived in the area. The great swamp here, where buffalo fish jump, herons stalk, and ruddy ducks glide on black water, is all that remains of a swamp created by the 1811 New Madrid earthquake. Its force caused land to sink 50 feet in places, made the Mississippi flow backward, and rang Boston's church bells.

Mingo National Wildlife Refuge is an exceptionally beautiful relict of a change in the course of the Mississippi about 18,000 years ago. It left behind a swampy region where the Mingo River flows, so winding, overhung, and islanded that it seems more like a series of oxbow lakes in an enchanted forest than a river.

The first non-Indian settlers here were French traders. Cape Girardeau began life as a trading post in 1733. Up river, Ste. Genevieve is Missouri's oldest permanent settlement on the west bank. Many of the old homes are in the French Creole style from the 1780s.

New Madrid, at the tip of an almost 360-degree bend in the Mississippi River, felt earthquake aftershocks for two years. It has interesting earthquake displays at the town museum, along with displays recalling the town's role in the Civil War. The Hunter-Dawson State Historic Site preserves a wealthy merchant's 15-room home as it would have been in the 1850s.

West of Ste. Genevieve are the old silver and lead mines of Bonne Terre, with a billion-gallon underground lake. Nearby is St. Francois State Park, a fine place to sample Ozark hill country. The drive south from Potosi, along scenic SR 21, goes through ravishing scenery to the massive boulders of Elephant Rocks State Park. The highest peak in the Missouri Ozarks is Taum Sauk Mountain.

Bollinger Mill State Historic Site (*above*) This yellow poplar single-span bridge in Burfordville was started in 1858 but delayed by the Civil War and not finally completed until ten years later. It is one of four covered bridges in Missouri and one of only two still used by traffic. Just beyond the bridge is the four-story Bollinger Mill, which was built in 1867 by Solomon Burford.

Bubble Bath (*right*) The foaming water of the rapids at Johnson's Shut-Ins State Park is the perfect place to cool off on a hot summer's day.

Slow but Snappy (*left*) The common snapping turtle, which is often over 18 inches long and 30 pounds in weight, likes quiet, muddy waters. These useful scavengers feed on fish, aquatic animals, and decaying matter.

SITES TO SEE

● **Glenn House** (Cape Girardeau), built 1883, has classic Victorian decorations with stenciled ceilings and period furniture. The Mississippi's bygone days as a steamboat river are recalled with displays and memorabilia.

● **Cape Rock** (Cape Girardeau) offers splendid views along the Mississippi River.

● **Trail of Tears State Park** (north of Cape Girardeau) covers 3,415 acres, including part of the trail that the Cherokee Indians followed when they were forced to move from southern Appalachia to Oklahoma. A monument marks the spot where Princess Otahki is supposedly buried. This is the only Missouri state park on the Mississippi River; it offers camping, hiking, picnicking, swimming, and fishing facilities.

● **Elephant Rocks State Park** (Graniteville) contains a 1-mile trail signposted with descriptions of the natural sites in Braille and English. The park gets its name from the massive granite Elephant Rock, estimated to be 1.2 billion years old. It is about 27 feet tall, 35 feet long, and 17 feet wide.

● **Ste. Genevieve** preserves many of the early homes from its days as a prosperous riverboat community, with a strong French influence in the architecture. Visitors can walk through **Amoureaux House**, built 1770 and one of the oldest surviving Creole houses, with an outstanding display of fine silver, glassware, and china. The **Felix Valle Home State Historic Site**, built 1818, is a stone structure with 2 entrances so the original owners could both live there and use the building as an office. **Guibourd-Valle House**, built 1785, demonstrates the fine craftsmanship that went into building early log homes, with hand-hewn beams and wooded pegs.

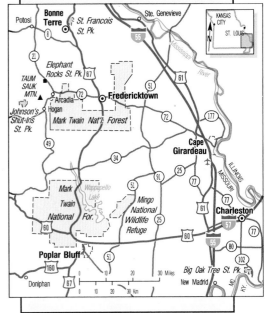

AN INDEPENDENT STYLE
Around Kansas City and St. Joe

By the early 1800s, Kansas City was a staging ground for expeditions going west. The region has retained its character as a place of departure ever since. The dissenting Mormon prophet Joseph Smith was jailed in Liberty; the Pony Express chose St. Joseph as its eastern terminus; and local outlaw Jesse James was shot dead there. Amelia Earhart, pioneer aviator, was born in Atchison, Kansas, and Harry S. Truman, who ushered the world into the Nuclear Age, began his career in Independence.

When Joseph Smith was jailed in 1838, his good fortune was that William A. Doniphan headed the state militia. This most independent-minded general in U.S. military history flatly refused to execute Smith and his followers as ordered. Historic Liberty Jail, where Smith was kept, is open.

Nearby Independence is the Reorganized Mormon Church headquarters, with its splendid gold-domed Auditorium. The Mormon (LDS) Visitors' Center offers displays and films on Mormon history.

In the early 20th century, a more famous soldier, Douglas MacArthur, lived across the river at Fort Leavenworth, Kansas. The Main Parade is beautifully restored, and the Frontier Army Museum has the best collection of horse-drawn vehicles in the nation. While MacArthur was in residence, his political nemesis, Harry Truman, was a Missouri county judge. Memorabilia of their dispute over whether U.S. troops should be allowed to attack communist bases in Manchuria during the Korean conflict is at the Harry S. Truman Library and Museum in Independence. The Truman family home is also open to visitors, and guided walking tours of the neighborhood are offered.

In Kearney, visit the cradle of another cussedly independent Missourian, Jesse James. There are mementoes of the outlaw at the family home in Kearney, and at the St. Joseph Museum, too, including the bloodstained floorboard on which he died. The museum also displays memorabilia of William Quantrill's raiders, the Confederate guerrillas with whom James rode during the Civil War. They attacked Lawrence, Kansas, in 1863, burning the town and murdering 150 civilians.

East of Kearney, Watkins Woolen Mill State Historic Site preserves the only 19th-century woolen mill with all its original machinery intact in the U.S., as well as weaver Waltus Watkins's house. The mill was built in 1861, and although it no longer operates, a wide selection of spinners, twisters, and looms are on dis-

play. Restored buildings include the summer kitchen and fruit-drying house.

The St. Joseph Museum is in a 43-room 1879 sandstone mansion overlooking the Missouri River. It was decorated in 1887 by New York designer Louis Comfort Tiffany. The collection covers North American Indians and wildlife, as well as local history. Visitors can see birch-bark canoes, period fashions, military artifacts, and stuffed native animals. Windows on the staircase landings contain Tiffany-designed stained glass.

As the railroads made their way west, so did surveyors and naturalists. The fossil beds of western Kansas were among their discoveries. The Museum of Natural History at the University of Kansas in Lawrence has one of the nation's finest fossil collections and extensive exhibits of mounted animals, including the horse Comanche, the sole cavalry survivor of Custer's Last Stand.

The Thinker by Rodin (*left*) Sculpture forms a significant part of the Nelson-Atkins Museum of Art in Kansas City, MO. The collection also includes Oriental artifacts, international paintings, and antiquities.

Harry S. Truman National Historic Site (*above*) lies on a quiet residential street in Independence, MO, former President Truman's home town. The spacious 14-room Victorian house, filled with Truman's furnishings, personal belongings, and memorabilia, was the childhood home of his wife. After their marriage in 1919, the Trumans lived here until they died. Once Truman was elected, the city gave the family a flagpole for their yard, and the house became known as the "Summer White House." The Union and Pacific Railroad Station in the center of town featured heavily in Truman's "Whistle Stop" campaign of 1948 and his many trips to Washington and back.

Agricultural Hall of Fame and National Center, Bonner Springs, KS (*right*) The displays of farm machinery and implements provide a unique look at the development of farming in the past and its prospects for the future.

SITES TO SEE

● **Atchison, KS**, has several mementoes to Amelia Earhart, its pioneering aviatrix who flew solo across the Atlantic in 1932. The local airport, named in Earhart's honor, contains a statue of her. The **International Forest of Friendship** is a living memorial, with trees from all U.S. states and territories, foreign countries, and a "moon tree" grown from seeds carried back by the Apollo 14 space mission.

● **Hallmark Visitors Center** (Kansas City, MO) has tours explaining the creative process, from idea through production of the cards, wrapping papers, and novelty items that Americans have grown up with. Demonstrations show how unusually shaped cards are cut.

● **Toy and Miniature Museum of Kansas City** (Kansas City, MO) displays charming antique dolls and exquisite hand-carved miniatures. Highlights include dollhouses with each item made to scale.

● **Spencer Museum of Art** (Lawrence, KS), on the University of Kansas campus, ranks as one of the nation's top university art museums. A collection of American paintings and sculptures from the 19th and 20th centuries is outstanding, as are the American, European, and Oriental decorative arts. The university's **Spencer Research Library** contains manuscripts and rare 15th- to 17th-century European books in its large collection.

● **Jesse James Bank Museum** (Liberty, MO) has some of the original bank furnishings that were here when the notorious gang robbed the bank.

● **Frontier Army Museum** (Ft. Leavenworth, KS) displays a carriage that Abraham Lincoln used and numerous pioneer wagons, along with historic military uniforms.

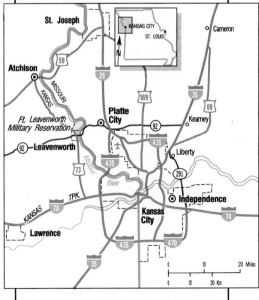

ST. LOUIS

The first structure at St. Louis was a landing built by French fur trapper Pierre Laclede in 1764. About 40 years later, Lewis and Clark passed through the settlement that had grown up around the spot on their way west; within years they were followed by thousands of men and women seeking a new life beyond the Mississippi. St. Louis had become not only a staging post for the pioneer, but the gateway to a new life.

Today, St. Louis is the nation's second largest inland port, a hub of transportation, and a leader in the aerospace and automobile industries. In many ways, it is also still a gateway city, served by four interstate highways and looking equally to the East, West, and Gulf coasts. Although attractions are scattered throughout the metropolitan area, the riverfront, downtown, and Forest Park have the most to offer visitors.

The riverfront is the place to begin exploring St. Louis. At Laclede's Landing, 25 brick buildings, many with cast-iron facades, are registered National Historic Landmarks and are lively with restaurants and stores. Just south of the area is the riverfront Jefferson National Expansion Memorial, dominated by the Gateway Arch. The nation's tallest monument, it towers 630 feet above the city and gives the visitor panoramic views from its observation deck.

St. Louis's downtown area is where you will find Busch Stadium, home to the St. Louis Cardinals, as well as the convention complex. Farther west is Forest Park, site of the 1904 world's fair, where the art museum and part of the zoo remain from the exposition celebrating the Louisiana Purchase. Recreational opportunities include ice skating and summer roller skating in the Steinberg Memorial Skating Rink, one of the nation's largest.

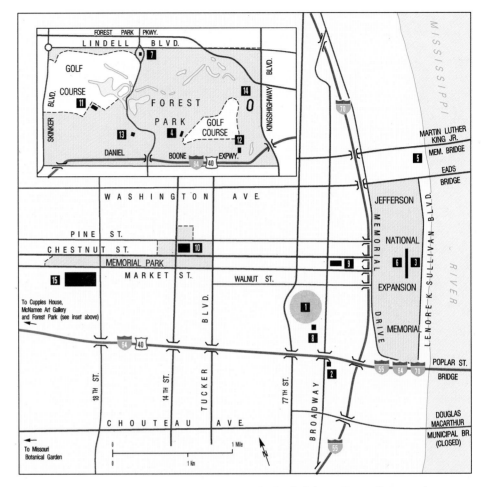

Gateway Arch (*left*) was conceived by the Finnish-American architect Eero Saarinen, whose design for the soaring, stainless steel curve won a national competition in 1947. In its finished state, 40 feet higher than originally planned, it is supported by its own structural form, without the aid of an inner frame or skeleton, and its width and height are the same. In a chamber directly below the arch, the Museum of Westward Expansion honors Thomas Jefferson, who brought St. Louis into the U.S. with the Louisiana Purchase, and the brave settlers whose march west led them here.

Climatron at Missouri Botanical Garden (*far left*) Another amazing architectural construction is the geodesic dome. This one contains a fine collection of orchids and various other subtropical and tropical plants.

MUSEUMS

Eugene Field House and Toy Museum The author of "Little Boy Blue" and other poems lived here as a child. The house now contains antique toys and dolls, and Field memorabilia.

Soldiers' Memorial Military Museum A 7-block tribute to St. Louis men and women who died during both world wars, as well as in Korea and Vietnam. Two museums are devoted to military activity of St. Louisians since 1800.

National Bowling Hall of Fame offers video exhibits and memorabilia.

The Magic House A children's museum with hands-on science, communications, and computer exhibits.

St. Louis Art Museum A varied collection, strong in pre-Columbian art and German Expressionism, with many works by Max Beckmann.

Missouri Historical Society The collection provides a fascinating account of life in St. Louis since its founding. The Lindbergh Collection contains items used on the historic transatlantic flight and personal belongings.

St. Louis Science Center Demonstrations explain earth sciences, physics, and biology.

NOTABLE BUILDINGS

Cupples House and McNamee Art Gallery This Romanesque-style mansion, built 1890, displays paintings and sculptures in its former bowling alley.

Old Courthouse The Greek Revival building where the early stages of the Dred Scott slavery trial took place. Today, the building houses exhibits devoted to St. Louis's role in the nation's westward expansion.

Union Station A magnificent 19th-century structure, converted with its train shed into a stylish hotel, shopping, and entertainment area.

PARKS AND GARDENS

Jewel Box An Art Deco greenhouse with dazzling floral displays.

St. Louis Zoo Lakes, pampas, bluffs, glades, and jungles provide naturalistic habitats for 2,500 animals.

EISENHOWER'S ECCENTRIC HOMELAND

The Kansas Plains

The geographic center of the lower 48 states is located near Lebanon, where the landscape is days long and the sky is like an infinite blue dome. In the flatness of these plains, colors become topography: the fresh green of young wheat, the creamy spires of summer yucca, and the startling white of roadside outcrops are what hills and valley are in other states. Grain silos loom like cathedrals here, and in late summer, giant combines creep against the rim of the sky like walking castles. These are the essence of the heartland.

Abilene honors a man who once loomed over the stage of history. Dwight D. Eisenhower, or just plain Ike, was the modest Kansas boy who became supreme commander of the Allied troops in World War II, and then President of the United States. The Eisenhower Center contains a fascinating collection of the trappings that accrue to power, including Japanese armor and a Saudi Arabian gold sword. There is also memorabilia of Ike's military and presidential achievements. His boyhood home and grave are also preserved.

While Ike was growing up, Civil War veteran S. P. Dinsmoor was building the Garden of Eden at Lucas, a limestone log house with a garden of concrete sculptures in the folk-lunatic style. The price of admission includes a visit to the mausoleum, where Dinsmoor's embalmed body is displayed: this tour option was his idea of giving visitors good value.

In fact, the larger-than-life quality of this part of Kansas is kind to fanciers of the eccentric and idiosyncratic. The Fick Fossil Museum at Oakley features the collection of a Mrs. Fick. She not only gathered an astonishing number of fossils, but turned them into fascinating works of art.

Goodland, near the Colorado line, was once the Rainmaking Capital of the United States. The High Plains Museum here has memorabilia of such aficionados as Frank Melbourne, an Australian rain maker known as the Rain Wizard.

Lakeside tamarisks and prickly poppies are two of the surprises that can be found at Cedar Bluff State Park, near Hays.

The Pillars of Castle Rock (*right*), their weather-worn tops like the battlements of a medieval fortress, look out over prairies that stretch flat to the horizon in every direction. These amazing chalk pinnacles, and those of nearby Monument Rocks, are the remnants of an ancient seabed, and eons of wind and water erosion have revealed a variety of marine and reptilian fossils contained within layer upon layer of sediment. The sites can be reached by road from Oakley.

Similar formations and chalk cliffs are typical of the valley of Smoky Hill River and can be found as far east as Cedar Bluffs Reservoir.

The Large Statue of Dwight D. Eisenhower (*left*), in characteristic pose, towers over the Eisenhower Center, which is dedicated to the life and memory of the 34th President of the United States.

Covering 22 acres of landscaped grounds, the center contains the family home, a museum, and the Presidential Library, which houses papers collected by Eisenhower during his term of office. Also here is the Place of Meditation, where the President, his wife Mamie, and their son are buried. An informative half-hour film is shown at the Visitor Center.

SITES TO SEE

● **Historic Fort Hays** (Hays) contains restored buildings from the 1867 fort, 2 officers' homes, and the 1867 blockhouse, the oldest surviving building in northwestern Kansas. The fort marked the trailhead of the Ft. Hays—Ft. Dodge military supply road that ran to Dodge City. **Fort Hays State University** is located on part of the original grounds of the fort. The **Sternberg Memorial Museum**, on campus, provides an excellent picture of local history.

● **Lebold-Vahsoltz Mansion** (Abilene) is a Victorian house, restored to its former glory.

● **Goodland High Plains Museum** (Goodland) features such unique exhibits as a full-size model of the first patented helicopter built in the U.S.

● **The Gallery of Also Rans** (Norton) presents a somewhat light-hearted look at presidential candidates who did not make it to the White House.

● **Prairie Museum of Art and History** (Colby), spread over 24 acres, includes a furnished 1930 farmhouse, a sod house, and a unique doll collection, as well as homesteading memorabilia.

● **Museum of Independent Telephony** (Abilene) traces the history of the telephone in the hands of its independent operators.

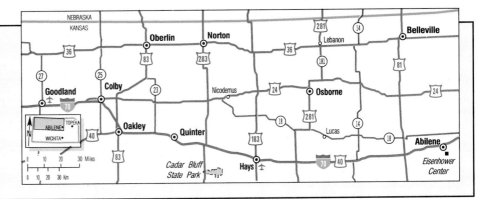

TRAILS ACROSS THE PLAINS

Southeastern Kansas

Armies of wagon trains once rutted the prairie where US 56 now crosses the rolling flint hills west of Council Grove. When the Mexican territories were opened, first traders, then settlers, set out along the Santa Fe Trail seeking a Promised Land. From Council Grove to Coffeyville and Wichita, the legacy of the area is a legacy of sodbusters and Mennonite farmers, of Osage and Kaw Indians, of cowboys driving the Chisholm Trail, and of outlaws like Billy the Kid and the Dalton Gang.

For traders and settlers going west, the narrow strip of forest along the Neosho River at what is now Council Grove was a welcome source of timber for spare axles and repairs, and a place to rest. The 1857 Last Chance Store still stands, and on Main Street a stump of the Council Oak is preserved. Here, for $800, Kaw Indians agreed to let Santa Fe Trail travelers cross their land.

Mennonite farmers were among those content to find their Promised Land in this part of Kansas. They are commemorated at Goessel's Mennonite Heritage Museum and Hillsboro's Pioneer Adobe House and Museum. The adobe house was built by a Mennonite family in 1880, and occupied, still with a sod roof, until 1956. At Independence, the most famous chronicler of life on the plains is commemorated at the Laura Ingalls Wilder homesite, where the author had her own little house on the prairie from 1869–71.

By the time the railroad reached central Kansas, settlers already in Oklahoma and Texas were ready to send beef back east. Cattlemen drove their cattle to the railhead at Abilene and wore a trail whose traces can still be seen. Look for Chisholm Trail markers near Caldwell and Wellington, where the Chisholm Trail Museum describes the cattle route and the region's agricultural development, as well as local history.

When a measure of wealth came to the area, nomadic desperadoes like Billy the Kid and the Dalton Gang came, too. The Coffeyville Historical Museum contains moneybags, safes, and guns of the bank-robbing Daltons, but the most extensive records of the area's past are preserved at Wichita. Historic Old Cow Town Museum covers 17 acres, and its 36 buildings, dating from 1865, include the city's first permanent house and church. At the Wichita Art Museum, paintings by Charles M. Russell give a vivid record of the cowboy-nomads who roamed the plains when the dust of westward-bound wagon trains cleared.

The "Madonna of the Trail" in Council Grove (*left*) stands on the site where, between the 1820s and 1880s, wagon trains were assembled and outfitted before they set off on the long, difficult Santa Fe Trail in New Mexico. The 16-foot-high statue depicts a pioneer woman with her children and commemorates the fortitude of these women, who endured immense hardships during the opening up of the West.

Nearby are the remains of the Post Office Oak, a tree which served as a mailbox for the pioneers. Letters left in a stone cache beneath the tree were picked up by the next wagon train along the trail.

Ancient Wooden Storage Barns (*right*), still to be found on farms in the Flint Hills, indicate that Kansas has long been one of the United States' top wheat-producing states; today it yields 20 percent of the nation's wheat for export.

Although the barns have largely been replaced by giant concrete grain elevators, Kansas remains a vast producer for other crops as well, including alfalfa, hay, soybeans, and sugar beets.

SITES TO SEE

● **Messiah Festival of Music and Art** (Lindsborg, *left*) has been an annual tradition during Easter week since 1882; concerts are held on the Bethany College campus.

● **Hays House Restaurant** (Council Grove), the oldest continuously serving restaurant west of the Mississippi, has catered to hearty appetites since Santa Fe Trail travelers ate here. Gen. Custer and Jesse James often stayed in the upstairs rooms, according to legend. Other historic buildings in town include **The Last Chance Store** and the **Old Indian School House**.

● **Dean Smith's Cutting Horse Training Stables** (Council Grove) prepares horses for competition across the U.S. Tours include training sessions and championship horse demonstrations.

● **Greenwood County Historical Society Museum** (Eureka) pays tribute to early Kansas pioneers.

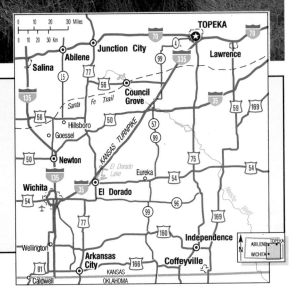

THE MIDWEST

The northern boundary of these heartlands lies in the gray, green, aquamarine waters of the Great Lakes, edged by their dark forests and polychrome cliffs, by towering dunes, agate beaches, and wooded islands. South of the great manufacturing cities that rim the lakes—Milwaukee, Chicago, Detroit, Cincinnati—are great checkered quilts of farmland and (even today) miles of the once horizon-wide prairie, sweet-smelling and splashed with summer flowers. Here the continent takes a deep breath and begins to turn west; here lawyer Lincoln learned his trade, great harvests of grain were gathered and shipped across the lakes, and here Thomas Edison learned to "converse in lightning."

Toward the west of the Midwest, where Wisconsin borders the Mississippi and Cornish lead miners settled, is the Dairy State's playground, the Dells of the Wisconsin River. In the region's deep south are ravines, caves, and limestone hills reaching to the winding banks of the wide Ohio. The Midwest's archaeology—the mound-cities and great earth-effigies of the Hopewell Indians—is perhaps the richest in the nation, with cut-stone blast furnaces buried deep in the southern forests, looking as though they were built by wandering Assyrians.

CANADA

LAKE SUPERIOR

**PAGES
182-183**

**PAGES
172-173**

ST. IGNACE

**PAGES
176-177**

ESCANABA

**PAGES
174-175**

TRAVERSE CITY

LAKE HURON

WISCONSIN

GREEN BAY

LAKE
MICHIGAN

MICHIGAN

LAKE ONTARIO

**PAGES
180-181**

LANSING

BUFFALO

**NEW
YORK**

MADISON

MILWAUKEE

DETROIT

**PAGES
178-179**

SANDUSKY

CLEVELAND

PENNSYLVANIA

CHICAGO

**PAGES
160-161**

**PAGES
162-163**

AKRON

**PAGES
170-171**

**PAGES
168-169**

PITTSBURGH

FORT WAYNE

ILLINOIS

INDIANA

OHIO

COLUMBUS

**PAGES
158-159**

**PAGES
166-167**

**WEST
VIRGINIA**

SPRINGFIELD

INDIANAPOLIS

CINCINNATI

HUNTINGTON

CHARLESTON

**PAGES
164-165**

ST.
LOUIS

LOUISVILLE

LEXINGTON

VIRGINIA

**PAGES
156-157**

KENTUCKY

PADUCAH

**NORTH
CAROLINA**

TENNESSEE

NASHVILLE

LITTLE EGYPT
Southern Illinois

Long horizons yielding to the forested hills and rugged gorges in this part of southern Illinois give the region one of its nicknames: the Illinois Ozarks. Little Egypt, however, is an older and more fanciful name for the area. It was probably coined by the same settlers who dubbed their town Cairo. Perhaps they thought the mighty, bicolored confluence of the Ohio and Mississippi rivers resembled the Nile. Or, perhaps the sandstone outcrops and tumbled monoliths scattered through the lush green woods reminded them of obelisks and pyramids.

Lake Egypt is the most southerly of the lakes that make Shawnee National Forest a magnet for boaters and anglers. Bird watchers flock to the Crab Orchard National Wildlife Refuge on Crab Orchard Lake, 43,000 acres on the Mississippi flyway.

For backpackers and hikers, there are miles of wilderness trails. Fern Clyffe State Park is famous for its trails through strangely canyoned terrain. Giant City State Park, west of Devils Kitchen Lake Park, was named for its jumbles of house-sized sandstone blocks. Knights of the Gold Circle, a pro-Southern group, met here secretly during the Civil War.

The Garden of the Gods is a remote rock garden of weathered sandstone, explored via catwalks and winding trails. Nearby Pounds Hollow Recreation Area is a typical "Illinois Ozarks" hollow, with a picturesque lake, magnificent oaks, and rugged outcrops. At Cave-In-Rock State Park, a great cave overlooks the Ohio River. For many years, this 150-acre site was the lair of river pirates and robbers, and today it offers recreational and picnicking facilities for the whole family. There

are superb views from Tower Rock, a 160-foot-high limestone bluff downriver.

Some of the strange landscapes in this part of Illinois are the joint work of man and nature. Old Shawneetown, the oldest non-Indian settlement in Illinois, was all but destroyed by a 1939 flood. A ghost town is left, unmatched for its curious, river-lapped melancholy. The town's First State Bank of Illinois State Historic Site has a historical marker recalling the time when newly founded Chicago was considered a poor credit risk. Southwest along the Ohio is Mound City National Cemetery, the final resting place of nearly 5,000 Confederate dead.

Nearby Cairo was a bustling steamboat town whose strategic position on the Ohio and Mississippi rivers assured its importance during the Civil War. Today, the color and commotion of the riverboat days are gone from the town's quiet streets. Magnolia Manor, however, an 1869 merchant's showplace, has been restored and still echoes the boisterous days when this little river town believed it could surpass Chicago as the midwestern center of American commerce.

Garden of the Gods Recreation Area (*left*) The spectacular effect of the sun at day's end mellows the rock bluffs on this ancient trail. Some of these weathered rock formations are 200 million years old.

Pounds Hollow Recreation Area (*right*) Idyllic Pounds Hollow on the Saline River offers the occasional glimpse of a deer or fox in the sunlight that breaks through the trees in the Shawnee National Forest. Saline springs at nearby Old Shawneetown were first used by prehistoric Indians, and led to Illinois' first important' industry, salt processing.

SITES TO SEE

● **Fort Massac State Park** (Metropolis) contains a reconstruction of a fort built by the French in 1757. Gen. George Rogers Clark passed through here in 1778, and he is remembered with a statue. In 1805, Aaron Burr and Gen. James Wilkinson, Commander of the Western U.S. Army, met at the fort, allegedly to plan treason and the conquest of the southwestern United States and Mexico. The park was Illinois' first state park. Today, it offers facilities for hiking, camping, boating, and picnicking.

● **Crab Orchard National Wildlife Refuge** (Marion) is the seasonal home of more than 120,000 Canada geese each fall, along with thousands of loons, herons, turkey vultures, and bald eagles.

● **Willis Allen House** (Marion), built 1851 in the Italianate style, is on the National Register of Historic Places. The exterior walls are 4 handmade bricks thick, and the interior is noted for its fine hand-crafted oak beams. The rooms have been restored with period antiques.

● **Metropolis** hosts a Superman Festival each June in honor of its most famous "son." Visitors to town can receive free copies of *The Planet*, and speak to the mild-mannered hero from a special telephone booth.

● **Old Slave House** (Junction) is an 1834 Greek Revival mansion built for a local farmer and businessman, who illegally kept slaves imprisoned in small cubicles on the third floor. The first two floors have been restored with period antiques, and the third floor has been partially restored to show the horrific conditions the slaves had to endure, including the whipping post. Abraham Lincoln is said to have spent a night at the house, unaware of the slaves sleeping above him. Locals maintain the house is haunted.

● **Cairo Public Library** (Cairo) displays local antiques and a collection of Civil War records.

● **John Marshall Bank and House** (Shawneetown) was built in 1818 as a private residence and served as the state's first bank. It has been restored.

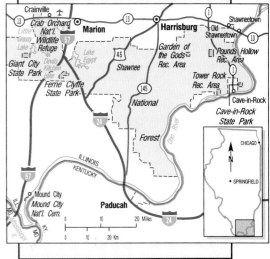

LINCOLN LAND

Central Illinois

The placid fields, woods, and small towns of central Illinois—as amiable and unsurprising as apple pie—were Abraham Lincoln's home ground for 17 years. He arrived here in 1830 as a 21-year-old country boy; he left as president-elect, destined to preserve the nation's unity. Many shrines, monuments, and museums throughout the area commemorate this most modest of American heroes. Yet none is more poignant than the region itself. This is a place whose fertile croplands, close communities, and long horizons serve as the role model for the American heartland.

Great flocks of geese settle along the marsh pastures of the Illinois River between winter and summer to gather strength between north and south. The best views of the geese, along with ducks, shore birds, and bald eagles, is on Chautauqua Lake's reedy shores in the Chautauqua National Wildlife Refuge.

Springfield, one of the most interesting state capitals in the nation, offers the best insight into Abraham Lincoln, Illinois' adopted son. Lincoln's Springfield home was the only one he ever owned. He and his family lived in it for 17 years, and the scrupulously restored Lincoln Home National Historical Site reflects their tastes and lifestyles. Original furnishings include Abe's lap-desk and shaving mirror. The site attempts to re-create the environment Lincoln knew. Walk along wide streets and visit the homes of his friends and neighbors: Solomon Allen kept livestock in a nearby barn; political ally Jesse Dubois was a neighbor; the Harriet Deane House is built on land once owned by Lincoln.

Elsewhere in Springfield, visit the Lincoln-Herndon Law Offices, where the 16th president had his law practice, the family pew in the First Presbyterian Church, and the tomb where he, his wife, and three of their children are buried.

For a glimpse of a younger Lincoln, travel northwest to Lincoln's New Salem State Park, a reconstruction of New Salem when Lincoln lived here from 1831–37. Onstot Cooper Shop, where Lincoln studied law in the evenings, and John Kelso's log cabin, where the philosopher introduced the future president to the classics of English literature, have been restored. Ann Rutledge, once Lincoln's great romance, is buried in Oakland.

Lincoln traveled widely in central Illinois as a young man. Long before he became famous, he established land ownership in the town of Lincoln—and christened it with watermelon juice. Later, as a lawyer on the Eighth Judicial Circuit, Lincoln visited the Logan County courthouse in the town regularly. It is now reconstructed as the Postville Courthouse State Historic Site. A fine collection of memorabilia is on display at Lincoln College's Lincolniana and Presidents Museums. Pekin is another town famous for its association with Lincoln's early career and foreshadowing his fame. Here he took on—and won—the case of "Black Nance," an escaped slave.

Lincoln's Tomb (*left*) is a state historic site. A 117-foot granite obelisk rises above the monument; on the base are statuettes of Lincoln at various times during his life. Lincoln's body originally lay in a white marble sarcophagus inside the tomb, but after an attempt was made in 1876 to steal it, his remains were buried beneath the floor.

The Kitchen of the Lincoln's Clapboard House (*right*) looks just as it must have when Mary was busy in it, producing the preserves, pies, and tasty meals that earned her a reputation as a superb cook. Furniture, pots and pans, and equipment, such as the washboard on the wall and the flat-iron on the range, give a strong flavor of the period. All that is missing is the aroma of fresh-baked bread.

SITES TO SEE

● **Dickson Mounds Museum** (Havana) comprises a burial mound and excavated Indian village overlooking the Illinois River. The archaeological museum features prehistoric Indian cultures, and numerous artifacts are on display.

● **Edgar Lee Masters Memorial Museum** (Petersburg) is the restored home of the author of *Spoon River Anthology*. The poet is buried in the cemetery at the edge of town, near Ann Rutledge.

● **Springfield** hosts the Illinois State Fair, one of the nation's major agricultural fairs, each August. Highlights include tractor pulls and pie-baking and husband-calling competitions. The elaborate LincolnFest, held on July 4th weekend, appeals to historians as well as those with a casual interest in Lincoln's life.

● **Dana-Thomas House** (Springfield), built 1902–04, was one of Frank Lloyd Wright's first Prairie-style homes. The house still contains the original stained-glass windows, as well as much of the furniture and many of the decorative furnishings Wright designed for the interior.

● **An original draft of the Gettysburg Address**, in Lincoln's handwriting, is on display in the lobby of the **Old State Capitol**. In 1858, Lincoln delivered his "House Divided" speech here, and his body was brought here from Washington, D.C., to lie in state after his assassination.

● **Historic Clayville** (Springfield) is a living museum re-creating country life in the mid-19th century. The **Broadwell Inn** was a stagecoach inn which has been restored.

CHICAGO

A city of various reputations—Queen City of the Lakes, Windy City, Toddling Town, and as Carl Sandburg saw it, a "wheat stacker, player with railroads, city of the big shoulders"—Chicago stacks Lake Michigan's shore with America's most extraordinary architectural accomplishments, several world-class museums, public beaches, parks and gardens, and all the ethnic diversity the immigrant waves of the 19th and early 20th centuries could fling against the Great Lakes and once endless prairie.

First visited by explorers Joliet and Marquette in 1673, laid out on a grid pattern in 1830, and connected by rail with San Francisco in 1869, Chicago quickly became the Midwest's principal broker. The Great Fire of 1871 destroyed most of her buildings, but her position as the region's freight center for crops and livestock was unshaken. Great fortunes were made, and the new riches made the city into a treasure house. Those who came here from Europe also brought great cultural vitality, and their heritage is evident in a variety of ethnic museums unsurpassed in the United States.

Above all, it is Chicago's buildings that express the excitement of the city, its adventurous sense of being on the frontier. The country's first skyscraper, the 11-story Home Insurance Building, now demolished, was built here, and today Chicago boasts the world's tallest building, the Sears Tower. Master designers like Louis Sullivan, Frank Lloyd Wright, and Mies van der Rohe set the pace for architectural experiment. In recent years this experimentation has produced the towering curved facade of the First National Bank building and the cylindrical 60-story apartment buildings of Marina City, overlooking a boat basin.

Chicago's plazas are adorned with murals and sculpture by many of the 20th century's great artists, including Pablo Picasso, Henry Moore, Joan Miró, Isamu Noguchi, and Alexander Calder.

Academic and cultural energy is supercharged here, too: the first atomic reaction took place at the University of Chicago. The city also has more than 50 colleges and universities. With about 7,000 acres of public parks, and with extensive beaches, Chicago is a town that plays hard, too—as if the Midwest invested a good part of its urge for recreation, as well as its crops, money, and creativity, in its major city.

Skyline, Lake Michigan
(*below*) The Great Fire of 1871, supposedly ignited when a cow kicked over a lantern in a wooden barn, raged for two days and destroyed 2,000 acres of the downtown area. Halted by rain and Lake Michigan, it left 90,000 people without homes and more than 17,000 buildings in ashes. The city's recovery proved as astonishing as its sudden devastation: new buildings valued at $40 million rose from the ruins in the first year after the disaster. Spurred by necessity, Chicago's urban development continued unabated, straight into the 20th century, and the history

of modern American architecture is written in the present skyline.

The Sears Tower, a cluster of nine rectangular shafts of different heights, is the world's tallest building, measuring a monumental 1,454 feet. The Reliance Building, completed in 1895, provided an archetype for the many glass-walled structures that succeeded it. Domestic buildings by Frank Lloyd Wright dot the western suburbs, and the imposing arch Louis Sullivan designed in 1894 to grace the Stock Exchange now stands in Grant Park. Tours of such landmarks begin at the ArchiCenter in the downtown area.

MAP REFERENCE

1. Adler Planetarium
2. ArchiCenter
3. Art Institute of Chicago
4. Chicago Historical Society
5. Du Sable Museum of African American History
6. Field Museum of Natural History
7. John G. Shedd Aquarium
8. John Hancock Center
9. Marina City
10. Merchandise Mart
11. Museum of Science and Industry
12. Reliance Building
13. Sears Tower
14. Soldier Field
15. University of Chicago

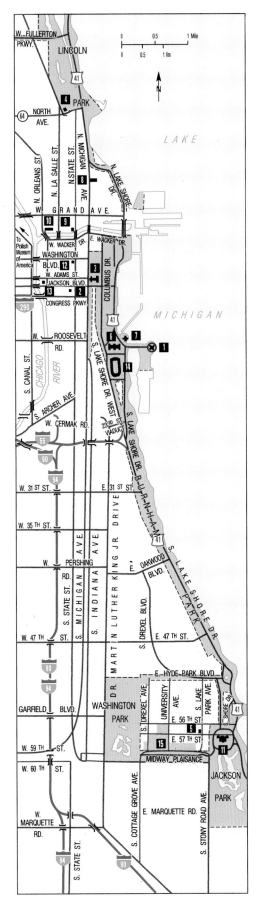

MUSEUMS

Adler Planetarium Exhibits include the telescope used to discover Uranus and moon rocks collected by the Apollo 15 mission. Visitors can watch sky shows.

Art Institute of Chicago World-famous collection that includes outstanding Impressionist and post-Impressionist paintings, Oriental and primitive art, textiles, and armor. Seurat's *Sunday Afternoon on the Island of La Grande Jatte* is here.

Du Sable Museum of African American History First U.S. museum devoted to African-American history; annual arts and crafts fair is held in July.

Field Museum of Natural History Not to be missed: Egyptian tomb chapels and the towering skeleton of the albertosaurus, plus outstanding exhibitions about North American Indians.

Museum of Science and Industry One of the world's largest museums devoted to contemporary science and technology. About 2,000 major exhibits include the Apollo 8 space capsule and a German U-505 submarine.

Polish Museum of America includes fine art, folk art, stamps, coins, and memorabilia of such famous Polish-Americans as Revolutionary War patriots Thaddeus Kosciuszko and Casimir Pulaski.

NOTABLE BUILDINGS

John Hancock Center Visitors can enjoy the views from a 94th-floor observation deck in this 100-story building of shops, offices, and apartments.

Merchandise Mart One of the world's largest commercial buildings, with about $7\frac{1}{2}$ miles of corridors and hundreds of wholesale showrooms. A $1\frac{1}{2}$-hour guided tour is available.

PARKS

Burnham Park Site of the 1932 Century of Progress World's Fair. At the north end of the park is Soldier Field, home of the Chicago Bears.

John G. Shedd Aquarium The world's largest indoor aquarium, with more than 8,000 aquatic animals and a Caribbean coral reef.

Lincoln Park Chicago's largest park contains St. Gaudens' statue of Lincoln, as well as a zoo, a conservatory covering $3\frac{1}{2}$ acres in 19 buildings, and a 9-hole public golf course. The Chicago Historical Society is here.

INDUSTRIAL PIONEERS
Indiana's Northeast Lake Country

Although it is difficult to think of the neat, well-groomed villages of northeastern Indiana as pioneering country, pioneering is a tradition here. Even the ground—the "Indian" land of flat acres, low hills, wandering streams, and shallow lakes—is a relative newcomer, created by glacial outwash dumped at the end of the Ice Age. First a province of the Potawatomi and Miami Indians, and later of French fur-trappers and traders, the region became part of the Northwest Territory in 1787 and gained statehood in 1816.

Non-Indian settlers arrived in great numbers in northeastern Indiana in the 1830s, encouraged by road and canal building that briefly bankrupted the young state. By the 1850s, when the Amish, pioneers in reverse, moved here, the Studebaker Company had created "Wheel City" in nearby South Bend. By the 1930s, northeastern Indiana was famous for the automobiles it produced and the airplane parts it manufactured.

The pioneering days are commemorated at Angola by the Little River Railroad, which runs trips featuring mock train robberies between Steubenville and Pleasant Lake. Steuben County Courthouse, modeled on Boston's Faneuil Hall, is a reminder of Angola's early prosperity.

Pokagon State Park, northwest of Angola, was named for Chief Pokagon of the Potawatomi Indians. In the early 1800s, he sold the U.S. government one million acres of land here, including the park, for three cents an acre. The park offers swimming beaches on Lake James, meadows for picnicking, and a $\frac{1}{4}$-mile toboggan slide on which speeds of 35–40 m.p.h. can be reached.

Speed enthusiasts will also want to visit the Auburn-Cord-Duesenberg Museum, housed in the former factory showroom of the Auburn Automobile Co. in Auburn. Built in 1930 for $450,000, the building has been restored to its original Art Deco splendor.

Fort Wayne, established by General "Mad" Anthony Wayne as the first American fort in this part of the Northwest Territory, contains reminders of the region's history. The Landing, a gas-lit street built in the 1830s along the Erie-Wabash Canal, and exhibits at the Allen County-Fort Wayne Historical Museum recount the canal's history. Baer Field Aviation Museum is devoted to local aviation achievements.

The Amish have always eschewed modern technology. At Amish Acres in Nappanee, Amish homes and farm equipment coexist with non-Amish period pieces and such turn-of-the-century technology as a steam-powered mint still, a relic of Indiana's days as the leading producer of peppermint and spearmint oils.

Mennonite Buggy on a Gravel Road, Johnson County (*right*) A sect of Protestant Christians that established its first American settlement in 1683, the Mennonites believe in the rejection of worldly concerns. Living in self-contained communities, they often travel and farm using horse-drawn vehicles.

The Exhibits in the Auburn-Cord-Duesenberg Museum (*left*) transported more self-indulgent and profligate travelers as well as sportsmen. Car manufacturing began in Auburn around 1900, and the Auburn Automobile Company produced the famous front-wheel-drive Cord here until 1937.

SITES TO SEE

● **Midwest Museum of American Art** (Elkhart) has a collection which includes works by Norman Rockwell, Grandma Moses, and Alexander Calder, as well as a good photography collection.

● **Ruthmere Museum** (Elkhart) is housed in a Beaux Arts mansion with a wrap-around marble verandah, built in 1908. Plush furnishings include silk wallcoverings, china from 3 presidential administrations, and original Tiffany lamps.

● **Johnny Appleseed Memorial Park** (Fort Wayne) is the grave site of John Chapman, the itinerant nurseryman who became a folk legend. The largest orchard he planted is near Fort Wayne.

● **Historic Fort Wayne** (Fort Wayne) includes a replica of the 1816 fort, with barracks, officers' quarters, and the fort kitchen, the neighboring Frontier Village, and an Indian village. Costumed guides explain everyday fort and domestic life in the early 19th century.

● **Fort Wayne Children's Zoo, African Veldt, and The Australian Adventure** (Fort Wayne) covers 38 acres, including 22 acres of African veldt, which can be toured by electric cars or walking along an elevated boardwalk.

● **Louis A. Warren Lincoln Library and Museum** (Fort Wayne) is an unusually fine collection of Lincoln memorabilia, including personal possessions and displays explaining the Lincoln era.

● **Allen County-Fort Wayne Historical Society Museum** (Fort Wayne) is in the old Fort Wayne City Hall, an 1893 Richardson Romanesque building. The collection highlights local history, featuring the building of the Erie-Wabash Canal.

● **Huddleston Farmhouse Inn Museum** (Cambridge City), an 1840 3-story Federal-style home, is refurbished with period furnishings. The complex also includes a restored barn and a smokehouse.

INDIANA'S DEEP SOUTH
Around Hoosier National Forest

The last Ice Age never reached southern Indiana. Glacially tilled central prairies farther north give way to limestone hills and deep woods, to a land of vast caves, steep meadows, and broad lakes. It is as if the state's midwestern decorum were relaxing in the southern air in this region of Indiana's superlatives: the biggest park, lake, and cave, and in that cave, for good measure, the world's largest underground mountain. Some of Indiana's earliest settlements are along the winding Ohio River, and the boyhood home of Abraham Lincoln is preserved in the state's southwest corner.

Indiana's non-Indian settlements followed the Ohio River. The first capital, at Corydon, is less than ten miles from the river bend where Harrison Crawford State Forest, one of the largest pieces of land, lies. Indiana's constitution was drafted under Corydon's Constitution Elm, now just a trunk. On July 4th, at the annual Old Settlers Days celebrations, visitors can watch the re-enactment of Indiana's only Civil War engagement, when Gen. John H. Morgan's Confederate Raiders crushed the home guard.

Jeffersonville's Howard Steamboat Museum is housed in a mansion built 1890–94 and lavishly furnished by the founder of the Howard Shipyards. It contains paddleboat and river memorabilia; the furnishings provide a fascinating reminder of the Ohio's gilded years.

Indiana's largest caves are at Wyandotte, near Corydon. Gunpowder was manufactured at Big Wyandotte Cave during the Civil War. It has extensive tunnels and chambers, and what is boasted

of as the world's largest underground cave. Marengo Cave is famous for its onyx chambers. The Squire Boone Caverns were discovered in 1790 by Daniel and Squire Boone, and are now part of a complex that include's the midwest's largest collection of Indian artifacts.

Nationally important collections at Indiana University in Bloomington house Shakespeare folios and Jefferson's copy of the Bill of Rights, the Elizabeth Sage Costume Collection in Wylie Hall and murals by Thomas Hart Benton.

At Spring Mill State Park, near Mitchell, a restored village commemorates a typical community that sprang up to support farmers who brought their grain to the local gristmill.

Around Bedford, limestone was quarried for some of the nation's most famous buildings, including New York's Empire State Building. Visit the quarries and take a one-hour underground cruise at Bluespring Caverns to see how nature quarried the limestone.

The Lincoln Boyhood National Memorial (*left*) stands on the farm where Lincoln lived from 1816 to 1830. A replica of a pioneer cabin like the one he inhabited and the activity on nearby Living Historical Farm, where frontier farming methods are used, paint an evocative portrait of life in this rugged wilderness.

Brown County (*above*) contains some of Indiana's most picturesque woodland scenery. The hills are thick with dogwood and redbud, and the vast expanse of limestone that spreads from the Ohio River to Bloomington is laced with mineral springs and rushing streams that appear suddenly and vanish underground just as unexpectedly.

SITES TO SEE

● **Hoosier National Forest** (Bedford) encompasses 188,000 acres, with camping, picnicking, boating, fishing, and horseback-riding facilities, including 13,000 acres of primitive forest for hiking.

● **Hillerich and Bradsby Co. Inc.** (Jeffersonville) are manufacturers of the legendary Louisville Slugger baseball bat. A museum displays bats belonging to the biggest names in baseball.

● **Culbertson Mansion State Historic Site** (New Albany) is the 1869 French Second Empire-style home of one of the state's early entrepreneurs. The interior features Italian marble fireplaces and an exquisite mahogany and rosewood staircase. The mansion is in a neighborhood of Victorian homes known as the **Mansion Row Historic District**.

● **Virgil I. Grissom Memorial** (Spring Mills State Park) honors the local astronaut who died on the launchpad at Cape Kennedy in 1967. In addition to his personal memorabilia, the site includes the Gemini III space capsule.

● **T. C. Steele State Historic Site** (Belmont) preserves the home and studios of landscape painter Theodore Clement Steele, founder of the Brown County Art Colony. More than 150 of his paintings are on display, and nature trails are marked out on the grounds, where picnicking is permitted.

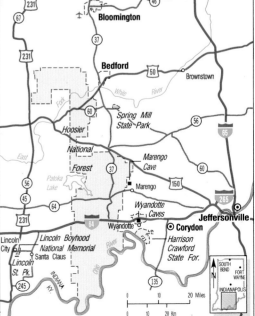

MOUND-BUILDERS AND IRON-MAKERS
Ohio's Southern Forests

Ohio's Hanging Rock iron region was once dotted with massive furnaces. The truncated sandstone pyramids, resembling Mayan temples, devoured trees for charcoal and turned the abundant ore into pig iron. When they fell cold, they soon succumbed to the underbrush and became crumbled mounds. At Chillicothe, there are other mounds, the ancient Hopewell Indians' ceremonial centers. Like the furnaces, these mounds spurred a great network of trade and, for a time, fused diverse cultures into a durable civilization. Then the rituals cooled, and the mounds became, like the old iron furnaces, massive tokens of cultural brevity.

The most fully restored of Ohio's 19th-century ironworks is the Buckeye Furnace in Wayne National Forest. The site contains a magnificent blast furnace, the stockpile building, the bridge loft from which the furnace was charged, and the casting shed where the molten iron was fed through a channel known as the "sow" into molds known as "pigs." The former company office has been re-created in the old company store. It contains a wide variety of period goods, from lunch pails to spittoons.

The tons of wood, ore, and limestone these furnaces consumed like angry woodland gods were carried in horse- or ox-drawn wagons. The mountains of earth which the Hopewell Indians piled up at Mound City Group National Monument, their ceremonial center near Chillicothe, were carried in baskets on human backs. These mounds were built over cremation sites, and this place became a city for the dead. It was also the center of a vast trade network that allowed the dead to be adorned with precious goods from the Rockies, Chesapeake Bay, Ontario, the Smokies, and the Great Lakes. The excellent visitor center displays objects such as copper antlers for a headdress, necklaces, and pipes that are bird- and animal-shaped.

North of Chillicothe and the Buckeye Furnace are the remarkable rock formations, gorges, cliffs, and waterfalls of Hocking Hills State Park. The park, one of Ohio's most popular tourist areas, is a wonderland of erosion: a spectacle of nature's impermanence, which the old mounds and furnaces faintly echo.

Picturesque Waterfalls (*below*), caves, and rock formations in a winding, wooded ravine make up the Old Man's Cave unit of Hocking Hills State Park. Five other units include Ash Cave, a huge rock shelter 100 feet deep, 700 feet wide, and 90 feet high, formed by erosion beneath an overhang of harder rock.

Serpent Mound (*right*), four miles from Locust Grove, is one of the finest Indian effigy mounds. The sinuous body of the serpent, in the act of swallowing an egg, is ¼-mile long and three to five feet high. Excavations show that the serpent's body was first outlined with stones, then built up with clay and earth.

SITES TO SEE

● **Death Mask Mound** (Mound City Group National Monument) is the oldest and largest mound in this prehistoric Hopewell burial site along the Scioto River. When the site was excavated, 13 individuals were found buried here along with copper falcon effigies. This was the only one of 23 mounds not damaged when a World War I training facility was built here. The **Mound of Pipes** contained such a marvelous collection of exquisitely carved pipes that about half the originals are now on display in the British Museum in London, with replicas in the visitors center. Marked trails and trailside exhibits help visitors explore the site.

● **Vesuvius Furnace** (Wayne National Forest) is one of the many 19th-century iron-producing furnaces that dotted this region of Ohio. In operation from 1833 until 1906, the furnace has been restored. **Wayne National Forest**, covering 190,000 acres, is known for its spectacular scenery, with spring and fall colors the highlights.

● **Our House** (Gallipolis) is a restored 1819 inn with period furnishings and an Americana Museum. This Ohio River town had noble beginnings when French Royalists, fleeing mob rule at home, settled here in 1790. Most were unprepared for the rugged lifestyle and moved on within 2 years.

● **Hocking Valley Scenic Railway** (Nelsonville) takes passengers on 10- and 25-mile round trips through rural countryside, with stops at Robbins Village, a pioneer community with log cabins.

● **Ohio University** (Athens) is the state's oldest university, founded in 1804. This pretty college town contains many attractive 19th-century homes.

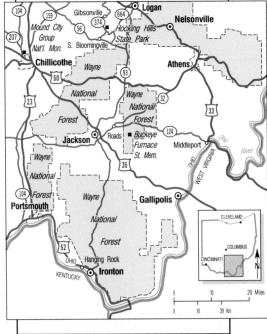

NATURE'S BUFFER BETWEEN INDUSTRIAL GIANTS

Cuyahoga Valley National Recreation Area

One of the United States' first urban recreation areas was established in 1974 between Cleveland, Lake Erie's old port city, and Akron, the world's tire-making capital. The Cuyahoga Valley National Recreation Area is 32,000 acres of land along a 22-mile section of the Cuyahoga River, which contains remnants of the old Ohio and Erie Canal, preserving a rich diversity of natural, cultural, historical, and recreational resources.

The CVNRA is a wilderness buffer between metropolitan areas north and south. It preserves floodplain, ridgetop forest, tall-grass prairie, meadows, and mature woods, making them accessible with trails for horseback riding, hiking, and bicycling. Wildflowers and birds are abundant; Deep Lock Quarry Park is a well-known gathering place for warblers on their spring migration. In the Virginia Kendall unit of the park, the Ledges Trail leads past outcroppings of "luckystones," and from its Ice Cave, a cooling breeze issues all summer long.

In addition to these gentle wilderness pleasures, the CVNRA preserves some of the first encroachments on its wildness as monuments. The park headquarters occupies the former Company Store and some mill workers' modest houses at Jaite, a turn-of-the-century company town. Tracts of the dried-up Ohio and Erie Canal are also preserved.

Hale Farm and Village at Bath are the most elaborate preservations. The farmstead was built in 1826 by Jonathan Hale, modeled after farms in his native Connecticut. Today, the house contains memorabilia and artifacts.

At The Village, historic buildings have been collected to re-create a 19th-century village, complete with village green. A splendid barn, built like a fortress from massive notched logs, houses a glass factory. The complex also has a small farm and a pottery which makes traditional salt-glazed stoneware.

South of the recreation area in Akron is Stan Hywet Hall and Gardens, an extravagant mansion. The home of Frank Sieberling, co-founder of Goodyear Tire and Rubber Co., it was designed as a faithful reproduction of an English Tudor manor house—even the stone-flagged corridors were artificially worn to suggest great age. The balconied Great Hall and delightful gardens create a mood of rough Elizabethan glory.

The Yellow Warbler (*left*) is a common species in the park, and in spring thousands of these little birds gather in the Deep Lock Quarry area before migrating. The occasional pair will, however, remain behind to nest and raise their young.

Steam Locomotives (*right*) on the Cuyahoga Valley Line offer enthusiasts a chance to indulge their nostalgia. Starting from Independence on Saturday and Sunday mornings, June to October, excursion trains run through the park, alongside the river and the Ohio and Erie Canal, to Quaker Square in Akron. Here, in a restaurant in the former Railway Express Agency building, a collection of railroad memorabilia is displayed. Trains return from Akron in the late afternoon.

SITES TO SEE

● **Blossom Music Center** (north of Akron) is the summer home of the world-renowned Cleveland Orchestra. Open-air concerts by the orchestra and other performers, catering for all tastes, are offered almost every night. Set in woodland, seats are available in the pavilion or on the lawn; picnicking is a popular way of passing pre-concert time.

● **H.S. Wagner Daffodil Trail** (CVNRA) is bright with blossoms in April.

WORTH A DETOUR

● **Cleveland**, on the shores of Lake Erie, has much to offer visitors. The redeveloped **Flats** area, along the riverfront, is buzzing with restaurants and stores. The **Cleveland Museum of Art** is world famous for its collection that spans the story of art from ancient Egypt to contemporary works. It houses outstanding early Picassos, along with works by Van Gogh, Monet, and Jackson Pollock.

● **Chagrin Falls** (east of CVNRA) is a charming town with many 19th-century homes and stores. There is a path along the falls in the center of town.

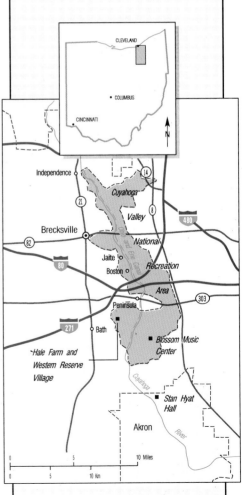

PLEASANT ISLANDS AND CALM LANDSCAPES

Lake Erie's Southwestern Shore

The landscapes are calm and peaceful where Lake Erie's gray waters make an inland sea against the flat fields of northern Ohio. It is as if this quiet kernel of the American heartland has always been immune to change. But this is an illusion. Glacial paths like the tracks of snakes can be seen on Kelleys Island; and offshore from Put-in-Bay on South Bass Island, on 10 September 1812, 28-year-old Oliver Hazard Perry aimed his fleet point-blank at the seasoned British and blasted them into surrender in the Battle of Lake Erie. Thomas Edison, whose inventions changed the world, was born in Milan, nine miles south of the lake.

Ferries depart regularly from Marblehead and Sandusky for the pleasant islands just north of the Marblehead Peninsula. On Kelleys Island, named for two brothers who owned the entire island in the middle of the 19th century, rent a bicycle for an easy ride to Glacial Grooves, formed 25,000 years ago, when glacial action scored parallel channels several inches deep in the limestone bedrock. Excavation has exposed an area some 400 feet long to show the finest example of such grooving in the western hemisphere.

A shorter ride, past some fine old lakeside homes, takes you to Inscription Rock State Memorial, a huge weathered slab of limestone, which was engraved with enigmatic pictographs some 400 years ago, probably by Erie Indians. The carvings, whose significance is unknown, include at least eight human figures, some wearing headdresses and smoking pipes, and animal and bird forms. They are now nearly obliterated from the rock, but in 1850 Captain Seth Eastman of the U.S. Army made a sketch of the pictographs, and a copy of his sketch is displayed at the site.

On South Bass Island, Perry's Victory and International Peace Memorial commemorates the United States' naval victory and the ensuing peace between Britain, Canada, and the U.S. Heineman Winery at Put-In-Bay offers tours and a visit to Crystal Cave, an enormous geode—a hollow rock with strange crystalline forms of celestite—in which the largest crystal is 24 inches long by 18 inches wide and weighs around 200 pounds.

The orchards of the Marblehead Peninsula on the mainland are famous for their apples and peaches, and the area produces most of Ohio's wine. Northwest of Locust Point, the lush marshes and woods of Crane Creek State Park line the lakeshore. The 79-acre park offers boating, fishing, and swimming, and there are both hiking and bicycle trails; hunting is allowed with a licence.

To the south is the rich farmland of the Western Reserve, given to residents of New England in 1792 to compensate them for property which had been destroyed by the British during the Revolutionary War. These so-called "Firelands" are featured in the collections of Norwalk's Firelands Museum.

At Milan, visit the birthplace of Thomas Edison, America's most ingenious inventor. Among the memorabilia are several of his inventions, including an electric light bulb with a filament of charred bamboo, and a talking doll. Behind the modest house is the grassy channel of the old Milan Canal. When Edison was a boy, the canal carried vast tonnages of grain to Lake Erie's docks. A walking tour of historic houses in the town is available.

In charming Vermilion, the Great Lakes Historical Society Museum depicts the history of shipping on the Great Lakes.

Put-In-Bay (*above*) on South Bass Island, is one of Ohio's main recreation centers. During the summer, its fine marina and sheltered moorings are crowded with sailing boats. Swimming and fishing in the lake also attract thousands of local people and tourists. Put-In-Bay can be reached April to November by ferry.

Grooves in the Rock (*left*) on Kelleys Island give a graphic insight into the region's geological past. Glacial erosion a million years ago cut through the rock to reveal marine fossils, indicating that all the land bordering Lake Erie was once underwater.

Apple Orchards (*right*), peach orchards, and vineyards clothe much of the western part of the Marblehead Peninsula. In the summer, when the trees yield their luscious bounty, crates of fruit are packed to find their way to the nation's supermarkets.

The 20-mile drive around the peninsula, which forms the northern shore of Sandusky Bay, affords fine views of the lake and surrounding countryside. The town of Marblehead, at the tip of the peninsula, is a delightful summer resort and fishing center.

SITES TO SEE

● **Hayes Presidential Center** (Fremont) preserves Spiegel Grove, Rutherford B. Hayes's home from 1873 until he became president in 1877, then again after he left Washington, D.C. On a 25-acre estate, the large Victorian home contains family furniture and belongings, along with the former president's personal letters, papers, and library. The property is guarded by six gates that were in position at the White House during the Hayes administration. Hayes and his wife, Lucy, are buried on the grounds.

● **Perry's Victory and International Peace Memorial** (South Bass Island), 352 feet tall, is reached by ferry from Port Clinton or Catawba Point. The column, made of pink granite, has an open-air observation deck on top.

● **Train tours of South Bass Island**, lasting about 1 hour, depart from Put-In-Bay in the summer.

● **Harbour Town** (Vermillion) is the restored riverfront, recalling the heyday of Great Lakes shipbuilding here, when many of the town's residents were ship captains.

● **Cedar Point** (Sandusky) is the region's largest and most popular amusement park. Over 100 years old, the park contains hair-raising roller coaster rides, as well as more than 40 other rides and African safari shows with exotic animals; beaches and picnicking facilities are also available.

● **Follett House Museum** (Sandusky), housed in an 1837 Greek Revival mansion, displays domestic memorabilia from the 19th century, and artifacts from the Johnson's Island Confederate Officers' Prison across the bay; an estimated 12,000 prisoners were kept here.

● **Marblehead Lighthouse** (Lakeside), built in 1821 at the tip of the Marblehead Peninsula, is reached via scenic SR 163 from Port Clinton.

● **Wineries** dot the countryside on the mainland as well as on the islands. Most welcome visitors, and many have free tastings.

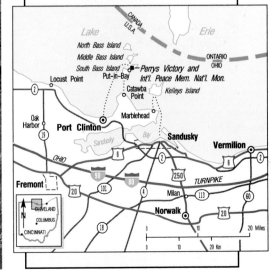

LAND OF LONG HORIZONS

Michigan's Upper Peninsula

Bounded by three of the five Great Lakes, covered by wide tracts of boreal forests and sparkling with lakes, rivers, and waterfalls, Michigan's Upper Peninsula is a wild place. It is spacious, clean, and lonely, a land of long horizons chilled in winter and cooled in summer by Canadian winds. By virtue of a remarkably well-preserved heritage of fur-trapping, iron mining, and maritime commerce, the Upper Peninsula is also one of the most interesting and diverse corners of the United States; its history is equally fascinating.

After the War of 1812, explorer Henry Schoolcraft and several companions sailed along the Upper Peninsula's northern shore. As they passed what is now Pictured Rocks National Lakeshore, Schoolcraft wrote, "There was no one who could recall such a scene of simple novelty and grandeur in any other part of the world." These eroded, polychrome-on-yellow cliffs and submarine outcrops lend shades of green to Lake Superior's blue waters.

It was via the Great Lakes that the first non-Indian trappers came to the Upper Peninsula, and by way of the lakes that the region's iron was later shipped to the foundries back east. The lakes are still a major thoroughfare; at Sault Ste. Marie, giant freighters, 1,000 feet long, pass through Soo Locks.

Southwest of Sault Ste. Marie is the forestland that provided charcoal for Michigan's blast furnaces. Historic Fayette Townsite in Fayette State Park is a picturesque ghost town with a restored charcoal kiln on the peninsula's southern shore.

A much greater port—once the world's biggest for shipping pine lumber—was at Menominee, the Upper Peninsula's most southerly town. The Mystery Ship Seaport here is home of the *Alvin Clark*. It sank in 1864, was recovered intact, and is claimed to be the world's oldest floating merchant ship; it is also a museum of Great Lakes history. Menominee County Historical Museum contains interesting memorabilia of the iron and lumber industries.

On the Keweenaw Peninsula, Michigan's northernmost tip, Calumet's historic district preserves streets and buildings from the town's heyday. Hancock and Houghton, its sister city, are linked by the Portage Lake Vertical Lift Bridge which forms part of the Keweenaw Waterway. Portage Lake was dredged, and a canal was cut through to Lake Superior, so boats could avoid difficult waters off the point. The area attracted many European immigrants during the copper boom of the mid-1800s, and their influence can still be felt today.

Pictured Rocks National Lakeshore (*right*) Although this picturesque parkland hugs more than 40 miles of the shoreline of Lake Superior, it is only three miles across at its widest point. The forest which covers much of the park area is a mixture of spruce, fir, pine, hemlock, and northern hardwoods. Along the shore, the spectacular effects of erosion by wind, ice, and waves can be seen in the 200-foot Pictured Rocks cliffs that rise above the lake. The Grand Sable Banks, at the northern end of the park, are the result of a retreating glacier from the close of the last Ice Age, about 10,000 years ago. The five square miles of sand dunes which surmount the banks mark the edge of the predecessor of the present lake. The park provides year-round recreation possibilities: hiking, camping, fishing, boating, and picnicking in the warmer months, and cross-country skiing throughout the winter.

Tahquamenon Falls State Park (*left*) The Upper Falls on the Tahquamenon River are a popular destination for boat trips. The Tom Sawyer Riverboat Cruise provides regular scheduled trips which leave from Slater's Landing, near Hulbert and last about 4½ hours. There is also a combination boat and narrow-gauge train ride which departs from Soo Junction. At the crest, the Upper Falls are 48 feet high and 200 feet wide. Farther downriver, a series of cascades and rapids forms the Lower Falls, which are divided by an island. You can also reach both the Upper and Lower Falls by car, via SR 123 between Newberry and Paradise.

SITES TO SEE

● **Sault Ste. Marie**, Michigan's oldest town, preserves several historic districts. Self-guiding walking tours are available along the waterfront, through the original commerical district, and through a restored neighborhood. Explorer Henry Schoolcraft's home is preserved, along with other 17th-century buildings.

● **Boat trips through Soo Locks** (Sault Ste. Marie) are available at the docks. East of the locks, the **Tower of History** provides sweeping views of the locks, the town, and St. Mary's River from an observation point 21 stories up. A small museum here recalls the history of Great Lakes shipping and the town's development.

● **Museum Ship Valley Camp** (Sault Ste. Marie) is housed on a former Great Lakes freighter.

● **Historic Fayette Townsite** (Fayette State Park) is the ghost town abandoned in 1891. The site includes the restored charcoal kilns, a hotel, and homes built when the town was a prosperous pig-iron smelting community.

● **Coppertown, U.S.A.** (Calumet) explains the influence of copper mining on the region's history with a simulated mine and old equipment displays. There are also photographic exhibits and miners' memorabilia. The **Calumet Theatre**, opened at the turn of the century as an opera house, is preserved and still used for concerts.

● **Copper Harbor**, Michigan's northernmost community, is a popular resort that has retained much of its charm and atmosphere from yesteryear. In the boom days of copper mining, this now quiet harbor prospered as the region's leading port. Nearby **Ft. Wilkins State Park** contains the partially restored fort, built in 1844 and abandoned in 1870. Restored officer quarters are among the log buildings open to visitors.

● **Historical Museum** (Marquette) displays Indian and pioneer artifacts, as well as memorabilia of the lumber and mining industries and Great Lakes shipping.

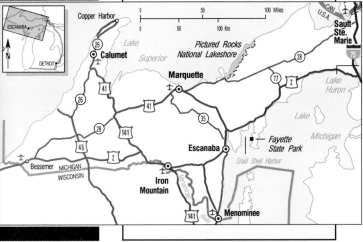

SLEEPING BEAR AND CHERRY PIES

Sleeping Bear Dunes National Lakeshore

When Frenchman Jean Nicolet set out to explore Lake Michigan in 1634, he was so sure *michi gami* (great water) would be the fabled Northwest Passage to the Orient that he took a damask coat to wear when he met the Chinese emperor. Michigan's northwest shore may not be a land of spice and silk, but it is rich with forests and orchards, scenic harbors, and tranquil beaches that have shifting sand mountains and sparkling water. It whispers with romance. Indeed, it may be impossible to find any place more unlike the conventional image of the sensible Midwest than this stretch of Michigan, where only the friendliness of the people and the prevalence of fresh-baked cherry pies give the location away.

The Chippewa Indians, whose narrow birch-bark canoes once plied these offshore waters like graceful waterfowl, have a legend about the great sand dunes on Michigan's western shore. Once, they say, very long ago, a great forest fire swept across Wisconsin. To escape, a mother bear and her two young cubs dived into Lake Michigan, hoping to swim to the far shore. The mother reached safety, but her cubs drowned. Greatly saddened, Manitou, the great spirit power, created North and South Manitou islands to mark the cubs' graves. The mother bear, it is said, still waits for her cubs to reach shore: her sleeping golden body forms the 480-foot Sleeping Bear Dune.

The best way to see the bear's wonderful park is via Pierce Stocking Scenic Drive. It traverses the dune tops into

forested valleys and provides great views of the shore's bays and inlets, the islands, and the inland ridges and lakes to the east. At sunset on a calm day, the lake is silvery and traced with a fine texture of currents.

The 35 miles of trails crisscross the tops of the dunes. You can climb the dunes and scramble down the steep face of Sleeping Bear Dune to a tiny beach, but the return climb is very arduous. The 130-foot Dune Climb, near the start of the Pierce Stocking Scenic Drive, is easier.

The Sleeping Bear Point Coast Guard Station at Glen Haven houses the Maritime Museum, which was built in 1901 when the Manitou Passage was a major shipping route.

To the north, the coast dips into Grand Traverse Bay. Traverse City lies at the base of this "great crossing," bounded by cherry orchards that bloom in early May. North of the city, the Old Mission Peninsula, whose tip is halfway between the Equator and the North Pole, is named for a reconstructed 1836 Indian mission. The Chateau Grand Travers Vineyards overlook the bay and offer tours.

Northeast of Traverse City, scenic US 31 follows the water's edge through silver woods along the path French voyagers used in the 1790s. Sometimes, especially when the morning and evening fogs stir along the shore, it seems as if the spirit of the Great Manitou still breathes here.

Birch Forest in Winter
(*left*) When nearly all of Michigan was covered with forests, animals like beavers provided the fur trade with a valuable stock of pelts. In the 1930s, the growing lumber industry attacked the forests for raw materials. The hard wood of these white birches makes excellent flooring and beautiful furniture.

South Manitou Island Lighthouse, Sleeping Bear Dunes National Lakeshore
(*right*) In 1871, this lighthouse was built to guide ships safely into the island harbor. Fog bells, whistles, and sirens were all 19th-century lighthouse innovations, but ships were still wrecked on the rocks, and their ruins can still be seen here.

SITES TO SEE

● **Sleeping Bear Point Coast Guard Station Maritime Museum** (near Glen Haven) was built in 1901, when the Manitou Passage was a major Great Lakes shipping route. By 1931, drifting sands threatened to engulf the building, so it was dragged by horses over the dunes to its present location. Displays feature memorabilia from the U.S. Lifesaving Service, U.S. Coast Guard, and Great Lakes shipping. The boathouse has been restored to its 1901 condition, including period rescue boats and equipment. Equipment includes a Lyle gun, used to shoot lifelines to people stranded on a shipwreck.

● **The Visitor Center for Sleeping Bear Dunes National Lakeshore** (Empire), open year round, explains the natural and cultural history of the region, and a slide program highlights the park's features; rangers are on hand to answer questions.

● **Valley of the Giants** (South Manitou Island) is 80 acres of virgin white-cedar trees, some 500 years old. Ferry services from Leland are available from May through mid-October. The *Francisco Morazan* freighter wreck is visible from the island's south shore; the best viewing point is signposted off the trail leading to the cedars.

● **Clinch Park** (Traverse City) features native wildlife and fish in a zoo and aquarium; steam train tours of the zoo are available.

WORTH A DETOUR

● **Interlochan Center for the Arts** (Interlochan) is home of the National Music Camp and the Interlochan Arts Academy on a 1,200-acre campus. Established in 1928, the center gives year-round classes in music, art, dance, and drama. Highlight of the year is the 8-week Interlochan Arts Festival each summer with more than 400 concerts, art shows, plays, musicals, and operas. Visitors can attend the festival's events, and visit classes and rehearsals.

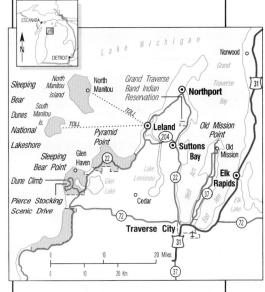

TIP OF THE MITTEN

Michigan's Dire Straits

Summer fogs, autumn storms, and thick wintry ice besiege the wild, windy passage of the Straits of Mackinac. When the French first explored the area in the 1630s, Ojibwa and Huron Indians fished the waters from their birch-bark canoes. By the 1930s, great freighters steamed up the Lake Huron shore to pass through the straits and turn south to the busy port of Chicago. The lighthouses that guided them are empty now, but modern voyagers still flock to the region's quiet resort towns nestled amid birch and pine.

St. Ignace was still wilderness when, in 1671, the Jesuit missionary Father Jacques "Père" Marquette built a bark-covered chapel here and made friends with the resident Ojibwa. The mission village soon became an important base for the exploration of the Midwest and for the booming fur trade. To see the country as Father Marquette saw it, visit Wilderness State Park on Waugoshance Point across the straits from St. Ignace, or the Father Marquette National Memorial and Museum in Straits State Park.

The garrison at St. Ignace moved to Detroit in 1701, and the Jesuits abandoned their mission several years later and moved on. The Fort de Buade Museum, built on the original site of the old fort there, contains fascinating depictions of the French settlers' lives.

In 1715, the French built a new fort, Michilimackinac, where Mackinaw City now stands. Beside the impressive span of the Mackinac Bridge, wooden palisades still buttress the restored houses and offices of the old fort against the fierce winds. Mackinaw Maritime Park adjoins the fort, and the Old Mackinac Point Lighthouse serves as a small museum of shipping in the Straits area.

The British moved the fort to Mackinac Island in 1781, 20 years after they took control of the straits. Perched on cliffs above the blue water, Fort Mackinac preserves the history of its 115 years of Indian, British and American occupation. The restored fort includes original buildings and touching curiosities, as well as regular cannon and musket firings.

Among the other interesting sites on the island are the original headquarters of John Jacob Astor's American Fur Trading Company, and the stately Grand Hotel, which dates from the island's early days as a fashionable resort.

Automobiles are not permitted on the island, but horse-and-carriage tours are available and bicycles can be rented, making SR 185 around the island the safest highway in the nation.

A Tour in a Horse-drawn Carriage (*left*) is the best way to see Mackinac Island. Tours, starting from the center of the shopping district on Main Street, take 1¾ hours and visit major scenic and historic points of interest, including Fort Mackinac, Arch Rock, Skull Cave, Governor's Mansion, and the Grand Hotel.

Mackinac Bridge (*above*), with its long, graceful curve, joins Mackinaw City with St. Ignace on the straits' northern shore. Opened in 1957, it unites the two parts of the state. Edged by four of the Great Lakes, Michigan contains more fresh-water shoreline than any other state, and fishing boats dot every cove.

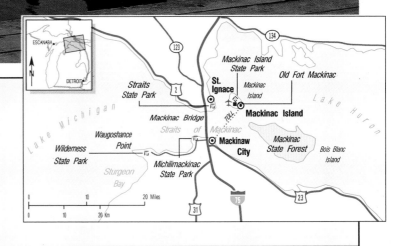

SITES TO SEE

● **Mill Creek State Historic Park** (Mackinaw City) features the excavation of an 18th-century industrial complex, possibly the oldest in the area. Log-cutting demonstrations are given in the rebuilt water-powered sawmill that cut lumber for the construction of Fort Mackinac. Guides in period costume give various craft demonstrations.

● **Mackinac Bridge** spans 5 miles, making it one of the world's longest suspension bridges.

● **Mackinac Island** contains numerous restored buildings in addition to the fort. The **Beaumont Memorial** preserves the 1820 medical practice of Dr. William Beaumont, a U.S. Army surgeon who specialized in the human digestive system. **Biddle House**, believed to be the island's oldest original building, contains 19th-century furniture.

DETROIT

After its establishment in 1701 as Fort Pontchartrain du Detroit, to protect the French fur trade, the next 124 years of Detroit's history tell of regulating the passage of trade goods, of the city's changing hands rapidly between the French, British, and Americans, and of its being the center of Indian land annexation: from the start, Detroit knew a lot about mobility.

In 1825, completion of the Erie Canal cut travel time between New York and Detroit, and commerce with the East rapidly increased, changing Detroit into a thriving port.

The real change in Detroit's fortunes, however, came one day in 1896, when a young Detroiter, Henry Ford, drove a motorized four-wheel bicycle nine miles from the city to his family's homestead in Dearborn. Although he did not know it, he was about to give Detroit, and the rest of the nation, its wheels. With a large pool of cheap immigrant and black labor, the great auto plants followed Ford's lead, and the city grew wealthy. The richest of the rich moved to the lakeshore communities around Grosse Pointe, which still has some of the most valuable real estate in the country.

Meanwhile, Detroit sprawled around the parks, galleries, and great buildings that wealth had brought, obliterating all but a few traces of an elegant city plan inspired by L'Enfant's Washington, D.C.; a suggestion of the early formality remains in the convergence of the roads at Grand Circus Park. Today, this most heavily industrial of the United States' great cities is also one of its most fascinating, not only for its cultural facilities, but also for the record it preserves of a town responsive to its location, resources, and opportunity, a very American town—Motown.

Paddleboat Travel (*below*) is a leisurely pleasure of the past. But old steamers still navigate the Detroit River, now one of the world's busiest international waterways, as far as Boblo Island.

Belle Isle (*above*) When children have exhausted the extensive outdoor pleasures of slides, tunnels, and climbing structures of wood and heavy net, they can be entertained indoors at the Dossin Great Lakes Museum. Among the exhibits are scale models of the first sailboat and steamboat that sailed the Great Lakes. The massive restored lounge from a 1912 luxury steamer is also on display.

HISTORIC SITES AND DISTRICTS

Fort Wayne Built in the 1840s to protect the U.S.-Canadian border, this fort was only abandoned by the military in the 1960s. Restored buildings include the 1848 Georgian-style barracks that now houses a museum of military history in Detroit; the 1906 married officers' quarters contain the Great Lakes Indian Museum.

MUSEUMS

Detroit Institute of Arts An outstanding collection of paintings, sculpture, silver, and 18th-century furniture. A 27-panel mural by Diego Rivera, focusing on Ford's River Rouge plant, fills an entire room.

Detroit Science Center Hands-on exhibits, as well as technology and science workshops and demonstrations. The space theater uses the $67\frac{1}{2}$-foot tilted dome as a screen for films.

NOTABLE BUILDINGS

Detroit Public Library A 1921 Renaissance Revival building known for allegorical murals.

General Motors Building When built in 1922, this was the nation's largest office building. Designer Albert Kahn also designed Packard, Ford, and Chrysler plants.

Moross House The city's oldest brick house, built in the 1840s in Federal and Greek Revival styles. Today it houses the Detroit Garden Center and contains 1850s furniture.

PARKS

Belle Isle Park A 1,000-acre park in the Detroit River with beaches, boating facilities, formal gardens, and a children's playground, as well as an aquarium and a zoo, with an elevated walkway through exhibits of uncaged animals.

Boblo Island An amusement park with three roller coasters on a 272-acre site in the Detroit River. Moonlight cruises start from here.

WORTH A DETOUR

Edsel and Eleanor Ford House In suburban Grosse Point Shores, this 1929 house was built for Henry Ford's only son and his family in the rural style of the English Cotswolds. Furnishings are English, 18th-century French, and Art Deco, with Old Masters and Impressionist paintings.

Fair Lane On the University of Michigan's Dearborn campus, this house was built in 1914 for Henry and Clara Ford; rooms today are furnished in 1920s style. One of Mrs. Ford's rose gardens has been restored.

Henry Ford Museum and Greenfield Village In neighboring Dearborn, these two sites comprise the nation's largest museum complex; the scope, variety, and quality of displays are extraordinary, and a visit could easily last several days. The museum covers most aspects of America's cultural and technological history. Curiosities and memorabilia include George Washington's campaign chest and the chair Abraham Lincoln was sitting in when he was assassinated. Major agricultural, industrial, transportation, and communication exhibits include a replica of the first steam train, and oil-burning engines as large as houses. Domestic and decorative arts are also fully represented. Greenfield Village is a world of its own, with wide, tree-lined streets and numerous historical buildings brought here from their original locations, including the Wright brothers' cycle shop from Dayton, Ohio, and Thomas Edison's laboratory from Menlo Park, New Jersey.

Cranbrook Educational Community Established in the 1920s by newspaper publisher George G. Booth, this cultural center in Bloomfield Hills includes an art academy, a science institute, 40 acres of formal gardens, and Booth's mansion, **Cranbrook House**, which was designed by Albert Kahn.

MAP REFERENCE

1 Detroit Institute of Arts
2 Detroit Public Library
3 Detroit Science Center
4 Fort Wayne
5 General Motors Building
6 Moross House

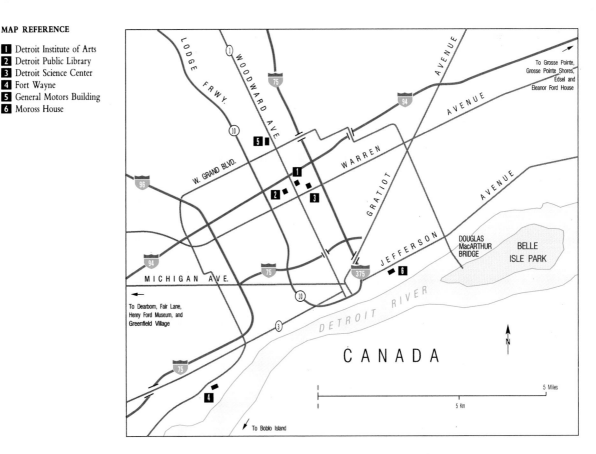

THEATER OF THE DELLS

Wisconsin's Dairyland

If south-central Wisconsin's dairyland image seems a little bland, dispel it by visiting the Dells. Here Holsteins and cheddar are upstaged by sites and pleasures that include gilded circus wagons, a dragon-festooned church, buried treasure in a blue hill, and a real house with a giant merry-go-round and waterfalls, perched on a 400-foot-high rock. Winnebago Indian legend identified the area as the track of an enormous serpent. Today, this picturesque region is known as the spectacular Dells of the Wisconsin River.

The first circus came to Wisconsin in 1847, a year before statehood. In 1884, the Ringling brothers staged their first show at Baraboo, and the town soon became the circus's winter home. Baraboo's Circus World Museum has one of the world's largest collections of circus wagons—trundling masterpieces of gilded carving and ornate decoration—as well as shows under the Big Top.

Just a few miles from Baraboo is a quite different showplace, Devils Lake. Ringed on three sides by quartzite cliffs created by glaciation, the lake is fed by springs and has no visible outlet. In the surrounding park, one of several areas forming the Ice Age National Scientific Reserve, there are exhibits and naturalist programs explaining features of the landscape that are the result of glacial action

At North Freedom, the Mid-Continent Railway Museum offers a restored 1894 depot, antique locomotives and rolling stock, and steam-train rides through the rolling valley.

The beautiful Wisconsin River wanders between eroded cliffs and isolated, top-heavy columns of rock. At Stand Rock, a natural amphitheater is used for authentic Winnebago ceremonies, and the Winnebago Indian Museum has a fine collection of artifacts and ceremonial items.

There are also theatrics at Wisconsin's most remarkable house: The House on the Rock, south of Spring Green, an eccentric masterpiece perched on a 400-foot-high rock, with interior waterfalls and pools, a 350-foot-long observation deck, and a giant carousel. Blue Mounds offers a house inside a rock—the colorful Cave of the Mounds. Discovered during quarrying in 1939, it is notable for its theatrically lit, multi-colored formations. Blue Mound is the site of buried Winnebago treasure, according to legend, and in 1828, a prospector named Ebenezer Brigham began to mine valuable lead here.

Little Norway is a traditional farmstead in Nissedahle, in the wooded Valley of the Elves. The showpiece is the dramatic *stav-kirke* (stave church), a reproduction of a 12th-century Norwegian church, with gaudy dragon heads breathing "fire" underneath the eaves.

Picturesque Kilbourn? (*right*) In a determined effort to lure more visitors to the area, the town of Kilbourn City changed its name to Wisconsin Dells in 1931. This was only one change in a series of local events that produced this beautiful town, set along the banks of the Wisconsin River. Originally the local center of commerce in the area was the thriving town of Newport. When the railroad came through in 1856 and chose a location two miles north to cross the river, a good part of the town literally up and left for the new location called Kilbourn City. Today, Wisconsin Dells is the perfect starting point for exploring the unique rock formations of the Upper and Lower Dells. The area's geological features were extensively recorded by the landscape photographer H. H. Bennett between 1865 and his death in 1908. The striking images of his black-and-white photographs attracted tourists from near and far. Much of his work can be seen at the museum in the H. H. Bennett Studio Museum Foundation.

Circus Museum (*left*) The town of Baraboo, home of the Circus World Museum, took its name from Baribault, a 19th-century French fur trader. Later, five brothers, the sons of a German harness maker, presented their first show under the banner of the "Classic and Comic Concert Company." Eventually, this became the Ringling Brothers Circus, which had its winter home in Baraboo from 1884 until 1918, when it merged with the Barnum and Bailey Circus. The museum features live performances, a range of circus memorabilia, and a collection of circus wagons that is one of the largest in the world.

SITES TO SEE

● **Wisconsin Dells** is a popular starting point for visits to the spectacular Dells of Wisconsin. Numerous boat trips depart from here for scenic cruises along the Upper and Lower Dells of the Wisconsin River, and horse-drawn wagon trips take visitors through Lost Canyon with its 80-foot walls. There are also several family-style amusement theme parks in the area.

● **Frank Lloyd Wright's hillside house at Taliesin** (Spring Green) was the center of the Prairie School of architecture when Wright lived and taught here. Some of Wright's models and drawings are on display, along with large murals of his buildings.

● **Garrison School** (Portage), on the site of Fort Winnebago, is furnished with McGuffey readers and antique school desks. The nearby **Old Indian Agency House** is an 1832 house built for the U.S. Agent who dealt with the local Winnebago Indians, and the house was the hub of social life at Fort Winnebago. The 2-story building has been restored and furnished with 19th-century items.

● **Wollersheim Winery** (Prairie du Sac), producing wine since 1857, offers tours and tastings.

● **U.S. Forest Products Laboratory** (Madison) pioneered research into the efficient use of wood and wood products in 1910. The research continues today, and tours are available.

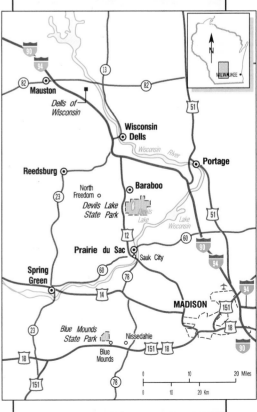

LAND OF NORTHERN LIGHT

Around Apostle Islands National Lakeshore

When Al Capone wanted peace and quiet, he left Chicago's mean streets for his North Woods hideout in sleepy Couderay. A sturdy little retreat, with its own machine-gun tower and blockhouse, it still contains some of Capone's personal belongings. This is perhaps the only reminder of life's darker side in this region of northern light, wide horizons, and clear water. There are still deep woods in this rich lumber country, but it is the soft northern clarity of the light, reflected from innumerable rivers, kettle lakes, and Lake Superior itself, that gives these landscapes their restful beauty. Even law-abiding people feel encouraged to come here for peace and quiet.

At Fred Smith's Wisconsin Concrete Park in the village of Phillips, you will encounter the brides and grooms at a 1901 double wedding, bears that look like frogs, and the chariot race from *Ben Hur*. Made by a retired logger and pulp cutter, the figures are formal, austere, and enigmatic; and in the glacier-scrubbed region that Fred Smith helped to log, they are perfectly at home.

From the picturesque harbor at Bayfield, the Apostle Islands seem to float like fat pancakes, or a mirage of flat clouds, on Superior's blue waters. All except Madeline Island, the largest, belong to the Apostle Islands National Lakeshore. Boat tours from Bayfield go to Stockton, Raspberry, and Manitou islands, prime ground for primitive camping and hiking. There is also a frequent ferry from Bayfield to La Pointe on Madeline Island.

In summer, Big Bay State Park, less than five miles from La Pointe, is a special place, with wide beaches, dunes clad with sand cherry and blue-green agropyron grass, a lagoon fringed with cattails and water lilies, woods carpeted in bracken, reindeer moss, and tasty thimbleberry patches.

In the southwest, there is another lake: a lake of grass, with islands of marsh, heath, meadow, and prairie, called Crex Meadows Wildlife Area. White-tailed deer, and even black bear, chest deep in waving marsh grass, can be seen here, as well as numerous birds: osprey, bald eagle, the stately but faintly preposterous sandhill crane, pheasant, grouse, and several hawks and herons.

North, south, and west of the reserve are the winding waters of St. Croix National Scenic Riverway; on its east bank is the Governor Knowles State Forest.

Big Bay State Park (*left*) Located on the largest island in the scenic archipelago, the state park attracts thousands of visitors every summer. Sheltered bays with shallow water provide suitable locations for swimming in mid-summer, however, the dangerously cold waters just offshore can cause swimmers to suffer hypothermia.

Hayward (*above*) The American Birkebeiner cross-country ski race, which runs from Hayward to Mount Telemark just outside Cable, is one of the largest events of its kind in North America. The race is held annually in late February. Horse-drawn carriage tours of Hayward recall the town's past as a lumbering center.

SITES TO SEE

● **LaPointe Historical Museum** (Madeline Island) is where the American Fur Co. post was established in 1816. Four log buildings are preserved with displays on Indian life, French voyageurs, and the fur-trading and fishing industries. The island's Indian burial ground contains graves covered with small house-like structures intended to provide protection for spirits.

● **Fairlawn Mansion and Museum** (Superior) has splendid views of Lake Superior and Barker's Island. Built in 1890 in the style of a French chateau, the mansion displays Victorian furnishings, shipping memorabilia, and rare Indian photographs.

● **Hayward** hosts the Lumberjack World Championships each July. Visitors can watch log-rolling, tree felling, and amazing sawing feats. The **National Fresh Water Fishing Hall of Fame** here has over 4,000 specimens.

● **Amnicon Falls State Park** offers scenery that is a textbook display of strata, upthrusts, and weathering.

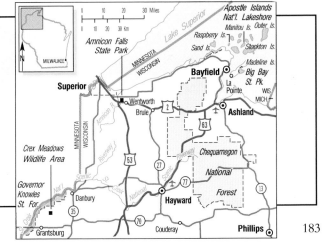

THE NORTHERN PLAINS

The northern plains states are the pivot on which America turns. To the west, beyond the flatlands of Wyoming and Montana, the Rocky Mountains thrust up like a wall above the plain. To the east are the Great Lakes, and beyond them, the worn stumps of the Appalachians. Lying placidly between these ranges, the plains are a respite: if you need to catch your breath, this is the place to do it, where Dakota buffalo once roamed in shaggy majesty, and the fields of Iowa and Nebraska mirror the sky's bowl in green and gold images of calm and plenty.

Of course, there is drama here, too. Spiritual descendants of the *voyageurs* still paddle the waterways of Minnesota's northern lakes, the clang of the iron-miner's pick still rings in the Mesabi range, and on clear nights in the great woods, if you're lucky, you can still hear wolves howl. The grasslands are still rodeo country, and the trails of America's great thrust west still rut the prairie. And in the Badlands of the Dakotas, where Teddy Roosevelt learned his rough-riding, red, gray, blue, and chalk-white pinnacles rear up to the sky, as if the world had been stripped of its grassy floor, and you were allowed to see into the great basement of gnome-carved pillars that once supported it.

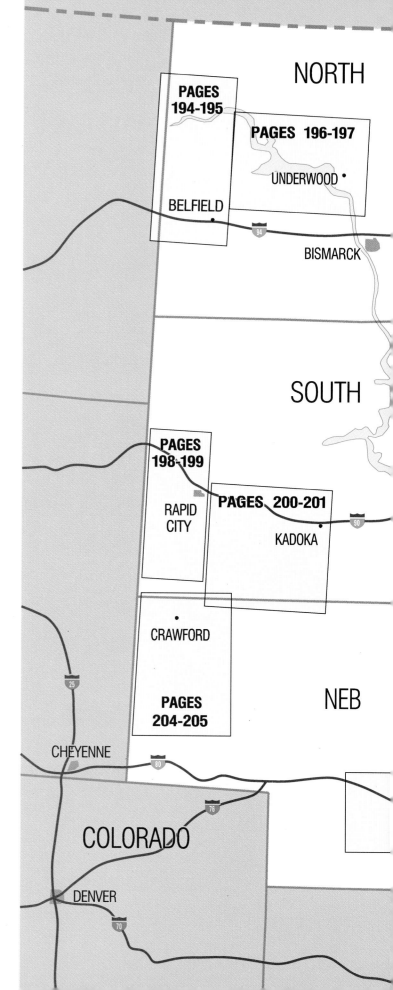

184

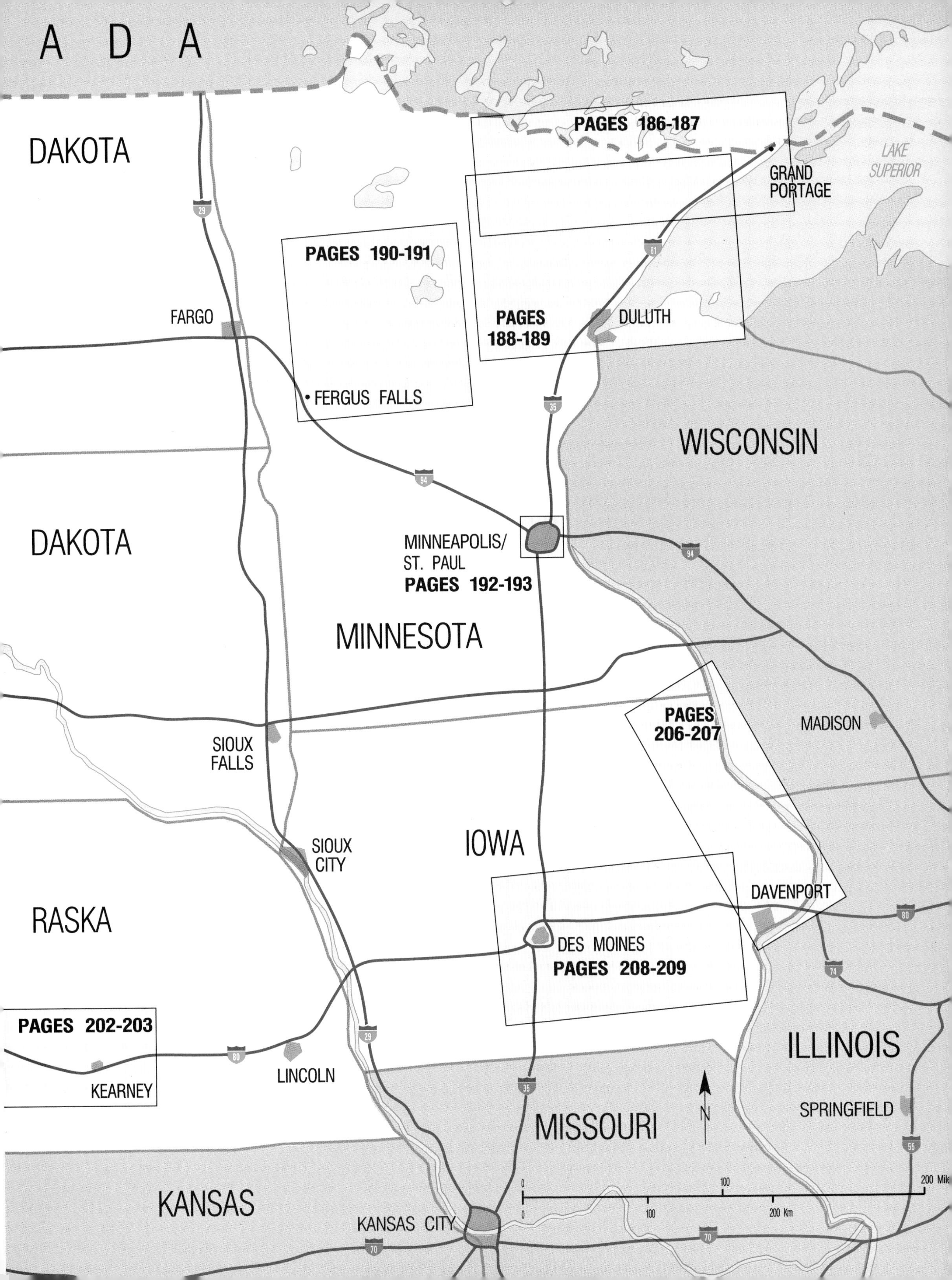

A D A
DAKOTA
PAGES 186-187
LAKE SUPERIOR
GRAND PORTAGE
PAGES 190-191
PAGES 188-189
DULUTH
FARGO
FERGUS FALLS
WISCONSIN
DAKOTA
MINNEAPOLIS/ ST. PAUL
PAGES 192-193
MINNESOTA
PAGES 206-207
MADISON
SIOUX FALLS
SIOUX CITY
IOWA
DAVENPORT
RASKA
DES MOINES
PAGES 208-209
PAGES 202-203
KEARNEY
LINCOLN
ILLINOIS
MISSOURI
N
SPRINGFIELD
KANSAS
KANSAS CITY
0
100
200 Miles
0
100
200 Km
29
61
94
35
80
74
55
70

VOYAGEURS' COUNTRY
Lake Superior's Northwestern Shore

Lake Superior's northwestern shore was once a major terminus for the fur trade. Beyond it lay a forest wilderness, rich in fur-bearing animals and laced with rivers and lakes that the voyageurs navigated by canoe; to the east lay the shipping lanes of the Great Lakes, which connected the wilderness with the east coast. Today, this part of Minnesota is changed—but not much. In vast tracts of wilderness where dense forests and island-dotted lakes are the order, loons cackle and wolves howl to each other across moonlit valleys. An 18th-century voyageur would still feel quite at home.

Grand Portage National Monument is where voyageurs carried their 90-pound packs along an 8½-mile trail to the Pigeon River and the wilderness network of lakes and rivers now constituting the Boundary Waters Canoe Area (B.W.C.A.). The peace and quiet of this picturesque area of islands is guaranteed by the restriction of motorboats along this particular section of the U.S./Canada border. Until the fur-trading North West Company left Grand Portage in 1803, this was the site of the annual July rendezvous, when furs and other goods were exchanged and old acquaintances were renewed amid great festivities. The monument includes replicas of the company's Great Hall, a kitchen filled with period utensils, and the stockade with a lookout tower open to visitors.

Outside the stockade is the warehouse, with two birch-bark canoes and other trading memorabilia. Canoes at this time were often up to 42 feet long and capable of carrying four tons of goods.

Ely, a resort town, is the site of the January All-American Dog Sled Championships and the starting point for winter dog-sled trips into the B.W.C.A.

To the northwest is the aptly named Voyageurs National Park. Here, four major lakes and 30 smaller ones lie within 219,000 acres, sprinkled with islands of marshland, water meadow, and forest.

Instead of canoeing into the national park, it is possible to fly over it on a sightseeing tour from International Falls. This town celebrates its famously harsh winters during January's Ice Box Days festival, featuring the always-popular Freeze Yer Gizzard Blizzard Run.

Rivers and Lakes (*right*) abound in Superior National Forest, and the Boundary Waters Canoe Area, lying along the Canadian border, is a federally protected wilderness canoe area. Throughout the forest, there are marked canoe trails that follow the paths the Indians and voyageurs used to take through this watery wilderness.

This Moose Cow (*left*) is probably descended from a herd that swam out to Isle Royale in the early part of this century. The moose flourished, and when the first wolf pack crossed the ice to the island in the winter of 1948-9, it found plenty of prey. But moose are also strong swimmers who take to the water in self-defense. The wolves then prey on smaller animals, like beavers. The best chance now of seeing wolves in the wild is almost certainly on the island.

SITES TO SEE

● **Isle Royale National Park** (Lake Superior, MI), reached by ferry from Grand Portage, is the biggest island in the world's biggest freshwater lake. Forty-five miles long, it is home to wolves, lynx, foxes, and martens, as well as wildflowers that include 34 kinds of orchids. Cars are not permitted.

● **Grand Mound History Center** (International Falls) is at one of the midwest's largest Indian burial mounds, and includes artifacts relating to the Laurels, who lived here until about A.D. 800.

WORTH A DETOUR

● **Lake of the Woods**, one of the world's largest lakes, has 65,000 miles of shoreline. Fed by the Rainy River,

with two-thirds of its area lying in Canada, it is 90 miles long and 55 miles wide with 14,000 islands.

● **Northwest Angle State Forest**, separated from the rest of the state by Buffalo Bay and a portion of Canada as a result of a surveyor's error in 1822, is the most northerly point of the lower 48 states.

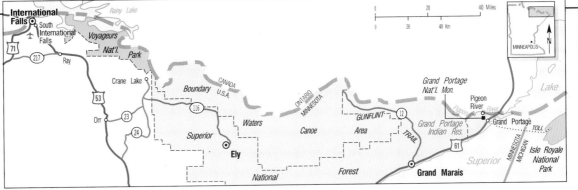

IRON COUNTRY

Northeastern Minnesota

Although iron mining has helped shape the last 100 years of northeast Minnesota's history, the landscape survives as one of the nation's great unspoiled wilderness regions. In fact, its mining heritage adds an unexpected piquancy and interest to the region. The Lake Superior shoreline remains outstandingly beautiful, all the more interesting for the ports and lighthouses that serve the ships carrying iron ore. In the same way, the character of the old iron towns gives a lively, human dimension to the clear lakes, miles of forest, rugged hills, and tumbling streams that still dominate the region's interior.

Minnesota's vast iron deposits were first discovered in the Vermilion Range in 1865. In 1890, even larger deposits were discovered in the Mesabi Range. Cuyuna, the smallest of the state's three iron ranges, is farther to the southeast. To get a sense of the scale of these mining operations, visit the Hibbing/Chisholm area, site of the world's largest open-pit iron-ore mine and the state's excellent mining museum.

Hibbing's Hull Rust Mahoning Mine was a conglomeration of 50 mines, which have produced an excavation three miles long, two miles wide, and 535 feet deep. During World War II, one fourth of all the iron ore mined in the U.S. came from this pit. It is still active, and summer visitors can witness the operations, including 18-cubic-yard shovels and 170-ton trucks nibbling away at the rust-colored escarpments.

From midair over this "man-made Grand Canyon of the north," it is possible to see where the town of Hibbing once stood; it was moved to its present site in 1918 to make way for the mine.

The Minnesota Museum of Mining at Chisholm, open May through September, displays a life-size underground model of part of the Mesabi Range mine drift, antique panoramic photographs, a unique

1910 Atlantic steam shovel, and the giant tires used on ore trucks; each tire is more than 10 feet across and weighs 5,700 pounds. Ironworld U.S.A., also near Chisholm, a park at the edge of an open-pit mine, offers excellent cultural displays and entertainment.

The Great Lakes' shipping lanes have always been essential to Minnesota's iron industry; today they are equally valuable for the shipment of grain brought by rail from the state's rich farmlands to Duluth.

Duluth is an international port, where giant ore carriers and ocean-going freighters pass beneath the massive Aerial Lift Bridge to dock in the harbor, with 49 miles of waterfront dominated by ore dumps, grain elevators, and shipyards.

Among the city's gems are Glensheen, a lakeside Jacobean-style mansion built 1905–8, and The Depot, which houses art and history displays, including a replica of an early fur-trading post, in a renovated 1892 railroad depot.

Near Duluth are a number of fine state parks. Jay Cooke, almost within city limits, has wonderful river and hill scenery, and 50 miles of trails. The George H. Crosby Manitou State Park has a variety of wilderness hiking trails, wolves, moose, and ravishing cascades.

SITES TO SEE

● **First Settlers' Museum** (Hibbing City Hall) explains how all the town's buildings were moved to their present location in 1918 to make way for the Hull Rust Mahoning Mine. Many buildings were mounted on steel wheels and trundled 2 miles south.

● **Canal Park Marine Museum** (Duluth) describes the workings and the history of Great Lakes shipping.

● **Split Rock Lighthouse State Park** (Two Harbors) preserves a 1910 lighthouse, one of the highest in the United States, and has a restored keeper's house.

● **Skyline Parkway** is a 16-mile road above Duluth with fine views of the city and harbor.

● **Lake Superior Zoo** (Duluth) is home for animals from around the world. It also has a nocturnal house and children's petting zoo.

● **United States Hockey Hall of Fame** (Eveleth) pays tribute to the sport's players and coaches on all levels from high school through college, professional, and international. Visitors can re-live exciting matches on film; classic antique hockey memorabilia is displayed.

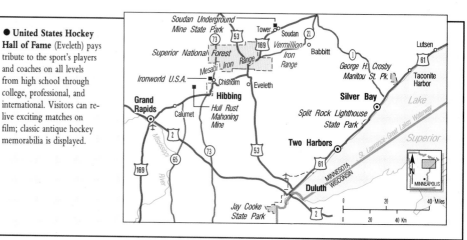

Black Bears (*top*)
roam here in fall, gorging
themselves on wild cherries
and other woodland fruit
before their long winter
hibernation.

**The Rocky, Cliff-ringed
Shores of Lake Superior**
(*above*) are clear evidence of
the area's glacial past, as are
its fertile plains and dense
evergreen forests.

Open-pit Iron Mines
(*right*) scarred the land
terribly, but many old
workings are now pastoral
recreation areas.

PAUL BUNYAN'S BACKYARD
Minnesota's Birthplace of a Legend

In this part of Minnesota, there are a wonderful number of lakes and trees. The prosaic explanation is that the low hills and numerous kettle lakes were produced by glaciers, and the forest is the primeval climax vegetation of these latitudes. More knowledgeable Minnesotans, however, have another explanation: the lakes fill the hoofprints of Paul Bunyan's blue ox, Babe, a beast with horns 42-axe-handles-and-a-plug-of-chewing-tobacco wide. Bunyan, who used four-foot logs for toothpicks and ran a logging camp somewhere between Winter of the Blue Snow and the Spring That The Rain Came Up From China, was a figure spun from the labor of those who logged here. He was "born" near Akely, where those with the eye of faith can see his "cradle."

The numerous waterways here were indispensable to the early loggers. At Grand Rapids, a former logging town at the most northerly navigable point on the Mississippi River for steamboats and other large boats, the excellent Forest History Center describes life in these northern woods from prehistoric times to the 20th century, and includes a 1934 forest ranger's cabin.

Near Brainerd, another lumber town on the Mississippi, Lumbertown U.S.A. re-creates a small Minnesota town in the 1870s, with a maple syrup mill, schoolhouse, furniture store, blacksmith and cobbler shops, and livery stable. There are rides on a replica of a Northern Pacific Railroad train and on the *Blue Berry Belle* riverboat. Helicopter sightseeing trips are available from the Paul Bunyan Amusement Center at Brainerd.

Lake Bemidji State Park offers boardwalk access to a great variety of delicate bog-dwelling plants.

Historically, the most interesting park in this area is Itasca State Park, whose 30,583 acres include virgin forest and 157 lakes. The largest is Lake Itasca, where Henry Schoolcraft discovered the source of the Mississippi in 1832. The Wilderness Drive, a paved loop road, crosses through the park.

West of Lake Itasca, in the White Earth Indian Reservation, is Tamarac National Wildlife Refuge, a prime area for ducks and geese during the spring and fall migrations. Bald eagles nest here, and golden eagles sometimes pass through on their way south in the fall. The easiest way to see the refuge is via the 10-mile Blackbird Auto Tour, which runs past wide lakes, meadows, marshes, and early-melting "potholes," where wood ducks nest in spring. The gravel road also gives easy access to the Old Indian Trail, which leads past a Sioux burial ground. The Ojibwa Indians of the Leech Lake Reservation still harvest wild rice by hand using centuries-old traditional methods.

Tranquil Lake Itasca (*right*) is the largest within the Itasca State Park, which lies on US 71 north of Park Rapids. The park has stands of virgin Norway pine, as well as specimens of almost every type of wild animal, plant, and tree found in the state, many of which can be seen along the 11-mile Wilderness Drive. Year-round naturalist programs are offered, and for the active, there are 17 miles of bike trails. Other attractions include cruises on the lake, fishing, and riding, and in winter cross-country skiing and snowmobiling are available.

The Blacksmith's Forge (*far right*) in the Forest History Center in Grand Rapids is one of many exhibits helping to re-create the atmosphere of a turn-of-the-century logging camp. Other exhibits include a modern forest management display, showing genetically improved trees, and there are two miles of self-guiding nature trails, which in winter can be followed on skis. Guided tours are also available.

Statues of the Outsized and Mythical Paul Bunyan and his Blue Ox, Babe, (*left*) stand on the lake front at Bemidji. Originally – and now again – a lumber town, Bemidji is also a great tourist center, and on July 4th weekend, when the water festival is held, attractive, old-fashioned horse-drawn carriages appear on the streets, adding to the festive atmosphere. The main event of the winter is the Finlandia Ski Marathon, held in late February.

SITES TO SEE

● **Maplewood State Park** (near Pelican Rapids) has one of the state's largest ironwood trees with a circumference of 53 inches. These trees in this state are usually only a few inches across, and botanists are not sure why this one is such an exception. The park's 9,000 acres include hills, woods, meadows, and lakes, with trails for hiking, skiing, snowmobiling, and horseback riding. The fall colors are spectacular.

● **Bemidji** hosts the annual Paul Bunyan Water Festival around the Fourth of July.

● **Walker Wildlife and Indian Artifact Museum** (Walker) displays specimens of regional wildlife, as well as a full-scale Indian village. The **Cass County Historical Museum** recaptures the past with pioneering and logging memorabilia. The town is at the edge of **Chippewa National Forest**, 663,000 acres which surround Leech Lake, one of the state's largest. Scattered tracts of virgin pine, which once covered much of the state, are preserved within the forest. Numerous camping, hiking, fishing, and boating facilities are available.

MINNEAPOLIS–ST. PAUL

More than any other major metropolitan area in the U.S., Minneapolis-St. Paul breathes a northern invigorating air. Although the Twin Cities are not, in fact, any farther north than Yellowstone National Park, only a few sizeable towns lie between them and the lake-splashed wild country stretching 1,500 miles north to the Arctic Circle. These northern miles, almost as much lake as land, impose their own character on Minneapolis-St. Paul, bringing fresh winds and punctuating the metropolitan area with more than 1,000 lakes.

At first, St. Paul was the lustier of the twins, thriving on its status as a steamboat terminus with an influx of immigrants — largely of Swedish, Norwegian, and French-Canadian origins—who served the fur, lumber, and agricultural industries. Minneapolis began to grow after the Civil War, when St. Anthony Falls was harnessed to drive lumber and flour mills. Today, St. Paul preserves a more diverse ethnic heritage (mostly German, Irish, Polish, and Italian) than predominantly Scandinavian Minneapolis, and Minneapolis has the more modern skyline with the 57-story IDS Tower, the tallest building between Chicago and San Francisco, and the 1929 obelisk of the Foshay Tower.

As lakes, parks, two rivers, and appealing ethnic diversities liven the Twin Cities, so does their cultural variety. The two cities have some 130 art galleries, 90 repertory and dinner theaters, 15 museums, and nine dance companies. St. Paul's Winter Carnival typifies how the Twin Cities embrace the natural scene, and how it embraces them.

HISTORIC SITES AND DISTRICTS

Historic Fort Snelling (M) A restored limestone fort built 1819 on a bluff of the Minnesota and Mississippi rivers. Costumed guides demonstrate blacksmithing, drilling, and baking.

MUSEUMS

American Swedish Institute (M) A turn-of-the-century mansion with Swedish glass, pewter, copper, textiles, porcelain fireplaces, pioneer tools, and memorabilia.

Children's Museum (SP) Hands-on exhibits include a car-repair shop, TV studio, a doctor's office, and a store.

Gibbs Farm Museum (SP) Antique agricultural tools and craft demonstrations illustrate urban-fringe farming from 1849 to the early 1900s.

Minneapolis Institute of Arts (M) Period furnishings, paintings, statuary, and photography are among the arts represented in this collection.

Science Museum of Minnesota (SP) Natural science exhibits, with films about space projected on a domed screen.

Walker Art Center (M) Collections featuring 20th-century American and European paintings. The interior is noted for its high-ceilinged exhibition area; adjoins Guthrie Theater.

PARKS

Eloise Butler Wildflower Garden and Bird Sanctuary (M) Displays of native Minnesota plants and flowers.

Como Park (SP) Site of a zoo and Victorian conservatory known for its floral displays, as well as an amusement park and golf course.

Indian Mounds Park (SP) Picnic facilities near mounds supposedly raised to mark burial sites of Sioux chiefs.

Minnehaha Park (M) Site of the 1849 John H. Sevens Home, the city's first permanent settler's home, now an interpretive museum.

Minnesota Zoo and Gardens (M) A model of an ideal zoo with about 1,700 animals in naturalistic environments, and 2,000 plant varieties. Five trails explore different habitats, and there is a dolphinarium.

NOTABLE BUILDINGS

Alexander Ramsey House (SP) A French-Renaissance style limestone mansion with a mansard roof. Built 1868–72, this was the home of the first governor of the Minnesota Territory, and contains a fine collection of family furnishings.

Cathedral of St. Paul (SP) Modeled after St. Peter's in Rome, the massive structure is topped with an impressive Beaux Arts dome which, with its cross, stands 280 feet tall.

Guthrie Theater (M) An architecturally unusual theater, named for the director Tyrone Guthrie, with the stage projecting into the steeply-banked 1,441-seat auditorium, so no member of the audience is more than 15 rows from the stage.

Landmark Center (SP) A cultural center occupying the former federal court building, built 1892–1902 in the Romanesque Revival style.

State Capitol (SP) Built 1896–1905, the chief splendor is the interior with its numerous examples of marble and limestone.

Ice Palace, Winter Carnival (*left*) Massive ice palaces were built in St. Paul over 100 years ago. The carnival now lasts 11 days and includes a fierce ice-fishing competition.

Dandelion fountains (*above*) and modern sculpture decorate the parks and the Minneapolis Sculpture Garden.

MAP REFERENCE

1 Alexander Ramsey House (SP)
2 American Swedish Institute (M)
3 Cathedral of St. Paul (SP)
4 Children's Museum (SP)
5 Foshay Tower (M)
6 Gibbs Farm Museum (SP)
7 Guthrie Theater (M)
8 Landmark Center (SP)
9 IDS Tower (M)
10 Minneapolis Institute of Arts (M)
11 Science Museum of Minnesota (SP)
12 State Capitol (SP)
13 Walker Art Center (M)

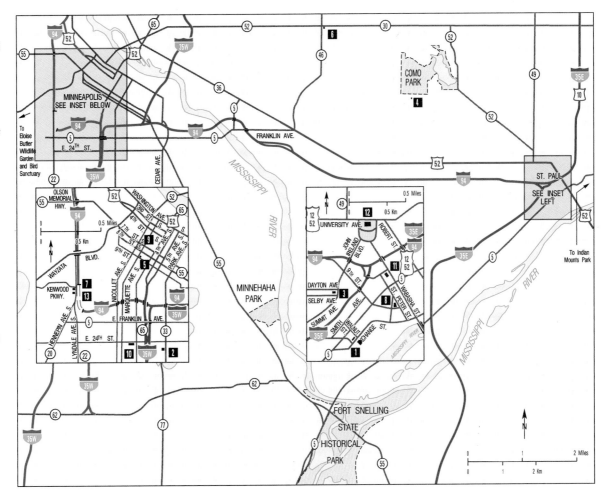

ROUGH RIDER COUNTRY
North Dakota's Badlands

An Indian-fighting general who passed dyspeptically through these Badlands thought they were "hell with the fires put out," but most visitors think they are among the most beautiful landscapes in the United States. More colorful than South Dakota's majestic Badlands, more verdant than eastern Montana's superb Makoshika Badlands, the best of North Dakota's Badlands are preserved in Theodore Roosevelt National Park. It uniquely honors the president who ranched here, established the first five national parks, and set aside 125 million acres of national forest.

In rough-rider country, the barren and the fertile interpenetrate: beyond river bends clothed in shimmering willows and cottonwoods are the polychrome striations of arid tablelands; earth colors and the colors of vegetation are juxtaposed; above soft hillsides where bison go about their quiet, prehistoric business, loom surreal pinnacles, spikes, and castellations of eroded earth.

Theodore Roosevelt came here to hunt buffalo in 1883, bought a share in the Maltese Cross Ranch, and stayed to raise cattle. His neighbor, the colorful Marquis de Mores, tried raising and slaughtering beef here to ship directly to eastern markets. At Medora, named for the marquis' red-haired American wife, he built a meatpacking station and the Chateau de Mores. This two-story, 26-room mansion was staffed by French servants, and visitors could entertain themselves with copies of *La Vie Parisienne* or with butcher knives and bear traps. It has been lovingly restored.

East of Medora, US 85 heads north toward the park's North Unit through fields of wheat and sunflowers, oddly distinguished by occasional buttes. Here a 15-mile scenic road goes to the Oxbow

Overlook. Along the way, visitors are likely to see longhorns like the ones raised during Roosevelt's time in this region.

Northwest, at the Fort Union Trading Post National Historic Site, beaver pelts and buffalo hides were traded for beads, guns, and blankets. Among those who made the 1,900-mile paddleboat journey here from St. Louis was John James Audubon, the great illustrator of America's birds and animals, and Karl Bodmer and George Catlin, Indian and western landscape painters. Established by the American Fur Company in 1829, the fort was for many years a center of civilized living, with formal dinners served on fine china and accompanied by excellent wines. Foreign guests were often impressed by the luxuries available at the fort. The U.S. Army bought the fort in 1869 and it was dismantled so all that remained were the stone foundations. Today, the foundations of several buildings have been excavated, including the main house with the kitchen, the icehouse, palisades, and Indian reception buildings.

Fort Burford State Historic Site, in nearby Williston, is where Chief Sitting Bull surrendered in 1881. A museum is located in the original officers' quarters.

Painted Canyon (*above*) Called "bad lands to travel across" by the French fur traders, this collection of clay cliffs and gullies paints a map of geological time. Eroding at the rate of an inch a year, the desolate landscape is dissolving rapidly and may only survive another few million years. The prairie dogs (*left*) who inhabit it construct separate sleeping and storage chambers in an extensive network of tunnels. They mark each burrow, or colony, with a mound of earth.

Maltese Cross Cabin (*right*) "I never would have been President if it had not been for my experiences in North Dakota," Theodore Roosevelt once claimed. This substantial cabin was the main house on the Maltese Cross Ranch in which he became a partner in 1883. The following year, he established his own private ranch, the Elkhorn, whose maintenance provided him with invaluable experience in business management.

SITES TO SEE

● **Petrified Forest** (Theodore Roosevelt National Park), can be reached on foot or horseback; the Park's largest concentration of petrified wood is here.

● **Scenic drives** on paved roads, with interpretive signposting, are available in both units of the park. In the North Unit, a 15-mile-long paved road crosses the park from the North Unit Visitor Center to Oxbow Overlook. Along the way, it passes River Bend and Bentonitic Clay overlooks; look for longhorns like the ones Roosevelt raised between the visitor center and Squaw Creek Campground. In the South Unit, the 36-mile Scenic Loop Drive begins and ends at the Medora Visitor Center. Boicourt Overlook has some of the best views of the Badlands.

● **Elkhorn Ranch Site** where Roosevelt had his second ranch, is off US 85 between the park's two units. Inquire at a ranger station or visitor center before going to the undeveloped site.

● **Museum of the Badlands** (Medora) has exhibitions about North American Indians and fur-trading days.

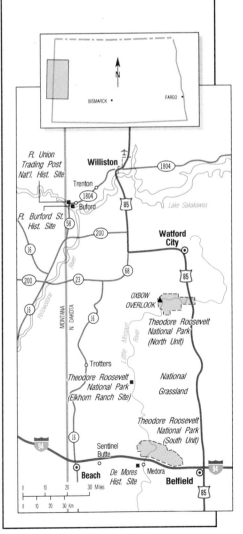

RECREATION AND POWER PLANTS

Around Lake Sakakawea

For almost 200 miles, Lake Sakakawea explores farmland and Badland bays, making a silver and gray wedding with the arid, colorful bluffs drowned years ago by the great Garrison Dam. The Lewis and Clark expedition came this way in 1804, and met Sakakawea (or Sacajawea), the Shoshone woman who guided them across the continent and for whom the lake is named. Fishermen flock to the lake for its giant walleye, and boaters for its marinas and innumerable bays. South of the lake a rolling landscape of power plants and lignite mines jostles farms and prairie.

Garrison Dam at Riverdale is one of the world's biggest earth-filled dams. It impounds the Missouri River to create the 609 square miles of Lake Sakakawea. Tours of the power plant, which generates 400,000 kilowatts of hydroelectric power, are given in the summer.

South of the dam are several sites associated with Lewis and Clark, and the now extinct Arikara, Hidatsa, and Mandan Indians they met. These include a re-creation of Fort Mandan, where the explorers spent the winter of 1804-05; Fort Clark, a fur-trading post; and the Knife River Indian Villages National Historic Site, where Sacajawea joined the expedition. Cross Ranch State Park preserves the landscape much as Lewis and Clark saw it. In the adjacent Cross Ranch Nature Preserve, there are good views, fine cottonwoods, untouched prairie, a herd of bison, and over 100 archaeological sites.

Between Washburn and Kildeer, SR 200 passes through prairie landscapes underlain by great deposits of lignite. The Antelope Valley Station power plant,

Great Plains Coal Gasification Plant, and the Coteau Properties Freedom Mine near Beulah are among the giant power plants and mines offering tours.

In utter contrast are the area's wildlife refuges. Lake Ilo National Wildlife Refuge, in the dry plains, is an oasis for water birds on the central flyway. Audubon National Wildlife Refuge, northeast of Garrison Dam, has eight miles of gravel roads and offers a chance to see Canada geese and sandhill cranes.

For people in need of refuge, the Little Missouri Bay Primitive State Park offers Badlands scenery, primitive camping, horse rentals, and 75 miles of backpacking and riding trails. For the less active, a gravel road leads off SR 22 to a picnic shelter that affords panoramic views over the surrounding countryside.

In Four Bears Memorial Park, near New Town, a museum presents the history of the Madan, Hidatsa, and Arikara Indians. On Indian Day, in late May, demonstrations are given of dance, music, games, and crafts.

Canada Geese (*left*) The isolated lakes and marshes amid the vast prairie grasslands provide essential stopover points for migrating birds making the long journey from northern Canada to their winter homes in the south. In total, about a hundred million waterfowl migrate south each fall. Canada geese in their familiar V-shaped flight formation are a common sight during the spring and fall.

Little Missouri Bay (*above*) Lake Sakakawea, created behind the Garrison Dam, was built to control the flood waters in the Missouri River Basin and has become a major recreation area. The Fort Berthold Indian Reservation surrounds much of the lake, which is home to a wide variety of wildlife and birds attracted by the stable and welcoming environment the reservation offers.

SITES TO SEE

● **Garrison** is easily distinguished from neighboring towns by "Wally Walleye," a giant model of the popular local walleyed pike perched high above town; the **North Dakota Fishing Hall of Fame** is nearby. **Fort Stevenson State Park**, south of town, is the location for an annual walleye fishing contest held each July.

● **Garrison Dam National Fish Hatchery** (Riverdale) maintains a large aquarium for viewing, and produces salmon, bass, pike, and trout.

● **Knife River Indian Villages National Historic Site** (Stanton) preserves the remains of 3 historic and prehistoric Hidatsa Indian villages, last occupied in 1845. Plains Indians artifacts are on display, and there are demonstrations of Indian culture.

WORTH A DETOUR

● **Minot**, home of the North Dakota State Fair each July, is also near the **J. Clark Salyer and Upper Souris national wildlife refuges**. Headquarters of both provide self-guiding auto tours and advice on wildlife viewing. **The Pioneer Village and Museum**, on the fairgrounds, recaptures the spirit of life on the prairie with restored buildings and farming and domestic antiques.

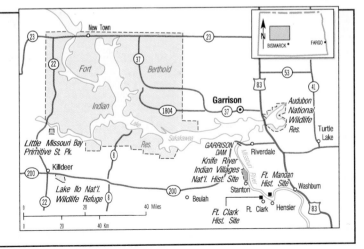

197

PLACE OF COMMEMORATION

South Dakota's Black Hills

The Black Hills, which rise clothed in dark conifers and pale meadows from South Dakota's prairies, are rich in monuments. Some, like Mount Rushmore, speak in giant tones on epic themes, but others are more abstract and eloquent. Bear Butte is one of these, and so are the multicolored, iron-hard stone logs that dot the hills. In the spectacular honeycomb caves, flowing stone and slow-growing crystals commemorate time itself. Black Hills' gold, which visitors can take away as jewelry, commemorates why treaties were broken in these hills.

Bear Butte, northeast of Sturgis, stands aloof above the plain like a Black Hills outrider; buffalo graze on its slopes, lapped to the north by reed-fringed Bear Butte Lake. The mountain is an upthrust of magma that stopped short of being a volcano. To the Indians, it was a sacred place they called *Maho Pata*. Chiefs Sitting Bull, Red Cloud, and Crazy Horse made pilgrimages to the summit.

The Crazy Horse Memorial at Thunder Mountain, near Custer, was begun in 1947 by Korczak Ziolkowski and is still in progress. It will eventually be the world's largest carving. Only 17 miles from Mount Rushmore, the monument juxtaposes the Indian hero with Gutzon Borglum's giant carvings of presidents at Mount Rushmore.

Gen. Custer is also remembered in these hills. At Custer State Park, where buffalo roam and the magnificent Needles Highway climbs to 6,200 feet, there is a replica of Gordon Stockade. This fort was built illegally in 1874 by prospectors drawn to the area by Custer's report that there was "gold around the roots of the grass."

Deadwood's Historic District preserves the authentic atmosphere of the gold rush days. Its original buildings include the saloon where Wild Bill Hickock was shot. The Adams Memorial Museum contains memorabilia of Wild Bill, Calamity Jane, and other Deadwood dignitaries. At Lead, the Homestake Gold Mine is one of the biggest in the western hemisphere.

Visitors cannot go down the Homestake's 1½-mile-deep shafts, but subterranean appetites can be satisfied in numerous caves. Wind Cave National Park, with a 28,000-acre wildlife reserve, is outstanding. So is Jewel Cave National Monument, one of the world's longest caves with more than 80 miles of tunnels.

At Spearfish from June to September, one of the region's greatest commemorations is the traditional Black Hills Passion Play, recounting Christ's last week of life.

Days of '76 (*above*) A buckskinned nostalgia buff joins in Deadwood's annual celebration of 1876, the roistering year when 25,000 prospectors stormed into town looking for gold, and Jack McCall shot Wild Bill Hickok.

Jeep Tour, Custer State Park (*left*) Mule deer, elk, and bighorn sheep roam the park's 73,000 acres, but the biggest draw is the bison herd, best seen on the 18-mile Wildlife Loop; visitors are also welcome at the November Bison Auction. The Park's Needles Highway (SR 87) climbs to the highest point between the Rockies and the Alps.

Summer in Deadwood (*right*) Visitors tread sidewalks where Calamity Jane and Wild Bill Hickok once strolled.

SITES TO SEE

● **Homestake Gold Mine** (Lead) claims to be the world's oldest continuously operating gold mine, and one of the largest in the Western Hemisphere. Guided tours provide a fascinating glimpse of the scale and complexity of its operations. Tours begin on the hillside opposite the huge Open Cut surface mine. It was here in 1876 that America's largest deposits of gold were discovered. This cut-in-half mountain is picturesque with red, cream, and blue-green strata.

● **D.C. Booth Historic Fish Hatchery** (Spearfish) was founded in 1899; before then there were no trout in the Black Hills. The original hatchery building and the **National Fish Culture Hall of Fame** are open to visitors.

● **National Museum of Woodcarving** (Custer State Park) is home of one of the world's largest collections of animated woodcarvings. They were created by an original Disneyland animator and include 36 scenes with life-size characters. Visitors can see how the carvings are made in a studio.

● **Mount Moriah Cemetery** (Deadwood) is the final resting place of the town's most notorious residents, such as Wild Bill Hickok and Calamity Jane. Follow the signs from the center of town.

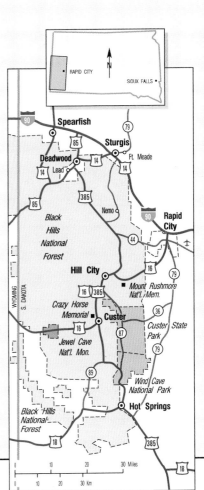

THE EARTH UNDRESSED

South Dakota's Badlands

About 30 million years ago, the Badlands were a place of lush grass and dense woods, where primitive and now extinct animals roamed. Then floods covered the plain, burying its plants, animals, and red earth in deep sediment. Erosion began, as millennia of wind and rain undressed the land, stripping the mud, the fossilized vegetation, and the flesh of earth down to the rocky bones. Simultaneously, the clay and mud began to divulge strange forms, rearing up in trunk-like pinnacles and becoming veined with canyons and rivulets. Stripped bare by the passage of time, the earth revealed sky colors and disclosed itself to be splotched and banded in myriad pastel shades, as delicate as the first pale streaks of dawn or the last tints of sunset.

The Badlands National Monument, created in 1939, was doubled in size in 1976 to 225,000 acres by the addition of new areas in the Pine Ridge Indian Reservation. In 1978, its status was elevated to that of a national park in recognition of the value of the Badlands to the national heritage.

Turning south off I-90 at Cactus Flat for the park, there is high plains grassland, a feature of the land here for many miles. Even after entering the park, it is about six miles before the Badlands take visitors by surprise—which they do as soon as you pull into an overlook and peer 200 feet down the highly eroded Badlands Wall.

Spread out below and far into the distance lies another world. French fur traders gave the region its name, calling it *les mauvaises terres à traverser*, "bad lands to pass through." The route they found to the west is today's Badlands Loop (SR 240) which crosses the North Unit before rejoining I-90 at Wall.

However arid the Badlands seem in high summer, there is water here, and it, along with wind, is mostly responsible for the fantastic gallery of Gothic-style spires and pinnacles. To see the landscape in winter, covered with a sprinkling of snow, is to see it with the extra clarity gained when shelves and cap rocks are limned with white.

In late summer, prairie grass clothes the high tables in tawny gold. From Sheep Mountain Table, visitors can enjoy some of the park's finest views.

There are many turnoffs on the Badlands Loop, giving access to scenic overlooks and trails. The Door Trail, partially accessible to disabled people, lets visitors wander among small canyons, nodules of volcanic ash, and sharp pinnacles. In contrast, the Cliff Shelf Nature Trail leads through a cliffside oasis, where gaunt juniper, sumac, and buffalo berry grow, and cattails wave in a desert pool. At the Cedar Pass Visitor Center, detailed exhibits explain the most fascinating features of Badlands' geology.

Badlands National Park (*right*) contains spectacular landscapes formed by water and wind. Eroded fossil beds contain the bones of saber-toothed cats, early camels, early horses, and a giant rhinoceros-like creature, the Titanothere, that lived here many millions of years ago. Today, the park supports coyotes, bighorn sheep, deer, golden eagles, pronghorns, prairiedogs, and a herd of some 400 bison.

Prairie Homestead (*left*), a genuine dugout sod house, stands near the park's northeast entrance.

SITES TO SEE

● **Wounded Knee Massacre Site** is south of Badlands National Park near Pine Ridge. Here, on Dec. 29, 1890, an estimated 300 Indian men, women, and children were shot by 7th Cavalry troops and buried in a mass grave.

● **Black Hills Petrified Forest** (Piedmont) A guided tour takes visitors along a ½-mile walk where numerous petrified stumps and logs of pine, cypress, and primitive palm trees lie where they fell, or where movements of the earth have brought them to rest. Some are still upright, and many are still half-buried in a matrix of sandstone.

● **Wall**, the northern gateway to Badlands National Park on I-90, is best known for the **Wall Drug Store**. Founded in 1931, it claims to be the world's largest drugstore and the first to advertise free glasses of ice water. In summer, it attracts up to 20,000 people a day. When you get there, pause for a 5-cent doughnut and a cup of coffee in the restaurant with a live tree. The walls are decorated with snapshots from around the world, including one from Bin Hoa, Vietnam, with the information that it is only 10,659 miles from this unique emporium. The ice-water well is still in the backyard, and there are also a Traveler's Chapel, western clothing store, trail supplies, and animated displays for children. Across the road is the **Wild West Historical Wax Museum**, with famous Westerners such as Calamity Jane, Wild Bill Hickok, Wyatt Earp, and Jesse James.

● **Wall Roundup Days**, with an authentic western rodeo and a parade, are held annually in July.

● **The Heritage Center** (Pine Ridge) is a Jesuit educational center, built in 1888 to teach Indian children. The Red Cloud Indian School, the schoolhouse, was named in honor of the Oglala chief who supported the school's foundation. Displays include Indian artwork and artifacts.

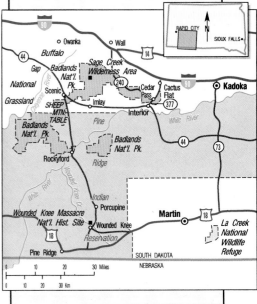

TOWNSCAPE ADORNED WITH HISTORY
The Platte River Road

Between Grand Island and North Platte, pioneers on the Oregon Trail thought of the prairie grasslands they saw as "The Great American Desert." One hundred years or so have transformed the Nebraska prairie into rolling farmland. The townscapes here—Grand Island, Kearney, Gothenburg, North Platte—are like the landscapes: pleasant, peaceable, and as virtuously American as anything Norman Rockwell painted in Vermont. Yet, they have a curious property lacking in the east, but still truly American. It is something these prairie towns share with their surrounding fields of wheat and corn—the character of being simultaneously recent and well established.

The main building of the Stuhr Museum of the Prairie Pioneer at Grand Island stands in a circular moat where ducks and geese swim. Inside, relics and memorabilia of the pioneers who passed this way and settled here range from sod-busting plows and hand-pumped vacuum cleaners to a set of Limoges china. These items chart the course of settlement like the most precious documents of tenure, as if they were made good by sweat and certified by pride.

Down the road at Kearney, the elements of new arrival and comfortable establishment found repeatedly on this stretch of the road west are still in place. Fort Kearney, southeast of town and now walled by beautiful cornfields, was the first fort on the Oregon Trail. Built to protect settlers on their way west, it later served to guard the Union Pacific Railroad; replicas of the palisade and stockade now guard trees and flowers, a blacksmith's shop, and military

escort wagons. The George Frank House, on the grounds of Kearney State College, was built in 1889 for the entrepreneur from New York City who modernized Kearney, bringing it an electrical plant, a streetcar service, and the Kearney Canal. His three-story mansion set the seal of arrival on the little prairie town.

At Minden, south of Kearney, the Harold Warp Pioneer Village documents the American pioneer spirit in every field of technology; the collections are excellent, and of stupefying size and variety.

At Gothenburg, farther west on the Platte River Road, stands a restored Pony Express station, complete with memorabilia and Indian artifacts, such as moccasins and stone arrowheads. Aviation buffs will not want to miss the annual Nebraska Antique Airplane Association Fly-In each September, with precision flying drills and flour bomb contests.

Buffalo Bill's Home (*left*)
This 19-room, gingerbread-trimmed house is located 3½ miles northwest of North Platte in the Buffalo Bill State Historical Park. William F. Cody was hired to provide meat for the construction crews on the new railroad crossing the continent. His lengendary marksmanship earned him the nickname "Buffalo Bill."

Platte Valley Farmstead (*above*) The first farmstead in Lincoln County was the Erickson home built in 1869. The transformation from prairie grasslands to well-established agricultural resource is a tribute to the will of the dedicated homesteaders.

SITES TO SEE

● **Robert Henri Museum and Historical Walkway** (Cozad) pays tribute to the town's native son, born Robert Henry Cozad. Henri, a founder of the Ash Can School of painting, was an artist at the beginning of this century. The museum is housed in the family home, formerly a hotel, and furnished in period style. A brick walkway leads to a park with a Pony Express station, rural church, and century-old school.

● **Harold Warp Pioneer Village** (Minden) has 26 buildings on the site, including an original Pony Express station, an 1869 Indian fort, and a railroad depot from the 1880s. There are also restored antique cars, tractors, and airplanes. Demonstrations are given of rarely practiced crafts such as broom making, as well as spinning, glassblowing, and weaving.

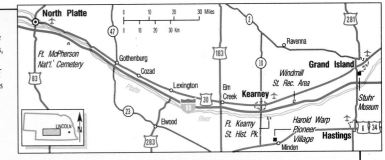

TRAIL COUNTRY
Nebraska's Frontier Land

In northwestern Nebraska, the Great Plains gradually give way to rugged bluffs that welcomed the pioneers who struggled west on the Oregon and Mormon Pioneer trails in the mid-1800s. As non-Indian settlers poured into the area, the Sioux rebelled, and the Plains Indians Wars unrolled their bloody course. Ranchers, cowboys, and railroad builders made towns like Crawford the roistering focus of frontier hurly-burly, but soon they became peaceable communities, leaving the grasslands, buttes, and pothole lakes to the cattle, coyotes, and migrant waterbirds.

The North Platte River marked the course of the Oregon Trail along its the south bank. The Mormon Pioneer Trail, opened by Brigham Young and his followers in 1846–47, followed the north bank. Both trails followed routes pioneered by mountainmen and fur traders, such as the Sublette Expedition, which in 1830 first took a wagon train across the Rockies.

Scotts Bluff National Monument, an 800-foot-high escarpment of sandstone, siltstone, and volcanic ash, was a towering landmark for travelers, and a welcome campsite where firewood and good water were found. The one-and-a-half-mile road goes to the top of the bluff, from where there are fine views of the North Platte valley and spectacular Chimney Rock, another pioneer landmark, which

evening light illuminates in summer until late at night. There is a trail to the top.

In Wildcat Hills State Recreation Area, buffalo and elk can still be seen. Oglala National Grasslands, in the state's extreme northwest corner, preserves 94,334 acres of native prairie where there were once great herds of buffalo.

The great bastion against the Sioux in this area was Fort Robinson, near Crawford. Fort Robinson State Park's 23,000 acres preserves many of the fort's original structures, including the 1874 officers' quarters and the guardhouse where Chiefs Crazy Horse and Dull Knife were killed trying to escape. A museum in the former post headquarters preserves pioneer, Indian, and military relics, and the Trailside Museum displays natural history.

Looking West (*left*) After the long trek across the prairies, Chimney Rock marked the beginning of the next leg on the journey westward. Rising almost 500 feet above the North Platte River, this was a natural landmark along the Oregon Trail.

Settlers' Dream Home (*right*) A sod homestead on the open prairie of the Oglala National Grasslands illustrates the harsh life of the early settlers. The native grasses which have covered this land for centuries survive the climatic extremes of baking sun in the summer and freezing cold in winter.

SITES TO SEE

● **Museum of the Fur Trade** (Chadron) commemorates the days when Indians and non-Indians coexisted peacefully here. Set in a landscape of buttes and canyons, the museum includes a reconstruction of the 1833 Bordeaux Trading Post, with displays of tanning equipment, trading goods, and weapons. The town's annual Buckskin Rendezvous and Fur Trade Days is celebrated each July with tomahawk throwing, tanning demonstrations, and tests of flintlock marksmanship.

● **Chimney Rock National Historic Site** (Bayard) is a 500-foot-high rock, a towering landmark for thousands of early traders and pioneers. The tall spire indicated that the second difficult, mountainous part of the trip west was about to begin. A gravel road off SR 92 takes visitors to within half a mile of the rock; hiking boots are recommended for the walk to the mountain.

● **Agate Fossil Beds National Monument** (SR 29) contains the fossilized remains of now-extinct animals and plants from about 19 million years ago. A self-guiding trail leads to the fossil beds.

● **Knight Museum** (Alliance) preserves western Nebraska's history with displays of Indian artifacts, farming equipment, and railroad supplies.

WORTH A DETOUR

● **Ash Hollow State Historic Park** (Lewellen) was a rest point for the covered wagons after they crossed the dangerous Windlass Hill to the south. Some of the tracks are still visible. Nearby **Blue Creek** was the site of one of the first major battles between the U.S. Army and North Plains Indians in 1854.

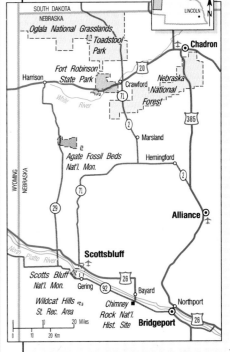

LAND OF THE UNEXPECTED

Northeastern Iowa

If, on a summer day, you climb the 500-foot bluff at Pikes Peak State Park and gaze toward the hazy Mississippi River, dotted with wooded islands and irregular inlets lush with reeds, it is easy to suppose you have strayed from Iowa to a wilder, more exotic region. This northeastern corner of the state was untouched by the last Ice Age, and its rough limestone hills and ridges produce a landscape quite unlike the horizon-wide quilt of cornfields that covers the southern part of the state. And, if the rest of the nation claims the southern tableland for its breadbasket, native Iowans claim this northwestern corner as their Little Switzerland.

Northeastern Iowa has been popular for a long time. Artifacts found at Effigy Mounds National Monument, north of Marquette, indicate a settlement there about 500 B.C. Indians of the Red Ocher Culture, so called because they sprinkled their grave chambers with iron-ore dust, dotted the region with their conical burial mounds. Prehistoric Effigy Mounds people constructed the region's huge effigy mounds in the shapes of birds and animals. The most notable is the 137-foot-long Great Bear Mound. Some of the trails crossing the monument's 1,475 acres offer good views of the Upper Mississippi Wildlife and Fish Refuge, which stretches 284 miles from Wabasha, Minnesota, to Rock Island, Illinois.

One of the first non-Indians to exploit Iowa's natural resources was Julien Dubuque, who in 1785 began mining lead in the neighborhood of the city now named for him. The Old Shot Tower still stands as a monument to the old industry. Built in 1856, it produced lead shot throughout the Civil War. Today, Dubuque is a river town and proud of its heritage. A sailboat race on the Mississippi is held here in mid-summer, and September's city-wide RiverFest features a Venetian boat parade and international dragon boat races. Paddleboat cruises leave from Dubuque for Bettendorf and McGregor.

West of Dubuque, at Strawberry Point, is one of the parks that gives the area its distinctive charm. Backbone State Park, named for the vertebral appearance of its boulder-strewn central ridge, has springs, caves, and cliffs.

Decorah, to the north, is famous for its alpine scenery and is now a center for canoeing and skiing. Settled by Norwegians, the town holds a NordicFest in late July. Nearby Spillville has a Czech heritage, and it was here in 1893 that composer Anton Dvořák finished his "New World Symphony." His former house contains the Bily Clock Exhibit.

Pikes Peak (*right*), in the state park of that name, is the highest bluff on the Mississippi River. It offers splendid views over the river, with its islands and bayous, to the open country beyond. The 500-foot limestone and sandstone walls of the bluff are full of fossil remains, and the debris at its foot forms a treasure trove for intrepid fossil hunters.

Lying just four miles from McGregor, the 970-acre park provides fine recreational facilities, from camping and hiking to winter sports. The Bridal Veil Falls are worth a visit, as are several Indian effigy mounds within the park.

Vesterheim Norwegian-American Museum (*left*), in Decorah, contains antique belongings of the Norwegian immigrants who settled in this area, attracted by the abundant water power provided by the Iowa River. Vesterheim means "western home," and the collection is, appropriately, housed in restored farm buildings.

Today, the river is still well used – for recreational activities, especially canoeing.

SITES TO SEE

● **Fred W. Woodward Riverboat Museum** (Dubuque) recaptures the spirit of 300 years of life along the Mississippi with wide-ranging displays. Nearby, the sidewheeler *William M. Black*, a 277-foot ship built in 1931, is an example of one of the last steam-powered sidewheelers to sail the Mississippi.

● **Mathias Ham Historic House** (Dubuque), a 23-room Italianate mansion, is furnished to reflect gracious pre-Civil War living in Dubuque.

● **Laura Ingalls Wilder Park and Museum** (Burr Oak) is the restored childhood home of the author of *Little House on the Prairie*.

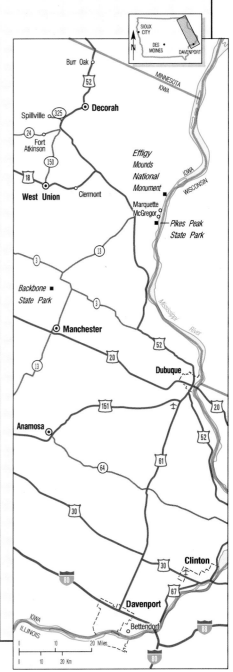

WHEN TILLAGE BEGINS

Southeastern Iowa

The orderly fields and picture-perfect farmsteads of southeastern Iowa are the image of good husbandry and stability. Along the wide rivers flowing into the Mississippi River, fine old water-powered mills still grind grain, and you can still see antique threshers and steam tractors having their day alongside the behemoths of modern tillage. Though Iowa is blessed with the richest farmland in America—where the land's fertility also sustains a rich and harmonious cultural tradition—it is more than America's bread basket.

In the Parks Library of Iowa State University at Ames, a series of murals illustrates a Daniel Webster quotation: "When tillage begins, the other arts follow." These murals were designed by Grant Wood, Iowa's most famous artist, and painted by a team of art students, in 1934–7. They show land being cleared and plowed in the 1840s, and illustrate industrial arts, veterinary medicine, and home economics.

A few miles southeast of Ottumwa is the village of Eldon. Here in 1930 Wood made what is perhaps the most famous American painting of the 20th century, *American Gothic*. The background house is still here, now called the American Gothic House.

At West Branch, about 85 miles northeast of Eldon, is a more practical instance of how art and agriculture are entwined in Iowa. President Herbert Hoover was born here. Although he is remembered for presiding over the first years of the Depression, he has something better to his credit. After World War I, Hoover worked on committees that helped avert famine in Europe. At the Herbert Hoover Presidental Library and Museum, there is touching evidence of his success: American flour sacks, returned to Hoover after being embroidered with pictures and messages of thanks by Belgian children.

Visitors can take a 14-mile round trip through the Des Moines River valley on the Boone and Scenic Valley Railroad from Boone. Just northwest of town is one of the world's highest and longest double-track railroad bridges.

Lively evidence of the diverse ethnic and religious groups that heped Iowa to grow can be seen at Amana Colonies, seven communities founded over 100 years ago by a European religious sect.

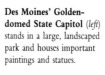

Des Moines' Golden-domed State Capitol (*left*) stands in a large, landscaped park and houses important paintings and statues.

The Museum Complex at Homestead (*right*) includes an early Amana house furnished in typical style and a blacksmith shop. The village is one of seven, known as the Amana Colonies, established in the 1850s by a German religious sect that believed in divine revelation through inspired prophets. The Amanaites once operated a completely communal system—even meals were prepared in a central kitchen; today they are joint stockholders in a corporation making kitchen appliances and heating and cooling systems. They also produce woolens, furniture, and wines made from fruit and blossoms. A map for a self-guiding tour of the villages and businesses is available at the visitor center in Amana.

SITES TO SEE

● **The Herbert Hoover Presidential Library and Museum** (*left*) preserves the 31st president's papers and administration archives. The library is located at the **Herbert Hoover National Historic Site**, with the restored humble 2-room house Hoover was born in, as well as a replica of the Quaker Meetinghouse he attended as a child. Hoover and his wife are buried overlooking the site.

● **John Deere Ottumwa Works** (Ottumwa) is open to visitors for tours.

● **Czech Museum, Library and Immigrant Home** (Cedar Rapids) displays a wide variety of Czech, Moravian, and Slovak heirlooms and crafts, preserving the city's immigrant heritage.

● **Kalona** was founded by Amish settlers and still celebrates its heritage every September with a Fall Festival.

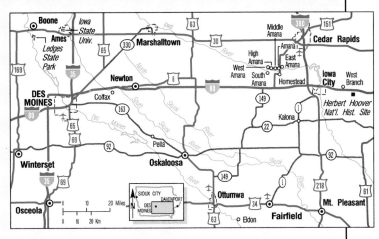

THE ROCKY MOUNTAIN STATES

The Rocky Mountain states offer the most extreme landscapes in the continental United States. In their eastern reaches, the rolling farmlands of Colorado, Montana, and Wyoming belong to the Great Plains. Southwestern Idaho slides into the Oregon desert, and in the northwestern part of the state are wheatfields and prairie. Between these flat extremes, the land tilts toward the Rockies and then rises abruptly into snowfields and glaciers. These peaks are among the planet's youngest mountains, and most visitors have a sense here of being in landscapes of dazzling newness, where alpine meadows and precarious cliffs, dark conifer forests, and bright stands of aspens seem freshly painted on the sides of the mountains.

The explorers Lewis and Clark were the first non-Indian travelers to cross the Rockies, en route to the Pacific, and they were soon followed by fur trappers and mountainmen, miners, and pioneers going west, surveyors and geologists. The best of what they saw is preserved in some of the nation's most dramatic National Parks—Yellowstone, Glacier, and Grand Teton—and in less famous, but outstandingly beautiful tracts like Wyoming's Wind River country, famous for its cowboy lore. And scattered among these areas of great natural beauty are such works of ancient man as Wyoming's Medicine Wheel and the magical Anasazi cliff dwellings at Mesa Verde, Colorado.

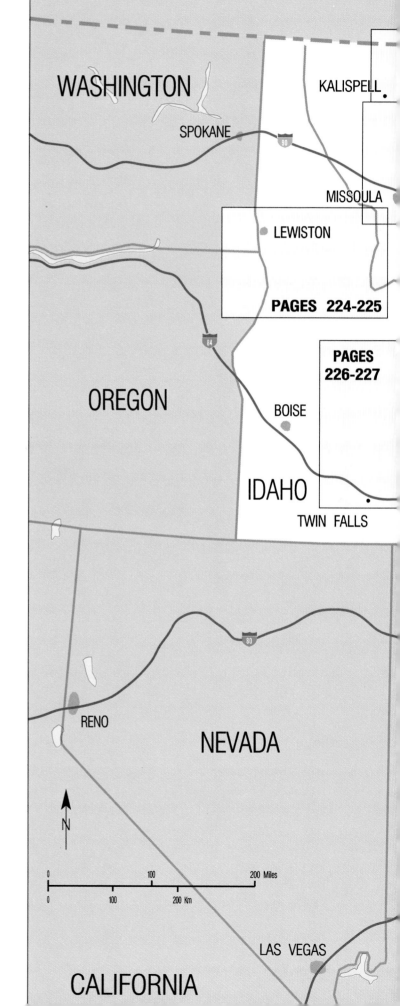

C A N A D A

NORTH DAKOTA

BISMARCK

MONTANA

HELENA

BUTTE

SOUTH DAKOTA

RAPID CITY

SHERIDAN

CASPER

WYOMING

JACKSON

NEBRASKA

NORTH PLATTE

CHEYENNE

SALT LAKE CITY

DENVER

COLORADO
SPRINGS

UTAH

KANSAS

GRAND
JUNCTION

COLORADO

OKLAHOMA

ARIZONA

NEW MEXICO

TEXAS

SANTA FE

GOING-TO-THE-SUN ROAD

Glacier National Park

When the mountains wear their coat of wildflowers under skies of pure sapphire, the million acres of Glacier National Park provide some of the most breathtaking and primitive scenery in America. Millions of years ago, geological processes sculpted these peaks and left in their wake an inheritance of some 50 glaciers and 200 lakes. The high peaks and sheer precipices show the effect of glaciation vividly, while the perpetual snowfields allow visitors to enjoy their beauty while basking in the warm summer sun.

More than 700 miles of horseback and foot trails cross Glacier National Park, but most visitors first drive the spectacular Going-to-the-Sun Road, which cuts north and then east across the park from West Glacier to St. Mary. Skirting Lake McDonald, the road climbs toward the Continental Divide, which cuts diagonally across the park. From the Visitor Center at Logan Pass, a raised boardwalk leads visitors to the delicate alpine flowers of the Hanging Gardens, and on to Hidden Lake Overlook. Garden Wall contains a variety of rock colors and patterns, and divides Grinnel Glacier from Josephine Lake. Naturalist-guided tours take place from Logan Pass.

East of Logan Pass, the Going-to-the-Sun Road passes through a tunnel and descends to St. Mary Lake. Perhaps the most startling feature of the park is the difference in vegetation on each side of the Divide. On the east side, Engelmann spruce and lodgepole pine are a sign that the weather is colder and drier here. On the west side, warm, moisture-laden Pacific winds give rise to more luxuriant growth. At the western end of McDonald Valley, grizzlies come to feast on September's McDonald Creek salmon run in a mature forest of fragrant, 200-foot-high red cedars.

Spectacular St. Mary Lake fills the 10-mile-long scoop of a glacial valley; there are excellent views of the lake from the mile-high peaks of the Lewis and Clark Range that rim the basin. From Babb, a road leads to the Many Glacier region and the impressive Many Glacier Hotel, built in the summers of 1914 and 1915 by the Great Northern Railroad Company. To the north are the wild Belly River Country and Canada's contiguous Waterton Lakes National Park, which, with Glacier, makes up the Waterton-Glacier International peace Park.

Nearby Browning is the tribal headquarters of the Blackfeet Indians. The fine Museum of the Plains Indians includes an exhaustive collection of Blackfeet artifacts such as beadwork, bags, and riding gear. Blackfeet Indian Days are held the second weekend in July.

St. Mary Lake, Glacier National Park (*above right*) As still and sparkling as glass, this lake is so often whipped into white-capped waves that the Blackfeet Indians once thought it the home of the Wind Maker. **Rocky Mountain Goats** (*left*) rely on the wind to uncover their winter food when it lies buried under the snow. Nimble and fearless, the goat has hooves that are specially designed for traction, with nonskid pads. **The Glaciers** (*below right*) that carved this landscape covered the park four times, following the path of least resistance and casually rearranging nature as they passed.

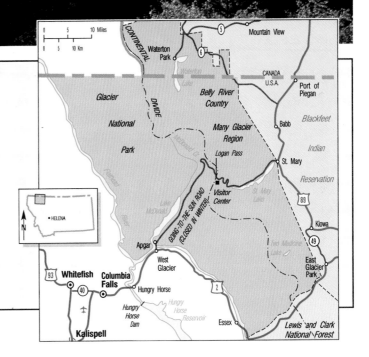

SITES TO SEE

● **Avalanche Creek** in the park is a river gorge running through a red mudstone canyon. A 2-mile trail leads to **Avalanche Creek and Basin**, a semi-circular amphitheater with 2,000-foot cliff walls.

● **Bob Scriver Studio and Wildlife Museum** (Browning) includes the artist's works in The Hall of Bronze, as well as other artists' paintings and taxidermy exhibitions.

● **Conrad Mansion Historic Site Museum** (Kalispell) is a sumptuously restored 23-room 1895 Victorian mansion built for a Missouri River trader.

● **Hungry Horse Dam** (Kalispell) is one of the world's highest.

● **Big Mountain Ski Resort Chairlift** (Whitefish) takes visitors to the 6,770-foot summit of Big Mountain in the summer for spectacular views of the surrounding Rockies and Canada.

WHERE THE BUFFALO ROAM

Montana's Flathead Valley

Sprawling between the Mission Range of the Rockies and the fierce Bitterroot Range, the Flathead Valley provides a gateway to mountain wilderness areas and to islands of wildlife preserved in a long, narrow valley of rich farmland. Here, firs and pines, orchards, and mountains crowd the shores of glacial Flathead Lake. Most of the region remained unsettled until prospectors flooded it during the gold rush of the 1860s. For today's visitors, it offers irresistible combinations of wildness and cultivation, history and recreation.

US 93 skirts the western shore of Flathead Lake, the largest natural freshwater lake in the West, curving through evergreen forests punctuated by orchards. Motor cruises tour the lake regularly from Polson, and visitors can also explore it on the racing sloop that sails from Bigfork. Boats can be rented from many of the lake's marinas, and a popular lakeland destination is Wild Horse Island State Park, whose 2,165 acres are home to bighorn sheep, deer, water birds, eagles, and coyotes.

Island-like wildlife domains lie south of the lake, too. On the National Bison Range, nearly 19,000 acres of prairie, marsh, woods, and high grassland set in the irrigated farm country between Ronan and Dixon, 300 to 500 bison wander in the company of elk, deer, antelope, mountain goats, and bighorn sheep. A 19-mile self-guiding car tour reaches the reserve's high country.

In nearby St. Ignatius, within the Flathead Indian Reservation, stands the St. Ignatius Mission, first established as a Jesuit mission in 1854. Its church was erected in 1891 and decorated about 10 years later with frescoes by Joseph Carignano, the mission's cook. But the real beauty of the brick church lies in its assured, isolated stance against the backdrop of the Mission Mountains. It was, and remains, an island sanctuary. Artifacts and exhibits relating to the Flathead Indians, also known as the Salish Indians, can be seen in Polson at the Flathead Historical Museum in summer, and at Miracle of America Museum throughout the year.

North of the bison reserve are the Ninepines and Pablo national wildlife refuges, home for hundreds of thousands of migratory waterfowl. Between Ronan and Condon lies the wild and beautiful Mission Mountains Wilderness area. To the south, on Missoula's doorstep, are the 60,000 acres of the Rattlesnake Wilderness National Recreation Area.

Missoula was built by and for the prospectors who came through Hell Gate Canyon in the 1860s. Logging became—and remains—important. At the U.S. Forest Service's Smokejumpers Base Aerial Fire Depot, "smokejumpers"—the paratroopers of forest-fire fighters—are trained.

Buffalo (*left*) The American bison, usually called the buffalo, carries the distinction of being the largest and most dangerous animal in the Rocky Mountains. Adult male buffaloes can reach a shoulder height of five feet or more and weigh more than a ton, but they can still outrun humans. Nearly 200 years ago, vast herds numbering 60 million animals roamed North America freely. By 1900, the buffalo was nearly extinct in that area, having been slaughtered for their tongues, then thought a great delicacy, and shot by sportsmen from trains. Laws enacted around that time protected the two surviving herds, from which today's noble beasts are descended.

National Bison Range (*above right*) Created in response to the combined efforts of the American Bison Society and President Theodore Roosevelt, this vast fenced site received its first seven bison in 1909. Two of them came from Texas, two from Montana, and three from New Hampshire. The herd has now grown so large that it is thinned annually by auction.

Pronghorn Antelope (*below right*) True antelopes only inhabit Asia and Africa, but the pronghorn is often called one as well. These are grazing in the high grasslands of National Bison Range, while elk and bighorn sheep roam the higher ground.

SITES TO SEE

● **Flathead River Gorge** (Polson) has perpendicular walls 200 to 500 feet high, with water flowing at the rate of 50,000 gallons per second out of Flathead Lake. According to legend, the gorge was dug by Paul Bunyan.

● **Miracle of America Museum** (Polson) has a collection of posters from both world wars, as well as pioneer memorabilia. The town hosts the annual Montana State Fiddlers Contest at the end of July.

● **Polson-Flathead Historical Museum** (Polson) contains artifacts and exhibits relating to Flathead Indians, also known as Salish Indians.

● **Lakeside** is a year-round recreational area, with boat charters and cruises around Flathead Lake available all year from the town's harbor.

● **SR 83** south from Swan Lake is a scenic drive that passes the Swan River National Wildlife Refuge between Flathead and Lolo national forests.

● **Lolo National Forest** has 2,100,000 acres sweeping east from Missoula to the Montana-Idaho border, with almost 2,000 miles of hiking trails. Several ski centers, such as Montana Snowbowl, are in the forest.

● **Historical Museum at Fort Missoula** (Missoula) is housed in the 1877 fort from which the military fought the Nez Perce Indians under Chiefs Joseph and Looking Glass.

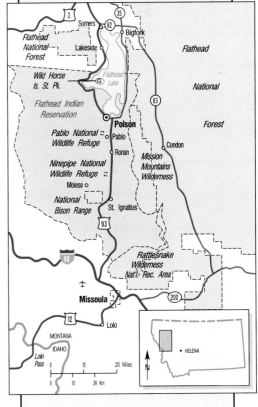

THE SOURCE OF THE MISSOURI
Beaverhead and Gallatin

In this generously forested section of southwestern Montana lies a central valley protected by the towering peaks of the Madison Range to the east, and the Snowcrest and Ruby ranges to the west. To the north, I-90 follows the route of the old Lewis and Clark Trail to mineral-rich Butte, where the "richest hill on earth" eventually yielded 19 billion pounds of copper. Around Alder Gulch, in the center of the region, visitors can still pan for gold and step back in time on the tree-lined boardwalks of Virginia City, with its authentic old stores and offices.

In 1864, John Bozeman brought the first wagon train into this area to settle the Gallatin Valley. His companions named their town for the explorer, and its Museum of the Rockies, near the campus of Montana State University, provides an excellent introduction to the region. It has fine displays of geology, archaeology, ethnology, and Western art, as well as outstanding dinosaur and history exhibits and an 1889 homestead.

South of Bozeman, in the valley the Indian hunters called the Valley of Flowers, is Big Sky. From here, visitors can raft on the Gallatin River or ride a gondola to Lone Mountain ski resort for wonderful panoramas of the Spanish Peaks Wilderness and Gallatin National Forest. South of Livingston on US 89 is forest scenery of a more unusual kind—the 40 square miles of Gallatin Petrified Forest, containing stone trees from forests buried by volcanic eruptions millions of years ago.

At Butte, copper mining has also left its mark with a mammoth hole in the ground, the spectacular 1,800-foot-deep Berkeley Open Pit Mine. At the World Museum of Mining, a collection of buildings re-creates life in an early mining village. East of Butte, along I-90, are the Lewis and Clark Caverns, where visitors can see how much more prettily nature does her mining; the historic Madison Buffalo Jump where Indians herded bison to their death; and, at Three Forks, the confluence of rivers that form the Missouri.

South of Butte, in the Beaverhead Valley, the gold towns that brought the mining boom to this part of Montana in 1863 nestle. Visitors can sense gold fever in Nevada City, re-created with period buildings from around the state, and at historic Virginia City, which was the territorial capital for over a decade. Among the restored 19th-century buildings here is Montana's first newspaper office. In Alder Gulch, where the boom began, it is still possible to pan for gold, see a gold dredge, and ride the Anchor Gulch Short Line work train.

Cattle Drive (*far left*) Once the preserve of the buffalo, the prairie grasslands provide perfect grazing for the herds of cattle that are regularly rounded up and taken to market.

Berkeley Pit Mine (*left*) By the mid-1950s, after more than 70 years of continuous production, the high-grade ore from the tunneled mines was just about played out. Then excavation began on the massive open pit mine to extract low-grade ore from the mineral-rich earth.

The Missouri River (*above*) High in the Rocky Mountains, fed by winter snows, lies the source of the rambling Missouri River. At Three Forks, the principal headwaters join together to form the river itself; from there, it winds its way through scenic mountain landscape. Great Falls marks the start of 10 miles of cataracts which end at Fort Benton, marking the farthest point of navigation by 19th-century river boats.

SITES TO SEE

● **Madison River Canyon Earthquake Area** (West Yellowstone) recalls the night of Aug. 17, 1959, when an earthquake deposited half a mountain in the canyon. Within 30 seconds, 60 million tons of rock and dirt fell, forming a dam 400 feet high, killing 28 and creating Quake Lake. A nearby ridge, now known as Refuge Point, sheltered 250 survivors.

● **Copper King Mansion** (Butte), an 1888 mansion built for William A. Clark, the town's leading copper baron, has been lovingly restored with lavish Victorian furniture. Clark's son's mansion, **Arts Chateau**, also reflects the town's former glory. Both lend an air of refinement to this still-rugged mining town.

● **Beaverhead Rock State Monument** (off SR 41 north of Dillon) is the site of a massive beaver-shaped rock recognized by Sacajawea as she guided Lewis and Clark westward.

WORTH A DETOUR

● **Big Hole National Battlefield** (west of Wisdom) commemorates a 2-day battle in the 1877 Nez Perce War. Although the Indians won this bloody battle, they were only 2 months away from surrender.

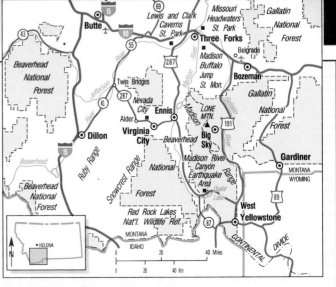

LAND OF ENDURING LEGENDS

Cody, Crow, and Custer Country

By the time fall comes to the valleys, Wyoming's Bighorn Mountains are already white with snow, and they remain snow-covered long after spring flowers have come to the Montana uplands where Custer and his men died at Little Bighorn. Things endure in this land of legends. Parades of strange creatures still march pictographically across the wall of a sandstone cave in the Bitter Creek Valley, Chief Plenty Coups is still the unexcelled Crow chief, and Buffalo Bill Cody is still the best showman in buckskin.

Cody, Wyoming, laid out by Buffalo Bill and his business partners in 1896, is full of fond memories of the swashbuckling showman. Queen Victoria, thrilled by his Wild West show, gave him the $100,000 bar at the Irma Hotel. The Chamber of Commerce occupies a replica of his T.E. Ranch, and the Buffalo Bill Historical Center is a complex of four excellent museums: the Buffalo Bill Museum; the Plains Indian Museum; the Whitney Gallery of Western Art; and the Winchester Arms Museum.

Northeast of Cody, across the Bighorn Mountains in Montana, is Custer Battlefield National Monument, a memorial to a far less fortunate showman. Here, above the valley of the Little Bighorn River, Lt. Col. George A. Custer and his men made their famous last stand against the Sioux and Cheyenne, whose determination to leave their reservation was matched, in 1876, by the U.S. government's resolve to return them to it.

Having divided his regiment in three, hoping to conquer his well-concealed opponents by attacking from several directions at once, Custer led more than 200 men in a direct charge. Hopelessly outnumbered by roughly 8,000 Indian warriors, he and all his men were killed. Visitor center displays describe the course of the battle and explain why it happened. Among the relics are Custer's revolver and Chief Sitting Bull's knife sheath, covered with coup-marks. As the youngest general in the Union Army during the Civil War, Custer had led a brigade of cavalry during the Gettysburg campaign, but his distinguished history had been subsumed in its final, bloody chapter.

West of the Crow Indian Reservation is the home of Plenty Coups, the Crow chief who urged peace and forbearance. At the Chief Plenty Coups State Monument, a small museum houses relics. The first dude ranch in the area was built in 1903 at Barry's Landing, in what is today the Bighorn Canyon National Recreation Area in Montana.

East of Lovell on Medicine Mountain is a mysterious Medicine Wheel, a spoked 250-foot circle of limestone boulders; its age and purpose are unknown.

Birthplace of a Legend (*right*) Although William "Buffalo Bill" Cody was born in Iowa, the legend he worked so hard to embellish associates him firmly with a wilder west. The state of Wyoming gave him a ranch in the town of Cody, and his boyhood home was moved there in 1933, 16 years after his death. A gateway to Yellowstone National Park, to neighboring dude ranches, and to the colorful history and flavor of old frontier towns, Cody still preserves many relics of the great man. During a lifetime crammed with adventure, he worked Colorado's gold fields, rode for the Pony Express, and hunted buffalo on the Great Plains. In 1883, he organized his famous Wild West Show, with which he toured the U.S. and Europe for many years, establishing himself as a memorable showman. The fine museums in Cody concentrate on the Old West and its cowboys and Indians, and authentic rodeos are held here every year.

Twentieth Century Cowboy (*left*) Wyoming is still prime cowboy country and riding and roping still the prime skills of the busy cowhand. But when temperatures plummet, wily wranglers now give their steeds a break and get out their snowmobiles. In this scene, a rancher heads for open country as he starts his winter herding in the Big Horn mountains.

The Boyhood Home of...
WILLIAM FREDERICK CODY
"BUFFALO BILL"
Built By his Father in 1841
AT LeCLAIRE, SCOTT COUNTY, IOWA
MOVED TO CODY, WYOMING IN 1933

SITES TO SEE

● **Chief Black Otter Trail** (Billings) is a scenic drive north of the city around the Rimrocks, which tower 400 feet. **Oscar's Dreamland**, in Billings, has one of the world's largest collections of steam and gasoline tractors as well as an entire main street of pioneer stores and homes, the state's first oil rig, the one-time tallest windmill in Kansas, and antique automobiles and wagons.

● **Pictograph Cave State Monument** (south of Billings) in the Bitter Creek Valley contains strange memorials of the region: cave drawings, in grease, charcoal, blood, and plant dyes, of animals and not-quite-human figures. Buffalo bones and stone tools in one cave indicate it was probably inhabited 1,500 years ago.

● **The Bradford Brinton Memorial Museum and Historic Ranch** (south of Sheridan) is an example of how the wealthy lived. Built in 1892 as the Quarter Circle A Ranch, this property was bought in 1923 by millionaire Brinton as a summer home. Beautifully maintained, it contains his furnishings and western art collection, and there are gardens with great views of the Bighorn Mountains. **Trail End Historic Center State Historic Site** in Sheridan is a restored home.

● **Cody** hosts several festivals during the year: Buffalo Bill's Birthday Ball in February; the Frontier Festival in mid-June; the Plains Indian Pow Wow in late June; and Stampede Days in early July with rodeos, a carnival, and concerts.

● **Greybull**, a bentonite-mining town, is named for an Indian legend about a massive albino buffalo that wandered here. **The Greybull Museum** contains Indian artifacts, western memorabilia, and giant ammonite fossils. The Days of '49 festival is held the second weekend in June.

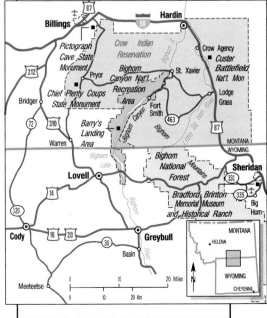

ON THE OREGON TRAIL

Eastern Wyoming

Wyoming is a land of legible signatures, the broadest of which lies in the arc of the North Platte River. Flowing north between the Seminoe and Shirley mountains to Casper, it then skirts the Laramies to flow east to Douglas and on to Nebraska. The river marks the route of the Oregon Trail, the great westward migration that followed its south bank. The pioneers left their marks here, too, in the cliffs where they carved their signatures, in the river crossings and campsites that served them, and in the military forts that protected them.

In 1834, the fur trader William Sublette found a site for a trading post at Laramai's Point, near the confluence of the Laramie and North Platte rivers. Within 15 years, the trickle of pioneers passing through along the Oregon Trail became a flood. As their relations with the Indians worsened, the government bought Fort John, as it was called, from its civilian owners and turned it into Fort Laramie, a military outpost. Visitors will find a fascinating collection of buildings at Fort Laramie National Historic Site, including "Old Bedlam," erected in 1849 as officers' quarters, which is the oldest military building in the state.

An estimated ten percent of those heading west died along the trail. Thousands of their names are carved in Register Cliff State Historic Site near Guernsey. At nearby Oregon Trail Ruts State Historic Site, the deep grooves cut into the sandstone by iron-rimmed wagon wheels can still be clearly seen, as can the paths worn by muleteers walking beside the wagons. To the north, near Lusk and its interesting stagecoach museum, stand the red cliffs that supplied local tribes with the material they used for paint.

In the late 1800s, moss agate was discovered in the Guernsey area and exported in large quantities to Germany. But ranching was the major business here and in the grasslands to the north. Douglas prospered as a supply center for the cattlemen. The Wyoming Pioneer's Memorial Museum here displays an impressive collection of local memorabilia. Nearby Fort Fetterman State Historic Site holds a living-history festival during Fort Fetterman Days in the summer.

Now a supply center for the oil, coal, uranium, and natural gas industries, Casper began life in 1847 as a ferry landing operated by Mormons. In the 1850s, a toll bridge replaced the ferry, and a fort was soon built to protect it. Almost forty years later, discovery of the Salt Creek oil field initiated an oil boom best known for the 1927 Teapot Dome scandal.

West of Alcova is the "Great Register of the Desert," Independence Rock State Historic Site. Covering 27 acres and rising from the plain in a giant hump, the rock bears about 5,000 names, painted or carved by travelers or incised for them by Mormon stonecutters. In 1847, nearly 1,000 pioneers celebrated the Fourth of July here.

Personal Reminders (*below*)
Register Cliff State Historic Site, south of Guernsey, marks a cliff where pioneers carved their names in stone as they rested on their long and arduous journey west. In the twenty years between 1840 and 1860, thousands of families passed this point with hopes of a prosperous future as a reward for their efforts. Today, this silent monument reminds us of the courage and determination of those early settlers who developed our nation.

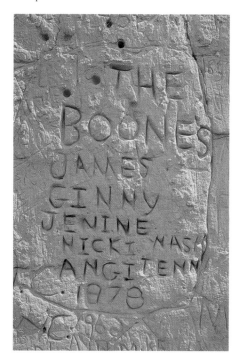

Lake Marie (*above*) The unspoiled beauty of this crystal-clear lake is one of the many natural attractions of the Medicine Bow National Forest. The five distinct units of the park cover a combined area of 1,665,000 acres in the eastern part of Wyoming. In summer, hikers, campers, hunters, and anglers take advantage of the various features and districts of the forest. Winter snows provide a range of activities from cross-country and downhill skiing to snowmobiling. The Pole Mountain unit of the park has outstanding unusual rock formations.

SITES TO SEE

● **Ayres Natural Bridge** (near Douglas) is a 50-foot-wide, 30-foot-high arch, naturally produced by the waters of La Prele Creek.

● **Laramie Peak Museum** (Wheatland) recaptures the spirit of travel along the Oregon Trail with a collection of pioneering memorabilia.

● **Stagecoach Museum** (Lusk) displays such intriguing items as a restored Concord stagecoach. The route of the Cheyenne and Black Hills Stage Line—once a frequent sight in the area—is marked with white posts.

WORTH A DETOUR

● **Cheyenne**, the state capital, has preserved some reminders of its boom days in the late 1860s. The **Cheyenne Frontier Days Old West Museum** has Indian and pioneer artifacts, as well as exhibits illustrating the impact of the Union Pacific Railroad on the region. Almost 300,000 people come to town each July for one of the world's largest rodeos and the Frontier Days festivities. Indian dances, parades, and cowboy-style competitions are all part of the fun. Philatelists will not want to miss the **First Day Cover Museum**. The collection, valued in excess of $1 million, contains the first first-day cover issued in England in 1840.

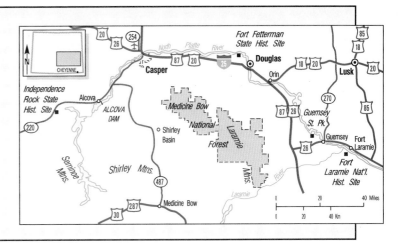

NEVER-NEVER LANDS
Yellowstone and Grand Teton National Parks

The first non-Indian to see the Yellowstone area was John Colter, who had accompanied Lewis and Clark across the continent. Although his reports of mudpots and spouting geysers were accurate, no one believed them, and easterners put Yellowstone in their mental file marked Never-Never Land. Had they received accounts of the Tetons, rising sheer from the plain like a jagged snowy wall, they, too, would have been tagged as fairy tales. And yet the easterners were partly right: these *are* Never-Never Lands, not quite believable even when seen.

These national parks, separated by less than ten miles, represent America's extremes of fire and ice. Yellowstone, a vast plateau rimmed by mountains, is the most thermally-active place in the world, with 10,000 geysers and hot springs. The Grand Tetons, to the south, whose highest peak is almost 2,000 feet above anything in Yellowstone, are the remains of a crustal tilting that rears high above Jackson Hole, a high wild valley that is completely surrounded by mountains. Yellowstone Lake, an inland freshwater sea with a 110-mile shoreline, is home to gulls and pelicans, and storms can whip ten-foot whitecaps against the shore.

In the Tetons, Jackson Lake and Jenny Lake adorn the flat valley known as Jackson Hole; in the mountains, spring comes to Lake Solitude around the Fourth of July with the glacier lilies.

To be reduced with the greatest possible speed to a state of incredulity, enter Yellowstone by Beartooth Scenic Highway (US 212) from Red Lodge, Montana, which passes through Beartooth Pass at 10,947 feet. It offers staggering views of the Grand Canyon of the Yellowstone. Or, take US 14/16/20 from Cody, which Teddy Roosevelt called "the most scenic 52 miles in America." This is one route to Old Faithful and the geysers, fumaroles, painted mudpots, prismatic springs, and thermal pools that make up the Geyser Basins regions of the park.

In the Teton Range, you may like to make your first surprise the Jackson Hole Aerial Tram ride from Teton Village. And, if these views are not staggering enough, there are several canyon trails.

Cascade Canyon Trail penetrates the heart of the mountains to Lake Solitude by way of a vast chasm. Death Canyon Trail explores alpine meadows filled with wild flowers for much of the season, and profound, awesome U-shaped canyons. Paintbrush Canyon Trail, named for its profuse trailside wildflowers, follows Paintbrush Canyon and joins the Cascade Canyon Trail at Lake Solitude. Often, however, the upper reaches of trails are closed by snow until mid-June or July.

Old Faithful (*right*) Every 77 minutes, on average, Yellowstone's most famous geyser shoots a 10,000-gallon plume of water up to 200 feet into the air. Each eruption lasts about 4 minutes, and along with the water, some 65 pounds of silica is lofted into the air. Drifting back to earth again, the cooling silica forms deposits of geyserite, predominantly gray, but sometimes blushed with pastel traces of rose and yellow, causd by iron and sulfur in the water. In time, geyserite will clog Old Faithfull's vent, but at present Park Rangers usually predict eruptions with an accuracy of plus or minus 10 minutes.

Old Faithful is one of some 300 geysers in the park, and they represent only a small part of the 10,000 or so fumaroles, hot springs, mudpots, hot lakes, and other features that make this the most thermally active area in the world. Indeed, several other geysers are almost as dramatic as Old Faithful. Castle Geyser has a two-phase eruption: for 20 minutes, an 80-foot plume of water is flung into the air, followed by an hour-long jet of steam. Excelsior Geyser, which last erupted in 1888, is now a hot spring, pouring 5 million gallons of blistering water a day into the Firehole River; in winter, the river here doesn't freeze, and elk come to its warm shores. The eccentric Riverside Geyser shoots an arching, 75-foot plume over the Firehole River.

Minerva Terrace at Mammoth Hot Springs (*left*) Deposits of travertine (limestone brought to the surface as a solution by Yellowstone's hot springs) form bulging, sugar-frosted balconies and fluted terraces on the slopes of Terrace Mountain; they can grow as much as twelve inches in a single year.

SITES TO SEE

● **Amphitheater Lake Trail** (Grand Teton) goes up the eastern slope of Grand Teton to Surprise and Amphitheater lakes at an altitude over 9,000 feet; there are panoramic views of Jackson Hole and the Wind River Mountains.

● **Grand Canyon of the Yellowstone**, up to 1,500 feet deep, has precipitous walls and magnificent falls. The most scenic sites are Artist's Point, Inspiration Point, and Lookout Point, which gives a good view of Lower Falls, twice the height of Niagara Falls.

● **Fountain Paintpot** (Yellowstone) is one of the most spectacular in the region, with rainbow-colored cones and constantly changing mini-craters.

● **Lynx, mountain lions, black bears, elks, mule deer, and moose** are found in Grand Teton National Park. One of the best ways to see lots of wildlife is to take an evening raft trip on the Snake River.

● **Gros Ventre Slide** (Bridger-Teton National Forest) is the site of a massive 1925 landslide that blocked the Gros Ventre River. Two years later, its partial collapse destroyed the town of Kelly.

● **Jackson** is well known for its Old West atmosphere. Nightly from Memorial Day through Labor Day, a mock robbery and shootout is held in the center of town.

● **National Elk Refuge** (near Jackson) is winter home to 7,000 elk. The shed antlers are collected by Boy Scouts and auctioned in Jackson Town Square on the third Saturday in May.

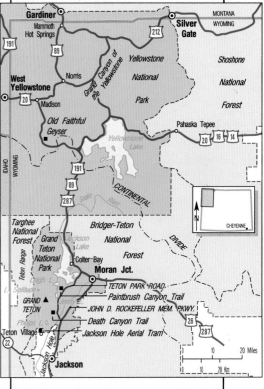

ON THE TRAIL WITH LEWIS AND CLARK
The Bitterroots and Beyond

Between the Seven Devils Mountains in Idaho and the Wallowa Mountains of Oregon, the Snake River winds through the black basalt walls of Hells Canyon, carving the deepest gorge in North America. Amidst these canyons and mountains lies the ancestral home of the Nez Perce Indians, who helped the Lewis and Clark expedition cross the almost impenetrable Bitterroot Range on the Idaho/Montana border in 1805. Since then, little has changed: the rivers still glint with trout, forests and meadows remain the territory of elk and falcons, and this remote corner of the Northwest keeps its beautiful secret.

Starting west from Missoula, Montana, the Lewis and Clark expedition embarked on the most challenging leg of its trek, crossing the razor-backed peaks of the Bitterroots at Lolo Pass and continuing along the Lochsa River, now designated a Wild and Scenic River Corridor. Not one town or village appears on this long stretch of US 12 (Lewis and Clark Highway.) between Lolo Pass and Kooskia, a wilderness where markers are the only signs of the great journey that founded the west.

At Orofino, a gold rush city in 1865, visitors can rest at the Lewis and Clark Canoe Camp, where the Nez Perce showed the strange white men how to make canoes from burned-out trees. It was in such vessels that Lewis and Clark completed their journey by river to the Pacific.

North of Lewiston, there are wheat fields and rolling prairies, and to the south, Hells Canyon National Recreation Area, where the wild Snake River winds between the black walls of the canyon. The best land views of the gorge are reached from the town of Joseph, Oregon, in the Wallowa Mountains. From here, it is a rugged drive to Hat Point Overlook, where the waters of the Snake sidewind 6,982 feet below. But the wildest stretches can only be viewed from the river itself, from jetboats and float trips that travel from Hells Canyon Dam along the 70-mile stretch of Scenic Waterway.

It is one of history's ironies that the help given to Lewis and Clark soon led to the settlement by whites on Nez Perce land. Soon after, the discovery of gold triggered the outbreak of the Nez Perce War at White Bird on the canyon of the Salmon River. Though the battle at White Bird was won by Chief Joseph and his people, they were finally forced to flee, only to be caught just short of freedom near the Canadian border. Despite such treatment of their forefathers, the Indians of the Nez Perce Reservation provide a warm welcome for visitors today.

Pumas (*left*) sometimes called cougars or mountain lions, are lone hunters and prey on animals as large as deer. The crags and caverns of this rugged area provide the ideal habitat for these wide-ranging animals.

Hells Canyon (*right*) Glistening from thousands of feet below at the base of Hells Canyon, the Snake River rushes to join the Columbia River on its way to the Pacific Ocean.

The Pale Brown Coloring of the Prairie Falcon (*far right*) enables it to blend into the rustic landscape. Although it seeks wide open country for its habitat, cliffs on the rock face provide a perfect perch to survey the surrounding landscape.

SITES TO SEE

● **Snake River** (*above*) float and jetboat trips give close-up views of Hells Canyon. For a different perspective, Heavens Gate, in a recreation area, is an overlook with panoramic views of Idaho and neighboring states from 8,407 feet.

● **Heart of the Monster** (Kamiah), a volcanic formation, is the legendary place of creation of the Nez Perce tribe. A recording explains the story.

● **White Bird Battlefield** (Grangeville) commemorates the first confrontation of the Nez Perce War in 1877; self-guiding auto tours are available.

● **Orofino** re-lives the past with the annual Lumberjack Days festival in September.

● **Weis Rockshelter** (west of Grangeville) is one of the region's oldest inhabited sites, first settled more than 8,000 years ago; ancestors of the Nez Perce continued to live here for the next 6,000 years.

● **Spalding Site** (Spalding) preserves the site of the second mission of the region's first settlers, missionaries Henry and Eliza Spalding, who arrived in 1838.

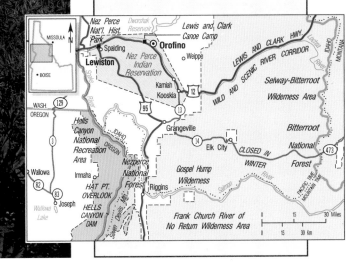

LAVA BEDS AND SAWTOOTHED MOUNTAINS
Idaho East of Boise

Natural treasures of fur and gold brought the first Europeans into this region of sawtoothed peaks and foaming torrents. Today, the wilderness rewards its visitors with year-round opportunities for recreation and adventure: hunting and fishing, rafting on the turbulent Salmon River rapids, or skiing on Sun Valley's majestic mountains. In the south, the lava flows belong to a long-ago world.

An excellent way to explore this region is on SR 75, which follows the course of the Salmon River south from Challis. At Stanley, it becomes the Sawtooth Scenic Route, bound for the snowy slopes of Sun Valley. Raft trips on the Salmon River begin in Challis and Stanley, and visitors can also swim in Challis Hot Springs. From Stanley, intrepid boaters launch rafts into the wild Middle Fork of the Salmon River, and backcountry expeditions spread out through the mountains, lakes, and streams of Sawtooth National Recreation Area.

Sun Valley, North America's first ski resort, was created as a winter sports mecca in the 1930s by Avril Harriman. He hired Count Felix Schaffgotsch to look for a site to rival the grandeur and beauty of the Swiss and Austrian Alps. Close to Shoshone, where many buildings have been constructed of locally excavated lava rock, the bizarre Shoshone Indian Ice Caves present the visitor with a more unusual snow scene: winds blowing through an ice-lined lava tube 1,000 feet long produce freezing temperatures even when the temperature outside soars.

Northeast of Shoshone lie the unearthly lavascapes of Craters of the Moon National Monument, which even moon-visiting astronauts have visited. Nearly unknown until 1921, the vast area of basaltic lava caves, cones, tubes, and desolate craters marks the remains of volcanic activity that began here about 15,000 years ago. Visitors encounter a vision of the Earth in its primordial infancy, sprouting spring flowers from cinder debris and lava flows.

More lava beds scar the earth near Twin Falls, where the Snake River plunges from a greater height than Niagara Falls. Evel Knievel tried, and failed, to leap the Snake River Canyon here on a rocket-powered motorcycle. Most people cross the canyon on the glorious Perrine Memorial Bridge or at Three Island Crossing State Park near Glenns Ferry, which was used by Oregon Trail pioneers.

Osprey in nest (*left*) An impressive bird of prey which is successful in nearly 90 percent of its forays, the osprey feeds solely on live fish and has evolved the ideal tool for catching them. The undersides of its toes are covered with tiny sharp spikes that grip the most slippery prey with ease. Osprey can carry fish weighing $4\frac{1}{2}$ pounds, which is often more than an adult bird's own weight. Nesting wherever there is water, it builds its nest of intertwined sticks and continues adding to it year after year until the structure becomes enormous.

Sawtooth Mountains, Lower Redfish Lake (*above*) This is the youngest range of the Rockies and one of three ranges—the White Cloud and Boulder mountains are the others—that tower over the Sawtooth National Recreation Area. A visitor center at Redfish Lake provides information about local history and geology.

Pahoehoe Lava, Craters of the Moon (*right*) Pronounced pa-hoy-hoy, this Hawaiian word means ropy and refers to the relatively smooth surface of hardened basaltic rock. The sharper, more stubbly surface into which more viscous lava hardened is called Aa (pronounced ah-ah), which means hard on the feet.

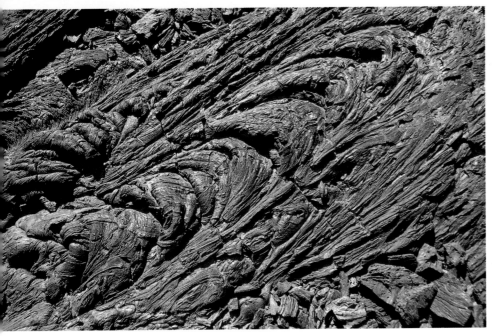

SITES TO SEE

● **Snake River Gorge** (Twin Falls) can be viewed from the 4-lane, arch-span **Perrine Memorial Bridge**. Walkways are available for pedestrians to take in the spectacular views of lakeside waterfalls, cliffs, and a park. The bridge, almost 500 feet high, is 1,500 feet long.

● **Devil's Orchard** (Craters of the Moon National Monument) is a group of lava fragments that possibly mark the vents of ancient cinder cones. Visitors can follow a self-guiding trail through these unusual features in the middle of a sea of cinders. Floral displays in spring are glorious, and in early summer dwarf monkey-flowers cover the ground in magenta. A 7-mile loop road takes in the park's main sites. Cave Area, reached via a trail from the loop road, has a series of lava tubes which can be explored. Be sure to take a flashlight and wear thick-soled shoes.

● **Craters of the Moon Wilderness** is a wild region inside the park which should only be crossed by serious explorers and hikers. Good hiking shoes are essential, and there is no water in summer.

● **Shoshone** hosts the Old Time Fiddlers' Jamboree each year, usually the second Sunday in July. Many of the city's buildings are constructed from the dark, porous, local lava rock. **The Community Methodist Church** is the prime example of this style.

● **Ketchum Cemetery** (Ketchum) is the site of Ernest Hemingway's grave. The novelist often visited Sun Valley, and a memorial to him has been erected along Trail Creek.

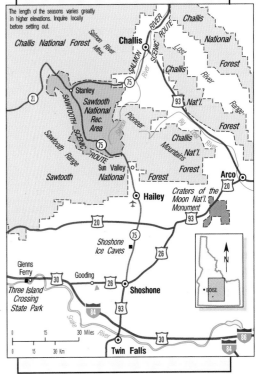

PIKES PEAK

Colorado's Gateway to the Rockies

During their arduous wagon trek over the western prairies, settlers and prospectors making their way to Colorado in the late 1850s held one vision in mind: the hope of seeing the tip of Pikes Peak. Beyond the mountain lay the promise of riches and new opportunities. For the Ute Indians, however, the mountain had a different significance; they believed Manitou, or the Great Spirit, lived there. Those who visit the mountain today—whether for recreation or to admire the view that inspired Katherine Lee Bates to write "America the Beautiful"—may think the Indians were closer to the truth than the pioneers.

Zebulon Montgomery Pike never actually climbed the mountain that bears his name. In an 1806 Army expedition mapping the Arkansas River, Pike and his company came upriver as far as Pueblo and saw the 14,110-foot peak "like a small blue cloud" to the northwest. Pike made one approach to the summit, in snow, but had to turn back. Fourteen years later, botanist Dr. Edwin James became the first non-Indian to stand atop the mountain. Today visitors can drive to the top or ride the cog railway from Manitou Springs. Pike National Forest, with campgrounds, wilderness trails, and winter ski resorts, abuts the Peak to the north and west.

In the late 1870s, railroad magnate William J. Palmer decided to make an area near the mining town of Colorado City into a vacation enclave for affluent easterners. Colorado Springs, as he called it, was soon the haunt of English aristocrats. They came to hunt, play polo and cricket, and "take the waters" at nearby Manitou Springs, where Tudor-style houses still

grace the city. Just beyond is the Garden of the Gods, a 1,350-acre expanse of twisted boulders that the Ute believed were giants turned to stone for daring to approach the abode of Manitou.

The wealth of Colorado Springs was based on the gold at nearby Cripple Creek, once billed as the "world's greatest gold camp." In its heyday, the town boasted a pair of opera houses and 14 newspapers. The Cripple Creek District Museum recalls the boom days with photographs and a working assay office.

The classic western mountain scenery has attracted artists and moviemakers as well as tourists. Albert Bierstadt, the great 19th-century landscape painter, thought the Rockies made "the finest compositions for the painter"; Tom Mix spurred the development of the Hollywood western by filming in the Cañon City area; and John Wayne came here to film *True Grit*. Only writers have a problem: as Teddy Roosevelt said during a visit in 1901, "the scenery bankrupts the English language."

Bighorn Sheep (*left*) The noble symbol of these craggy slopes, this wild breed is also called the Rocky Mountain Sheep. Heavy curling horns identify the male, and straight spiky ones mark the female. Once hunted nearly to extinction, the bighorn can now be roaming in the Rockies as it searches out natural mineral licks.

Garden of the Gods (*above*) Thrust through the earth's crust roughly 65 million years ago, the red Fountain Formation sandstone in this stony wilderness is frozen in rigid waves and sculptured shapes. Further eroded by wind and weather, some of these amazing natural sculptures bear descriptive names like Kissing Camels and Balanced Rock.

SITES TO SEE

● **U.S. Air Force Academy** (Colorado Springs) is set among rugged mountains. The starkly modern architecture of the Cadet Chapel, with its 150-foot-tall spires, is stunning. The grounds are open to the public during the day; maps of self-guiding tours are available from the visitor center. Cadets march in formation at noon during the academic year.

● **Buckskin Joe** (Cañon City) is a reconstructed 1850s mining town, made up of buildings collected from surrounding mining villages.

● **Miramont Castle Museum** (Manitou Springs), built in 1895, is an eclectic 46-room period stone house built as a mission by a French priest in Colorado.

● **Cave of the Winds** (Manitou Springs) is off US 24, west of town. The drive through Williams Canyon offers great scenic views.

● **Florissant Fossil Beds National Monument** (Florissant) includes petrified sequoia stumps from about 35 million years ago, when a large lake here was filled in with volcanic ash. An 11-foot-tall petrified sequoia is one of the largest known examples. The grounds also include a 19th-century homestead, recalling pioneer life.

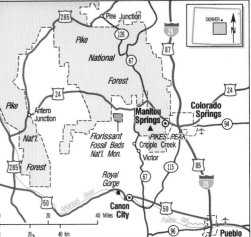

ALPINE WILDERNESS
Rocky Mountain National Park

"The shining mountains," as the Indians called the Rockies, rise like a tidal wave of stone above the western horizon of the Great Plains. In Rocky Mountain National Park, some of the most breathtaking of these peaks can be seen from Trail Ridge Road, one of the nation's highest highways. Below the snowy crests of Ypsilon Mountain and Longs Peak, which soars above 14,000 feet, are famous resort towns such as Vail, Dillon, and Frisco.

"Go West, young man, go West!," the headlines of Horace Greeley's *New York Tribune* declared in 1859. And, by the thousands they went, seeking the gold and silver then being discovered in Colorado and throughout the Rockies. They built towns—Empire, Georgetown, and Silver Plume—where the mansions of the successful can still be seen.

The old mines lie long exhausted, but the fall gold of the aspen trees, the clear blue of mountain skies, and the matchless scenery are still the hallmarks of Rocky Mountain National Park. Within its 410 square miles run more than 350 miles of trails, including the rugged path to Longs Peak, the park's highest at 14,255 feet.

Trail Ridge Road follows an ancient Ute Indian trail through the park for 45 miles along the mountain crests, reaching elevations of more than 11,500 feet. At the road's start, west of Estes Park, there are eastern views of distant plains. The 13,000-foot peaks of the Mummy Range, cloaked with permanent snow, glisten to the north. As the route circles the rim of Hidden Valley, it is possible to see Rocky Mountain bighorn sheep, or yellow-bellied marmots, wild roses, and huckleberries.

In winter, Hidden Valley is the park's major recreation area. (Trail Ridge Road is closed beyond the valley from October to May.) Near Rock Cut, the half-mile Tundra Trail goes to a wind-beaten alpine region where delicate-looking herbs and grasses cling tenaciously to bare stone at altitudes of 12,300 feet.

To explore the foothills of the Front Range, with their own striking beauty, it is impossible to do better than to visit Lory State Park, northwest of Longmont. Greeley, to the east, was founded by the Tribune editor. Its Centennial Village re-creates an entire settlement of the 1870s and the lifestyle of those who settled the Front Range.

Georgetown started as a gold-mining town but boomed when silver was found in the region in the late 1860s, becoming Colorado's third largest city by 1878. With the wealth came rapid building, and 200 Victorian structures still remain. The 1879 Howell House, built by a mine manager and local politician, was one of the most luxurious and state-of-the-art homes in all of the Colorado Territory. Long before most people had even heard of central heating, gaslights, and bathtubs, they were installed here. Maxwell House (not open to the public) is one of the nation's best examples of Victorian architecture. The town's downtown area has a variety of stores in restored 19th-century buildings.

Springtime in the Rockies (*left*) When spring and summer finally come to the Rocky Mountains, they come with a sudden rush of blue skies, green leaves, and abundant wild flowers.

Fresh Snow Near Dream Lake (*above*) One of the most accessible wild valleys in Rocky Mountain National Park lies between Flattop Mountain (12,324 feet) and Hallett Peak (12,723 feet). Between the peaks, and at the very lip of the Continental Divide, is Tyndall Glacier, whose meltwater feeds the stream that in turn has made two enchanting and aptly named lakes—Emerald Lake and Dream Lake. Farther down the valley is diminutive Nymph Lake and beyond that, Bear Lake. From the Bear Lake Trailhead, there are trails leading to Flattop Mountain, to Glacier Gorge, and, much easier walking, to Dream Lake and Emerald Lake. An Interpretive trail around Bear Lake has good accounts of the region's flora and fauna. Bear Lake Road is one of the few paved roads into a high alpine basin; for those who prefer not to drive the whole way, there is a shuttle bus to Bear Lake Trailhead.

SITES TO SEE

● **Hotel de Paris** (Georgetown) was established in 1875 by dashing Frenchman Louis Dupuy with characteristic French elegance and fine cuisine. The hotel's reputation as a civilized island in the rugged West was enhanced even more by fine wine cellars. The building is now a museum.

● **Georgetown Loop Historic Mining Area** has a steam locomotive which follows the path of mine cars used in the silver strike of 1884. Visitors can catch the train from both Silver Plume and Georgetown.

● **Aerial Tramway** (Estes Park) takes visitors in enclosed tram cars to Prospect Mountain's peak at 8,700 feet, giving spectacular views of the national park.

● **The Estes Park Area Historical Museum** contains Ute Indian artifacts, a cabin, displays from early settlers, and a Stanley Steamer automobile. The elegant Stanley Hotel on the town's outskirts was built by car maker F.O. Stanley.

● **Kauffman House** (Grand Lake) is a restored 1892 log hotel, now housing a museum of pioneer exhibits. The nearby **Grand Lake** is Colorado's largest natural lake; the mists that rise from its surface are, in Ute legend, the spirits of drowned people. The lake boasts the world's highest yacht club at 8,153 feet.

● **Loveland**, at the mouth of Big Thompson Canyon, is Cupid's hometown. Each Valentine's Day, thousands of cards are sent through the town to be postmarked.

● **Longmont Museum** (Longmont) chronicles the history of the St. Vrain Valley from before its use by French fur trappers up to the time of local astronaut Vance Brand. Exhibits include Indian spear points from 10,000 B.C.

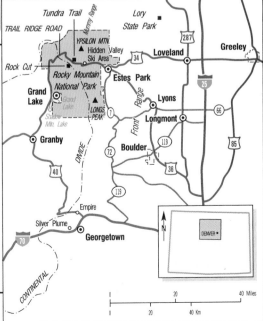

PEAKS AND PUEBLOS

Mesa Verde and the San Juan Mountains

Marked by peaks as jagged as dog's teeth, by sweeping valleys, steep-sided box canyons, and mountains that turn aspen-yellow in the fall, these landscapes are full of strongholds and secrets. Their legacy is of gold and silver; of bandits, gunslingers, and gamblers; and of Ute warriors feared even by the Navajo. In the north, the Black Canyon of the Gunnison National Monument forms an awesome abyss. In the south, ancient farmers made their homes in cliffside apartments.

Mesa Verde National Park rises 2,000 feet above the Montezuma Valley, seamed by canyons and cloaked in high grassland, pinyon pine, and juniper. Cliff dwellings are cut into the park's canyon walls. Most famous of these 13th-century homes is Cliff Palace, with its 220 rooms; Spruce Tree Ruin is also vast. Far View Ruins, easily reached from the park entrance road, typifies the mesa-top pueblos the Anasazi inhabited before they moved directly into the canyon walls.

Possibly because of a long drought, the Anasazi disappeared from the region late in the 13th century. The reservation of the Ute Indians, who came here 600 years later, surrounds Mesa Verde on the east, west, and south. All are welcome at their Sun Dance festival at Ignacio in July and at the tribal fair in late September.

Turning north at Durango, visitors pass through Purgatory and the spectacular San Juan Mountains on the way to Silverton, a quaint old silver-boom town. The Silverton, a narrow gauge, steam-powered passenger train, still follows the course of the rushing Animas River and offers an exciting 45-mile round trip from Durango to Silverton and back.

Ouray stands on the Million Dollar Highway, whose name may derive from the estimated worth of the gold tailings—refuse from the neighboring mines—that were used to build it. The town still thrives on the natural riches of hot springs and mineral ore that lie beneath it. Telluride grew so rich on mining that it could support a luxury hotel and an opera house 100 years ago. Both are well preserved, and the town is now a national historic landmark. Its fame today rests on its ski facilities and various celebrations, including a Hang Gliding Festival in the fall.

At Montrose, the Ute Indian Museum houses exhibits about the tribe and early exploration of the region. But most unforgettable here is the somber plunge of the narrow, deep Black Canyon of the Gunnison National Monument.

South of the multicolored Slumgullion Pass is the bonanza town of Creede, where silver is being mined again today.

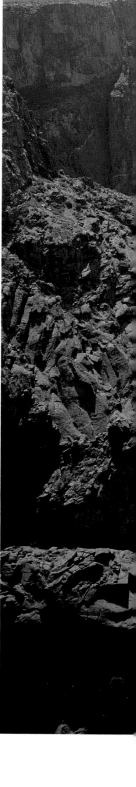

High-speed Chase (*right*) The Gunnison River, running along the bottom of Black Canyon, develops a ferocious speed as it tumbles down an average of 95 feet along every mile it travels within the gorge. This rate of fall is one of the highest for a river in North America. The steep canyon walls lining the riverbed offer the very experienced climber a challenge rewarded by breathtaking views of both landscape and wildlife. The two roads that run along the north and south rims of the canyon provide the less adventurous with stunning views from observation points perched on the cliff edges overlooking the gorge. Heavy snowfalls cut off the north rim road in the winter; however, the south rim road usually remains open up to the first two overlooks all year round. The visitor center at Gunnison Point provides hiking permits; a wealth of information about the park, its history, flora, and fauna; and current interpretive programs.

Silent Streets (*left*) The haunting remnants of the thousand-year-old Anasazi culture that flourished in the Mesa Verde give us a small insight into a past about which we still know relatively little. The evidence we have tells us that they were skilled artisans producing highly decorated baskets, earthenware, and cloth, who reached a cultural peak between 1100 and 1300. For mysterious reasons, they moved to the cliffside alcoves about 1200, and began to build their cliff dwellings. 1276 marked the beginning of a drought that lasted 23 years. In the end, the cliff dwellers, probably the ancestors of the Pueblo Indians of northwestern New Mexico, left in search of a more reliable water supply.

SITES TO SEE

● **Durango & Silverton Narrow Gauge Railroad** (*above*) One of the last of the steam trains that were once a frequent sight passes along the sheer Animas Gorge through spectacular mountain scenery.

● **Curecanti National Recreation Area** encompasses 3 reservoir lakes popular with fishers and hikers. Naturalist-led boat tours of Morrow Point Lake are available.

● **Lake City's national historic district** preserves the elaborate Victorian homes constructed during the region's mining boom days at the end of the last century. Self-guiding walking tours are available.

● **Pioneer Museum** (Gunnison) captures this part of Colorado's social and environmental history with displays of minerals, antique mining equipment, and farming tools. Visit a restored schoolhouse, a railroad depot from the 1880s, and an early post office.

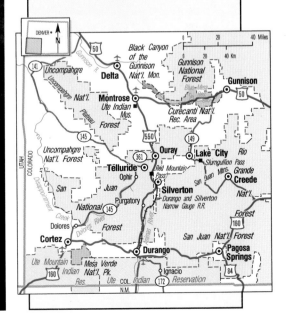

DENVER

Colorado's Queen City of the Plains sits against the Rockies' Front Range and regally commands all roads to the north, south, east, and west. Where the Granite Building stands in Larimer Square, Gen. William Larimer jumped a Cherry Creek land-claim staked by competing prospectors, named it Denver City, and, on what he then christened Larimer Street, built a log cabin with doors made from coffin lids.

Today, Larimer Square, the city's restored original block, is a preserved oasis of galleries, boutiques, courtyards, arcades, and restaurants, where the ghosts of former rough-and-tumble days can only be faintly seen. Lincoln Hall stands next to where the Apollo Theater—its second floor was built on springs to accommodate a dance floor—once was, and the 1873 Gallup-Stanbury Building was once the Tamblen Saloon, with the Antiers Hotel upstairs. An idea of Denver's Golden Age is visible in the soaring lobby of the Brown Palace Hotel in the downtown business district.

A park-like mall links the U.S. Mint, the Civic Center, and the State Capitol, whose golden dome commemorates the original source of the city's wealth. Almost directly between the Mint and the Capitol, as if placed to mediate between wealth and government, is the Denver Art Museum, a multi-sided building clad with more than one million glass tiles. It houses one of the nation's finest American Indian art collections, along with outstanding collections of European and pre-Columbian art, textiles, and costumes.

Like Denver's art galleries and museums, its parks and gardens stand between the city's colorful past and its modern sprawl. Among the best is Cheesman Park.

HISTORIC SITES AND DISTRICTS

Larimer Square The original city block was built in 1858, and today contains 13 historical buildings. Self-guiding tours start from the information booth. The square is listed with the National Register of Historic Places.

MUSEUMS

Molly Brown House Museum This 1889 home of *Titanic* survivor "the unsinkable" Molly Brown is made of Colorado lava stone with sandstone trim. It is furnished in turn-of-the-century style.

Children's Museum of Denver Hands-on fun for youngsters includes a face-painting circus tent and a playroom filled with 80,000 plastic balls.

Denver Museum of Natural History This is the nation's seventh largest natural history museum, with more than 90 dioramas of natural wildlife habitats, as well as 7 dinosaurs and more than 90 fossilized mammals. The Coors Mineral Hall displays one of the largest gold nuggets found in Colorado, weighing $8\frac{1}{2}$ pounds.

Firefighters Museum Located in Old Firehouse No. 1, this collection includes antique firefighting equipment and memorabilia.

Museum of Western Art The collection, housed in an 1880 building, includes works by Bierstadt, O'Keefe, Remington, and Russell.

NOTABLE BUILDINGS

Grant-Humphreys Mansion A 42-room house completed in 1903 in the Classic Revival style.

Pearce-McAllister Cottage This 1899 colonial revival was built to satisfy Mrs. Pearce's wish to have a "perfect colonial cottage" like ones in the eastern U.S. The **Museum of Miniatures, Dolls, and Toys** is housed here.

U.S. Mint Visitors can watch presses stamping out $1·3 million worth of coins each day. This 1904 building is one of the nation's three gold depositories, and all the coins made here are identified by a letter "d" on them. The Gold Hall displays six $27\frac{1}{2}$-pound bars, with a total value of about $1 million. Tours are conducted daily.

PARKS

Denver Botanic Garden The 20 acres of this garden include native and exotic plants and trees, as well as a Japanese teahouse and alpine garden. The **Boetcher Memorial Conservatory** displays more than 800 tropical and subtropical trees and shrubs.

Denver Zoo Home to 1,500 animals and 400 species. Exhibits include ponds with waterfowl and a monkey island. Visitors can also enjoy camel and elephant rides.

Elitch Gardens This popular amusement park was opened in 1890 as a botanical and zoological garden. Rides include a thrilling roller coaster and log flume rides, and there is a children's playground.

WORTH A DETOUR

Golden Capital of the Colorado Territory for five years from 1862, this town just west of Denver once matched its larger neighbor in importance.

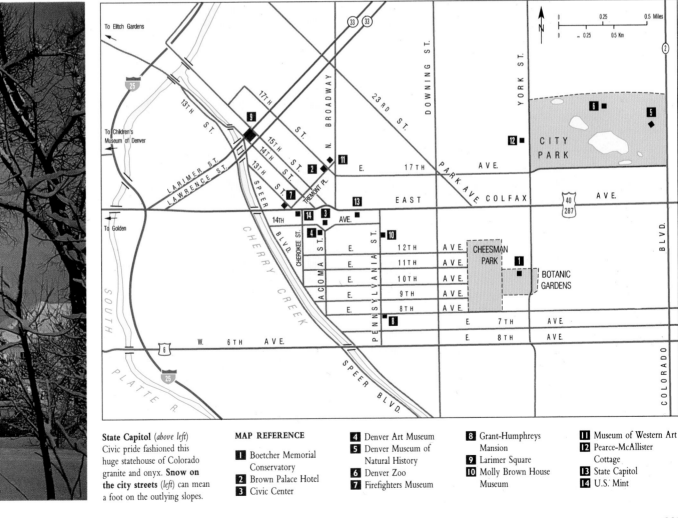

State Capitol (*above left*) Civic pride fashioned this huge statehouse of Colorado granite and onyx. **Snow on the city streets** (*left*) can mean a foot on the outlying slopes.

MAP REFERENCE

1. Boetcher Memorial Conservatory
2. Brown Palace Hotel
3. Civic Center
4. Denver Art Museum
5. Denver Museum of Natural History
6. Denver Zoo
7. Firefighters Museum
8. Grant-Humphreys Mansion
9. Larimer Square
10. Molly Brown House Museum
11. Museum of Western Art
12. Pearce-McAllister Cottage
13. State Capitol
14. U.S. Mint

THE SOUTHWEST

If the Pacific Northwest, with its coastal rainforest and snowcapped mountains, belongs to the domain of Water, these southwestern states—where the most famous forest is petrified and the predominant colors are red, brown, and yellow—are the province of Earth and Fire. The nation is baked here in landscapes where the earth is laid bare by erosion, and wind-blown dunes undulate across deserts of pure and formal beauty. In thousands of feet of tilted rock, the Grand Canyon records vast panoramas of time, and southwestern Utah celebrates them with the greatest concentration of National Parks and Monuments in America.

Of course, there are more than deserts and canyonlands in these primeval landscapes. There are mountains here, too, and lakes, though the most famous of those, the Great Salt Lake, is best known for its density. And there are the works of man. Before the Europeans came here, great Indian tribes—Apache, Hopi, Anasazi, and Ute—ruled these lands, and the most memorable habitations are the ones they made of earth or carved into living cliffs, as at Canyon de Chelly. The later Spanish missions and Mormon temples are also wonderful transformations of the native sandstone, and there are still newer adornments here: Lake Mead, tumbling through the Boulder Dam's turbines, fuels the non-stop fires of Las Vegas' neon, and great cities like Phoenix have created oases of stone, steel, and piped water in the barren desert. In the end, though, even they are only brief modulations of the Southwest's fundamental themes: Earth, Fire, and Time.

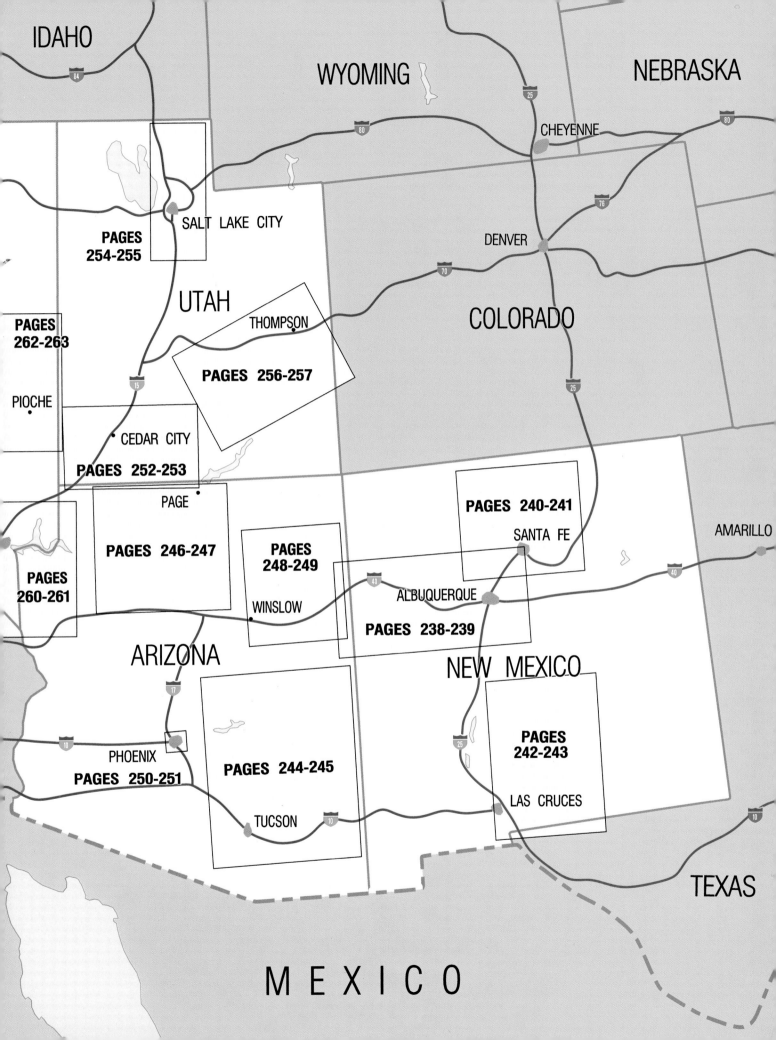

IDAHO

WYOMING

NEBRASKA

CHEYENNE

**PAGES
254-255**

SALT LAKE CITY

DENVER

**PAGES
262-263**

UTAH

COLORADO

THOMPSON

PAGES 256-257

PIOCHE

CEDAR CITY

PAGES 252-253

PAGE

PAGES 246-247

PAGES 240-241

SANTA FE

AMARILLO

**PAGES
248-249**

**PAGES
260-261**

WINSLOW

ALBUQUERQUE

PAGES 238-239

ARIZONA

NEW MEXICO

**PAGES
242-243**

PHOENIX

PAGES 244-245

PAGES 250-251

LAS CRUCES

TUCSON

TEXAS

M E X I C O

FROM ALBUQUERQUE TO ARIZONA

Central New Mexico

In central New Mexico, where the Spaniards came to find gold and stayed to farm, the desert light performs strange tricks, endowing everything with a startling clarity. It transforms the soft and tawny curves of adobe buttresses, the brilliant red peppers that hang to dry on whitewashed walls, and the fuzzy pink blossoms that sway on pale green tamarisks. This dramatic scenery provides a perfect setting for exploring the evidence of ancient Indian civilizations, or for modern adventurers to journey by river raft on the Rio Grande or by hot air balloon over the spreading desert.

Christmas Eve is when Albuquerque's Luminaria Festival is held. Then the streets in the towns nearby are filled with the scent from small bonfires of pinyon pine, and candle lanterns made from paper bags outline sidewalks, roofs, and windows. On any day of the year, if visitors take the aerial tramway to 10,378-foot Sandia Peak at dusk, they will understand the magic of this region. During October's balloon fiesta, the sky is filled with bright bubbles of color.

The historic heart of Albuquerque is the Old Town. Around 1598, Don Juan de Oñate, the first governor of New Mexico, founded a settlement here called El Paraje de Huertas, "the place of orchards." It was destroyed during the Pueblo Rebellion of 1680, but when the Spanish regained control of the region, a new settlement was built and named for the Duke of Alburquerque (the first "r" was dropped later). Today, the Old Town Plaza is a cluster of galleries, boutiques, and craft shops. The best place to see and buy Indian crafts is the Indian Pueblo Cultural Center owned by New Mexico's 19 Indian pueblos.

West of Albuquerque, Petroglyph State Park preserves about 15,000 prehistoric drawings of fantastic birds and human-like figures.

Perhaps the best known of central New Mexico's still-inhabited pueblos is Acoma, a mesa-top community dating from A.D. 600 or possibly earlier. It has three glories: its eagle-nest location on a 365-foot-high mesa, the San Esteban de Acoma Mission, built 1629 to 1640, and the cream and brown Acoma pottery, whose geometric hatchwork is hand drawn with yucca leaves.

At Zuni Pueblo, west of Acoma, you can see the celebrated Zuni jewelry, baskets, and carved animal fetishes. Each August, the tribal fair and Zuni-McKinley County Fair and Rodeo are popular events.

Between Zuni and Acoma lies the 1,278-acre El Morro National Monument. The main feature, Inscription Rock, is a 200-foot sandstone cliff bearing Indian petroglyphs and thousands of inscriptions carved by priests, soldiers, and pioneers, beginning in 1605. Below the cliff is a perpetual pool of fresh water that served for centuries as an oasis for travelers crossing the desert. Take the path to the summit to view the ancient Indian ruins and marvel at the desert spread far below.

Acoma (*right*) The renowned Sky City perched on top of this sandstone mesa is considered the oldest continuously occupied community in the U.S. Protected from intruders by their isolation 357 feet above the fields below, the ancient inhabitants descended the mesa's steep walls daily to farm.

Hot Air Balloons (*left*) Today's visitors leave the heat and dust of the desert even farther below when they ride the thermal air currents. Albuquerque's annual International Balloon Fiesta lasts nine days.

SITES TO SEE

● **New Mexico Museum of Natural History** (Albuquerque) has broad-ranging exhibits on geology and evolution, including full-size dinosaur models. Visitors can see a replica of an Ice Age cave and witness the simulated eruption of an active volcano.

● **Albuquerque** hosts an annual state-wide arts-and-crafts fair in June.

● **Indian Pueblo Cultural Center** (Albuquerque), a museum, restaurant, and crafts store complex cooperatively owned by New Mexico's 19 Indian pueblos, is based in the ruins of the 9th-century Pueblo Chaco Canyon. The central

plaza is decorated with huge murals by contemporary pueblo artists. A first-class museum, devoted to pueblo history and culture, contains displays on each of the state's pueblos.

● **Grants** is near the massive lava beds of El Malpais National Monument and those from the now-extinct volcano Mount Taylor, which towers 11,301 feet high. **Ice Cave**, with its year-round ice formations, was formed 5,000 years ago by a volcanic eruption. Nearby **Bandera Crater** straddles the Continental Divide at 8,000 feet. Wear strong footwear for exploring lava beds.

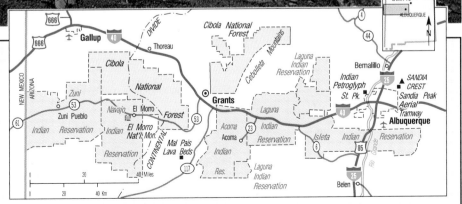

PAST AND FUTURE
Around Santa Fe

Although Santa Fe has been a capital city since Don Pedro de Peralta founded it in 1609 on the site of ancient Indian ruins, it asserts its charm in a quiet and graceful way. This is one of the most culturally vibrant cities in the U.S., and it looks to the future by conserving its past. The State Capitol is modeled on the style of a circular Indian kiva, and most buildings are painted to resemble adobe in the Pueblo style. With its Indian, Spanish, Mexican, and Anglo influence, the artistic character of this fascinating region reflects a beautiful and intriguing overlay of separate but harmonious cultures.

Traveling along Route 4 on the eastern edge of Bandelier National Monument in the early morning, it is possible to see clouds hovering in the canyons below, covering the green and yellow meadows like a patchy sea. Turn down the park road, and the mists clear, suddenly a cultural island from another time appears. In less than an hour, visitors can go from the prehistoric cliff dwellings in Bandelier's wild and beautiful Frijoles Canyon, where the air smells of the vanilla bark of ponderosa pines, to the Los Alamos laboratories where the Nuclear Age was born. Or, in just minutes, they can step from the Spanish Palace of the Governor's in Santa Fe, pass Indians selling jewelry and carved gourds, and cross the square where Anglo traders reached the Mexican end of the demanding Santa Fe Trail.

Four nations ruled New Mexico from the Palace of the Governors—the Spaniards who built it in 1610; the Pueblo Indians who ousted the Spanish briefly during the Pueblo Revolt of 1680; the Mexicans; and finally the Americans. Each period is the subject of historical exhibits inside the Palace and in other fine Santa Fe museums—the Museum of Indian Arts and Culture and the Museum of International Folk Art are memorable.

Outside Santa Fe, there are wilderness areas in the Jemez and Sangre de Cristo mountains. Outstanding pueblos include San Ildefonso, where the celebrated black pottery is made; Pecos National Monument, once the largest Indian settlement in the Southwest; and Taos Pueblo, an adobe village nearly 1,000 years old that seems to grow from the very earth of which it is made. The massively buttressed Mission of St. Francis of Assisi in Rancho de Taos is perhaps the most photographed building in New Mexico. In its rectory is an 1896 painting by Henry Ault, "The Shadow of the Cross." In a certain light, it shows Christ carrying a cross; at other times, the cross is not visible. Taos itself is a lively center for the arts, where even the fire department has a good collection of paintings. At the Ernest L. Blumenschein Home, visitors can see the restored adobe house of the famous cofounder of the Taos Society of Artists.

Mission of St. Francis of Assisi, Taos (*right*) Just as the church was probably the center of the adobe farming village, Ranchos de Taos, Taos itself was once an important center for Indian and Spanish trading activities. **Pueblo Comanche dancers at San Ildefonso** (*far right*) bring historic tribal rituals to vibrant life in the present.

Abo, Salinas Pueblo Missions National Monument (*left*) These ruins, abandoned late in the 17th century, contain a church which is a remarkable example of American medieval architecture.

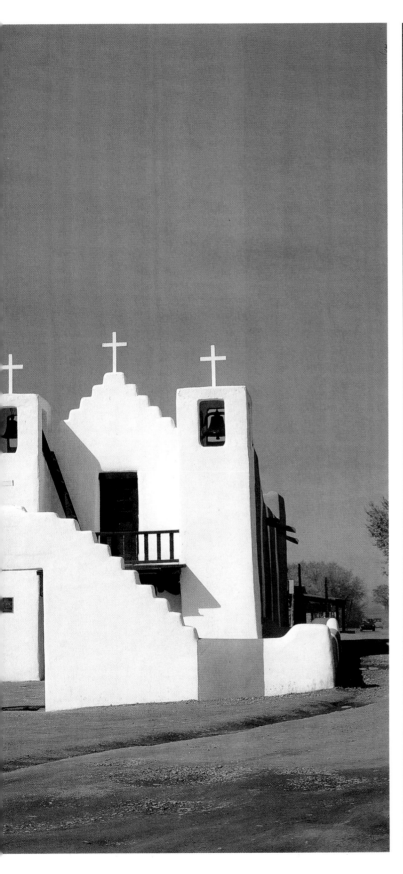

SITES TO SEE

● **Taos Pueblo** tribal members stage ceremonial dances open to the public throughout the year. Cameras are not allowed in the pueblo during these times.

● **SR 44** south from Cuba to San Ysidro passes through the Jemez and Zia Indian reservations.

● **Jemez State Monument** (Jemez Springs) contains the ruins of the 1622 San Jose de los Jemez Mission and the excavated ruins of Guisewa Pueblo.

● **Pecos National Monument** can be explored via a $1\frac{1}{4}$-mile trail from the visitor center. The route includes a restored kiva, ruins of 2 mission churches, the *convento*, where the priests lived, and the North Pueblo and partially excavated South Pueblo. Two thousand Indians once lived on the site of these now grass-covered mounds.

● **Bandelier National Monument** contains 70 miles of hiking trails through rough country, including walks from Upper Frijoles Crossing at 7,020 feet. Other attractions include Upper and Lower Falls and the Painted Cave.

● **Kit Carson Home and Museum** (Taos) is where this western legend lived from 1843 to 1868. The house is furnished with period items, including guns, saddles, cloths, and Indian artifacts. Carson is buried in the nearby Kit Carson Memorial State Park.

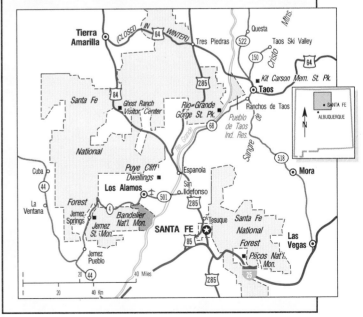

241

WHITE SANDS AND DARK CROSSES
New Mexico's Curious Terrain

Something mysterious colors the terrain of south-central New Mexico. The Organ Mountains loom like dark sentinels over the city of Las Cruces—The Crosses—named for a nearby graveyard of settlers killed by Apaches. Death-dealing Billy the Kid was captured here, and the Nuclear Age began when the first atomic bomb was tested northwest of Alamogordo in 1945. Some say the ghost of nuclear destruction still haunts the area, but the region's devout Spanish Catholics and Apaches have their own stories to explain this land's strangeness.

In 1896, 15 years after serving as Billy the Kid's defense lawyer at the courthouse on the dusty main square of Mesilla, Judge A. J. Fountain and his son rode out of town on local business. They were never seen again.

The Fountains' disappearance is just one of Mesilla's mysteries. The town's streets, lined with old adobe houses, look much as they did when the Butterfield stagecoaches stopped here in the 1850s. The Gadsden Museum contains a collection of Penitente religious objects that is both archaic and chilling. Churches, grottoes, shrines, and elaborate feast-day processions winding through the town are at the heart of Mesilla's Catholic culture.

From the heights of Aguirre Springs National Recreation Area, east of Las Cruces, look northward into the waterless valley of *Jornada del Muerto*— Journey of Death—along which many early pioneers died of thirst. The name took on new meaning when the first atomic bomb was detonated north of what is now White Sands National Monument. The great crater at ground zero is usually closed to

the public, but the visitor center at the White Sands Missile Range, near Las Cruces, displays missiles dating back to the 1940s and other relics. More rocketry is displayed at Alamogordo's International Space Hall of Fame.

The pure-white dunes of gypsum in White Sands National Monument are part of the world's largest gypsum desert. They do not show any evidence of the fateful atomic explosion, but explosions of a different kind mark the Valley of Fires State Park near Carrizozo. Here, volcanoes have created a moonscape of dark lava beds and twisted spires.

To the east, the cool heights of the Sacramento and Sierra Blanca mountains are preserved in the 1,103,441-acre Lincoln National Forest and the Mescalero Apache Indian Reservation. The area is dotted with ski resorts; one is Indian-operated.

Near Lincoln, most of which is preserved as a state monument, where gunslinging cowboys once fought on the streets and Billy the Kid escaped from jail for the last time, there are secluded snowmelt lakes and wilderness trails.

Bleached Earless Lizard (*left*) The plants and animals that live in the extraordinary environment of the White Sands have evolved in special ways to survive. Plants have developed elaborate root systems, some of them 30 feet long, and various animals, like this ghostly lizard, display a bleached coloration that is their best protection against predators.

White Sands National Monument (*above*) Covering the floor of the Tularosa Basin like heaps of granulated sugar, the sparkling white sands are the remains of Lake Lucero's constant evaporation. Dried and carried by arid southwest winds, the gypsum crystals form and reform as dunes, whose only stability derives from the vegetation anchoring them.

SITES TO SEE

● **Old Lincoln County Courthouse** (Lincoln), where Billy the Kid was once held, is now restored. The town's annual Old Lincoln Days in August include a re-enactment of the notorious escape.

● **Mesilla** is an historic village with a restored 19th-century plaza and buildings, including the courthouse where Billy the Kid was tried. Gadsden Museum has a local history collection and Indian artifacts.

● **White Oaks** (near Carrizozo) is a ghost town that was a thriving community at the turn of the century with 2,000 residents. Gold was struck here in 1880; the Old Abe Mine produced $3,000,000 of gold before it closed in 1960.

● **Space Center** (Alamogordo) has displays honoring U.S. and Soviet space pioneers. Fascinating exhibits include launch vehicles and spacecraft. At the Clyde W. Tombaugh Space Theater, visitors can view films and laser light shows on a giant wrap-around screen.

● **Ruidoso Downs** (Ruidoso) has quarterhorse and thoroughbred racing throughout the summer. The All-American Futurity, with a purse over $2,500,000, is held each Labor Day.

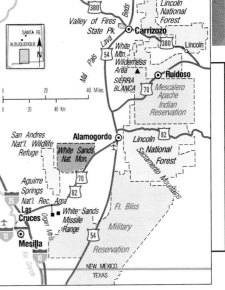

ARIZONA'S APACHE HEARTLAND
Ancient Cacti and Desert Trails

The bold land of the Apache is as enduring as the desert sun. Chief Geronimo and Chief Cochise, the great heroes of their people, once roamed these canyons and mountains and led their famous campaigns here. The Apache remain on the San Carlos and Fort Apache reservations today, now managing ranches and mountain resorts. They have endured, like the ancient cliff dwellings, the 200-year-old saguaro cactus, the 18th-century Spanish missions, and the legends of gold.

Among the strange rock formations and arid washes of the Chiricahua Mountains, Chief Geronimo and Chief Cochise fought the Apache wars of the 1860s and '70s against the U.S. Army. Two hundred years earlier, the Apaches' enemies had been the Spaniards and Mexicans, who came north from Mexico in the 1540s looking for gold along the Coronado Trail. Finding no gold, they took Apache slaves instead, and left behind horses, silversmithing, their language, and the graceful Moorish architecture of their missions. The stunning Mission San Xavier del Bac, or "White Dove of the Desert," is on a plateau that overlooks Tucson.

In Tucson Mountain Park, the native wildlife of these lands fills the Arizona-Sonora Desert Museum. In this wonderful combination of arboretum, aviary, zoo, and geological museum, exotic animals such as the margay and jaguarundi appear to roam free. Elsewhere in the park, on the dusty streets of Old Tucson, you can see the Old West wrapped in Hollywood's brand of legend: on a former movie set built by Columbia Pictures in 1939, cowboy shoot-outs are staged daily.

A little to the north, in the heart of the western section of Saguaro National Monument, towering saguaro cacti, some of them fifty feet high, ride the sloping *bajadas* for miles, and the sunsets blaze with neon pink and purple. The Apache Trail follows precipitous canyons to forests atop the Superstition Mountains.

The Apache and the Salado before them came to the shade of these mountains in the summer, and an ancient Salado tribe built cliff dwellings that are well preserved at the Tonto National Monument. Northeast lies Salt River Canyon—not as grand as the Grand Canyon, but easily its equal in beauty and color.

The Coronado Trail runs from Clifton to Alpine through the White Mountains. It passes miles of forests and green meadows before crossing the Mogollon Rim, an abrupt cliff stretching across the northern edge of the Apache reservation. Visitors who discover these highlands after a scorching stay in the desert will appreciate the eloquence of Chief Cochise: "I want to live in these mountains," he said, "I have drunk of their waters and they have cooled me."

Saguaro National Monument (*right*) The Monument has two sections. In the larger, eastern unit, the Rincon Mountain District, the saguaro forests are especially lovely and strange—thousands of towering, armed figures crowding the parched ground. In the western Tucson Mountain District of the Monument, the saguaros are taller: up to 50 feet high and weighing as much as two tons. This section of the Monument adjoins the northern edge of Tucson Mountain Park, home of the Arizona-Sonora Desert Museum. Hailed as one of the "great zoos of the world," this hillside combination of arboretum, aviary, zoo, and geological museum features animals in natural desert habitats, appearing to roam free behind hidden moats. Also well worth visiting in the Park is Old Tucson. It was built by Columbia Pictures in 1938 as the set for the movie *Arizona* and is everyone's idea of a town in the old wild west. To the delight of visitors, stagecoach rides, cowby shootouts, saloons, and entertainments still fill the dusty, atmospheric streets.

Mission San Xavier del Bac San Xavier (*left*), one of 29 missions between Sonora and the Gila River, was founded by Father Eusebio Francisco Kino in 1692. The present church dates from the 1780s and is the most dazzling example of mission architecture outside the California coastal missions established by Father Junipero Sera. Dramatically situated on a plateau overlooking Tucson, the church is a baroque masterpiece of Moorish and traditional Mexican styles. Its interior is richly furnished with a Byzantine array of statues, grottoes, and murals. Today the church functions for the local Papago Indians, and Mass is still celebrated there on Sundays.

SITES TO SEE

● **Pinal Pioneer Parkway** (SR 89) is a scenic drive along what was once the main road between Tucson and Phoenix. Roadside signs identify plants in the Sonora Desert.

● **Besh-ba-Gowah** ruins (near Globe) are the remains of a Salado Indian village from about 1225–1400.

● **Salt River Canyon** (northeast of Globe) offers brightly colored spires and sheer buttes that rise above the winding Salt River. A road down the canyon interior drops 200 feet in just over 5 miles. A picnic area is situated along the water.

● **Boyce Thompson Southwestern Arboretum** (Superior) contains 420 acres of semidesert plants from around the world.

● **Tucson** is one of the most historic towns in the Southwest. The **Arizona State Museum**, on the campus of the University of Arizona, has impressive collections illustrating the region's past and ethnic culture. **La Casa Cordova**, part of the complex of buildings that makes up the **Tucson Museum of Art**, is one of the oldest buildings in Tucson, dating from around 1850. Another important home, the **John C. Fremont House**, has period furnishings of the 1880s, when Fremont was territorial governor. The **Fort Lowell Museum** commemorates the same period, with reconstructions of the commanding officer's quarters and other rooms furnished as they might have been in 1885. The museum is in a park that preserves the ruins of the old fort.

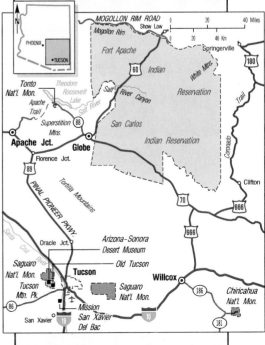

PAINTED CONTOURS OF EARTH'S HISTORY

Grand Canyon National Park, Arizona

Three million people visit the Grand Canyon each year, but those numbers should not deter crowd-shy travelers. Unimaginably magnificent, the canyon defies all expectations. No matter how many people may be peering over its rim, there is always room for more. The canyon opens up as though a vast drawer, miles across and a mile deep, had just been pulled out from beneath your feet. Miraculously revealed there are the richly painted contours of a hidden continent, and, in its plunging walls, the multicolored records of unrecorded time.

The Grand Canyon can be explored in a number of ways – by air, on foot, by raft, by mule-train, and by car. "Do it," as they say, in 20 minutes, or spend days savoring the two billion or so years consumed to produce its fantastic sculpture. At the rim's 7,000-foot elevation, the extraordinarily clear air is redolent of kaibab junipers and ponderosa pines. The desert sky is relatively cloudless, but the gradual shift of light transforms the canyon, making every view unique.

By far the most accessible part of the canyon is the South Rim. Its Grand Canyon Village includes a fine old lodge and comfortable accommodation. Driving from the lodge in either direction leads to many viewing points, each with its own history. All are well protected with barriers and protective walls.

The Watchtower, 25 miles east of the village, is a stone tower with wonderful views of the jade ribbon of the Colorado River far below, as well as the canyon, Kaibab National Forest and the Painted Desert's distant glories.

The North Rim is more remote. Reached by a 214-mile drive from Grand Canyon Village, it is undeveloped and often snow-closed October to May. Time and energy are well repaid by prodigious views downward and southward to the San Francisco Mountains, which harbor rugged trails and relative isolation.

A spectacular corridor through geological time, the Grand Canyon (*right*) has been eroded from a flat plateau by the torrential waters of the Colorado River. At the foot of the canyon, rocks more than 2,000 million years old have been exposed.

Bright Angel Trail (*left*) begins near Grand Canyon Village and winds nearly 8 miles to the river some 4,500 feet below.

River-running in dories (*right*) or white-water rafting on the Colorado offer both adventure and one of the best ways to view the grandeur of the canyon.

ARIZONA

SITES TO SEE

● **Yavapai Museum**
(Grand Canyon Village)
Follow explanations of the
canyon's timescale and the
forces that created it.

● **Cape Royal Drive**
(North Rim) Travel a 67-
mile route, which includes
prospects of the canyon and
ancient Indian dwellings.

● **Tusayan Ruin and
Museum** (near Desert View,
east of Grand Canyon
Village) See the remains of
homes and foundation walls
of a small Indian community
from prehistoric times.

WORTH A DETOUR

● **Navajo National
Monument**

● **Lipan Point**

● **Kaibab National Forest**

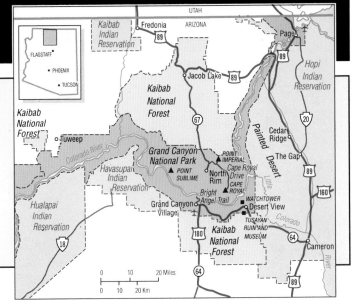

THE COLORS OF HISTORY
Navajo and Hopi Country

The lands of the Navajo and Hopi blanket 25,000 square miles of the arid reaches of the Colorado Plateau. The blazing colors that layer these rugged badlands are woven into Navajo rugs, and native jewelry captures the turquoise of the sky. Over 200,000 Navajo live here in an area the size of West Virginia. Within their territory lies the Hopi Reservation, traditional homeland of the descendants of prehistoric cliff dwellers, the Anasazi. Petrified Forest National Park and the Painted Desert, along with dusty cowtowns, borders this separate country.

Like the spirits that enter and leave Hopi kivas by different doors, visitors enter Navajo country through America's past and leave it by way of today's bright vacation lands.

When the Athabascan forefathers of the Navajo swept down from the north in the second century A.D., the Hopi were established farmers, living atop the mesas that tower above the desert. Then, as now, they descended to tend their crops of corn and squash in the sandy, red soil below.

Oraibi, on Third Mesa, is one of the oldest continuously inhabited villages in the U.S. Here the ancient Hopi ceremony of the Kachinas, rain-bringing spirits embodied by costumed men, is kept alive in the village plaza in summer. Other Hopi rituals are open to the public, too; the Snake Dance can be viewed at Mishongnovi or Shungopovi in August. Details of the dances, pottery, masks, and kachina dolls are displayed at the Hopi Tribal Cultural Center near Kykotsmovi.

Driving east into the land of "the people," or "Dineh," as the Navajo call themselves, the visitor may spot an Indian rodeo or see Navajo infants strapped to cradleboards, and the Navajo language is commonly spoken. The Hubbell Trading Post National Historic Site in Ganado was a center of trade between the Navajo and the white worlds from 1878; rugs and turquoise-and-silver jewelry are sold here. The post is named for John L. Hubbell, a self-educated New Mexican who built a trading empire out of his friendship with the Navajos. To preserve the colorful rug designs he was selling, Hubbell had them copied by artists, and these paintings still provide inspiration for weavers. The site also included a blacksmith shop, a bakery, and occasionally a one-room school.

To the north lies Canyon de Chelly National Monument, whose canyon walls, 1,000 feet high, are honeycombed with Anasazi cliff dwellings from the twelfth century. Scenic drives along the canyon's rims offer dizzying views of the sandstone ruins.

The spectrum of history runs from Window Rock, the headquarters of the Navajo nation, where visitors can observe tribal government at work, to once lawless and still popular spots like the Bucket of Blood Saloon in Holbrook. History is trapped in the reds, yellows, and blues of the stone trees—now 225 million years old—in Petrified Forest National Park, and in the nearby Painted Desert, where the spectacle of light and color reflects the essence of the Southwest.

Betatakin (*right*) This deep, south-facing natural alcove first provided shelter for the Anasazi around 1250; in the Navajo language, the word means "ledge house." Tree-ring dating techniques have shown that many timber-roofed dwellings were constructed within the cave, and that by 1286, it may have housed 125 people.

Petroglyphs (*left*) carved in sandstone and granite by the Anasazi, Navajo, and other tribes, often represented spirits of the animals and birds that surrounded them.

SITES TO SEE

● **Fort Defiance**, active during the Navajo uprisings of the 1860s, is today one of the major centers of Navajo affairs. Within the boundaries of the Navajo Indian Reservation, the town is at the mouth of the Canyon Bonito, with its sheer, perpendicular walls. Navajos live a very traditional life here, with many still living in hogans, round log-and-earth huts. The ceremonial Fire Dance is held every fall, and the more ancient Yei-Bei-Chai dance takes place during the winter.

● **Navajo Nation Fair** (Window Rock) is held during early September. Festivities include a powwow and traditional songs and dances, along with a parade and rodeo. Before entering any Indian reservation, visitors should be aware that the reservations are regarded as sovereign nations and have the right to make and enforce their own laws.

● **Little Painted Desert County Park** (Winslow) is known for its fabulous array of colors at sunset. There is a 2-mile scenic drive here that goes along the rim with views of part of the Painted Desert.

● **Petrified Forest National Park** contains several interesting sites that can be viewed from the 28-mile scenic drive through the park. **Puerco Indian Ruins** contain the partially restored remains of a community that lived here before 1400. **Newspaper Rock**, covered with petroglyphs, is viewed through a telescope from an overlook.

● **Canyon de Chelly National Monument** has prehistoric Anasazi Indian dwelling ruins, dating from 1100 to 1300, within red sandstone walls up to 1,000 feet deep in this spectacular canyon. The best ways to view the natural wonders and ruins are via the 36-mile South Rim Drive, or the 34-mile North Rim Drive. **Mummy Cave**, one of the most impressive dwellings, was occupied from 300 to 1300.

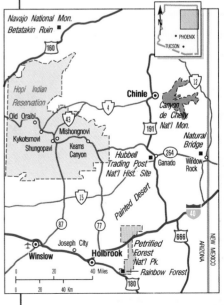

PHOENIX

With its outlying communities, Arizona's capital sprawls across the Salt River Valley, huge, glittering, and basking in the sun. Living up to its name, the city has risen from the homeland of the Hohokam Indians—whose prehistoric culture disappeared from the valley around A.D. 1400—to become the tenth largest conurbation in the U.S. and the largest city in Arizona. As if still bathed in rejuvenating fire, it offers the visitor some fascinating surprises. A young city, founded around 1868, Phoenix wears its youth like a coat of bright feathers that demand attention. In Heritage Square, the oldest part of the city, turn-of-the-century bungalows, an imposing old mansion, and a modern meeting area oblige the visitor to look at them with a fresh, unjaundiced eye.

In Phoenix, nature abuts the city with a sharpness unknown in the east, and the desert and mountains enter the city in novel ways. South Mountain Park is the world's largest municipal park, with 17,000 acres of peaks and canyons, and the Desert Botanical Garden in Papago Park is world-renowned for its collection of arid land plants. Scottsdale's seven-and-a-half-mile Green Belt has transformed the Indian Wash floodplain into a glistening chain of parks, lakes, and pools. So despite man-made steel and glasstowers and the profusion of shopping malls and ranch houses, nature lies down here with the urban lion quite happily.

The surrounding landscape blooms with cotton and with subtropical vegetables and fruits of all varieties, making agriculture a vital business for the city. Simultaneously,

industry thrives in research centers exploring new developments in aerospace, electronics, and communications. The sunny skies and comfortably dry air account for the many resorts and for the city's reputation as a winter leisure center. Leisure activities and cultural opportunities abound in every corner of the city. And just for good measure, this valley in the sun boasts a variety of interesting museums and sites that impartially preserve the archaic, the pioneering, and the futuristic aspects of the city's history.

250

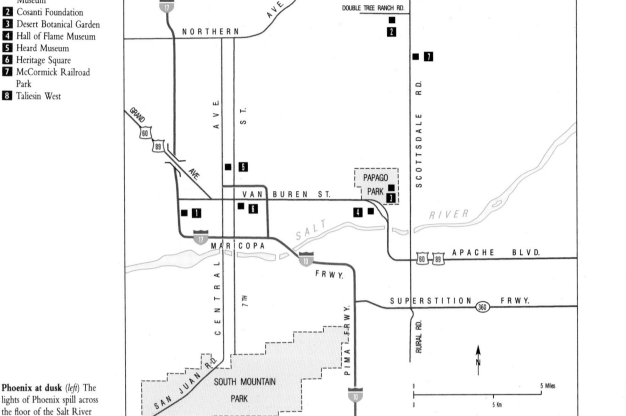

MAP REFERENCE

1 Arizona State Capitol Museum
2 Cosanti Foundation
3 Desert Botanical Garden
4 Hall of Flame Museum
5 Heard Museum
6 Heritage Square
7 McCormick Railroad Park
8 Taliesin West

Arabian Horse Sale, Scottsdale (*above*) Every February, breeders, trainers, and traders from around the world travel to Phoenix for this superlative show and sale. Interested spectators flock to admire the horseflesh, but the well-heeled come to buy.

Phoenix at dusk (*left*) The lights of Phoenix spill across the floor of the Salt River Valley like a shower of stars, stopping short where the deep darkness of the desert begins. The Hohokam Indians conquered the unyielding desert more than 3,000 years ago by threading it with an extensive network of irrigation ditches. In the 19th century, after the establishment of the present city, new ditches diverted water from the Salt River, and farmers put down tentative roots in the sandy soil. When the Roosevelt Dam was completed on the Salt River in 1911, it transformed the area again.

HISTORIC SITES AND DISTRICTS

Heritage Square The heart of the original city. Only Rosson House, a restored Victorian mansion, is open to the public on a regular basis.

MUSEUMS

Arizona State Capitol Museum houses the restored legislative chambers, period offices, and changing exhibits about political history.

Hall of Flame Museum One of the nation's most comprehensive collections of firefighting equipment, dating back to 1725.

Heard Museum Anthropological and primitive art including American Indian artifacts.

Pioneer Arizona Living History Museum Restored buildings re-create the gradual development of the old Southwest. Traditional melodramas are staged in the Opera House.

NOTABLE BUILDINGS

Cosanti Foundation (Scottsdale) Concrete complex by sculptor-architect Paolo Soleri, whose workshop is here, as is a scale model of his solar city, Arcosanti.

Taliesin West (Scottsdale) Studios and workshops of Frank Lloyd Wright's School of Architecture.

PARKS

Desert Botanical Garden, Papago Park Over 1,000 varieties of desert and arid land plants. The Phoenix Zoo is also in the park.

McCormick Railroad Park (Scottsdale) Trains on a scale of five inches to a foot carry passengers through a park built to the same scale.

South Mountain Park Look down on the city from Dobbins Lookout, 2,330 feet high.

OTHER ATTRACTIONS

Arizona State Fair Livestock shows, concerts, and rides for the entire family. October.

Heard Museum Guild Annual Fair Experience the rarely displayed culture and ceremonies of the Indians of the Southwest. March.

Parada del Sol Parade and Rodeo (Scottsdale) Everyone rides a horse or is pulled by one in the spectacular parade that kicks off a rough-riding rodeo.

THE EXUBERANT EARTH
Southwestern Utah

In no other part of the United States is the unadorned earth as exuberant and wildly beautiful as in southwestern Utah. As the light shifts, bare rocks become forests of strange trees, gaudy zoos, or assemblies of silent giants. These are landscapes scattered with monoliths decked in circus colors. The canyons are immense or sinuous and so deep that you expect to find earth-goblins perched on their towering walls. This is a land of the unexpected, where water slides, tumbles, and lunges in flash floods, and vegetation ranges from subarctic spareness to subtropical lushness.

According to Paiute Indian legend, the rock formations of Bryce Canyon were the work of Coyote, known as The Trickster. Dissatisfied with his followers, he assembled them in the canyon and turned them into its pillars, spires, and pinnacles. He created, as settler Ebenezer Bryce put it, "a hell of a place to lose a cow."

Bryce Canyon is a series of natural amphitheaters cut into the eastern side of Paunsaugunt Plateau. The top is forested with a variety of trees, including spruce, mountain lilac, and aspen.

Colors blaze at Cedar Breaks National Monument, where cliffs and arches of an almost 2,500-foot-high natural amphitheater are stained red, yellow, and purple by mineral oxides. Wildflowers blaze here, too. The monument's rim is 10,000 feet above sea level; roads are usually snow closed from mid-October through May.

Zion National Park, whose beauty beggars language, is open year round. Zion Canyon Scenic Drive follows the course of the Virgin River and Zion Canyon. In places, springs and waterfalls jet from Zion Canyon's towering cliffs, especially after the spring melt and summer storms. At Weeping Rock, streams seeping from the canyon wall create oases of ferns and moss.

Checkerboard Mesa (*right*) Near the eastern entrance to Zion National Park looms the butte of Checkerboard Mesa. The rugged sculptural quality of this eroded sandstone mountain is a spectacular example of the constant efforts of nature to affect the landscape. The orange-reds and pastels of the rock face highlight the fantastic patterns etched by time on the mountainside. Cracks in the rock face containing no more than a pocketful of soil provide a grip for flowers such as the slickrock paintbrush.

Weeping Rock (*left*) The wide variety of landscape in the vast area of the park ranges from bleak windswept rock outcrops to cool hidden sanctuaries of clear water pools ringed with moss and wildflowers. Spring water from deep within the mountains seeping through the porous stone nourishes the lush vegetation clinging to the sheer stone walls of these almost secret gardens.

SITES TO SEE

● **A scenic drive** along the Bryce Canyon rim touches Fairyland Point, Sunset Point, and the famous Rainbow Point at 9,105 feet, with its panoramic views of the entire park.

● **Floral wonderlands** thrive in Zion National Park. Cool, damp side canyons are colorful with bright red monkey and cardinal flowers, while drier environments are homes of claret cup and purple torch cacti, desert phlox, the yellow trumpets of puccoon, and white sego lilies.

● **The Temple of Sinawava**, narrowest section of Zion Canyon reached by car, is 300 feet wide. A mile-long trail called Gateway of the Narrows continues up the canyon.

● **St. George** is in a region known as "Dixie" because of its unusually warm year-round climate; cotton was grown and milled here during the Civil War. **The Mormon Temple**, the first in Utah, was built 1869–1877 of hand-quarried granite. **The Brigham Young Winter Home**, where the Mormon leader lived while the temple was being built, has period furnishings.

Another house with furnishings from the 1880s is the **home of Jacob Hamblin**, a Mormon missionary who had notable success securing peace with the Indians.

● **Pah Tempe Springs** (Hurricane) is one of the world's largest natural hot springs.

● **Moqui Cave** (Kanab) has dinosaur tracks and a replica

of cliff dwellings believed to have been inhabited around A.D. 900. Nearby **Heritage House** was built in 1894 of local materials.

● **Rim Trail** (Bryce Canyon) wanders for 11 miles through sagebrush, pinyon, and cliff roses.

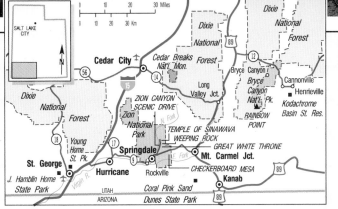

PEAKS AND BASINS
Utah's Mormon Country

From the crusty flats of the Great Salt Lake to the alpine meadows and snowfields of the Wasatch Range, the land the Mormons made their own is a kaleidoscope of topographic, climatic and cultural diversity. The first non-Indians to see the region were members of a 1776 expedition led by Franciscan priests. By 1847, when Brigham Young and the Latter-day Saints arrived at the Great Salt Lake, the territory belonged to Mexico. Within a year, it had passed to the U.S.; and by the 1860s, silver prospectors were setting up camp. Today, Utah is a popular vacation site, with out-of-staters flocking to winter resorts for deep-powder and wilderness skiing.

Migrants—birds and people—settle at the eastern edge of the Great Salt Lake. Most ancient of all settlers at the lake's margin are the birds—over 200 species include white pelicans and whistling swans.

The greatest testimony to the faith and hard work of the area's human settlers is the Mormon Temple in Salt Lake City, but the region holds many other Mormon sites. At Brigham City, where Brigham Young gave his last address in 1877, there are guided tours of the Box Elder Tabernacle and pioneer relics at the Brigham City Museum-Gallery. Brigham Young University in Provo was founded by the Latter-day Saints in 1875 and is now one of the nation's largest private universities. On campus, be sure to see the 112-foot carillon.

From Provo, a short ride via US 189 takes you to Provo Canyon and Bridal Veil Falls, where a 1,753-foot aerial tram ride offers spectacular views of the falls. Continue to Heber City for a ride on the Heber Creeper antique steam train through Heber Valley. A museum at Heber City depot displays railroad memorabilia; a re-created frontier town is nearby. The Alpine Scenic Loop (SR 92), with its fall colors, branches off US 189 and passes Mount Timpanogas. It also passes actor Robert Redford's Sundance Ski Resort and Timpanogos Cave National Monument, with its many pools and rock formations.

To the north of the region, near Logan, lies striking and easily reached mountain scenery. The folded sedimentary rocks of Logan Canyon contain numerous fossils, and, if you go 17 miles up the canyon from Logan and take a $5\frac{1}{2}$-mile trail, you can see the 3,000-year-old Jardine Juniper, believed to be the world's oldest and largest juniper tree.

Wind surfers on Deer Creek Reservoir (*left*) The Wasatch Mountains and Mt. Timpanogos overlook these colorful wind-powered craft. Elsewhere in the Wasatch-Cache National Forest, fishermen cast for trout in the glacial lakes, and water-sport enthusiasts swim and sail in picture-book settings of sun and sky.

SITES TO SEE

● **Timpanogos Caves National Monument** contains 3 limestone caves for exploring with a guide. A dazzling array of stalactites, stalagmites, and the bizarre, bright white helictites is found in each cave. Pools reflect these geological wonders, adding to the mystery. Most

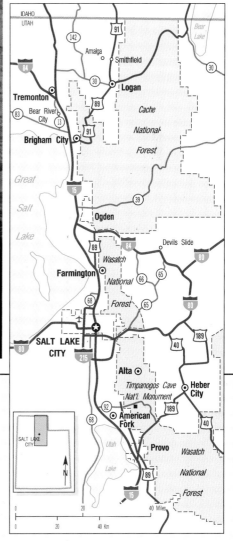

Salt Lake City at the foot of the Wasatch Mountains (*left*) When the Mormons left their city at Nauvoo, Illinois, to travel west with Brigham Young, no one knew where their migration would lead them. With the famous words "This is the place," in 1847 Young chose the valley where Salt Lake City now stands for their new community. The city proudly celebrates its founding on Pioneer Day, July 24, and it is now the world headquarters for the Church of Jesus Christ of Latter-day Saints. Called Great Salt Lake City until 1868, it is also the largest city in Utah and an important processing center for the products of the farming and mining regions that surround it. Visitors can view Brigham Young's home, called Beehive House, and his grave, as well as the mighty Temple, which took 40 years to build, and the vast Tabernacle, which seats 6,500.

incredible features include the Great Heart of Timpanogos, the Frozen Sunbeam, and the Chocolate Fountain. Access to caves is by ticketed tours only; there is a steep 1½-mile walk along a trail to the caves. **Canyon View Nature Trail** offers a leisurely walk through American Fork Canyon with good views.

● **Mt. Timpanogos' peak** can be reached via 2 hiking trails in Uinta National Forest.

● **Ronald V. Jensen Historical Farm** (Logan) is designed to resemble a 1917 Mormon farm. Traditional farming methods, such as sheep shearing, are often demonstrated.

● **Inspiration Point** (Brigham City) offers panoramic views that extend into Nevada on a clear day.

● **Harris Fine Arts Center** (Provo), on the campus of Brigham Young University, contains European, 19th-century American, and scenic Utah paintings, as well as a collection of musical instruments.

● **Pioneer Museum** (Provo) displays western art as well as artifacts from Utah's early days.

● **McCurdy Historical Doll Museum** (Provo) displays costumed dolls wearing folk costumes from around the world as well as American Indian and First Lady dolls.

CANYONLANDS
Southeastern Utah

Utah's canyonlands are a textbook of geological time. Time unwinds in serpentine canyon walls, rears up in massive striated waves above the twisting gorges of riverbeds, and stands in monstrous wind-worn arches, curving eternally over the lonely desert. The strange plants and animals that survive in these harsh and desolate environments bring to mind countless centuries of extraordinary evolution, and the ancient cliff drawings represent numerous mythological creatures older than recorded time itself.

Arches National Park boasts the world's greatest concentration of natural arches—there are more than 200 of them. Landscape Arch—105 feet high and spanning 300 feet—is one of the world's largest.

Southwest of Arches, the Colorado and Green rivers divide Canyonlands National Park into three sections. In the north is the Island in the Sky, a broad mesa lying between the two rivers. As its name promises, Grand View Point affords a fine vista of their confluence. A 100-mile jeep route, the White Rim Trail, follows a ledge 1,000 feet below the spectacular plateau; reservations are required for primitive campsites along the trail.

In the Needles region, named for its jumbled pinnacles of orange-and-white-ringed rock, Salt Creek provides water for cottonwoods and tamarisk trees. Grassy meadows bloom in Chesler Park, turning the desert into a prairie. On view in Salt Creek Canyon is the internationally known All-American Man pictograph, decorated with what looks like an American flag.

The park's most remote region is the Maze, a labyrinth of colorful canyons, ridges, and standing stones. Spiny blackbush shrubs dominate this arid wilderness, as do many varieties of reptile, including the leopard lizard, whose long legs keep its belly off the desert's burning floor. In Horseshoe Canyon, a collection of strange, life-size pictographs known as the Great Gallery depict the ancient spirits who visited this haunting landscape in prehistoric times.

Capitol Reef National Park, situated west of Canyonlands, takes its name from the white-capped outcrop—thought to resemble the Capitol building in Washington, D.C.—atop its long, pleated ridge, or reef. Navajo Indians called the colorful cliffs "sleeping rainbows." Before they disappeared around 1250, the Fremont Indians made pictographs and petroglyphs here representing distinctly non-human figures.

Other highlights of the park include Cathedral Valley, discovered during a search for a missing plane after World War II, and Hamburger Rocks near Muley Twist Canyon.

Inspired Lookout (*right*) The extreme ferocity of nature can hardly be imagined on a clear calm day, and yet only natural forces have carved this weird and contorted landscape. The soft pastel hues color the overwhelming vista in a surreal glow that could only be nature's handiwork. The canyons are rimmed by breathtaking observation points which delight the eye and inspire the mind. To descend into the heart of the canyons is to plunge into a world of extreme contrasts. The turbulent rush of wild-running rivers hurtling along their path to the sea provides the adventurer with the promise of superb white-water rafting. As the riverbed softens, the rushing river slows, giving the rafter the ideal vantage point for observing the variety of wildlife attracted to the oasis of the riverbank.

Landscape Arch (*left*) The natural stone arches create an awe-inspiring landscape which is a favorite of hikers. Cracks allowed the wind and rain to begin the laborious task of wearing away the exposed rock. Some of the enlarged cracks isolated long fins or narrow walls of stone. Eventually, due to the unending cycle of freeze and thaw, the arches we see today developed. As this process continues and the arches break down, the resulting buttresses will be the only reminder of these examples of nature's architecture.

UTAH

SITES TO SEE

● **Glen Canyon National Recreation Area**, on the banks of the Colorado River, connects Grand Canyon and Canyonlands national parks. In addition to camping and picnicking sites, the park features boating, fishing, swimming, and horseback riding. The auto ferry that crosses Lake Powell stops at Bullfrog Basin and Halls Crossing marinas.

● **Devils Garden Trail** (Arches National Park) is a 2-mile hike to the spectacular **Double O Arch**. Hikers of all levels of fitness will find trails with magnificent sights throughout the park. **Wolfe Ranch**, near Delicate Arch Viewpoint, is the remains of a cattle station started in 1888 that managed to function in the rugged conditions for 20 years.

● **Shafer Trail** (Canyonlands National Park), once a cattle trail, provides a passage for 4-wheel-drive vehicles to Shafer Canyon.

● **Goblin Valley State Reserve** contains thousands of rock formations ranging from the strange to the grotesque, but usually described as "gnomish."

● **Green River** is the center for expeditions on the Green and Colorado rivers. The town's annual Melon Days celebration is held the second weekend in September.

● **Moab** hosts the Jeep Safari every Easter and is the starting point for many jeep, raft, canoe, jet-boat, and airplane tours of the region. One of the more unusual tours is the 2-hour Canyonlands by Night trip on the Colorado, featuring illuminated cliffs.

● **SR 128** from Moab to Cisco follows the Colorado and offers spectacular scenery along the way.

WORTH A DETOUR

● **Rainbow Bridge National Monument**

● **Natural Bridges National Monument**

● **Newspaper Rock State Park**

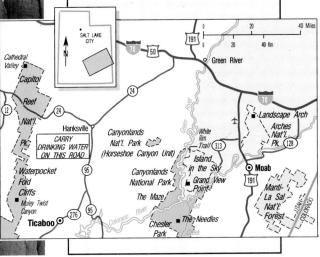

257

BIG SMOKY VALLEY AND TOIYABE NATIONAL FOREST

Central Nevada

US 50 follows the route of Pony Express riders, switchbacking its lonely way across north-south mountain ranges. It climbs summits more than 7,000 feet and descends to broad valleys that late sunlight turns golden and patterns with the long shadows of sagebrush. The Big Smoky Valley, running south from US 50 between the Toiyabe Mountains and Toquima Range, gains the spectacular aridity of the southern gold and silver fields around Tonopah. Here the hills crumbled under millennia of fierce sun, and here and there the desert gapes with long-abandoned mineshafts. In these beautiful, empty, archaic landscapes, the towns and ghost towns have a strangely remote quality. Like the petrified sea monsters that "swim" in shale at Berlin-Ichthyosaur State Park, they seem not merely old, but preserved from a different world.

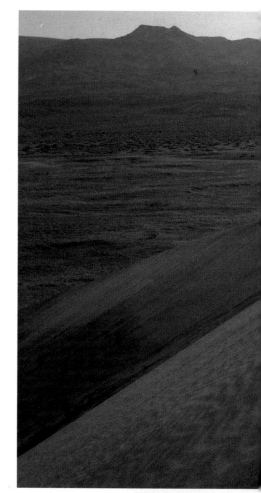

In 1862, a Pony Express rider (or, if the legend is true, his horse) discovered rich veins of silver in the foothills of the Reese River valley. Within two years, the original mining camp had grown into the town of Austin, with a population of 10,000 and 11 ore-reduction mills. Today, the town has only a few hundred inhabitants, but its main street is redolent of the boom days: It preserves—as surely as the gravemarkers of the Cornish, Scottish, and Irish mineworkers in the cemetery at the western edge of town, or the tower of Stokes Castle, the eccentric home of an eastern financier do—a memory of something foreign and far-removed. Gridley Store, the Methodist Church, and the International Hotel are buildings left from the heady mining days.

The steep climb of US 50 from Austin to the pinyon pine-clad coolness of Austin Summit at 7,484 feet, precedes a long descent to the northern end of Big Smoky Valley. If you turn south from US 50 and enter the valley on SR 376, you enter a different world, where the broad desert is bounded east and west by the hazy Toiyabe Mountains and Toquima Range, and the austerity of the land requires a marshaled precision of the vegetation. Like unsociable people, the desert plants keep their distance.

The turnoff to Kingston Canyon lies a few miles south of the junction with US 50. In true Nevada style—which is to heap startling contrasts on the entirely unexpected—the road will take you to a tranquil place of pure enchantment, a place of aspens, meadows, soft green mountains, a trout stream, and a mirror-like lake.

Farther south, a few miles north of Carver's, is another sort of oasis, Darrough's Hot Springs. Once stagecoaches stopped here at a hotel, saloon, and restaurant. Only the hot springs now re-main, but you can still bathe in them.

In Tonopah, the old Mizpah Hotel, once billed as The Finest Stone-built Hotel in The Desert, is still a fine place to come in from the heat and to eat a steak in the evening after crossing the desert. Here you can imagine, in the shade of the slot machines, the ghosts of Jack Dempsey, who worked as a bouncer; of Wyatt Earp, who dealt cards and his reputation; and of Jim Butler, who started it all. Butler was the prospector whose mule ran off one day in 1900 and, as good equines do in Nevada, led him to the veins of silver that made Tonopah, for a time, the Silver State's most important town.

The legend comes to life every Memorial Day weekend, when the town celebrates Jim Butler Days with parades, barbecues, old-fashioned mining contests, and burro and camel races.

Big Smoky Valley (*above*) In this long slab of arid desert wedged between two mountain walls, the dunes can sparkle with frost or glitter like gold dust in the sun. Too dry to support much plant life without assistance, valleys like this one prove bounteous when irrigated.

The prickly poppy (*left*) has developed a thick stem and spines instead of leaves in order to absorb and retain water.

Tonopah (*right*) struck silver in 1900, but many towns that boomed overnight have since gone bust. Historically, Nevada's riches lie deep beneath the earth's surface. Gold, silver, and copper have poured out of the ground since the mid-1800s.

SITES TO SEE

● **Spring Mountain Scenic Loop** (Toiyabe National Forest) climbs to 8,500 feet. National hiking trails through the forest are the Pacific Crest National Scenic Trail, Toiyabe Crest National Recreation Trail, and The Mount Charleston National Recreation Trail. Hikers can reach the top of Charleston Peak at 11,918 feet.

● **Central Nevada Museum** (Tonopah) covers the state's heyday as a mining center. Displays include heavy industrial and mining equipment.

● **Berlin-Ichthyosaur State Park** (Gabbs) displays fossils of reptiles that swam in a now-extinct ocean 180 million years ago. Although similar ichthyosaur fossils have been found worldwide, the collection here contains the largest examples, with some up to 50 feet long. The park takes the first half of its name from the former company mining town of Berlin. Established in 1897, Berlin was abandoned in 1910 and is now a ghost town within the park.

● **Hickison Petroglyph Recreation Site** (Austin) has petroglyphs from 1000 B.C. to A.D. 500. Nearby is the former Pony Express Trail.

WORTH A DETOUR

● **SR 305** northward from Austin to Battle Mountain is a scenic drive through the picturesque Reese River valley. Minerals were discovered near Battle Mountain in 1870, then the town grew as a center for supplying mining equipment.

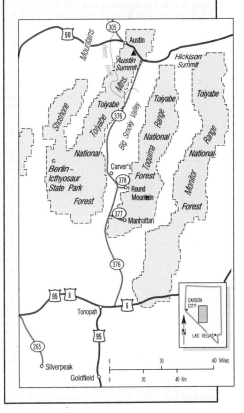

LAND OF FIRE AND WATER
Nevada's Southern Tip

Before Hoover Dam was completed in 1936, this was a land of fire. Summer temperatures soared into the 100s, as they still do, and the red Jurassic sandstone was the desert's most beautiful emblem. Then the dam was built, and Lake Mead shifted the balance of nature. Now, eight million visitors a year come to Lake Mead National Recreation Area, drawn by the fires of Las Vegas's neon and the blue–on–blue of the amazing lake.

In the early morning or late afternoon, bighorn sheep come to drink at the edge of Lake Mead. In the nearby desert, where the annual rainfall is usually less than six inches, jack rabbits, lizards, and roadrunners only venture out during cooler hours. Beyond the waterline, where huge striped bass do their submarine cruising, there is a theater of wings alien to desert climes: pelicans, geese, herons, cormorants, ospreys, and bald eagles hunting delicacies.

The creator of all this flap and spray, of the lake and the 550-mile shoreline that separates the worlds of the bighorn and the bass, is an arc of concrete across the Black Canyon of the Colorado River: the Hoover Dam. Towering 726 feet, it provides water for 14 million people, irrigates more than one million acres of land, and provides enough electricity to power half a million homes.

On the way south to Cottonwood Cove, visitors can find evidence of quieter days at Searchlight, a town, according to one legend, that was named for a brand of matches. In 1907, it was a flourishing gold-mining community; then the mines ran out. Today, visitors can see the old mine headshafts and historic buildings nestling among the modern ones.

At Overton, a town founded in 1865 by Mormon pioneers, the Lost City Museum of Archaeology displays finds from the 2,000-year-old Lost City pueblo. The town makes a good base from which to explore Lake Mead's fiery counterpart, the Valley of Fire State Park. In this showplace of glowing red sandstone, just beyond the lake's turquoise crater, ancient petroglyphs of horned sheep and lizards inhabit an eroded landscape of extraordinary beauty.

Hitting the Jackpot (*below*) The lure of the slot machines and the gaming tables is intensified by the shimmering light of the Las Vegas casinos. The visual bonanza of flashing neon and garish spotlights creates an image of a mothership from another world hovering just above the desert floor.

Putting Out the Fire (*right*) The Hoover Dam, which was known as Boulder Dam until 1947, was completed in 1935. It stilled the river and allowed the mud to settle, producing the crystal-clear Lake Mead at the heart of the nation's first national recreation area.

SITES TO SEE

● **Hoover Dam** offers 35-minute tours throughout the day, including the powerplant. When it was completed in 1935, it was the world's largest dam, 726 feet high. A small exhibition center features a model of Lake Mead with a recorded description of the dam's functions. Films of the construction project are shown at the **Boulder City Visitors Bureau**.

● **North Shore Scenic Drive**, along Lake Mead, takes visitors through countryside bright with red rock formations, as well as offering stunning views of the crystal blue waters against desert colors of brown, black, and red.

● **Old Mormon Fort** (Las Vegas), an 1855 Mormon agricultural mission, originally offered shelter for travelers on the Salt Lake-Los Angeles trail headed to the California gold mines. Part of the fort is reconstructed and furnished with antiques to show Mormon lifestyle in the early 1900s.

● **The Liberace Museum** (Las Vegas) is a shrine to one of the city's most popular performers. In addition to personal memorabilia, the collection includes Liberace's priceless customized car collection and flamboyant wardrobe.

● **Las Vegas's casinos** are glittering gambling palaces open 24 hours. At **Circus Circus**, built to resemble a circus tent, clowns, trapeze artists, and animal tamers entertain visitors around the clock. **Binion's Horseshoe** has one of the most-expensive facades in the world: 100 $10,000 bank notes are pressed between panes of bullet-proof glass.

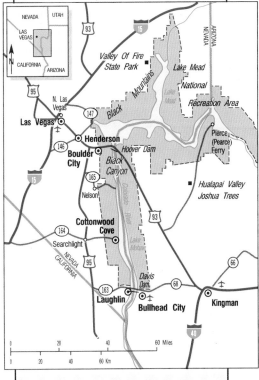

PITS AND PEAKS
East Central Nevada

The mountains of east-central Nevada culminate in Wheeler Peak, the highest mountain entirely within the state and the focal point of Great Basin National Park. Hiking trails begin where the Wheeler Peak Scenic Drive up the mountain ends, at an altitude of 10,000 feet. Visitors can follow them to shimmering alpine lakes, through a venerable forest of bristlecone pines, or directly to the summit— 13,063 feet high—to enjoy panoramic views of distant valleys, plains, and ranges. Like so much of east-central Nevada, Wheeler Peak shows the visitor a world of multiple perspectives.

The distance from the terraced depths of the Kennecott Copper Pits near Ely and the depths of Teresa Lake to the summit of Wheeler Peak is less than 50 miles. Pit and peak are thus neighbors, and each is the other's inverse.

The five gigantic open pits that stretch in a line six miles long were abandoned about 1978, and the massive ore trucks that once crawled along their neat terraces are gone. But they have become important symbols of the region's mining legacy. Wheeler Peak is an equally potent symbol of the state's natural wildness. The bristlecone pines on its upper slopes, gnarled and polished by wind and weather, testify to thousands of years of lonely isolation. At the base of the peak, Lehman Caves contain a subterranean wonderland of stalactites and stalagmites, limestone columns, flowstone streamers, and cave corals.

Traveling southwest from Ely, visitors pass through Currant and across a corner of Humboldt National Forest, where the desert seems to have been planted by a scrupulous gardener. At Lunar Crater, a huge black-rimmed caldera scoops a hole 430 feet deep in the soft prairie, which is dotted with volcanic craters called maars. The maars rise abruptly from the plain to stand like surreal guardians, their smooth sides oddly hollowed by partial collapse.

Lincoln County's infamous Million Dollar Courthouse still stands in Pioche, once considered the toughest town in the West. Begun in 1871, when its cost was estimated at $26,400, the courthouse was completed a year later, by which time the cost had reached $88,000. Refinancing and corrupt officials caused the debt to climb steadily. By 1937, when the debt was finally paid off, the county had lost nearly $1 million. Four years earlier, the building had been condemned. It was sold in 1958, with the four lots it stood on, for $150.

The attractive courthouse, now under restoration, is open to the public, as is the local cemetery, Boot Hill. The first 75 people buried here were murdered, many of them by a small army of gunmen hired to protect mine claims. As profits peaked, Pioche became a pit of vice.

Bristlecone pines on Wheeler Peak (*right*) While sagebrush and cacti bloom in some parts of Great Basin National Park, another area is a freezing Arctic-Alpine tundra life zone. An ancient and very uncommon forest of bristlecone pines contains some of the earth's oldest living things.

The Parachute formation in Lehman Caves (*left*) has become the symbol of this fantastic natural collection of colorful stone shapes. Drop by drop, calcite-laden water has hardened over time into intricate patterns of lacy crystals and columns as smooth as weathered wood.

262

SITES TO SEE

● **Ward Charcoal Ovens Historic State Monument** (south of Ely) consists of six 30-foot-high beehive-shaped ovens that are 27 feet wide at the base. Made of fieldstones in the 1870s, each blast furnace operated 24 hours a day, producing charcoal for mine smelting operations at nearby Ward. This 160-acre site is often inaccessible during winter.

● **Nevada Northern Railway Museum** (Ely) preserves rolling stock of the Nevada Northern line from several eras, as well as a dispatcher's office and a machine shop. Visitors can ride in restored rail cars through Ely, a ghost town, Robinson Canyon, and the Keystone mining district.

● **The White Pine County Public Museum** (Ely) houses Indian relics, as well as local mining memorabilia. Exhibits include steam locomotives from 1909 and 1917.

● **Garnet Hill** (west of Ely) has a garnet-studded rhyolith outcrop at the summit.

● **Delamar** (near Caliente) is a ghost town with a few rock buildings left from its populated days. There are also the ruins of a mill and a cemetery.

● **Lehman Caves** (Great Basin National Park) have candlelight tours in the summer.

● **Pioche** celebrates its mining and gun-slinging past with the Heritage Days festival each July.

● **Cathedral Gorge State Park** (Panaca) is located just off a scenic part of US 93. The park covers 1,633 acres and has camping and picnicking facilities.

WORTH A DETOUR

● **Eureka** was once a major lead-smelting town with a population of 11,000. It supported 100 saloons and even an opera house, along with several newspapers and fire-fighting companies.

● **Elko**, a cattle town, hosts the annual Cowboy Poetry Gathering every year at the end of January.

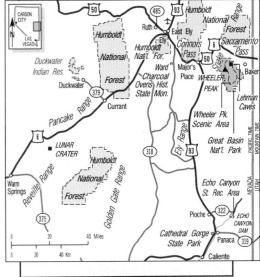

PACIFIC SHORES

At the rim of the continent, California fronts the Pacific with a coastline variously magnificent (the towering crags of Big Sur), romantic (the mist-shrouded seastacks of the northern coast), and enticing (the exotic beaches of Venice and Malibu). To the east, the Golden State climbs to the dizzyingly beautiful ranges, forests, and lakes of the Sierras. A rich plaid of flower and vegetable farms covers the central valley, and in the southwest, citrus orchards and shimmering date palms gradually yield to the dry exotics of the Mojave Desert. Within the compass of these wonderlands are two of the world's great cities: Los Angeles, where dreams are business, and San Francisco, the city of wondrous light and irresistible charm.

Two thousand five hundred miles west-southwest of California, the islands of tropical Hawaii rise sharply from the Pacific, born of volcanic fires and lying in the multi-colored sea like a counterpart of Eden. Except where the high calderas are washed in other-worldly shades of plum, terracotta, and molten red, or where dark, almost sheer cliffs fall into the sea, the islands are cloaked in infinite shades of green—rolling pastels in the Big Island's ranch country, dark rainforest shades splashed with bright flowers in Waimea Canyon, and almost luminous ones on the fern-shaggy pinnacles of Maui's Iao Valley. As for the towns and villages of Hawaii, they range from upbeat Honolulu, to former whaling harbors and the haunts of royalty; at their best, they have an old-world quality found nowhere else in the United States.

NIIHAU

KAUAI
PAGES 290-291

OAHU

HONOLULU
PAGES 292-293

PACIFIC OCEAN

N

0   50   100 Miles

0   50   100 Km

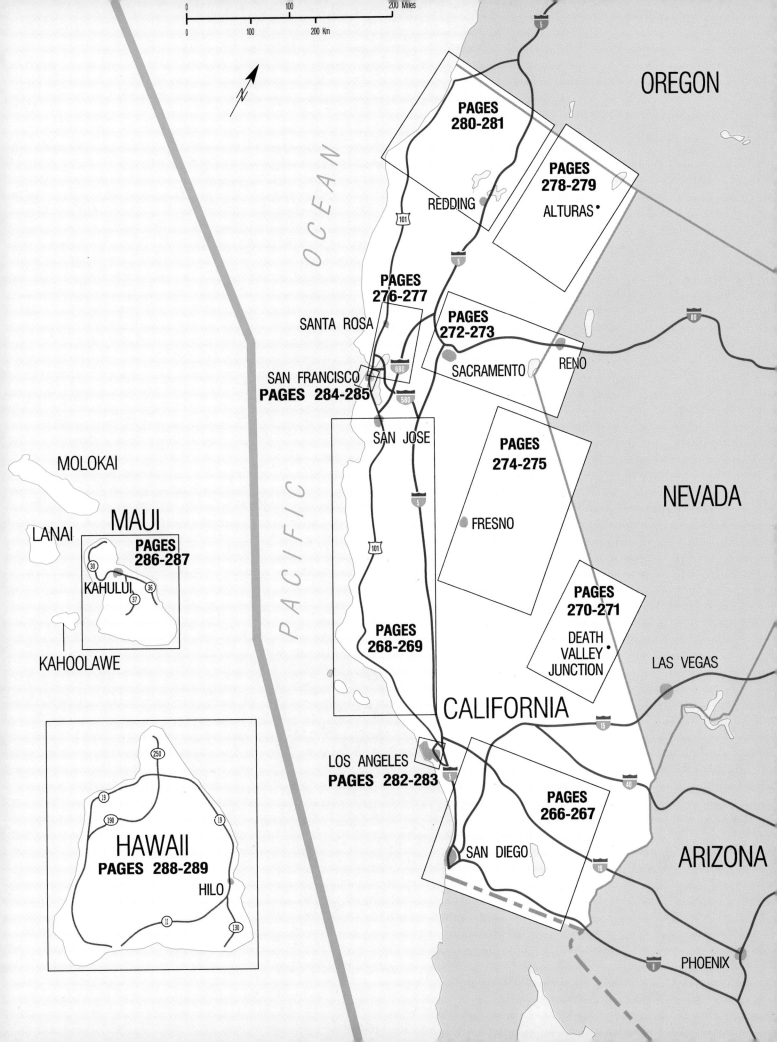

OREGON

PAGES
280-281

PAGES
278-279

REDDING

ALTURAS

PAGES
276-277

PAGES
272-273

SANTA ROSA

RENO

SACRAMENTO

SAN FRANCISCO
PAGES 284-285

PAGES
274-275

SAN JOSE

PACIFIC

PAGES
268-269

FRESNO

NEVADA

PAGES
270-271

DEATH
VALLEY
JUNCTION

LAS VEGAS

OCEAN

MOLOKAI

LANAI

MAUI

PAGES
286-287

KAHULUI

KAHOOLAWE

CALIFORNIA

LOS ANGELES
PAGES 282-283

PAGES
266-267

HAWAII
PAGES 288-289

HILO

SAN DIEGO

ARIZONA

PHOENIX

0   100   200 Miles

0   100   200 Km

N

DESERT TREASURES
East of San Diego

The Mojave Desert spreads across southern California, a shimmering plain whose southern arm runs into the drier Colorado Desert. Hidden away in the desert are oases of giant palm trees fed by tiny trickles of water and stony ranch country. Tucked away here, too, are the curious wonders of Joshua Tree National Monument and the opulent city-oases of Palm Springs and Palm Desert. To the south, towns of a radically different character—Calexico and Mexicali—hug the Mexican border, surrounded by distant rings of dark mountains.

Travelers who drive east over the coastal hills around San Diego and head north on SR 79 from I-8 pass through the gnarled oaks of Cleveland National Forest to Cuyamaca Rancho State Park, where resinous ponderosa and Coulter pines shade huge boulders, and clear streams flow through green hills and grassy meadows. West of the Santa Rosa Mountains are the stark flats of Anza-Borrego Desert State Park.

Still, there are visions to be had in these arid plains. Clumps of ocotillo and cholla and barrel cacti bloom after the spring rains with colors as brilliant as the sun. Along I-8 toward Yuma, Arizona, golden folds of vast sand dunes shimmer along the roadside. And, if the emptiness and solitude of the desert here are too much, head north to Salton Sea, one of the world's largest salt water lakes. Its crusty shores, marshes, and ponds are home to various waterbirds, and Salton Sea State Recreation Area has a beach and other recreational activities.

North of the lake, near Indio, row upon row of towering date palms conjure up visions of the Arabian Nights. Many date farms here are open to the public; visitors can walk beneath luscious bunches of Black Abadas, Deglet Noors, and Medjools dates. Still farther north are the less luscious marvels of Joshua Tree National Monument. Its Joshua trees—some 40 feet high—wave their spiny arms like guardians of these pink and golden wilds. Several natural palm oases, where animals come to drink greedily, lie within the monument.

For those won over by the clarity of desert light, there are mementoes in the diamond trays of the Palm Springs jewelry stores. The sparkling mineral springs are a valuable attraction, too, but the real treasure in this city of wealth and country clubs is the Palm Springs Aerial Tramway. It leads straight from the desert floor to the alpine heights of the Mount San Jacinto Wilderness State Park, a breathtaking 5,873-foot ascent into the San Bernardino National Forest and another world filled with treasures.

Joshua Tree National Monument (*left*) The Joshua tree and other slow-growing plant life form the basis of the fragile desert food web. These trees, host to infesting insects, also provide nesting sites for birds feeding on the insects, and shelter for lizards. Even dead, the trees' fibers sustain termites which convert the plant's energy to animal energy in another step along the food chain.

Quenching a Thirst (*above*) The blazing sun can prove fatal even to a traveler with a canteen full of water. After too long in the open desert, humans simply lose their desire to drink. When rain does fall, the cacti root systems suck up water almost as soon as it hits the ground, fleshing out as the water fills their internal reservoirs to tide them over the long hot periods to follow.

SITES TO SEE

● **Rim of the World Drive** (San Bernardino National Forest) covers 40 miles of spectacular views from 5,000 to 7,200 feet.

● **Indio** hosts the annual National Date Festival each February. Highlights include an Arabian Nights pageant, and camel and ostrich races.

● **Palm Canyon** (south of Palm Springs), on the Agua Caliente Indian Reservation, gives visitors the chance to see 3,000 washington palms, most at least 1,500 years old. Fifteen miles long and narrow and winding, the canyon has facilities for hiking, picnicking, and horseback riding.

● **Palomar Observatory** (Palomar Mtn.) lets visitors see the 200-inch Hale telescope, along with several smaller types. **The Greenway Museum** exhibits astronomical photographs.

● **Palm Springs Desert Museum** (Palm Springs) displays contemporary and western American art.

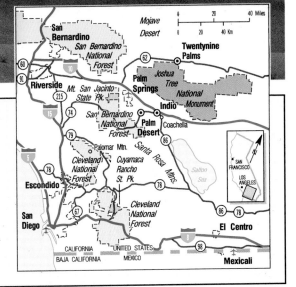

THE MISSION COAST
From Ventura to Santa Cruz

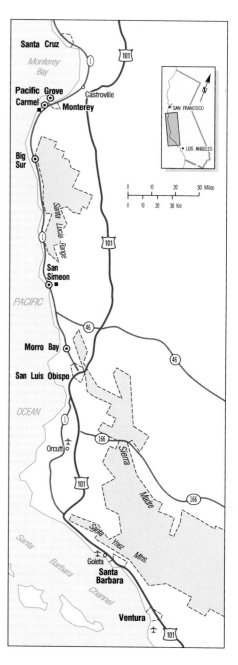

California fringes the Pacific with a ragged coast that runs from the subtropical streets of Santa Barbara to the magnificent, surf-pounded cliffs of Big Sur. At Ventura, the scent of citrus groves perfumes the beach, while the hills behind Santa Cruz tower with imponderable stands of colossal redwoods. Between these leafy extremes, fields of flowers stretch for miles around the seed farms of Lompoc, and neat rows of artichokes connect the beach at Castroville to coastal SR 1. Punctuating all these are the old Spanish missions of the Camino Real.

The jagged green peaks that rise from the fog along SR 1 are the crumpled result of the earth's movements along the San Andreas Fault over millions of years. For the Indian nations that lived in this region of violent change—the Chumash, Salina, and Costanoan—the myth of Coyote the Trickster, the great Changer of Things, was potent and widespread. Perhaps he prompted them to welcome Father Junipero Serra to their rugged coast when he and his Franciscans marched north from Mexico in 1769.

Father Serra and Father Fermin Lasue established a chain of missions, each a day's ride from the next, stretching north from San Diego along the route dubbed El Camino Real, the Royal Road. Many of them still stand, tucked away in the middle of the cities that grew around them. Mission Santa Barbara, the "Queen of the Missions," was founded in 1786. Stroll beneath its bell towers into a serene courtyard with graceful arcades and rest by a fountain amid bird-of-paradise flowers.

North of the Lompoc Valley flower fields, La Purísima Mission State Historic Park, and the hills north of Morro Bay, San Simeon towers over its vast grounds. But nowhere is the scenery along the Californian coast more spectacular than at Big Sur. The Santa Lucia Mountains plunge hundreds of feet into the sea, and flowery meadows, redwood groves, and clear streams ornament the clifftops.

At Point Lobos State Reserve, the sea is sapphire, and stands of cypress jut from windswept cliffs clothed in flowering succulents. Past Point Lobos, the land descends into dunes and tidepools best explored between Carmel and Pacific Grove. At Santa Cruz, an antique seaside boardwalk amusement park brightens the sheltered beach.

Mission San Carlos Borromeo del Rio Carmelo (*left*) Founded by Father Junipero Serra in 1770 at Monterey, the Mission was moved to Carmel the following year. It became Father Serra's headquarters, and he was buried in front of the altar when he died in 1784. Memorabilia of the padre, a candidate for canonization, are on exhibit.

San Simeon (*right*) When newspaper magnate William Randolph Hearst built his dream house, he chose a plot atop La Cuesta Encantada (The Enchanted Hill), overlooking the Pacific. Work began in 1919 and was incomplete when Hearst died in 1951; shown here, his Greek temple and mosaic pool. **Pacific Surfer**, (*far right*) plays in bigger, bluer waves.

SITES TO SEE

● **Ventura** is a good take-off point for **Channel Islands National Park**, where primitive camping is allowed on Anacapa and Santa Barbara islands; visitors must arrange their own transportation to the islands.

● **Santa Barbara's County Courthouse** is a fine example of Spanish-Moorish architecture, with a sculptured facade and sunken gardens; the interior has murals and Tunisian tile work. The town's historic adobes include **Casa de Covarrubias** and **Historic Fremont Adobe**. The **El Presidio de Santa Barbara State Historic Park** is a complex inlcuding the state's second oldest building, **El Cuartel**. **Stearns Warf**, dating from 1872, has stores and restaurants, and offers fine views of the harbor.

● **Mission San Luis Obispo de Tolosa** (San Luis Obispo) is known as "The Prince of Missions." Built in 1772, it includes a museum with Chumash Indian artifacts and memorabilia of early settlers.

● **Solvang**, a Danish community, offers tours in streetcars pulled by Belgian draft horses. The town's Danish Days festival is held in September. East of town is the Old Mission Santa Ynez, dating 1804.

● **Pfeiffer Big Sur State Park** has beaches and several hundred acres of chaparral and redwoods.

● **Monterey** is an old port and fishing town gone upscale. **Cannery Row**, made famous by John Steinbeck's novel of the same name, is now rather chic, but **Monterey State Historic Park** preserves several historic buildings. They include the **Custom House**, California's oldest government building, and **Larkin House** (1835), which combines New England and Spanish colonial styles in what became the Monterey manner. The excellent **Monterey Bay Aquarium**, one of the world's largest, includes a 90-foot model of Monterey Bay, a two-storey sea-otter tank, a three-storey kelp tank, and a shorebird aviary.

● **Salinas**, John Steinbeck's hometown, lies in the center of a rich farming area and boasts 33,000 acres of grapes. The Festival of Monterey County Wine and Food is held in August; the California Rodeo, held on the third weekend in July, is one of the nation's largest. The John Steinbeck Public Library contains manuscripts and memorabilia of the Nobel Prize-winning author.

DEATH VALLEY DAYS
California's Outback

Death Valley is a place of great distances. There is the distance from the lowest point in the United States near Badwater to the 11,049-foot summit of Telescope Peak. There is the height of the mercury in midsummer, when temperatures climb to well over 100°, and there is the long measure of months between one rainfall and the next. Greatest of all is the distance between Death Valley and everywhere else in the world.

Sunk beneath the foreboding shadows of the Panamint and Armagosa mountains, Death Valley National Monument stretches over 3,000 square miles, one and a half times the area of Delaware. In addition to landscapes of austere and even phantasmagoric beauty, it includes the lowest point in the U.S., the Panamints, and Mount Williamson's peak (over 14,000 feet high), dazzling salt flats, and summer heat of dangerous intensity. All visitors should heed Park Service warnings about the hazards of travel here, in summer or winter.

Many of the Valley's geological wonders are near Furnace Creek Visitor Center. Artist's Drive loops through brilliantly colored red, orange, and ocher badlands. On a dry lake bed to the south is the vast jumble of salt crystals known as Devil's Golf Course. From the panoramic overlook at Zabriskie Point, the shimmering peaks of Golden Canyon melt into the distance. From Dante's View, the highest peaks of the Sierras can be seen.

These are the valley's major panoramas, but the desert is a subtle place, too. Look closely for the details that make it so: widely spaced creosote bushes seemingly planted by an attentive gardener, a hidden canyon sheltering delicate tracks of fox, coyote, and other hardy survivors in the world's hottest desert, where summer ground temperatures can reach 180°.

Stovepipe Wells and Scotty's Castle offer food, drink, and fuel. Near Stovepipe Wells is the shifting yellow ocean of the Sand Dunes area; near Scotty's Castle (a beautifully furnished stone mansion built in 1922 by a wealthy and eccentric midwesterner) is the immense volcanic bowl of Ubehebe Crater, 2,400 feet in diameter, and the Racetrack, where boulders from high cliffs move across the desert with imperceptible slowness, leaving strange, mysterious trails behind them. But take a lesson from William Manly, and avoid the desert in the summer heat. Manly and a group of other pioneers accidentally wandered into the area on their way to the gold fields in the winter of 1849. When they finally escaped, Manly looked back, raised his hat, and spoke the name for the first time: "Goodbye, Death Valley!"

Death Valley (*above*) This fierce, enchanted corridor of folded rocks and salt flats, pinnacles and dunes, was pushed up (and down) three million years ago by the faulting and drifting of the earth's crust. Eruptions, erosion, and the evaporation of vast lakes added the final details to this magnificent, infamous landscape of sun and stone.

Flowers of Death Valley (*left*) The Valley's best-kept secret is that it's more than a wonderland of rock and sand. Snow often covers Wildrose Peak, where trails cross forests of pine, juniper, and mountain mahogany. On remote trails, you may sometimes glimpse rare desert bighorn sheep.

SITES TO SEE

● **Dantes View** (near Badwater) at 5,475 ft. provides spectacular panoramas that include the valley, the Panamints, and Badwater, the lowest point in the U.S.

● **Furnace Creek Visitor Center** includes the **Death Valley Museum** with excellent exhibits describing the geology, climate, archeology, history, and natural history of the valley.

● **Harmony Borax Works** (near Furnace Creek) has an interpretive trail leading visitors through the old borax processing works, now mostly in ruins. In the heyday of borax works, teams of 20 mules would pull loads weighing up to 36½ tons. The nearby **Borax Museum** highlights the minerals of Death Valley and the history of mining here. It occupies original ranch buildings at Furnace Creek Ranch.

● **Ubehebe Crater** (near Scotty's Castle) was formed by a volcanic steam explosion probably not more than 3,000 years ago.

● **Wildrose Canyon**, with high pine-covered mountains, birds, and wildflowers, is the area of the park least like the rest of Death Valley. Charcoal kilns from the last century are found here. A trail leads from the Mahogany Flat campground to **Telescope Peak**, the highest point in the park at 11,049 feet.

● **The Racetrack** is southwest of Scotty's Castle. Here, boulders, fallen from high cliffs, continue to move with imperceptible slowness, leaving mysterious trails behind them.

● **Sand dunes** are a mark of the valley. Arid mountains provide a backdrop for the golden sand sculpted and rippled by the wind. The dunes east of Stovepipe Wells are easily reached by walkers on a casual stroll. Early dawn and late afternoon are when the light is considered best for photographing the dunes.

● **Mosaic Canyon** can be reached by car or on a 3-mile-long trail from Stovepipe Wells. The canyon is noted for its narrows of polished marble.

WORTH A DETOUR

● Eureka Springs Sand Dunes National Natural Landmark

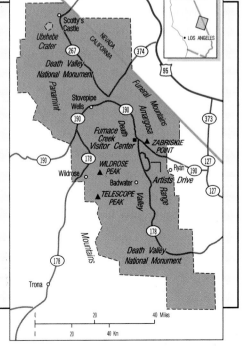

A HEART OF GOLD

The Northern Sierras

In January, 1848, James Marshall saw "some kind of metal...that looks like gold" while inspecting a millrace near Coloma, California, on the American River. In a matter of months, the great gold rush was on. Today's visitors to Mother Lode Country can explore its early mining towns and pan for gold in the tumbling streams. To the east, where Lake Tahoe shines like a sapphire set in slopes dotted with ski resorts, the granite peaks of the High Sierra rise majestically. In Nevada, only a few miles farther east, the glittering casinos of Reno and Sparks attract players still willing to gamble for the promise of gold.

The discovery of gold in the Sierras brought California its first great wave of immigration and captured the imagination of the world. Gold seekers even traveled from New York and Europe, through the malaria-ridden swamps of Panama, or around Cape Horn.

Today, I-80, SR 49, and US 50 take modern prospectors more smoothly to the old gold fields. SR 49 winds through the rounded hills and scrubby valleys that follow the American and Yuba rivers into the heart of Gold Country. In Coloma, where it all began, visitors can explore a reconstruction of Sutter's Mill, while greenhorns can pan the rocky shores of the American River. Rambling Victorian inns, wooden sidewalks with hitching posts, and the tunnels of abandoned mines mark former boom towns such as Auburn and Grass Valley.

I-80 climbs quickly from the broken foothills to the evergreen clarity of the Sierra crest. From Emigrant Gap and Donner Pass, the Golden State stretches below—the same promised land that brought pioneers this way in the 1850s.

The lands of the Eldorado National Forest contain the world-famous ski resort of Squaw Valley. In summer, its wilderness reserves, Granite Chief and Desolation Wilderness, cut through by glacial streams and granite ravines, open their pine-scented interiors to the adventurous. Lake Tahoe beckons like a jewel between jagged mountains. At the foot of picture-perfect Emerald Bay, the waters of Eagle Falls plunge from steep cliffs with an abandon that seems to echo the spirit of a land once ruled by chance and daring.

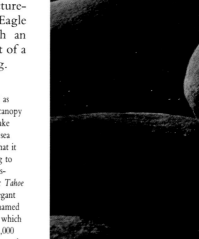

Lake Tahoe (*right*)
Sparkling, serene, and as clear and blue as the canopy of sky above it, this lake rests 6,228 feet above sea level, but is so deep that it never freezes. Cruising to Emerald Bay, the glass-bottom paddlewheeler *Tahoe Queen* passes many elegant resorts and the aptly named D.L. Bliss State Park, which embraces more than 1,000 acres of spectacular forested mountains.

Former Glory (*left*)
Although James Marshall tried to keep his discovery of gold a secret, the news spread like wildfire. Farms and ships were abandoned, and tiny settlements of prospectors sprang up like weeds. Such wealth flooded some of these towns that wooden buildings destroyed by fire were sometimes replaced by sturdier, more costly brick ones with iron shutters.

CALICO SPICE SHOP

PRIVATE

SITES TO SEE

● **Sacramento**, the state's capital, has christened itself "Camellia Capital of the World" and celebrates every March with a 10-day Camellia Festival. **The Capitol building** was built 1860–74 in the Greek Revival style. A variety of tours are offered daily, and there are historical exhibits in the restored main building. **Old Sacramento** is a 4-block area that has been redeveloped to capture the atmosphere of the gold rush days. The **California State Railroad Museum** here displays over 20 restored train cars and locomotives.

● **Auburn** has a charming historic central section with restored buildings from the gold rush days of the 1880s; the town's post office is the oldest continuously used one in the state. Old mining equipment is displayed at the **Gold Country Museum**.

The museum also contains artifacts of local California Indians.

● **Malakoff Diggins State Historic Park** (Nevada City) was once the site of the largest hydraulic gold mine in the world. Today, visitors can watch a 20-minute film about how miners lived and the technique of hydraulic mining: streams of water were blasted against the side of a mountain to extract gold. Although the technique was successful for extracting gold, it had devastating consequences for the environment and was banned in 1884. The park also includes a town with a museum in the former dance hall.

● **Empire Mine State Historic Park** (Grass Valley) is at the location of a mine that produced 6 million ounces of gold before it closed in 1956; there are 367 miles of passageways in the mine. The park features the restored surface works of the mine, including the office, blacksmith's shop, machine shop, and owner's cottage. The nearby **Pelton Wheel Mining Museum** contains the hydroelectric Pelton Wheel used to produce power for the mine and other old mining equipment, such as a Cornish pump designed to remove water from the floor of the mine.

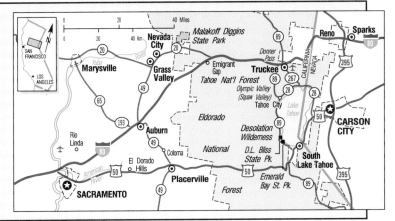

SIERRA WONDERS

Yosemite, Sequoia, and Kings Canyon National Parks

Before 1851, few non-Indians had seen Yosemite, the awesome valley on the western slopes of the Sierra Nevada Mountains where the Merced River flows beneath towering cliffs. When they did, they quickly heralded it as a sublimely beautiful place. The sheer face of Half Dome and the monolithic wall of El Capitan loom above the valley floor. The voice of the wilderness sighs in the wind and thunders in the roar of Yosemite Falls, plummeting 2,425 feet down the face of the valley's northern rim. To the southeast, in Sequoia and Kings Canyon national parks, giant sequoia trees stand like vast pillars holding up the sky.

If wind and water sound the primeval music of these high reaches, the mountains have other voices, too. John Muir, the great pioneer of American conservation, fell in love with Yosemite. His eloquent writings prompted the preservation and protection of many wild places. Muir imagined the voice of the glaciers before they created these harsh landscapes: "Here let us carve a basin," he heard the glaciers say, "there, a Yosemite Valley, here a channel for a river with fluted steps and brows for the plunge of songful cataracts..."

The best place to view the grandeur of the glaciers is from the 7,214-foot height of Glacier Point. Space suddenly turns upside down in dizzying views over the Yosemite Valley. Visiting Glacier Point at sunset and on nights with a full moon means going away with images that will last a lifetime. On moonlit nights, the soaring granite peaks take on the appearance of a fairyland. Signs identify the major peaks. Beyond the granite walls of the valley, the Sierra wilderness rises in a kaleidoscope of peaks and ranges studded with glaciers, glassy streams, crevasses, meadows, and alpine lakes.

From Tuolumne Meadows, the widest expanse of subalpine meadow in the Sierra Nevadas, with a magnificent array of wildflowers, a network of trails leads into the high peaks. Adventurous hikers can follow the footsteps of naturalist John Muir on stretches of the 200-mile John Muir Trail here.

In Sequoia and Kings Canyon national parks, some of the deepest gorges in the country crisscross the wild canyon of the Kings River. From Cedar Grove, within the canyon, hiking trails rise from the valley floor toward spectacular peaks and views.

Sequoia National Park embraces the Giant Forest, an ancient grove of *Sequoiadendron giganteum*, the giant sequoias that are the world's largest living trees. Foremost among them is the General Sherman Tree, a relic from the age of Moses and Buddha, which is 103 feet in circumference, 275 feet high, and more than 2,500 years old. More giants, a line of mountains rising more than 14,000 feet and known as the Patriarchs of the Sierra, tower over the eastern edge of the park. Among them is Mount Whitney, whose summit—14,494 feet high—marks the highest point in the contiguous 48 states.

Horses and Mules For Hire, Yosemite Valley (*left*) To find privacy and the wildest places in Yosemite National Park, go on foot or on horseback. Guided horseback tours are available; even inexperienced riders will probably find the animals docile enough for an expedition; they are for rent at the Valley stables, near Camp Curry. For the timid, bicycles can also be rented.

Mono Lake (*above*) This is the second oldest lake in America, the remnant of an inland sea that once filled Mono Basin. In 1941, Los Angeles began diverting water flowing into the lake for its own uses, and since then the lake has gradually shrunk and become increasingly salty and more alkaline. The survival of wildlife that depends on the lake is threatened, and the wind scatters pollution.

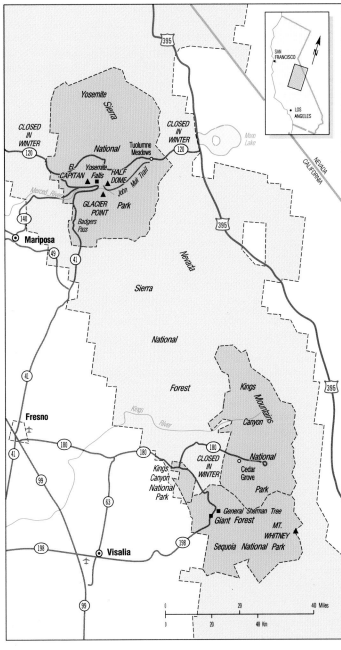

SITES TO SEE

● **Devils Postpile National Monument** (near Mammoth Lakes) consists of 60-foot basalt columns, resembling a large stack of posts set on their ends. A trail to the top reveals the mosaic pattern of the column ends. Jagged spires and waterfalls distinguish the surrounding countryside.

To the south, **Rainbow Falls** drops 101 feet.

● **Mariposa Grove** (Yosemite National Park) is a grove of giant sequoias, including Grizzly Giant, probably the oldest here at 2,700 years old.

● **Mariposa County Historical Center** (Mariposa) has a collection of gold rush-era memorabilia,

including schoolroom and Indian village replicas.

● **Half Dome** (Yosemite National Park) has a cable-and-step system to the summit. A spur of rock, The Visor, juts from the cliff 4,800 feet above Tenaya Canyon.

● **Yosemite Pioneer History Center** (Wawona) re-creates Yosemite's rugged

stagecoach days. This town of restored historic buildings and horse-drawn coaches is located in serene meadows. **Wawona Basin** is a popular recreation area, with saddle and pack animals for hire during the summer.

● **Moro Rock** (Sequoia National Park) gives spectacular views of the Great Western Divide to the

east and San Joaquin Valley to the west, 6,000 feet below.

● **Congress Trail** (Giant Forest Village) is a 2-mile loop trail through a giant sequoia forest.

● **Badgers Pass** (Yosemite) is a popular site for cross-country skiers because of the

good views of the high peaks and Bridalveil Falls.

● **Indian Cultural Exhibit and Indian Village** (Valley Visitor Center, Yosemite) features history of the Miwok and Paiute Indians from 1850. A nearby gallery sells art inspired by Yosemite sites.

VINTAGE PLEASURES
Napa Valley and Sonoma County

Driving through sun-drenched Napa Valley, visitors might think this is a sleepy, *mañana* place. But inside the blessedly cool interiors of one of the region's ever more numerous wineries, it is easy to sense the dedicated, passionate search for perfection at work here. This region has introduced more Americans to the pleasures of wine than anywhere else. The wineries have international ambitions—and the wherewithal to realize them. There are admirable table wines to please all pocketbooks; there are also wines to equal the world's best.

Although wine is made in many areas of California, the term "Wine Country" firmly indicates the wineries of Napa Valley and neighboring Sonoma County.

Napa Valley first gained fame as a gold-rush center in the 1850s, but its lasting wealth has come from the earth in another form. Industrious settlers planted grape-vines using cuttings supplied by priests from the missions at Sonoma and San Rafael. In time, the valley's conditions proved custom-made for grapes of all kinds, not just one or two varieties from the old world wine-growing regions.

Napa Valley vines are an extraordinary anthology of the best grapes Europe and the southern hemisphere have to offer. Here grow such classic reds as Cabernet Sauvignon, the soul of French Bordeaux; Barbera, which provides the Italian Piedmont with its meaty Barolos; and the Syrah on which the wine trades in South Africa and Australia depend.

Most remarkable among the whites is the unqualified success of the German varieties, notably Johannisberg Riesling, which could not have been expected to thrive in so different a climate.

The supremely versatile white Chardonnay provides local table wines, prize-winning vintages, and sparkling "California champagne." Among the reds, Napa Valley naturally features the state's native Zinfandel—a true Californian with a peppery personality.

On the road between Napa and St. Helena, many wineries are a joy just to look at: Sterling crouches like an Aegean fortress in the hills; Spring Mountain Winery was the setting for the "Falcon Crest" series. Rise above it all in a hot-air balloon or go antiquing at ground level, rooting amid quaint bottle openers and turn-of-the-century firkins.

Finally, to emulate the more self-indulgent San Franciscans, head for the spas of Calistoga. A session in the steam cabinets and mud baths, accompanied by some deep drafts of the local mineral water and capped by a pummeling on the massage table, should cancel out any notion of having over-indulged.

Replacing the stopper in a wine barrel, Chappellet Winery (*left*) Grape juice becomes wine through the carefully controlled process of fermentation. The natural sugary juice, called "must" in its original state, often begins the process spontaneously by interacting with the yeast in grape skins. In some wineries, cultivated yeast is added to the must instead. Fermentation can occur in open or closed containers. Oak barrels like these give a rich flavor to both red and white wines, but fine wine can also be made in stainless steel vats or in concrete ones, sometimes lined with glass or enamel.

Napa Valley: Weinterrassen Panorama (*right*) The fertile valleys that flow north from the Bay Area gained their first vineyard in 1838. Twenty years later, an ambitious, footloose Hungarian named Agoston Haraszthy founded the world-famous industry that flourishes there today. Near Sonoma, he created the first large vineyard in the state. Then, with the state's backing, he went to Europe to collect the best grapes for cultivation in the local climate. Swiss, French, and Italian winemakers came to the area around 1880, bringing with them age-old methods of irrigation, cultivation, and harvesting.

SITES TO SEE

● **Winery tours and tastings** are available all through Napa and Sonoma valleys. It is best to check times and costs with specific wineries; some of the best-known wineries require reservations.

● Numerous companies offer **hot-air balloon trips** over the wineries and surrounding counyryside. Balloons take off from Calistoga and Yountville.

● **Herd Beeswax Candle Factory** (St. Helena) is located on the grounds of Freemark Abbey Winery.

● **Marin County Civic Center** (San Rafael) was designed by Frank Lloyd Wright. Advance appointments are needed to tour the building and the 140 landscaped acres, which include a theater and fairgrounds.

● **Mission San Rafael Arcangel** (San Rafael) is a 1949 replica of a mission begun in 1817 as a health care center. The original bells and star window remain.

● **Robert Louis Stevenson State Park** (north of Calistoga) is an undeveloped park on Mount Saint Helena with rugged scenery and trails. It is named after the author, who spent his honeymoon here with his American wife.

● **Old Faithful Geyser of California** (Calistoga) is one of the world's few regularly erupting geysers, spewing a 60-foot-high jet every 40 minutes.

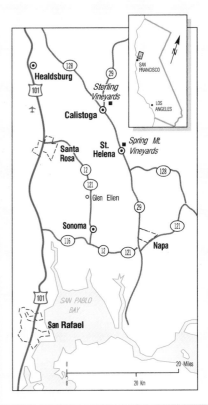

FIRE MOUNTAIN AND PLATEAU OF BIRDS

Lassen Volcanic National Park and Lava Beds

In the northeast corner of California lies a landscape shaped and scarred by volcanic eruptions. Lassen Peak, which the Atsugewi Indians called Amblu-Kai, the Fire Mountain, erupted 300 times from 1914 to 1921, and until the 1980 eruption of Mount St. Helens, it was the last volcano to erupt within the contiguous U.S. Fumaroles, sulfur pots, jagged "jumbles," and rivers of purple stones mark the presence of "fires" that still lurk near the surface here and at Lava Beds National Monument. To the north and east, near the Oregon border, lakes harbor millions of birds migrating along the Pacific flyway and make the sagebrush plateau a birdwatchers' paradise.

The easiest route to the craters and snowy peaks of Lassen Volcanic National Park is the 30-mile Lassen Park Road (SR 89). On its way through the park, the road passes the Sulphur Works area, where thermal springs and mud pots bubble with steam. Bumpass Hell, another spectacular area of intense thermal acitivity, is reached by a trail off Lassen Park Road beyond Emerald Lake. Lassen Park Road passes south, east, and north of Lassen Peak—a 2½-mile trail leads to the 10,457-foot summit—then passes the ancient lava plugs that form Chaos Crags and Chaos Jumbles, and Manzanita Lake. In the northeast corner of the park, SR 44 approaches Butte Lake and the multicolored formations of the Fantastic Lava Beds formed during the 1851 eruptions.

Just below the treeline in the park, tall stands of incense cedar, red fir, ponderosa pine, and mountain hemlock occur. Numerous trails skirt the woods or cross meadows often white with camas lilies or blue with lupins in springtime. As the snows melt, monkey flowers and arrowleaf balsamroot, or mule ears (*Wyethia mallis*) embroider the forest, and thick, scarlet stalks of snow plants spring from beds of pine needles.

North and east of Lassen are the arid plains of the Modoc Plateau. At Lava Beds National Monument, the scars of volcanic eruptions untold centuries ago are still evident. Purple and black streams, cinder cones, and lakes of solidified lava mark where rivers of fire once flowed. Some of the 200 lava tube caves sheltered Modoc Indians during the Modoc War (1872–3), during which the U.S. Army tried to force the Modoc tribe back onto the reservation only recently set aside for them. The Modoc fought fiercely to remain independent, and for nearly five months, a band of 52 Indians resisted an army that grew to more than 1,000 men.

The Tule Lake National Wildlife Refuge in the Klamath Basin provides feeding and breeding grounds for millions of waterfowl that travel the Pacific flyway. In March, the peak of the spring migration, Tule and Lower Klamath lakes have the largest concentration of waterfowl, including sandhill cranes, on the North American continent. Quiet footpaths skirt the swamps and marshes, and bald and golden eagles can be seen nesting in the scattered trees.

Lassen Peak (*right*) Although this towering inferno 10,457 feet high, is now quiescent, its rocky flanks testify to the terrible activity unleashed by its last eruption. Its position in the chain of volcanoes known as the Ring of Fire, which almost encircles the Pacific Ocean, accounts for its explosive history. Once hardened, molten lava erodes into soil that supports extensive plant and animal life. **Coyotes** (*left*) prowl the area stalking pikas or rock rabbits for food.

SITES TO SEE

● **Modoc National Wildlife Refuge** (Alturas) harbors one of the largest sandhill crane nurseries in the U.S. The refuge's 6,000 acres on the Pacific flyway are also home to other birds and waterfowl, along with mule deer, rabbits, and coyotes, among others. Birdwatchers flock to the refuge in April and September.

● **Modoc County Museum** (Alturas) records the development of this ranching area with a collection of Indian artifacts. The firearms collection includes guns from the 1600s to World War II.

● **McArthur-Burney Falls Memorial State Park** (Burney) is the site of a 129-foot multi-level forest waterfall over moss-covered lava rock. When Theodore Roosevelt saw the falls, he supposedly called it the eighth wonder of the world.

● **Cave Loop Road** (Lava Beds National Monument) links more than a dozen caves near the visitor center. Trails and ladders make many of the caves accessible for visitors, but only Mushpot Cave is illuminated. In the summer, ranger-led walks explore some of the caves; schedules are posted at the visitor center. To explore caves, it is recommended you always have someone with you, you wear protective headgear and hard-soled shoes, take along several light sources; free lights are provided at the visitor center.

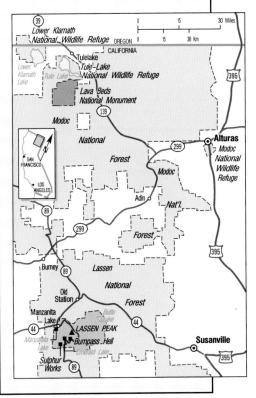

REDWOODS AND MOUNTAINS
North Coast and the Shasta-Cascade Wilderness

Between Eureka and the Oregon border, US 101 runs like a seam that sews the rocky coast to the forests of colossal redwoods. This rugged coastland is wetter than most of the state. When the rains cease in the spring, cloaks of fog replace them, shrouding the redwoods that stand like guards 200 feet tall above the gray sea. Wild azaleas and rhododendrons bloom beneath the great trees. Offshore, small vertical islands called sea stacks rise like stone trees from the swirling dark water. Between this misty coast and the snowy summit of Mount Shasta lie forests, rivers, and a magnificent wilderness of mountains.

An ideal way to see California's unique redwood forests is to visit one of the three state parks encompassed by the Redwood National Park, all of which lie off US 101. Roosevelt elk roam the grasslands of Prairie Creek Redwoods State Park, perhaps the prettiest of the three sites. Visitors can walk at the feet of giant trees, some of which are 800 years old and 20 feet in circumference. The James Irvine Trail leads to a magical and secret-seeming gorge named Fern Canyon, where five-fingered and sword ferns feather the 50-foot walls. The canyon empties onto Gold Bluffs Beach, named for the prospecting that took place here in the 1850s.

Inland, mists begin to clear as the slopes of the Klamath Mountains rise in evergreen robes to elevations of nearly 9,000 feet. Many rivers—most importantly the Klamath, Salmon, and Trinity—drain these craggy slopes, and they have long been in the main avenues into this largely uninhabited wilderness. Indians once followed migrating salmon up their rushing streams, and the coastal cities of

Eureka and Crescent City still support a lively ocean-fishing and crabbing industry.

Today, SR 299 from Arcata follows the rugged and beautiful Trinity River through forests of douglas fir and ponderosa pine. Experienced backpackers will penetrate this remote wilderness with greatest success, but even the most casual traveler will pause to wonder at the scale and variety of these landscapes. Alpine on the western slopes, they are almost desert-like on the more arid eastern side.

From the town of Willow Creek, go north into Klamath River country, a favorite haunt of fishermen and backpackers. Or continue on SR 299 southeast to French Gulch, a mining town dating from the 1850s gold rush.

Farther east, past the intricate shoreline of Whiskeytown Lake, the foothills of Mt. Shasta are easily visible from the city of Redding. Starting here, a main highway like I-5 feels like a country road as it travels north between the Klamath Mountains and the mighty Cascades, toward Mt. Shasta's 14,162-foot peak.

Roosevelt Elk (*left*), the mammal most frequently seen in Redwood National Park, was named after President Theodore Roosevelt.

Three State Parks—Del Norte Coast (*right*), Jedediah Smith, and Prairie Creek—were supposed to have formed the core of Redwood National Park, created in 1968. Ten years later, the area was enlarged to cover 106,000 acres. In addition to preserving the redwoods, the park offers sanctuary to a wide variety of wild creatures. Among them are the elusive mountain lion and the rare bald eagle, peregrine falcon, and brown pelican.

SITES TO SEE

● **Azalea State Reserve** (Arcata) is at its most colorful in May, June, and July.

● **Joss House State Historic Park** (Weaverville) preserves the oldest Chinese temple still in use in the state. Built about 1825, the Taoist temple has displays commemorating Chinese contributions to state history and explaining Chinese life. The **J.J. "Jake" Jackson Memorial Museum** explains regional history with an assortment of memorabilia, including Chinese weapons and old jail cells.

● **Castle Crags State Park** (Dunsmuir) is known for its towering granite crags over the Sacramento River; early Spanish settlers called them the Devil's Castle. During the Modoc War, Battle Rock was the site of a bloody battle between local Modoc Indians and gold miners.

● **Whiskeytown Unit of the Whiskeytown-Shasta-Trinity National Recreation Area** (Redding) is a mecca for water sport enthusiasts because of Whiskeytown Lake's constant level; boats and other water craft may be hired. Other popular activities include hiking, horseback riding, and nature studies. The **Tower House Historic District** preserves some of the atmosphere of the gold rush days, after gold was discovered in Reading's Bar in 1848. El Dorado Mine, now abandoned, was one of the mines that produced vast amounts of gold each month. Park rangers give gold-panning demonstrations, and visitors can try their hand at recreational gold panning (registration is required); any gold found cannot be sold.

● **Clarke Memorial Museum** (Eureka) displays one of the state's most outstanding collections of Indian baskets, as well as other Indian artifacts.

● **Blue Goose Short Line Railroad** (Eureka) takes visitors on 3-hour rides through the cattle-ranching country that surrounds this former gold-mining town, offering splendid views of Mount Shasta along the way.

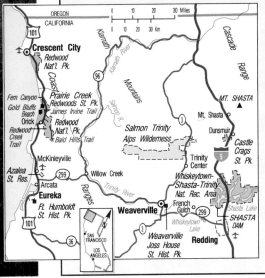

LOS ANGELES

The consistent climate, the diverse landscape, and the fascin-
ation of the entertainment industry prove an irresistible lure
to visitors of America's second largest city. Bordered by the
San Gabriel and Santa Monica mountains to the northeast
and west, and fringed by white, sandy beaches along the
south, the metropolis sprawls between the two in a multicultural melting pot. The startling variety and originality of
its architecture make this a city of delightful surprise.
Despite its big-city reputation, much of the land is lush and
green with palm tree-lined boulevards, subtropical splurges
of bougainvillaea, bird of paradise, and bottlebrush trees.

Los Angeles was first visited in 1769 by a Spanish expedition on its way to the port of Monterey; by 1781, Governor
Felipe de Neve had founded El Pueblo de la Reina de Los
Angeles, the Village of Our Lady the Queen of the Angels.
When Mexico finally won freedom from Spain in the early
19th century, Los Angeles became the last place to surrender
to the United States in 1848. Since that time, adventurers
have flocked here to seek their fortunes—be it in gold,
agriculture, oil, or the movies—and the entrepreneurial
spirit of the city became legend.

Relaxation, too, is a latter-day incentive, and the beach
communities from Malibu to Redondo Beach offer the
alternative laid-back lifestyle. Most colorful is Venice
Beach, founded by tobacco heir Abbott Kinney in 1904, and
intended as a replica of its Italian namesake. Musicians jostle
for space against a backdrop of sandy beach and the pounding Pacific. The sum of this variety is a paradox, for the
character of the city is both unmistakable for its color and
panache, yet anonymous for having no fixed character of its
own. Regardless of its size, however, Los Angeles is one of
the least overbearing cities, and a visitor to its hills, beaches,
parks, and campuses, studios and museums, can experience a
curious and exhilarating kind of freedom.

Manhattan Beach (*above*)
"Fun in the sun" could be
the official motto of the
beaches that lie along the
Pacific coast south of greater
Los Angeles. With its
neighbors, Hermosa Beach
and Redondo Beach, this
stretch of perfect powdery
sand represents to many the
California lifestyle,
popularized in song by the
Beach Boys and made up of
surf, music, and relaxation.
But nowhere in Los Angeles
is ever very far from the
movies. **A street-side
mural** (*left*) of an imaginary
Oscar ceremony studs the
audience with several
generations of Hollywood's
best-loved stars. Even the
man in the street dreams of
becoming one of those
legendary, instantly
recognizable faces, and of the
fame and fortune of stardom.

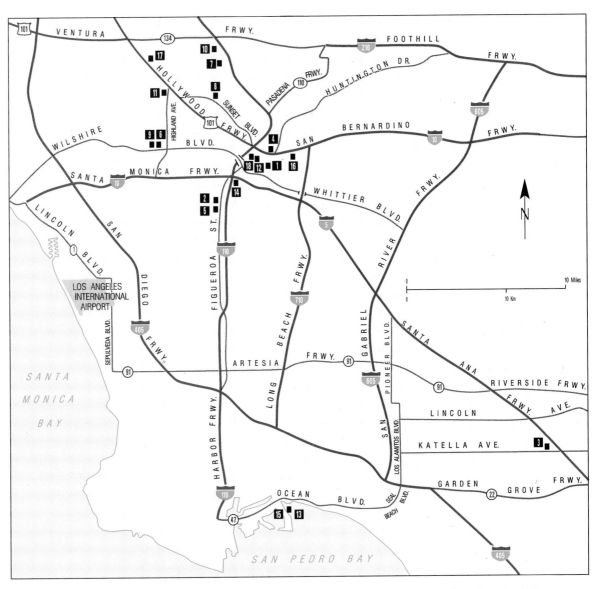

HISTORIC SITES AND MONUMENTS

El Pueblo de Los Angeles Historic Monument The Hispanic heart of the city.

Mann's Chinese Theatre, on Hollywood Boulevard, has the handprints and footprints of famous stars imprinted in the courtyard.

MUSEUMS

California Museum of Science and Industry Hands-on exhibits in areas of science, medicine, and technology.

George C. Page Museum of La Brea Discoveries Set alongside the Rancho La Brea Tar Pits where many fossilized remains have been discovered. The museum exhibits ice-age animals. Outside, an observation deck overlooks the pits.

Los Angeles County Museum of Art Major international collection. The Pavilion for Japanese Art houses an exquisite collection from the Edo period.

Museum of Contemporary Art Huge galleries display the work of modern artists.

Wells Fargo History Museum History and development of the West. Visitors can "board" a stagecoach and listen to an imaginary journey as it would have been in 1859.

NOTABLE BUILDINGS

Bradbury Building Built in 1893 and often used as a film location. Ornate iron railings line the five-story inner court, rising to a large skylight.

Hollyhock House One of Frank Lloyd Wright's most impressive works, set in Barnsdall Park. The hollyhock is used as an abstract motif.

St. John's Church Replica of an 11th-century church in Toscanella, Italy.

Union Station Built in 1939, it offers an impressive mix of mission-style architecture with art deco elements.

PARKS

Exposition Park A 114-acre recreation area. Home of the Natural History Museum of Los Angeles County and the California Afro-American Museum.

Griffith Park Over 4,000 acres, with hiking trails and wilderness areas. A model of an 1880s steam engine offers rides. The **Griffith Observatory and Planetarium** have star shows, simulated eclipses, and space voyages.

Los Angeles Zoo More than 2,000 animals, a children's zoo, Adventure Island.

SAN FRANCISCO

San Francisco is a dance of changes, the most magical city in America. From the Golden Gate to Nob Hill to Fisherman's Wharf and Twin Peaks, from the wild nasturtiums that grow along the cliffs to the redwood beams of the Mission Dolores and the Victorian brick of the Ghirardelli Chocolate Company, perspectives shift here like Pacific waves. And the life of the city, reflected from the ocean on three sides, has a luminosity that only Venice can match: bright and golden on some days, gray with swirls of fog on others, and sometimes with a diffuse pearliness that blends near and far like a magic lens.

Until the 18th century, however, this coastal gem was unknown to European settlers, although Sir Francis Drake sailed past in 1579, anchoring in a cove now known as Drake's Bay. Then, in 1776, when the Spanish established the Presidio, a military outpost, on the peninsula and Franciscan monks under Father Junípero Serra founded the Mission San Francisco de Asis, the seeds of modern San Francisco were sown. Known then as the pueblo of Yerba Buena (meaning good herb), life was relatively quiet until Russia spread its fur-trading industry, and dealers in hides, explorers, whales, and merchants put the port forever on the map. On February 2, 1848, Mexico surrendered California, the Stars and Stripes was finally raised over territory claimed from Mexico, and Yerba Buena was renamed San Francisco. Just eight years later, the discovery of gold changed the face of the city overnight when the newly rich and recently disappointed surged into town and decided to stay.

San Francisco has always welcomed strangers, and its cosmopolitan complexion reflects the trek of settlers from across the globe. The city's Chinatown, home for more than 75,000 Chinese, is known throughout the world for the authentic Asian atmosphere around its traditional buildings, temples, tea rooms, and restaurants.

The beauty of the skyline is further dramatized by its unpredictable location across 40 hills. Most notable are Russian Hill, named for the early traders, Telegraph Hill with its quaint wooden houses, Nob Hill, and Twin Peaks with its breathtaking views. Even today, these reminders of the past, like fine antiques in a modern store window, make San Francisco a jewel in the nation's crown.

San Francisco seen through the Golden Gate Bridge (*left*) A masterpiece of design and engineering, the bridge might never have been built. Many believed that the water depth, 318 feet at the deepest point, and the power of the tides rendered such a span impossible. Construction began in 1933, and the bridge opened four years later. 80,000 people crossed it on foot during its 50th anniversary celebrations.

Fisherman's Wharf (*far left*), originally the heart of a busy port where 300 fishing boats moored, is still full of fresh fish and local color. Tours to Alcatraz Island depart from here, and at Hyde Street Pier, nearby, visitors can board a schooner, a square-rigged vessel, and a World War II submarine. The shipping industry now operates from the Embarcadero.

HISTORIC SITES AND DISTRICTS

Jackson Square This block of beautiful 19th-century brick buildings survived the 1906 earthquake.

MUSEUMS

American Carousel Museum Carved wooden carousel figures from 1875–1927. Restoration demonstrations add interest.

Cable Car Barn Museum Powerhouse and museum for the famous cable cars.

California Academy of Sciences in Golden Gate Park includes the **Natural History Museum** where visitors can experience a simulated earthquake, **Steinhart Aquarium**, and the **Morrison Planetarium**.

Exploratorium More than 600 participatory exhibits explore science disguised as games.

San Francisco Maritime National Historical Park Maritime models and memorabilia.

San Francisco Museum of Modern Art Modern paintings, sculpture, and photographs.

NOTABLE BUILDINGS

Ghirardelli Square Named for the chocolate maker, this one-time factory is now a shopping center.

Haas Lilienthal House Queen Anne-style mansion is now a museum.

Palace of Fine Arts This building is a legacy of the 1915 Panama-Pacific International Exposition.

The Cannery An elegant example of converted industrial space.

The Old U.S. Mint Built in 1874 in Greek Revival style, one of the few buildings to survive the 1906 earthquake.

PARKS

Golden Gate Park includes a buffalo paddock, a windmill, lakes, and a children's playground, as well as the 1894 **Japanese Tea Garden**, the **Conservatory of Flowers**, modeled on Kew Gardens in England, and **Shakespeare's Garden**.

Lincoln Park Wonderful view of the Golden Gate area and home of the **California Palace of the Legion of Honor**.

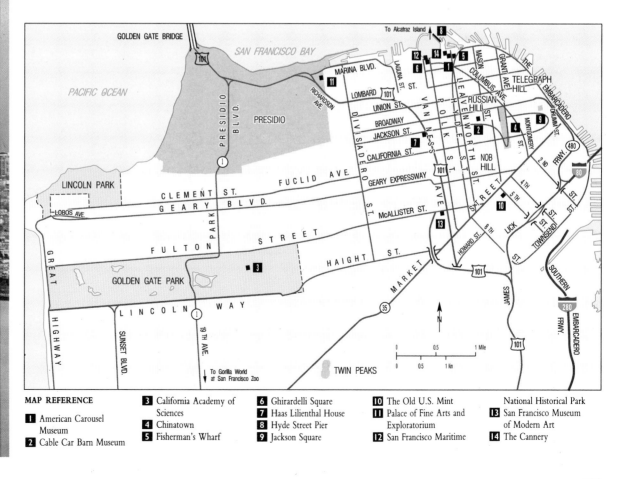

MAP REFERENCE

1. American Carousel Museum
2. Cable Car Barn Museum
3. California Academy of Sciences
4. Chinatown
5. Fisherman's Wharf
6. Ghirardelli Square
7. Haas Lilienthal House
8. Hyde Street Pier
9. Jackson Square
10. The Old U.S. Mint
11. Palace of Fine Arts and Exploratorium
12. San Francisco Maritime
National Historical Park
13. San Francisco Museum of Modern Art
14. The Cannery

THE HOUSE OF THE SUN

Maui

Long ago, according to legend, the demigod Maui went fishing and reeled the Hawaiian Islands out of the sea on his fishhook. Not satisfied with that, he then lassoed the sun from the 10,023-foot peak of the volcano Haleakala—the House of the Sun—and made it agree to move more slowly. Ever since, the sun has passed slowly over Maui, bringing sun-worshippers to the wonderful beaches and waving palm trees. In the mid-1800s, the sun—and the whale—also brought American ships to Maui to winter in the warm waters of Lahaina, once the Pacific's whaling capital. The charm of the town's old waterfront will persuade anyone that time really does pass more slowly here.

On the way to Haleakala National Park, you can drive through eucalyptus groves and pineapple fields toward the clouds. Near the mountain's peak, visitors can stand on the rim of the crater—2½ miles wide, 7½ miles long, and more than 3,000 feet deep—and peer across wind-sculptured cinder flats with 600-foot cones, to the Pacific and the misty peaks of Hawaii's other islands. On the mountain slopes outside the park, rare sandalwood trees grow, and a few goats wander among the scattered ruins of villages that have lain silent since the volcano's last known eruption about 1790.

West of Haleakala is Maui's second volcano, Puu Kukui, separated by the isthmus that gives the island its figure-eight shape. The town of Wailuku stands on the eastern slopes of the mountain at the head of the Iao Valley. Here in 1796 King Kamehameha I slaughtered the army of Chief Kalanikupule to take possession of the island. The western end of the valley is now a park graced by pavilions, pagodas, and Japanese gardens, all dwarfed by the Iao Needle, a spire of basalt cloaked in dense greenery rising 1,200 feet.

Lahaina lies on Maui's northwest coast. If you are adventurous—and have a four-wheel-drive vehicle—you can take the northern coast road from Kahului, but the easy way is south and west via SR 30. In Lahaina itself, the Pioneer Inn is a 1901 hotel redolent of Pacific romance.

The coast road from Kahului to Hana, the small village at the eastern end of the island, is challenging and prone to mudslides and wash-outs. But it offers spectacular scenery—ravines, promontories, fishing villages, waterfalls, bamboo forests, banana plantations, and one of the world's finest wind-surfing beaches, at Hookipa Beach Park. Here are fine panoramas of the Keanae Peninsula from the Wailua Valley Lookout. In Wailua, there is an 1860 church made of coral which was washed onto the beach.

***Carthaginian II* in Lahaina Harbor** (*far left*) In the mid-19th century, Lahaina was one of the centers of Pacific whaling activity, which flourished from 1820 until just before the Civil War. Today, the ship is a floating museum of whaling lore. Herman Melville came here in 1843 and later filled *Moby Dick* with details which he gleaned in this harbor.

Silversword, Haleakala National Park (*left*) Called ahinahina, gray-gray, in Hawaiian, this sunflower grows for up to 20 years, blooms only once, producing hundreds of bright blossoms, and dies.

Haleakala Crater (*above*) The highest point on this island, Haleakala stands like a gray and silent ghost, marking a geological region that once blazed with fiery eruptions. One of two volcano heads that emerged from the sea to form the basis of the island out of lava and windblown ash, Haleakala has been dormant for several hundred years. As the movement of the Pacific Plate carries Maui farther from the plume—the source of new lava—Haleakala moves closer to extinction.

SITES TO SEE

● **Silversword Loop Trail**
(Haleakala National Park),
leading to the rim of
Haleakala Crater, is one of
more than 30 miles of trails
in the park. For the more
adventurous, hiking and
horseback trips through the
crater are also available.●
**Leleiwi, Kalahaku, and
Puu Ulaula** overlooks have
interpretive exhibits
explaining the volcanic
scenery; silversword plants
can be seen at Kalahaku.

● **Whale watching** is a
popular pastime along the
coast at Lahaina; humpback
whales often winter here.
Windjammer cruises sail
from the port.

● **Baldwin House**
(Lahaina) is the restored
white stucco home of Rev.
Dwight Baldwin, a
Connecticut missionary who
became the community's
doctor.

● **Hale Paahao** (Lahaina) is
a coral prison, built in the
1850s, where fractious sailors
were often locked up.

● **Waiola Churchyard**
(Lahaina) contains the grave
of Queen Keopuolani, as
well as missionary families.

● **Tedeschi Vineyard and
Winery** (Ulupalakua) offers
tours and tastings; sample the
pineapple wine produced
here.

● **Helami Gardens** (west
of Hana) has 70 acres of
interest to weekend
gardeners, horticulturists, and
plant collectors.

● **Alexander & Baldwin
Sugar Museum** (south of
Kahului) recreates the history
of sugar production on the
island.

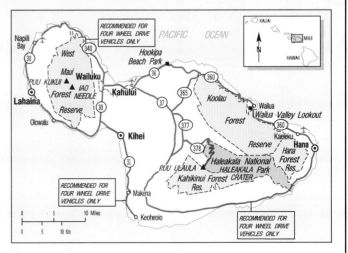

ISLAND OF MYTHS AND MONARCHS
Hawaii

Volcanic peaks of Mauna Loa and Mauna Kea may dominate the island of Hawaii, but feathery jungles of *ohia* trees, the colors of orchids, and memorials of the Polynesian islanders who made their landfall here adorn it. This is the Big Island, the domain of the fire goddess Pele, whose "mansion" is Kilauea's smoldering caldera. This is the Mother Island of the Hawaiian people, the home of her kings, and the fountain of her myths. For most visitors, soothed by scented breezes, ravished by black-sand beaches, and exhilarated by glistening ski slopes, this is a close approximation of paradise.

Visitors who follow SRs 11 and 19 around the island's coast pass through the bold geometry of sugarcane fields, past ancient temples, and beneath the hazy peak of Mauna Loa on a path through Hawaiian history. It began between A.D. 500 and 800 when Polynesians landed their canoes at Ka Lae; petroglyphs mark the site.

The Polynesians brought with them a vast pantheon of nature gods and goddesses. Legend says anyone who steals a stone from the Halemaumau, home of Pele, will experience years of bad luck.

To the east along the coast from Kaena Point is a natural stone pool at Kamoamoa, where Hawaiian queens once bathed. The road is covered by lava, but visitors can follow SR 130 inland to Hilo and some of the world's loveliest gardens.

To the north, the coast is quilted with sugarcane plantations and deeply bitten by gorges and tumbling rivers. Follow SR 19 inland to the Kamuela Museum at Waimea to see robes of woven bird feathers and other relics of Hawaiian royalty.

Near Waikui on the west coast, King Kamehameha built Pu'u Kohola Heiau, now a national historic site, to honor the god of war; he dedicated it with the sacrifice of his chief rival. Down the coast at Kealakekua Bay, south of the charming colonial city of Kailua-Kona, Captain James Cook made his Hawaiian landfall in 1779. At first, the natives supposed him to be a god, but they soon discovered their error and redressed it by killing the explorer. A memorial records the great man's arrival and tragic end.

A few miles south is Pu'uhonua o Hónaunau National Historic Park, a more than 500-year-old place of refuge for defeated warriors and breakers of taboos. Visitors can stroll along self-guiding trails here and view a reconstructed temple.

St. Benedict's Church on the Kona Coast (*right*) Known as the Painted Church, this structure was moved from the seashore to higher ground at the request of its missionary priest, Father John Velghe, who wanted to protect it from the elements. Legend says that, since many of his parishioners could not read, he painted key Bible scenes on its interior walls, so the church itself could help him teach the Gospel.

Mauna Loa Erupting
(*below left*) A seabed mountain more than four miles high, Mauna Loa includes several of the world's largest active craters. Polynesian mythology claims that one of them, Kilauea, is the home of Pele, the goddess of fire, who settled here when she fled from her cruel sister, the goddess of the sea. The lava that Pele has poured over the cliffs since the volcano's period of greatest activity in 1881 has reached all the way to the sea.

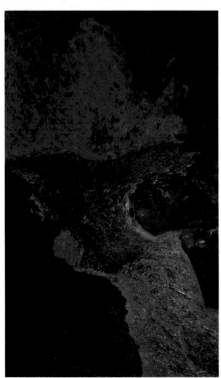

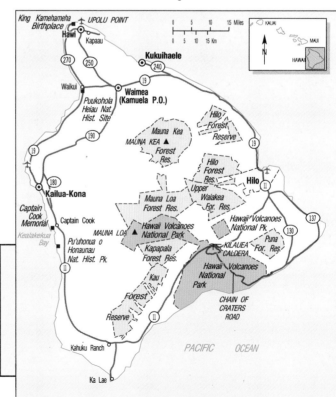

SITES TO SEE

● **Parker Ranch Visitor Center and Museum** (Waimea) recalls the history of Hawaii's first cattle rancher, Jim Parker. He settled here in 1809 to bring Kamehameha I's odd

collection of goats, sheep, and cows under control. Tours visit original buildings and historic homes; the museum has royal memorabilia.

● **Hulihee Palace** (Kailua-Kona) was used by Hawaiian kings and queens as a summer home. The two-story house has been restored with period furniture and decorations, including Kamehameha I's 180-pound exercise stone.

● **Hilini Pali** (Hawaii Volcanoes National Park) is an excellent site for views of the island's southeast coast. **Kipuka Puaulu**, the Bird Park, has a self-guiding birdwatching nature trail through dense native plants.

● **Nani Mau Garden** (Hilo) has over 20 acres of exotic tropical foliage. There are Hawaiian herbs and ginger trees, as well as orchids, air plants, flowering shrubs, and fruit trees.

● **The Naha Stone** (Hilo) lets visitors test their strength. Legend says Kamehameha I rolled the 1-ton stone over by himself; no one has done it since, although anyone can try.

● **Lava Tree State Monument** (south of Hilo) has shells of ohia trees submerged in the 1790 Kilauea eruption, forming a fern-covered and weathered forest.

THE SECRET GARDEN
Kauai

Kauai lures her visitors away from the main roads and popular resorts, encouraging them to find the secret pools and natural gardens that lie hidden beneath her jungle camouflage. She also entices them into misty caves and valleys, or beckons them to brilliant, unfrequented beaches reached by cliff-ledge paths. Some of her secrets are easily discovered, such as the Birthplace of Rainbows in Hanalei Valley, but others are more difficult to penetrate, such as the valleys of the beautiful Na Pali coast. Other of her secrets are places only shadows find, like the walls of 3,600-foot Waimea Canyon. Some secrets, such as the identity of the *menehunes*, known as the "small people," who left canals and pools and disappeared before the Polynesians came, remain a mystery.

From Lihue, where most visitors land, travel north toward opulent beaches, west toward the dramatic canyon lands of Waimea, or from Wailua, take a riverboat into the interior. There Fern Grotto and the natural bathing pools at the foot of Wailua and Opaekaa falls await you.

Choose to go north and you will find sublime views of the sea, pineapple plantations, and, near the lighthouse on Kilauea Point—from which there are wonderful views of the northern coast—albatrosses, boobies, and perhaps sea turtles, dolphins, and whales. Humpback whales migrate past the island between December and late March. If something seems familiar about the golden sands at Lumahai beach, it is probably because you have seen them before. The beach was featured as Bali Hai in the movie *South Pacific*.

West of Haena Point, the road ends at Ke'e Beach in Haena State Park, from where the two-foot-tall *menehunes* left the Hawaiian islands forever. Nearby is Mani-niholo Dry Cave, reputedly dug by the *menehunes* to catch a fish-stealing spirit. Its neighbors, Waikanaloa and Waikapalae wet caves, are said to have been dug by the goddess Pele in search of fire. When she found water instead, according to the legend, she quit the islands in disgust. Kauai's volcanoes have been cold ever since. The center of the island holds the world record for wetness.

If you head west and south from Lihue toward the island's drier side, SR 50 takes you to Alakoko Fish Pond. The *menehunes* are said to have built it in a single night, and it is still in use. Poipu, at the island's southern tip, is where Pele's sister Laka trained initiates in the sacred Hula dance.

Waimea Canyon is a must-see. Kokee Road crawls along the rim of this spectacular divide through mountain country clad in eucalyptus forest and flowering trees. Trout lurk in the streams, wild pigs in the woods. At Kalalau Lookout, one of the world's great views reaches across the 4,000-foot gorge to the Pacific. Here an 11-mile trail descends into the Kalalau Valley and meets the Na Pali Coast Trail from Ke'e Beach, thus traversing the heartland of Kauai's secrets.

Fern Grotto on the Wailua River (*left*) Many believe that hundreds of years ago Hawaiians worshiped in this amazing cave when the moon was full, gathering under the massive roof of the grotto's overhanging vegetation and listening to the splash of the 50-foot waterfall that drops from its heights. Botanical wonders are commonplace in Kauai, so the nickname "Garden Island" is well justified.

Na Pali-Kona Forest Preserve Along the Kalalau Trail (*right*) On the northern, windward coast of the oldest Hawaiian island, rugged cliffs called *pali* rise above the sea in splendid isolation. The rocky valleys still contain the temples and house platforms of their former native inhabitants. The tangled wilderness inland of these pristine beaches protects more than 200 endangered plant species.

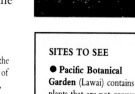

SITES TO SEE

● **Pacific Botanical Garden** (Lawai) contains plants that are not grown anywhere else in the U.S.; advance reservations are required for visits.

● **Kalalau Trail** (Haena State Park) is rich with orchids and exotic trees. It begins at Ke'e Beach and goes along the lava cliffs of the Na Pali Coast. Smaller trails lead to waterfalls; in wet weather, these trails are extremely treacherous.

● **Kauai Museum** (Lihue) presents this island's and neighboring Niihan's histories through ancient artifacts and recent photographs. Changing exhibits by local artists are often on display.

● **Grove Farm Homestead** (Lihue) is a restored plantation from about 1864.

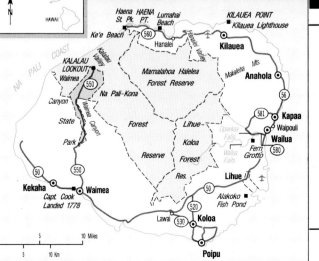

● **Wailua Falls** (near Wailua) plunges over a sheer canyon with a good pool for swimming at the base.

● **Waioli Mission House** (Hanalei) is a restored 1836 building with period pieces and memorabilia.

● **Mt. Waialeale**, at over 5,000 feet, gets about 500 inches of rain a year, earning it distinction as the world's wettest place. It can be reached by foot trails.

● **Kilauea Lighthouse** was built along the island's north shore in 1913.

● **Russian Fort Elizabeth State Park** (near Waimea) contains the remains of one of the two Russian forts built on the island in the early 1800s.

● **Kokee State Park** (Kokee) has 4,345 acres at almost 4,000 feet above sea level. The **Kokee Natural History Museum** here

covers the island's geology, including Alakai Swamp to the east.

● **Na Pali cliffs** (west of Ke'e Beach) rise 2,000 feet above the surf. The region is too steep for roads, but boat trips are a good way for visitors to view green valleys open to the sea. Helicopter tours set visitors down in a valley for a day's exploration.

HONOLULU

The name of this most diverse of American cities means "protected bay," and though small by mainland standards, it gives shelter and prosperity to a truly global variety of cultures, old and new, Western and Oriental, familiar and exotic. Along Waikiki Beach, where Oahu's chiefs once kept their fishponds and coconut groves, a man-made cliff of great hotels fronts the ocean. At night, though, the lights of sampans fishing off the reef bob on the dark water, and fishermen's torches blaze in the darkness, as they did for independent chiefs, united as a single kingdom by King Kamehameha I. Iolani Palace was the home of Hawaii's royal family from the time of its completion in 1882 until the monarchy was overthrown by local European and U.S. sugar interests in 1893.

However, in 1968 a new State Capitol was built: its open-crowned center and sunken-domed legislative rooms represent volcanoes; pools recall the ocean; and fluted columns are reminiscent of palm trees. In older sections of Honolulu, there are still streets that preserve frame homes in a new-England style dating from the island's missionary period.

The downtown section also includes the city's Chinatown, whose new Chinese Cultural Plaza celebrates Hawaii's multicultural heritage, and where colorful open-air stalls sell leis of fresh flowers. Even in the center of Honolulu, nature is never far away; there are panoramic views of the city and coast from the rim of Diamond Head's 760-foot crater, named for the shining volcanic crystals that early sailors mistook for diamonds. In Pearl Harbor, at the western edge of the city, the USS *Arizona* lies like the nave of a submerged cathedral, where it was sunk. In this most exotic of American cities, diversity and multicultural harmony has not been won without cost.

HISTORIC SITES AND DISTRICTS

Mission Houses Museum A complex that includes three of the oldest American buildings in Hawaii. **Frame House**, shipped from Boston in 1821, was the home of Hawaii's first Protestant missionaries and is furnished to reflect their way of life. **Printing House** has a replica of the Ramage Press on which, in 1822, the Hawaiian language first appeared in print. **Chamberlain House**, built of coral, was a home and warehouse.

Pearl Harbor The U.S. naval base, west of the city on H1, covers 10,000 acres at the mouth of the Pearl River. The USS *Arizona* National Memorial, which permits visitors to view the sunken battleship, is a memorial to those who died in the Japanese attack on Pearl Harbor, December 7, 1941.

MUSEUMS

Bishop Museum Extensive collection of Pacific art and artifacts. The planetarium has shows devoted to the Polynesian sky.

Hawaii Maritime Center Records history of Polynesia; also contains the *Falls of Clyde*, the last surviving full-rigged, four-masted sailing ship, built in 1878. Fine views from Aloha Tower.

Honolulu Academy of Arts Five courtyards and a sculpture garden; the Asian collection, which ranges from Japanese scrolls to Chinese furniture, is renowned. Also, art from Europe and the Americas includes the Kress Collection.

NOTABLE BUILDINGS

Iolani Palace State Monument The only former royal palace in the U.S.

Kamehameha Schools Established for native Hawaiian children by Princess Bernice Pauahi Bishop, last survivor of Hawaii's royal family.

Kawaiahao Church The city's oldest church, it was the royal family's chapel.

National Memorial Cemetery of the Pacific 21,000 graves of World War II and Korean War dead, on the floor of an extinct volcano, the Punchbowl.

Punahou School Founded in 1841; landscaped grounds and walls covered with night-blooming cereus flowers that open after 8 p.m., July to September.

Queen Emma Summer Palace Resembles a Mississippi plantation house. It is now a museum of the Hawaiian monarchy.

PARKS

Foster Botanic Garden Founded by Queen Kalama, wife of Kamehameha, in 1855.

Kapiolani Regional Park A magnificent 300 acres between Diamond Head and Waikiki Beach.

Nuuanu Pali State Wayside Spectacular views of coast and valley from an altitude of 1,186 feet.

OTHER ATTRACTIONS

Cherry Blossom Festival

Round Top-Tantalus Drive

Kewalo Basin

Orchid blooms (*above*) beautify Honolulu's residents and visitors alike, and give Hawaii its name, Orchid Islands.

Waikiki Beach and Diamond Head (*left*) Christened waikiki, which means spouting water, after the springs and streams that once fed into the swamps behind it, this two-mile strip of sand was a resort for Hawaii's natives for centuries.

MAP REFERENCE

1. Bishop Museum
2. Chinese Cultural Plaza
3. Diamond Head State Monument
4. Foster Botanic Garden
5. Hawaii Maritime Center
6. Honolulu Academy of Arts
7. Kamehameha Schools
8. Kewalo Basin
9. Iolani Palace State Monument
10. Kawaiahao Church
11. Mission Houses Museum
12. National Memorial Cemetery of the Pacific
13. Punahou School
14. Queen Emma Summer Palace
15. State Capitol
16. Waikiki Beach

THE PACIFIC NORTHWEST

Between southern Oregon and the Alaskan Peninsula, the great arc of the Pacific coast catches the warm sweep of the Japan Current. Inland, the Cascades and other ranges cause the moisture-laden winds to shed their burden as coastal rain, promoting abundant growth in the Oregon and Washington forests, orchards, vineyards, mint fields, and flower farms, and giving Mt. Rainier record-breaking falls of winter snow. Along Oregon's coast and in southern Washington, tidal poundings have carved picturesquely rugged cliffs and seastacks, sandy bays, and rockpools colorful with bright starfish and sea anemones.

Northwest of Portland, the great gorge of the Columbia River reaches the sea, and the coast begins to divulge the fret of islands that forms the inland passage between Puget Sound and the Gulf of Alaska. Whales spout along these fjord-cleft shores, and in their northern section, some of the world's great glaciers calve skyscraper-tall icebergs into the blue-green sea. A boat trip into Kenai Fjords National Park from Homer at the tip of Alaska's Kenai Peninsula is probably the easiest way to see them, as well as seals resting on ice floes, and mossy rainforest, nurtured even here by the Japan Current. There are also great landbound glaciers in Alaska, and in Denali National Park, some 250 miles north of Homer, one of the greatest, Muldrow, flows north toward the Arctic, its jumbled mouth within a few miles of the park road.

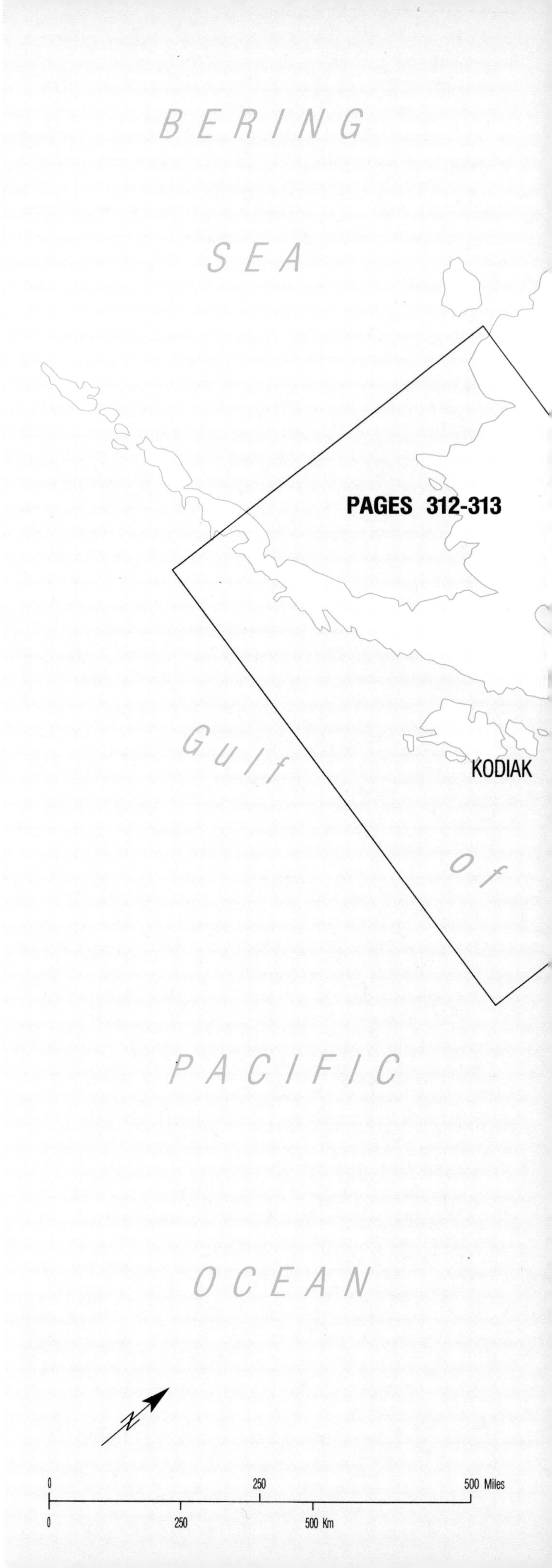

BERING

SEA

PAGES 312-313

Gulf

KODIAK

of

PACIFIC

OCEAN

N

| 0 | 250 | 500 Miles |
| 0 | 250 | 500 Km |

CANADA

ALASKA

PACIFIC

OCEAN

Alaska

CANADA

PRINCE RUPERT

JUNEAU

FAIRBANKS

**PAGES
316-317**

ANCHORAGE

PAGES 314-315

VANCOUVER

**PAGES
298-299**

BELLINGHAM

**PAGES
300-301**

PORT ANGELES

SEATTLE

PAGES 304-305

**PAGES
296-297**

**PAGES
302-303**

SPOKANE

WASHINGTON

PORTLAND

SALEM

**PAGES
306-307**

**PAGES
310-311**

OREGON

**PAGES
308-309**

EUREKA

CALIFORNIA

NEVADA

RENO

N

SAN FRANCISCO

0   100   200 Miles

0   100   200 Km

NORTH BY NORTHWEST

The Olympic Peninsula

Anchored to the continent by a strip of land barely 50 miles wide, this is the most westerly reach of the contiguous United States. The glacier-clad mountains and mossy rain forests of Olympic National Park lie quietly beneath the clouds at the heart of the peninsula. Along the coast, with its salmon-rich waters and wave-ravaged, picturesque shoreline, busy fishing communities and ancient Indian cultures still flourish.

Great rain forests once stretched all along this coast, from Canada to northern California. Today, the largest stand in Olympic National Park. Here, 300-year-old Sitka spruce and western hemlock encrusted with thick moss rise through the bottle-green light from a forest floor carpeted with ferns and Oregon oxalis. Only footfalls disturb the forest's primeval quietness.

US 101 circles these mountains and rain forests. From Hoquiam at Grays Harbor, SR 109 passes driftwood-strewn beaches where sea lions rest. On the peninsula's northern shore, SR 112 goes from Sekiu to Neah Bay and Cape Flattery, where a 30-minute walk leads to the most westerly point in the contiguous 48 states. The Makah Cultural and Research Center in Neah Bay houses archaeological finds up to 2,000 years old. The artifacts from a Makah village on Cape Alava were buried by a mudslide 500 years ago. The Makah, who now live at Neah Bay, were members of a whaling culture. Today, they and other Olympic Peninsula Indians make their living mainly by salmon fishing along this coast.

Along the national park's northern edge, the road skirts the deep turquoise waters of Lake Crescent before heading east toward Port Angeles, where a road leads into the wilds of the park. From the windswept promontories on Hurricane Ridge, the dark peaks of the Olympic Mountains rise in a jagged crown, framing the distant blue waters of the Strait of Juan De Fuca. To the south, Mount Olympus towers 7,965 feet, cloaked by Blue Glacier.

Visitors can hop on a ferry to Victoria, B.C., Canada, from the busy fishing piers of Port Angeles.

Farther east, at Sequim (pronounced Skwim), enjoy the dry weather of the Olympic rain shadow with its low annual rain fall; Sequim gets a paltry 17 inches of rain a year. On the historic streets of Port Townsend, lovely Victorian buildings remain from the town's early years as a classy resort.

Hoh Rain Forest (*above*) Outside the Pacific Northwest, temperate rain forests are found only in New Zealand and Chile. On the Olympic Peninsula, they grow in the west-facing valleys of the Hoh, Quinault, and Queets rivers; in these parts, an average of 12 feet of rain falls each year, and temperatures rarely reach freezing or go above 80°. The predominant trees here are Sitka spruce, some of which reach heights of 300 feet. Lush vegetation includes spike moss, sword ferns, and tropical-looking epiphytes, which grow on trees but take their nourishment from the damp air.

Jumping Salmon (*left*) abound in the waters of the Olympic Peninsula, allowing fishing communities to thrive, and providing excellent sport for keen fishermen.

Sea Stacks, Pacific Coast (*right*) The Olympic Peninsula's Pacific coast is marked by mysteriously looming sea stacks and arches; bald eagles soar here, and oyster catchers scamper in the tide. For human beachcombers, these beaches are unsurpassed: lucky finds can include glass floats used by Japanese fishermen.

SITES TO SEE

● **Olympic Game Farm** (Sequim) is home to hundreds of animal performers in Disney movies and other nature shows. Visitors can either drive through the farm or take guided walking tours.

● **Port Townsend's national historic district** contains some of the finest examples of American Victorian architecture outside of San Francisco; many of the restored homes operate as bed-and-breakfast inns. The Victorian Homes Tour allows visits to restored private houses on the first weekend in May and the third weekend in September. The **Jefferson Country Historical Museum** is in the old City Hall, built 1891, and contains memorabilia of the town's boom days at the turn of the century. An annual Rhododendron Festival is held in mid-May, and the Wooden Boat Festival is in early September.

● **Port Angeles** hosts the annual Salmon Derby over Labor Day weekend.

● **Hoquiam's Castle** (Hoquiam), a 20-room mansion, built 1897 for a local lumber baron, contains period furnishings, including lavish chandeliers.

● **Quinault Rain Forest** (Olympic National Park) is reached via 2 roads from glacial Lake Quinault. Trails from Graves Creek Ranger Station lead to the steep walls of the Enchanted Valley.

● **Mt. Walker Viewpoint** (near Quilcene) offers views of the high Cascades, Puget Sound, and Hood Canal to the east, and the Olympic Mountains to the west from the overlook atop this 2,800-foot mountain. There are camping facilities at the base.

● **Makah Days**, with Indian crafts, singing, and dancing, is held during late August at Neah Bay.

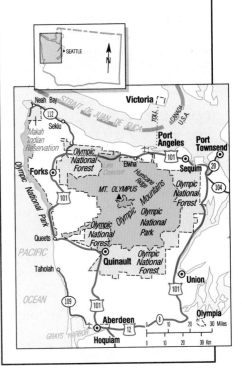

AN INLAND VOYAGE

Puget Sound

Puget Sound is a great inland passage stretching north to Vancouver Island and south along the eastern side of Washington's Olympic Peninsula. The wooded islands here have long attracted those in search of isolation. Sailors, bicyclists, and hikers still land in quiet harbors with white clapboard buildings reminiscent of New England; and beaches peppered with clams and mussels, glimpses of orca (killer) whales, rolling green farmland, giant rhododendrons, and the story of a pig all wait to be discovered.

For those without yachts, or even canoes, a good place to begin a Puget Sound voyage is on the ferry from Mukilteo to the southern tip of Whidbey Island. The island's fifty miles roll through attractive farm country, and Coupeville, little changed since 1880, offers a glimpse into local history. Deception Pass State Park, at the northern tip of the island, was perhaps named for the vicious currents that run beneath the bridge to Fidalgo Island.

On Fidalgo, 1,270-foot Mount Erie offers panoramic views of the sound and the Olympic Range. From Anacortes, the ferries pick their way through a maze of pretty islets to the San Juan Islands. Ferries stop at the four largest in the chain of more than 170 islands—San Juan, Orcas, Lopez, and Shaw.

Boaters will find numerous marinas and harbors along the San Juans, but none quite as popular as Friday Harbor on San Juan. Along its quaint and breezy streets, visitors can sample fresh seafood and visit the Whale Museum. Boat charters depart from here for offshore waters, where pods of orca (killer) whales can be seen, along with porpoises, seals, salmon, eagles, and thousands of water birds.

San Juan Island National Historical Park has self-guiding trails that tell the story of the "Pig War," the 1859 dispute between the U.S. and Britain over possession of the huge Oregon Country. Neither country accepted the other's legal authority over San Juan Island. When an American shot a pig owned by the Hudson's Bay Company and the British moved to arrest him, the U.S. citizens asked the U.S. army to protect them. The dispute was resolved in 1872, when the island became a U.S. possession. The British Camp on Garrison Bay has a formal garden and restored guardhouse and barracks. At the American Camp, vestiges of American defense works are preserved.

Orcas Island is a wild and wooded place. Moran State Park includes hiking trails through deep evergreen forests, inland freshwater lakes, a beach on the sound, waterfalls, boat rentals, and interpretive displays. It also has culture, art, and elegant resorts. On Shaw Island, Franciscan nuns run the general store and sell herbs grown at the island's Benedictine Monastery.

The sound's mainland coast also has its surprises. In Everett, the world's largest building (in terms of volume) is at the Boeing airplane assembly plant. The Tulalip, Swinomish, and Lummi Indians all hold reservations around the waters of the sound.

Deception Pass (*right*) Deception Pass State Park, at the northern tip of Whidbey Island, is named for the treacherous currents that race through the narrow strait between Whidbey and Fidalgo islands.

Harbor Seals, San Juan Islands National Wildlife Refuge (*left*) The Refuge includes 48 of the San Juan Islands, but only Matia and Turn islands are open to the public. Visitors can see the largest concentration of bald eagles in the lower 48 states, as well as great horned owls, puffins, dolphins, killer whales, and seals.

298

SITES TO SEE

● **The San Juan Islands National Wildlife Refuge** is spread out on 48 of the San Juan islands, with the sites on Matia and Turn islands open to the public. The Refuge contains bald eagles, great horned owls, puffins, and dolphins.

● **Orcas Island Historical Museum** (Eastsound) displays Indian and pioneer artifacts obtained from 6 homestead cabins.

● **Rosario** (Orcas Island), built 1904, is ornately furnished with a giant pipe organ, mahogany doors, and stained-glass windows. It is now a hotel, but the public is welcome on the grounds and in the lobby.

● **The University of Washington Oceanographic Laboratory** (San Juan Island) has tours in July and August.

● **Marysville** hosts a Strawberry Festival each June.

● **La Conner** is an old fishing port with a bustling dock and several interesting buildings, including an 1869 log cabin. **Skagit County Historical Museum** contains farming and logging equipment and a re-created blacksmith's shop and general store.

WORTH A DETOUR

● Peace Arch State and Provincial Park

● Ferndale

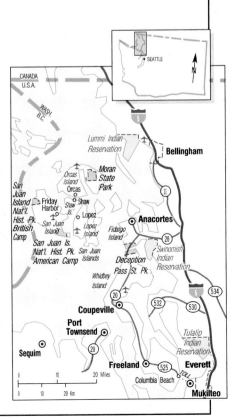

JAGGED PEAKS AND TRANQUIL LAKES
Washington's North Cascades

Only the lakes are smooth in the wilderness of saw-toothed peaks, glaciers, and wild rivers that forms North Cascades National Park. A single road, SR 20, unsurpassed among mountain roads, crosses the region. To its south, the tongue of Lake Chelan penetrates the wilderness, and to the north, Ross Lake juts into Canada. South of the park, US 2 threads across the ridges and valleys of the Wenatchee and Mount Baker-Snoqualmie national forests. Travelers on foot or by canoe are simply seized by the wilderness and find their perspective shuffled in ways they never forget.

For most of its passage between the two units of North Cascades National Park, SR 20 follows the valley of the Skagit River. In winter, highway access to this area is non-existent, but in summer, it is a kind of paradise. On clear days, some of the most spectacular views in the park can be seen along the road at Goodell Creek Viewpoint and Diablo Lake Overlook.

Out of Marblemount, the gravel road follows the Cascade River toward Cascade Pass. From it, you can eventually see the glaciers of Forbidden and Eldorado peaks. East of Marblemount, the road enters the Ross Lake National Recreation Area. Three dams across the Skagit River provide Seattle with hydroelectric power. Tours of the dams at Diablo and Newhalem include the Gorge powerhouse and a cruise on Ross Lake.

East of Ross Dam, SR 20 turns south toward Rainy Pass, where the Pacific Crest National Scenic Trail crosses the highway at just under 5,000 feet. The granite spires of Liberty Bell Mountain loom alongside Washington Pass. To the east, the jagged peaks of Silver Star and Gardner mountains rise, and to the south is Sawtooth Wilderness, a world of uprearing angles softened by snowcaps and aprons of evergreen forest. Farther east are Mazama, once a gold rush town, and Winthrop, a "Wild West" town with helicopter tours of the North Cascades on offer.

At the southern tip of Lake Chelan lies another world entirely: apple orchards produce bumper crops, and visitors sunbathe on lake beaches that get 300 days of sun a year. Excursion boats depart from Chelan and Fields Point to explore the 50-mile-long lake as far north as Stehekin.

South of Chelan, US 97 skirts the western shore of Lake Entiat to Wenatchee, the Apple Capital of the World, famous for its big Red and Golden Delicious apples. The Washington State Apple Blossom Festival is held here in late April and early May. The nearby Wenatchee National Forest offers breathtaking scenery in summer and superb skiing in the winter.

Bald Eagle (*above*) For these fish-eating eagles, which nest from Alaska to Arizona, and travel between the north and south bounds of their range along the Pacific flyway, the clear lakes and rivers of the Cascade Range offer abundant food, as well as isolated crags and trees for nesting. Mature birds have the distinctive white head; in adolescents, the head is brown like the rest of the bird.

Enchantment Basin, Alpine Lake Wilderness (*left*) The northern section of the Cascade Range contains more than half the glaciers in the lower 48 states, and glaciers have helped to carve the region's extraordinary landscapes, gouging lakes, basins and gorges among the lofty saw-toothed peaks.

Lake Clarence (*right*) The northern reaches of the Cascade Range offer almost as many lakes as peaks. Some of them, like Ross Lake and lake Chelan, are major waterways, creating their own weather and becoming mysterious or threatening when mists descend on them. Some, like Lake Wenatchee, are bordered by warm orchards; others are small alpine lakes, folded into the hills like turquoise handkerchiefs, quite jewel-like when spring flowers bloom on their shores.

SITES TO SEE

● **Thunder Creek Trail** (North Cascades National Park) begins at the Colonial Creek Campground on Diablo Lake and penetrates the glacial wilderness through Park Creek Pass. Hikers can continue to the northern tip of Lake Chelan.

● **Wenatchee** is an Indian name which means "place of the rainbow." **Ohme Gardens**, perched high on a cliff over the Wenatchee Valley, specializes in alpine plants; there are fine views from a lookout tower. **The Rocky Reach Dam** has a museum, picnic areas, and a glassed-in observation deck near the dam's 1,700 foot fish ladder. A good collection of Indian artifacts and local memorabilia is on display at the **North Central Washington Museum**.

● **North Cascade Smokejumper Base** (Twisp) is where the first airborne forest-fire fighting missions were launched. Daily tours are offered.

● **Chelan** has an historic downtown district that includes many early pioneer buildings. **Slidewaters** is a waterside park with a hot tub large enough for 60 people.

● **Mazama** is the starting point for a rugged 20-mile road to Hart's Pass that takes in fine mountain scenery on its way to the gold rush area around **Barron**, which was abandoned in 1907. Tunnels and ruined mine buildings dot the area.

● **Leavenworth** is a ski center decked out as a Bavarian village. From here, US 2 climbs into the wilds of the Wenatchee and Mount Baker-Snoqualmie national forests.

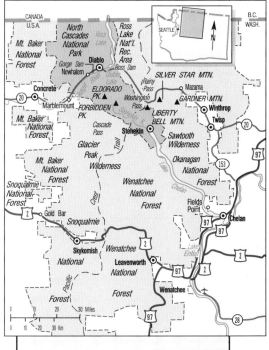

THE MOUNTAIN NEXT TO HEAVEN

Mount Rainier

Mount Rainier rises from near sea level to an icy summit towering 14,410 feet in the western Cascades. Indians called it Tahoma, "next to heaven," and it is often difficult to see the peak through its enveloping clouds. At least 27 glaciers hold a permanent hood of ice over Rainier's head. Because of this, the mountain makes its own weather; spring comes to the heights in mid-July, and deep winter returns to them in November. From national park visitor centers, winding trails penetrate alpine forests, and ski resorts dot the surrounding mountains, whose wilderness shelters secluded campsites.

Visible for more than 100 miles, "The Mountain," as Washingtonians call it, was sighted by Admiral George Vancouver in 1792. He named it for Peter Rainier, a colleague. Local Indians avoided the upper mountain slopes, no doubt recognizing its volcanic character in the tell-tale plumes of steam escaping from Columbia Crest on the summit. Like nearby Mount St. Helens, Rainier is dormant, not extinct.

There are fine mountain views from Mather Memorial Parkway (SR 410), which skirts the eastern edge of Mount Rainier National Park. The park's three main entrances are White River in the north, Nisqually in the southwest (near the park headquarters at Longmire), where an inn is open all year round, and Ohanapecosh in the southeast, where visitors can walk past waterfalls to virgin red cedar forests. Between Nisqually and Ohanapecosh is Paradise, where most of the park's visitor facilities are located. In summer, the trails that start here intersect subalpine meadows awash with lupines

and glacier lilies. In winter, trails are open for cross-country skiing and snowshoeing.

The northern White River park entrance is a favorite with hikers. From the rustic visitor center at Sunrise, Emmons Vista Trail leads to a lookout point overlooking Emmons Glacier, four miles long and a mile wide. Hikers following the 92-mile Wonderland Trail around Rainier's perimeter cross glacial moraines, meadows, and waterfalls; camp grounds are located every eight to ten miles. Also among the park's 300 miles of trails are excursions to suit all tastes and degrees of fitness. Before attempting to climb the mountain, though, the inexperienced should attend the famous mountaineering school at Paradise, where all the necessary preparations can be made to scale the peak in two days.

Outside the national park, there is fine skiing and a chairlift at Crystal Mountain, and wilderness campsites throughout the surrounding Mount Baker-Snoqualmie and Wenatchee national forests.

Glacial Grandeur (*far left*) With a glacier system comprising 34 square miles of ice—the largest single-mountain system in the lower 48 states—Mt. Rainier presents an awesome spectacle of massive and unearthly crags wreathed in halos of cloud. Continuous activity within the glaciers makes life potentially hazardous, but irresistibly exciting, for the intrepid climbers who tackle the craggy, irregular slopes. **More than 4,000 people** (*left*) make the two-day climb to the summit of Mt. Rainier each year.

Paradise Park (*above*) An icy wilderness and a peaceful parkland, Mt. Rainier soars over the spine of the Cascades, nearly 8,000 feet higher than any of its neighbors. Penetrating the upper atmosphere, it exerts a major influence on the park's climate, producing wet weather in the west and drier days in the east. In 1971–72, snow at the Paradise Ranger Station fell to a depth of 93½ feet, the greatest single year's snowfall ever recorded.

SITES TO SEE

● **Roslyn** retains the atmosphere of a booming coal-mining town with a number of restored buildings from the 1880s.

● **Mather Memorial Parkway** (SR 410) is a scenic drive from Enumclaw to Nile that passes north and west of Mount Rainier, taking in lofty Cascade scenery with many roadside overlooks and picnic spots. The road passes the White River park entrance.

● **Narada Falls** (Mount Rainier National Park) is a beautiful 168-foot cascade just a short walk from the park road between Cougar Rock and Paradise.

● **Mount Rainier Scenic Railroad** (Elbe) has 14-mile round trip rides in a steam locomotive with good views of the mountain.

WORTH A DETOUR

● **Tacoma**, a thriving Puget Sound port city, has an historical district showing where original buildings

were situated. St. Peter's Episcopal Church, built in 1873, is one of the few remaining early buildings. Other city buildings of note include the Old Tacoma City Hall (1893) and the former Northern Pacific RR Headquarters.

● **Fort Nisqually Historic Site** (south of Tacoma) is a reconstructed 1833 fort built by Hudson's Bay Company. The granary building is a good example of post-and-sill construction. The fort's history is explained in a museum.

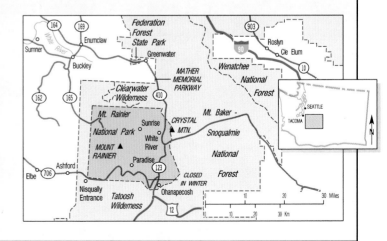

303

SEATTLE

Seattle occupies one of the most glamorous settings in the world. To the northeast stand the snow-capped ramparts of the Cascade Range, sentinels along the eastern border of the Olympic Peninsula's rain forests. To the south, the perfect volcanic cone of Mount Rainier seems to float weightlessly on the horizon, like a guardian deity watching over the serene landscape and waterways. The Olympic Mountains to the west provide protection from the ravages of the weather from the Pacific. But from the tip of the Space Needle, erected in 1962 for the world's fair, a bird's-eye view of the city 520 feet below reveals its intimacy with the sea and the outlines of the thriving partnership they share.

Puget Sound, a wriggling tendril of the Pacific Ocean, bears an archipelago of inviting islands that stretches away to the north. Boats and ships of every description travel from the open sea through locks to reach the heart of the city, and seaplanes use its urban lakes as casually as cars use freeways. One of the city's earliest settlers called the settlement on the Duwamish River New York, an ambitious name which was quickly modified with the Indian word *alki*, or "by and by."

Alki Point still exists, but within several years, the town had slipped to the eastern side of Elliott Bay and acquired the name Seattle in honor of a friendly local Indian chief. Brickworks and mills for the local timber sprang up, and the closer the Northern Pacific Railroad came from the midwest, the faster the population grew.

In 1889, a raging fire destroyed more than 30 blocks of the downtown area. Undaunted, the city rose from the ashes again in time to welcome the new settlers who flooded into town during the Alaska gold rush of 1897. Seattle played host to its first world's fair, the Alaska-Yukon-Pacific Exhibition, in 1909 and to the Century 21 Exposition, the world's fair of 1962, both of which spurred enormous urban development. Its history reflects its bold self-sufficiency, just as its museums and institutions reflect its European antecedents, its boom years, and its Indian, Asian, and pioneering maritime heritage.

Skyline at Night (*left*) The tip of the futuristic Space Needle, designed by a local architect, dominates every downtown view of Seattle. But the buildings surrounding it relate much of the city's history. The Smith Tower in pioneer Square was the tallest in town, at 42 stories, for 50 years after its construction in 1914. From the ground, walrus heads are easily seen on the facade of the restored Arctic Building.

MAP REFERENCE

1 Hiram M. Chittenden Locks
2 International District
3 Japanese Tea Garden
4 Klondike Gold Rush National Historical Park
5 Museum of Flight
6 Nordic Heritage Museum
7 Pike Place Market
8 Pioneer Square Historic District
9 Seattle Aquarium
10 Seattle Art Museum
11 Seattle Center
12 *Seattle Times*
13 Space Needle
14 Thomas Burke Memorial Washington State Museum
15 University of Washington Arboretum
16 Wing Luke Asian Museum
17 Woodland Park Zoological Gardens

HISTORIC SITES AND DISTRICTS

International District One of the oldest areas of the city, now the center of commerce and culture for its Asian population.

Pike Place Market Bustling marketplace, established as a farmers' market in 1907, for food, street entertainment, and arts and crafts.

Pioneer Square Historic District Thirty blocks of restored buildings, mostly erected after the fire of 1889. Pioneer Square, which is triangular, boasts a 60-foot Tlingit Indian totem pole.

MUSEUMS

Museum of Flight Thirty-five aircraft, dating from 1916 to a late 1960s Apollo command module, tell the story of aviation from its pioneer days to the space age.

Nordic Heritage Museum traces Scandinavian immigration from Europe to Ellis Island and across America, showing Nordic contributions to life in the Northwest.

Seattle Art Museum Renowned collection of Asian art, including ceramics, screens, and jade carvings, as well as paintings from the school of Northwest Mystics and one of the two Tiepolo ceilings in America.

Thomas Burke Memorial Washington State Museum A fascinating historical and scientific collection that examines the anthropology, zoology, and geology of the Pacific Rim cultures.

Wing Luke Asian Museum Seattle is the U.S. port closest to the Orient. This museum focuses on Asian folk art and the history of Asian-Americans in the Northwest.

NOTABLE BUILDINGS AND STRUCTURES

Evergreen Point Floating Bridge At 7,578 feet, the longest floating bridge in the world.

Lake Washington Ship Canal and Hiram M. Chittenden Locks Among America's busiest locks, these link Salmon Bay and the several lakes of the city to Puget Sound.

Seattle Center The grounds and futuristic buildings of the 1962 world's fair, highlighted by the soaring Space Needle, encompass three treats for children: Fun Forest Amusement Park, Pacific Science Center, and Seattle Children's Museum.

PARKS AND GARDENS

Klondike Gold Rush National Historical Park At the height of the gold rush of 1897–98, prospectors jammed the city and every available boat that might carry them to the Alaskan goldfields. Films, photographs, and artifacts capture the details of that rugged era.

University of Washington Arboretum The 200 acres include plants from around the world and an authentic Japanese Tea Garden, created by Japanese landscape architects.

Woodland Park Zoological Gardens Among the 1,000 animals and reptiles are golden tamarins, gorillas, night creatures, and animals of the African grasslands.

ATTRACTIONS

Seattle Aquarium An underground dome provides an unusual view on marine life in Puget Sound.

The Seattle Times Visit the pressroom, news department, composing, engraving, and mailing rooms of this busy newspaper.

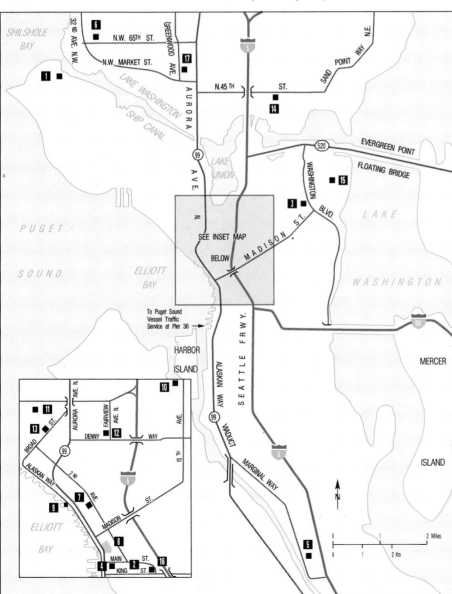

CLEAN AND GREEN
The Willamette Valley

This is Oregon's emerald heart, where the broad Willamette River flows 120 miles north to Portland, fed from the snow-laden Cascades. Along its winding banks are wide grasslands and orchards favored by birds and deer. To the west, the gentle slopes of the Coast Range produce Douglas fir and other valuable lumber—the backbone of the Northwest's economy. It was into this valley that Oregon's early settlers came in the 1840s; and here the population remains, in cities renowned for the quality of life and for air perfumed by the sweet tang of tree sap.

Signs of the hardy New England pioneers who settled the Willamette Valley are still evident along the rolling country roads with their numerous covered bridges. White clapboard churches and Woodsmen-of-the-World Grange halls dot tiny villages nestled amid orchards of walnuts and cherries and fields of pungent peppermint. Along SR 99, visitors can see old farms with distinctive Oregon barns, their roofs steeply pitched. These, and the moss-draped oak trees hung with mistletoe, offer an important clue to the valley's character. High rainfall makes the valley clean and green, and causes the Douglas firs along its gentle hills to grow to a monstrous size. The big logs from these hills feed the steaming sawmills sprawled on the outskirts of nearly every valley town from Eugene to Portland.

Portland, Oregon's leading city and one of the nation's busiest ports, is at the northern end of the valley, where the Willamette joins the Columbia River. A majestic mountain backdrop, many fine old buildings, and extensive forested parks make Portland an attractive place to visit. The city, which has adopted the rose as its symbol, holds a two-week Rose Festival in June, and one of the star attractions of the

145-acre Washington Park is the International Rose Test Gardens, where 10,000 rose bushes have been planted. From here, a zoo train takes visitors to nearby Washington Park Zoo, renowned for its breeding programs for rare animals.

Portland Museum of Art has collections of European and American art, and there is an exhibition of the state's history at the Oregon Historical Society.

Oregon's sparkling alps and rocky Pacific coast are just an hour or two away from most places in the valley. From Eugene, for example, the McKenzie Highway (SR 126) winds along the McKenzie River into the spectacularly lush Cascades. From Corvallis, whose name means "heart of the valley," US 20 heads to the coast through rugged logging towns such as Philomath, home of the Benton County Historical Museum with its pioneer exhibits and artifacts of the native Calapooia Indians. The valley is a great place for rivers—the Santiam, Crabtree, and Roaring rivers all have secret swimming spots and gentle rapids. North of Salem, the sleepy town of Aurora preserves traces of the utopian colony that was founded here in 1856. According to many Oregonians, utopia still thrives here today.

Mt. Washington, Willamette National Forest (*right*) Often the largest producer of timber in the country, the 1.6 million acres of this forest are so dense with trees that in some areas—and Mt. Washington is one of them—only hikers and horses can penetrate them. During the California gold rush, the fertile valley of the Willamette became the primary source of food for the west coast. After 1900, **lumbering** (*left*) replaced agriculture as the state's principal economic resource, which it remains to this day.

SITES TO SEE

● **Mission Mill Village** (Salem) is a complex of restored buildings set in a 4½-acre park. Notable buildings to visit include the **Thomas Kay Woolen Mill**, once water powered, the **Jason Lee House and Parsonage** (1841), and the **John D. Boon Home** (1847); both houses have period furniture.

● **Silver Falls State Park** (Salem) claims to have the largest series of waterfalls in the country within its 8,502 acres; 5 falls are higher than 100 feet.

● **Deepwood Estate** (Salem) contains an 1894 Queen Anne house, as well as a carriage house and formal and wildflower gardens.

● **Albany** has a selection of preserved Victorian buildings. Maps of self-guiding tours taking in many of the city's original buildings are available from the Chamber of Commerce office; some of the homes open to visitors the last Saturday in July. The World Championship Timber Carnival, with log-rolling, lumberjacking, and axe-throwing competitions, is held in early July.

● **Tualatin Vineyards** (Forest Grove) is one of the numerous wineries offering tastings and tours.

EAST OF THE ORIENT

The Oregon Coast

Between the Oregon coast and Japan lie almost 6,000 miles of Pacific Ocean. In all this expanse no island, nor any other barrier, impedes the onslaught of storms and waves. Sea and wind have carved this coast's precipitous cliffs and jagged headlands, and formed rock pools as colorful as tropical gardens. In the north, rain forests thrive atop mountains that rise abruptly from the sea. Farther south, beaches and miles of dunes border the edge of US 101. Following the drift of the broad Columbia River, numerous rivers flow from the green coastal hills, spilling into sheltered bays. Where they end, thriving fishing towns begin, and fleets of boats depart regularly for waters rich in salmon, trout, and shellfish.

Along with the waves from Japan and the daily fishing fleets, the Oregon coast has a history of memorable arrivals and departures. Captain James Cook made landfall here, and Lewis and Clark ended their epic cross-country journey on a beach southwest of Astoria, near the mouth of the Columbia. They spent the soggy winter of 1805–6 at Fort Clatsop, now rebuilt as a national memorial, recording in their journals lush landscapes rich in timber and furs. News of this wealth led John Jacob Astor to establish a fur-trading post here in 1811. The post and the colorful Victorian sea-captains' homes lend Astoria an air of old-time grace.

US 101 hugs the edge of Oregon for the coast's entire 400-mile length. In the north, it passes through resort towns such as Seaside and Cannon Beach, near dense forests of giant sitka spruce and cedar. At Oswald West State Park and Cape Meares,

the forest clings to narrow headlands that jut like dorsal fins from the misty surf.

South of the magnificent highlands of Cascade Head, US 101 stays within view of the ocean. Tidal pools, sea stacks, and offshore reefs that are home to sea lions are protected in the state beaches and parks along the popular central coast.

In Newport on Yaquina Bay, visitors can walk on the beach where Captain Cook came ashore. Visitors can also tour the Yaquina Bay lighthouse, one of the first on this coast. Newport's busy bay front is sharp with the smell of fish, fresh from the flotillas that crowd the piers.

South of Florence, the harsh stone cliffs give way to more than 40 miles of graceful sand hills in Oregon Dunes National Recreation Area. Windblown pines and wild rhododendrons border the dunes, which rise as high as 600 feet, and enclose a shining necklace of freshwater lakes.

Smelly Spectacle (*left*) The offensive smell given off when the cowl-shaped flower of this early spring flower is brushed has led to its common name, skunk cabbage. The corms of the plant were eaten by the Indians—the odor is removed by cooking. This useful plant is also a source of medicinal substances.

Cannon Beach (*above*) The craggy monoliths jutting out of the sea provide a sanctuary for coastal birds while breaking the crushing waves on their way to shore. This stretch of beach takes its name from a cannon that washed ashore after the U.S. Navy schooner *Shark* was shipwrecked in 1846.

SITES TO SEE

● **Cannon Beach**, one of the most popular along the coast, is the site of an annual sand castle-building contest each spring.

● **Columbia River Maritime Museum** (Astoria) recalls ocean- and river-going lore of the Pacific northwest. The lightship *Columbia* is open to visitors.

● **Whale-watching** is a popular local pastime, especially at **Cape Foulweather.**

● **Mark O. Hatfield Marine Science Center** (Newport), a facility of Oregon State University, is known for its aquarium of local sea life and exhibits of nautical history.

● **Coos Bay**, a busy timber port, has some of the most dramatic scenery on this coast.

● **Whitewater raft trips** along Rogue River depart from **Gold Beach**.

● **Three Capes Loop Scenic Drive** (Cape Meares State Park) connects 3 distinct promontories with spectacular coastal views.

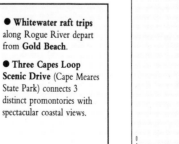

A GRAND JUNCTURE

The Columbia Gorge and Cascade Crest

The jagged spine of the Cascade Range divides the deep wet forests and valleys of western Oregon from the plateau of high desert that unrolls eastward. As the mountains divide, so they themselves are divided by the Columbia River, which cuts its wide gorge through the range and separates Oregon from Washington. Within a short distance in the zone formed by the great T-shaped junction of the river and mountain crest, you can climb the state's highest peak, walk beneath its tallest waterfall, and follow cool mountain passes to the east, where weekend skiers mingle with high-desert cowboys.

In this peak-and-gorge country, there are many landscapes: the dramatic overlooks and waterfalls of the Columbia River Gorge; the lush wilderness of the high Cascade Range; and the vibrantly colorful rockscapes of the eastern desert and the range country.

When the Columbia River Scenic Highway (US 30, paralleling I-84) was built in 1915, it was an engineering marvel. Today, the 24-mile stretch of road between Troutdale and the Bonneville Dam is a scenic wonder. It skirts the rim of sheer cliffs along the gorge, and visits rocky overlooks and wooded paths leading to waterfalls that include the two-tiered, 620-foot Multnomah Falls, Oregon's tallest.

Man-made marvels along the river include Bonneville Dam, where underwater windows allow close-up views of salmon negotiating artificial fish ladders.

Just east of Hood River, SR 35 heads south on its way to the year-round ski resorts and the trail heads to wilderness reserves.

US 26 also heads south through the Warm Springs Indian Reservation to join US 97 at Madras, a whitewater rafting center. US 97 runs north through high desert, almost paralleling the quick-flowing Deschutes River, and beside deep canyons through ocher plains studded with fragrant juniper and sage, until it crosses the Columbia River near Biggs. To the south, US 97 leads to Redmond, a lumber town with an annual rodeo and '50s festival. From here, the Sisters turnoff at SR 126 takes travelers to the Three Sisters Peaks—North, South, and Middle Sisters. With The Husband, a smaller mountain tucked behind them, they are the landmark mountains of the central Cascades. From the town of Sisters, SR 242 crosses McKenzie Pass at 5,324 feet. It winds across lava flows and marks the reach of the McKenzie River.

The Three Sisters, Smith Rock State Park *(above)* rise in stately splendor over the desert. The 623-acre park, with its brilliantly colored sandstone boulders, peaks, and cliffs provides opportunities for picnicking, rock-climbing, and hiking.

Hood River *(left)*, on the Columbia River, claims to be the sailboarding capital of the world, and there are good views of the sailboarders' activities from the Port Marina Park. The town's Independence Day celebrations include a regatta and the Columbia River "Cross Channel Swim."

Paddlesteamer Cruise Boat approaches Bridge of the Gods at Cascade Locks *(left)* Courageous immigrants to Oregon once risked their lives crossing the dangerous rapids on the Columbia River. The Cascade Locks were built in 1896.

SITES TO SEE

● **High Desert Museum** (Bend) has interpretive displays focusing on the ecology and creation of Oregon's high desert on the slopes of the eastern Cascades.

● **Lava Lands Visitors Center** (south of Bend) features a 500-foot cinder cone and a moonscape of dark lava beds traversed by easy trails.

● **The Dalles** is a historic 19th-century town that once marked the end of the Oregon Trail. Today, it is surrounded by wheatfields, cattle ranches, and orchards. The 1859 **Wasco County Courthouse** presents local history; self-guiding walking tours of the town start from here. **St. Peters Landmark** is an 1897 red brick Gothic-style church with 36 stained-glass windows. The town celebrates its cherry festival in late April, and Fort Dalles Days in July features a rodeo and other festivities.

● **Operation Santa Claus** (Redmond) is a reindeer ranch, whose animals are in demand in the holiday season. Visitors can see the reindeer at any time of the year, except Christmas when the herd is away busily working.

● **Smith Rock State Park** (Redmond) surrounds steep, beautifully colored rock canyons that rise from the banks of the Crooked River. This is a popular location with rock climbers.

● **The Cove Palisades State Park** (Madras) has colorful buttes and overlooks marking the confluence of the Crooked, Metolius, and Deschutes rivers.

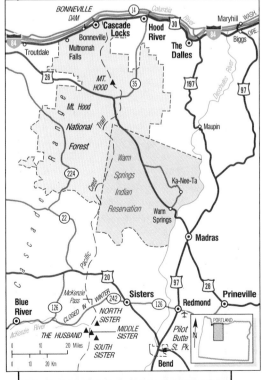

THE NORTHERN RIVIERA
Southern Alaska

Southern Alaska's maritime regions enjoy a surprisingly temperate climate. Anchorage winters are often no worse than winters in Denver, and the summer months are something like those in northern California. In everything else, though, this part of Alaska matches the rest of the state: the scale, variety, and beauty of its landscapes are overwhelming. Maritime Alaska, home of colorful Indian spirit-houses, onion-domed churches, dogsled races, and snowshoe-baseball, is an adventurer's paradise, as exotic as a South Sea Island.

Stretching southwest from the Alaska peninsula toward the U.S.S.R., the Aleutian Islands were the stepping stones that brought the first Russian fur traders to Alaska. Alexander Baranov, one of the most famous, built a fur-storage warehouse in the wet Sitka spruce forests at Three Saints Bay on Kodiak Island in 1793. The warehouse is now preserved as the Baranov Museum, with early Alaskan settler memorabilia and Eskimo artifacts.

You can take a ferry to Kodiak Island from Homer, but the only way to get to the spectacular Katmai National Park and Preserve, across the strait from Kodiak Island, is to fly there. The second biggest volcanic eruption ever recorded occurred here on June 1, 1912, filling the Ukak valley with 700 feet of ash and creating the fumaroles that made it the Valley of 10,000 Smokes. It no longer smokes, but it is still a beautiful desolation, with ash flows deeply incised by the wandering gorge of the Ukak River. The park is also home to the Alaska brown bear, the world's largest carnivore, weighing from 500 to 1,500 pounds.

North of Katmai, Lake Clark National Park and Preserve, bigger than Connecticut, encompasses still-unnamed peaks and an unexplored vastness. Lake Clark, the centerpiece, is rimmed by mountains, flower-covered slopes, and sparkling waterfalls. Along Cook Inlet, white whales wallow and great tidal floods rush with roaring noises.

Kenai National Wildlife Refuge, across Cook Inlet, is the home of moose, and in Kenai town, there is a fine onion-domed Russian Orthodox church. From Seward, you can take a boat trip to Kenai Fjords National Park, where seals lounge on ice floes, and icebergs plunge from the creaking glaciers into the sea. Puffins and kittiwakes are among the sea birds rearing their young on the steep cliffs here.

A good place to see icebergs close up, and to hear their submarine groans and rumbles, is at Portage Glacier Recreation Area between Seward and Anchorage. Icebergs up to 60 feet high float in a small, deep lake. By moonlight, the sights and sounds are especially eerie.

Dog Racers in Anchorage (*left*) Now Alaska's largest city and home to half the state's population, Anchorage was founded in 1915 and grew with the construction of the Alaska Railroad. An important defense center and a hub for the state's natural gas and coal industries, the city celebrates its colorful history annually with a winter festival. These dog racers have more fun with their sleds than the nomadic Eskimos, who used them to transport heavy loads over great distances.

The Snowy Peaks of Turnagain Arm (*above*) make a spectacular natural backdrop for the pinnacles of the city's sleek skyline. On nearly the same latitude as Leningrad, in summer Anchorage experiences the same pearly "white nights" of almost unending daylight.

Russian Orthodox Church in Ninilchik (*right*) stands as a graceful testament to the Russian settlers who first arrived in Alaska in 1784. This town was established as a fishing hamlet in the 1830s, and looks today much as it did 100 years ago. Several log houses survive, and the church bears the distinctive Slavic cross. The Russian government finally sold the territory to the U.S. in 1867, for $7.2 million.

SITES TO SEE

● **Anchorage** hosts the World Championship Dog Sled Races in February.

● **Anchorage Museum of History and Art** has a collection of items dating from prehistoric times. Exhibits include home scenes for Alaskan tribes and early settlers, as well as artists' interpretations of the state's natural beauty. The nearby **Oscar Anderson House**, built in 1915, was one of the first private homes here. Now restored, it contains period memorabilia, and offers excellent views of Cook Inlet.

● **Eklutna's cemetery**, next to a Russian Orthodox church, contains bright-colored spirit houses. These miniature houses were built on graves to house the souls and protect the possessions of the dead.

● **Exit Glacier** (Kenai Fjords National Park) can be reached via a $\frac{1}{2}$-mile trail from the Exit Glacier Ranger Station; there is access for handicapped people to $\frac{1}{4}$ mile from the glacier. In winter, the only way to get to the glacier is by dogsled or a snowmobile, or by using skis or snowshoes.

● **Harding Icefield** (Kenai Fjords National Park), one of the largest in the U.S., can be reached by airplane. Local air companies arrange charter trips.

● **Iceworm hunts** (Portage Glacier Recreation Area) are organized from the Begich–Boggs Visitor Center.

● **Lake Clark National Park** can only be reached by air; float planes land on lakes. There are no trails, but backpackers can enjoy dry tundra on western foothills.

● **Fort Abercrombie State Historic Park** (Kodiak) offers good views of the jagged coastline.

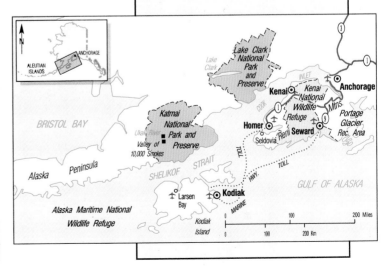

313

UNTAMED WILDERNESS
Alaska's Eastern Mountains

Alaska, more than three times the area of France, has great size, remoteness, and a northerly latitude which produces unmatched extremes of climate, landscape, and wildlife. To explore them is challenging, but in the state's eastern part, Alaska's magnificent variety is within almost easy reach.

Large tracts of Wrangell-St. Elias National Park and Preserve remain unexplored. The park, covering 13 million acres, is six times the size of Yellowstone National Park and is the largest in the United States. Three vast mountain ranges meet here, and the region contains nine of the 16 highest peaks in America. At the source of the many twisting streams and rivers, glaciers are still advancing and receding as nature continues to redefine itself. Malaspina Glacier, fed by an annual snowfall of more than 50 feet, covers 1,500 square miles and is bigger than Rhode Island.

One of the easier ways into the interior is the gravel road from Chitina to McCarthy, which was cut when gold was found in the vicinity. Before using the road, however, check at the ranger station in Chitina for details about weather conditions and the state of the road, because it is not regularly maintained.

From McCarthy, the Chitistone Canyon can be reached via an air taxi; the walls of the lower canyon rise 4,000 feet above the Chitistone River, and there is a 300-foot waterfall in the upper canyon. Some 10,000 Dall sheep live in the park, many of the ledges of the rocky canyon walls, where they can easily be seen because of their large numbers and their conspicuous white coats.

Among other wildlife to be seen in eastern Alaska are moose, humpback whales, and caribou. Birds include trumpeter swans, grouse, and peregrine falcons. Throughout these rich gamelands are the remains of prehistoric Athabascan Indian villages, camps, and hunting sites.

West of the Wrangells at Valdez, once the start of the Eagle Trail to the Yukon gold fields, is another kind of Alaskan wealth. The Trans-Alaska Pipeline unloads its oil into huge tankers here. Boat tours take visitors from Valdez to Columbia Glacier in Prince William Sound; 300 feet high and four miles wide, it calves icebergs the size of cathedrals.

North of Valdez, the highway crosses the Chugach Mountains via Thompson Pass, with panoramas of peaks and a roadside dotted with alpine flowers. Worthington Glacier, north of the pass, is a short walk from the road.

The Denali Highway (SR 8), Alaska's highest road, crosses the tundra between Paxson and Cantwell, offering distant, lonely views north to the Alaska Range.

Mount Drum (*above*) Rising 12,010 feet toward the clouds, Mt. Drum is only one of several dormant volcanoes in the Wrangell-St. Elias National Park and Preserve.

Farmers in the Matanuska Valley (*left*) till some of the richest farmland in the state and produce huge vegetables from it.

SITES TO SEE

● **Caribou bull** (*left*) commonly known as reindeer, survive the cold, arctic Alaskan winters feeding on lichens they uncover using their hooves to brush away frozen snow.

● **Cordova**, reached by air from Anchorage, is a small fishing community that was once the terminus for the Copper River Railroad. The town's annual February Ice Worm Festival features a colorful procession of 100-foot-long "ice worms" through the streets.

● **Richardson Highway** (SR 4), north from Valdez, is a scenic drive which follows the Trans-Alaska Pipeline route closely. It passes through Keystone Canyon with numerous waterfalls cascading down the towering walls; Horsetail and Bridal Veil are the most spectacular.

● **Ruins of Kennecott Mining Company**, one of the world's richest mines, which produced about $175 million worth of copper ore before being closed in 1938, is reached via a hand-operated cable tram over the Kennicott River.

● **Tok** is the site of the state's largest dog sled races each March.

● **Copper River Valley**, at the northern end of the park, is a region of bogs, tundra, and river shoals. From Porcupine State Campground, there are views across the valley to the Wrangell Mountains.

● **Kayaking and rafting** are popular sports on the Copper and Chitina rivers in Wrangell-St. Elias National Park. The Copper River flows 77 miles through some of the park's most spectacular scenery.

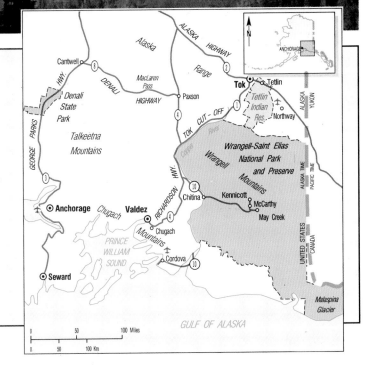

THE TOP OF THE WORLD

Denali National Park and Preserve

Denali is not the wildest national park and preserve. That distinction belongs to Gates of the Arctic National Park. Nor is Denali as big as the giant Wrangell–St. Elias National Park. But Denali does offer the visitor North America's highest mountain, the world's oldest protected ecosystem, and possibly the world's best chances for seeing grizzlies, caribou, moose, and Dall's sheep. It is also guaranteed to take your breath away.

In terms of sheer vertical relief, Mount McKinley is the world's highest mountain, towering more than 17,000 feet from its base—a mere 3,000 feet above sea level—to its 20,320-foot summit. The easiest and closest road approach is on a park service shuttle bus to Wonder Lake. However, Mount McKinley is usually cloud-covered in summer, and you often get a better view of its twin peaks from outside the park. There is a good vantage point on the Denali Highway (SR 8) about five miles east of Cantwell.

Visitors can drive only 14.8 miles into Denali unless they have a registered campsite. Even that small distance into a park 1,000 square miles bigger than Massachusetts can seem like a universe.

By the time summer comes, the pure white Dall's sheep have climbed into the mountains. The best place to see them is between Igloo and Sable mountains. The caribou have long since dispersed to their summer feeding grounds. Wolves roam everywhere except the high mountains. Grizzlies are relatively common, but dangerous; the best and safest chance of seeing them is probably from a bus tour in the Sable Pass area.

In summer, many migrant birds visit the park: terns from the Antarctic, jaegers from the Pacific, and golden plovers from Hawaii and southern Asia. Their songs and colors seem gathered from the globe's four corners to celebrate this park near the top of the world.

On the Northern Slopes of Mount McKinley (*right*), between the 20,320-foot south peak and the north peak, 850 feet lower, starts a chain of glaciers—Harper, Traleika, and Brooks—that eventually flow together to form the Muldrow Glacier. The glaciers were once the main route to McKinley's summit, which was first reached on June 7, 1913, but today climbers can board a ski plane which carries them 7,200 feet up the mountain. From there, the climb, made by more than 6,000 people, takes three days to three weeks. At least 12,000 climbers have attempted it, some just missing the peak.

In the fall, the wet tundra meadows at the foot of the mountain are bright with the magenta flowers of willow herb, and the ripening fruits of blueberry, cranberry, and bearberry provide a fall harvest for the bears.

Mount Foraker (*left*), at 17,400 feet, is a formidable peak by comparison with most of those in the Rockies, but here it is dwarfed by its towering neighbor to the north. For those who reach the top of Alaska's mountains, ice clad all year, it is possible to look out over a landscape devoid of all but miniature trees. In these high latitudes, the timberline lies at just below 3,000 feet, instead of the familiar 11,000 to 12,000 feet in the lower 48 states.

On the flat and seemingly endless tundra, with its web of waterways glinting in the almost continuous sunshine of summer, herds of caribou appear like ants and huge grizzly bears like toys. This is truly the last wilderness on earth, where nature still holds sway and human impact is of little significance.

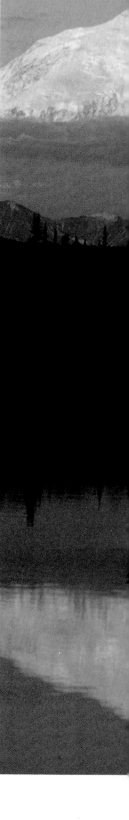

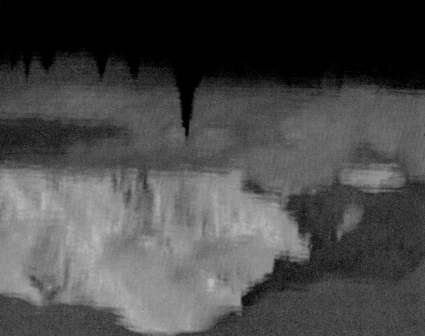

SITES TO SEE

● **Alaska brown bears** (*above*) frolic on the edge of a glacier-fed river in Denali National Park and Preserve. Also known as grizzly bears, the bears here weigh up to 750 pounds when fully grown. Visitors who come in contact with a bear should not do anything to startle it. Make sure no food or garbage is left out in campsites, because the scent will attract bears and other wild animals.

● **Denali State Park**, 324,240 acres lying to the east of the towering national park, is crossed by the scenic **George Parks Hwy. (SR 3).** The road climbs to 2,300 feet at Broad Pass and offers sweeping views.

● **Muldrow Glacier** (Denali National Park), 32 miles long, is the largest north-flowing glacier in the state. It can be viewed from the park road.

● **Various rafting and dog sled tours**, as well as tours specializing in wildlife watching, are available in and around the national park.

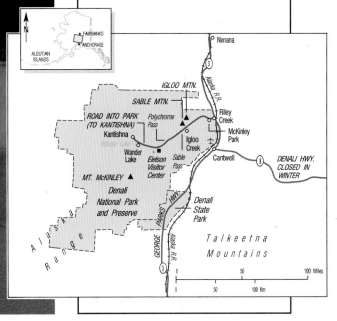

INDEX

PHOTOGRAPHIC CREDITS

r =right; *l* =left; *t* =top; *c* =center; *b* =bottom

1 David Muench; 2/3 Larry Ulrich; 4 David Muench; 6/7 Eric Horan; 12 Steve Raye/Taurus; 12/3 Gene Ahrens/Shostal/Superstock; 14 Clyde H. Smith/Peter Arnold; 14/5 Tony Stone Assoc.; 16 Eric Horan; 16/7 Margo Taussig Pinkerton/Photo Network; 18 John Kelly/The Image Bank; 18/9 Peter Miller/The Image Bank; 20 Clyde H. Smith/F. Stop Pictures/Colorific!; 20/1 Frank S. Balthis; 22 Hank Morgan/Rainbow; 22/3 Dan McCoy/Rainbow; 24 Charlotte Fuller-Bourdier/Colorific!; 24/5 D. F. Noyes/Rainbow; 26 Michael Manheim/The Stock Market/Zefa Picture Library; 26/7 Nathan Benn/Susan Griggs Agency; 28 Steve Dunwell/The Image Bank; 28/9 Elliott Varner Smith/International Stock Photography; 30 Steve Dunwell/The Image Bank; 30/1 Tom Algire/Shostal/Superstock; 32 Fritz Prenzel/Bruce Coleman; 32/3t Gene Ahrens/Shostal/Superstock; 32/3b Louis H. Jawitz/The Image Bank; 34/5 Robert D. Hagan; 38 John P. Kelly/The Image Bank; 38/9t Michael George/Bruce Coleman; 38/9b Audrey Gibson; 40 Ted Spiegel/Susan Griggs Agency; 40/1 Augusts Upitis/Shostal/Superstock; 42/3 David Muench; 44 © John McGrail; 44/5 Gene Ahrens; 46 Marvin E. Newman/The Image Bank; 46/7 Sepp Seitz/Susan Griggs Agency; 48 Thomas Nebbia/Aspect Picture Library; 48/9 Gene Ahrens/Shostal/Superstock; 50l Z. Leszczynski/Animals Animals; 50r Anne Heimann; 50/1 David Muench; 52/3 Gene Ahrens/Shostal/Superstock; 53 David Muench; 54 Lucian Niemeyer; 54/5 David Muench; 56/7 Heilmann/Zefa Picture Library; 57 J. L. Atlan/Sygma/The John Hillelson Agency; 58 Michael Melford/The Image Bank; 58/9, 60 Grant Heilman Photography; 60/1 Gene Ahrens; 61 Grant Heilman Photography; 62 Mark E. Gibson; 62/3 Ezra Stoller/Esto; 64/5 Fred J. Maroon/Susan Griggs Agency; 65 Bob Smallman/International Stock Photography; 66 Jim Howard/Colorific!; 66/7 Jeff Lepore; 68/9 Cub Kahn; 70/1 John Noubauer/Shostal/Superstock; 71 Mark Phillips/Shostal/Superstock; 74 Linda Bartlett/Colorific!; 74/5 David Muench; 76 Norman Tomalin/Bruce Coleman; 76/7 Tony Stone Assoc.; 77 G. E. Pakenham/International Stock Photography; 78 Erik Leigh Simmons/The Image Bank; 78/9 Lucian Niemeyer; 80/1 David Muench; 82 K. Kummels/Shostal/Superstock; 82/3 Suzanne A. Vlamis/International Stock Photography; 84/5 David Muench; 86l Sam Zarember/Stockphotos; 86r Grafton M. Smith/The Image Bank; 86/7 Tennessee Tourist Development; 88 D & I MacDonald/Photo Network; 88/9 John Guider/International Stock Photography; 90 David

Overcash/Bruce Coleman; 90/1 H. Morton/Shostal/Superstock; 92, 92/3t Bob Krist/Black Star/Colorific!; 92/3b J. Robert Stottlemyer/International Stock Photography; 94 Mike Yamashita/Colorific!; 94/5 David Forbert/Shostal/Superstock; 96 John Kelly/The Image Bank; 96/7 Tom Till; 98t Steenmanns/Zefa Picture Library; 98bl John Marmaras/Susan Griggs Agency; 98br Robert Harding Picture Library; 102 David Muench; 102/3 Gene Ahrens/Shostal/Superstock; 104 Charlotte Bourdier/Colorific!; 104/5 David Muench; 106 Steven Kaufman/Bruce Coleman; 106/7 Wendell Metzen/Peter Arnold; 108 John Elk III/Bruce Coleman; 109 Grant Compton/Colorific!; 110/1t Dan McCoy/Rainbow; 110/1b International Stock Photography; 112 Suzanne Engelmann/Shostal/Superstock; 112/3 Joe McDonald/Earth Scenes/Oxford Scientific Films; 114 David Muench; 114/5 Mary Fisher/Colorific!; 115 Patti McConville/The Image Bank; 116 Leonard Lee Rue/Shostal/Superstock; 116/7 David Muench; 118 Randa Bishop/Contact Press Images/Colorific!; 118/9 David Muench; 120 Michael Nichols/Magnum Photos; 120/1 Gene Lincoln/Aspect Picture Library; 122 Jeff Foott/Bruce Coleman; 122/3t Wendell Metzen/Bruce Coleman; 122/3b John Elk/Bruce Coleman; 124 Dan J. McCoy/Rainbow; 124/5 Momatiuk/Eastcott/Susan Griggs Agency; 126l Chad Ehlers/Photo Network; 126r Janeart/The Image Bank; 130 Ron Sanford; 130/1 David Muench; 132 Cletis Reaves/FPG/Pictor International; 132/3 Dale Kirksey/FPG/Pictor International; 134 Brian Parker/Tom Stack & Assoc.; 134/5 Matt Bradley/Bruce Coleman; 136t Robert Frerck/Susan Griggs Agency; 136b John Lewis Stage/The Image Bank; 138 Juan Alvarez/The Image Bank; 138/9 David Muench; 140 Breck P. Kent/Earth Scenes; 140/1, 142 Michele & Tom Grimm/International Stock Photography; 142/3 Garry D. McMichael/Photo Researchers; 144 Patti Murray/Animals Animals; 144/5t Tom Till; 144/5b C. C. Lockwood/Bruce Coleman; 146 Michele & Tom Grimm/International Stock Photography; 146/7 Photo Researchers; 147 Mark E. Gibson; 148 Robert Srenco/Shostal/Superstock; 148/9 Chad Ehlers/International Stock Photography; 150 Mark E. Gibson; 150/1 Tom Till/International Stock Photography; 152 Van Bucher/Photo Researchers; 152/3t Tom Till; 152/3b Bethay College; 156 Terry Donnelly/Tom Stack & Assoc.; 156/7 Richard Hamilton Smith; 158 D. Logan/H. Armstrong Roberts; 158/9 Robert Glander/Shostal/Superstock; 160/1 Zefa Picture Library; 162 Cathlyn Melloan/Click/Tony Stone Assoc.; 162/3 Kevin Magee/Tom Stack & Assoc.; 164 D. Muench/H. Armstrong Roberts; 164/5 Cathlyn Melloan/Click/Tony Stone & Assoc.; 166 David Muench; 166/7 Tony Linck/Shostal/Superstock; 168 John Shaw/Bruce Coleman; 168/9 Cuyahoga Valley NRA; 170 Tom Simon; 170/1 Mary Fisher/Colorific!; 171 Walter Rawlings/Robert Harding Picture Library; 172 James P. Rowan/Click/Tony Stone Assoc.; 172/3 T. Algire/H. Armstrong Roberts; 174 Rod Planck/Click/Tony Stone Assoc.; 174/5 Craig Blacklock; 176 Vic Cox/Peter Arnold; 176/7 K. Vreeland/H. Armstrong Roberts; 178 Mark E. Gibson; 178/9 Fred M. Dole/F. Stop Pictures; 180 Paul Damien/Click/Tony Stone Assoc.; 180/1 Richard Hamilton Smith; 182 Terry Donnelly/Tom Stack & Assoc.; 182/3 Richard Hamilton Smith; 186 Robert Villani/Peter Arnold; 186/7 Raymond G. Barnes/Click/Tony Stone Assoc.; 188/9t Richard P. Smith/Tom Stack & Assoc.; 188/9b Spencer Swanger/Tom Stack & Assoc.; 189 Richard Hamilton Smith; 190 Andrea Wade/Photo Network; 190/1 Gene Ahrens/H. Armstrong Roberts; 191 Andrea Wade/Photo Network; 192t Arthur Roslund/F. Stop Pictures; 192b Kay Shaw; 194 Entheos; 194/5 Stephen Trimble; 196 Jim Brandenburg; 196/7 Stephen Trimble; 198–9 Aspect Picture Library; 200 Jim Brandenburg; 200/1 David E. Ward; 202 H. Armstrong/Zefa Picture Library; 202/3 Tom Manglesen; 204/5 David Muench; 206 Dale Rosene/Bruce Coleman; 206/7 Tom Till; 208 H. Abernathy/H. Armstrong Roberts; 208/9t B. Vogel/H. Armstrong Roberts; 208/9b Doris De Witt/Click/Tony Stone Assoc.; 212 Michael Freeman; 212/3t M. P. L. Fogden/Oxford Scientific Films; 212/3b Michael Freeman; 214 Ernst Haas/The John Hillelson Agency; 214/5t & b Frank S. Balthis; 216l Miguel/The Image Bank; 216r, 216/7

Nicholas De Vore III/Bruce Coleman; 218 Martin Rogers/Colorific!; 218/9 Paul Conklin/Colorific!; 220 Mark E. Gibson; 220/1 Jim Cambon/International Stock Photography; 222 Monserrate J. Schwartz/Shostal/Superstock; 222/3 Frank S. Balthis; 224 Breck P. Kent/Animals Animals; 224/5 David Muench; 225 Stephen J. Krasemann/NHPA; 226 Pekka Helo/Bruce Coleman; 226/7 Ed Cooper/Shostal/Superstock; 227 Wardene Weisser/Ardea; 228 Francois Gohier/Ardea; 228/9 Spencer Swanger/Tom Stack & Assoc.; 230 Stephen Morley/Susan Griggs Agency; 230/1 Jim Hamilton; 232 Martin Wendler/NHPA; 232/3 Ed Cooper/Shostal/Superstock; 233 Anthony J. Lambert; 234 A. J. Hartman/Photofile International/Susan Griggs Agency; 234/5 Kay Muldoon/Colorific!; 238 Virgin Atlantic Airways; 238/9 Adam Woolfitt/Susan Griggs Agency; 240 Ted Schmoll/Photo Network; 240/1 George Hunter/Tony Stone Assoc.; 241 Stephen Trimble; 242/3 Bob McKeever/Tom Stack & Assoc.; 244 J. Canavosi/Bruce Coleman; 244/5 John Shaw/Bruce Coleman; 246l V. Phillips/Zefa Picture Library; 246r R. E. Dietrich/Shostal/Superstock; 246/7 Chad Ehlers/Photo Network; 248 Thomas Ives/Susan Griggs Agency; 248/9 Tom Algire/Shostal/Superstock; 250/1t John Bryson/The Image Bank; 250/1b Zefa Picture Library; 252 Wardene Weisser/Ardea; 252/3 David Muench; 254 Kent & Donna Dannen; 254/5 Dann Coffey/The Image Bank; 256 Frank S. Balthis; 256/7 John Shaw/NHPA; 258 Schneps/The Image Bank; 258/9t Stephen Trimble; 258/9b Frank S. Balthis; 260 Harold Hoffman/Photo Researchers; 260/1 David Muench; 262 Kent & Donna Dannen; 262/3 Ed Cooper/Shostal/Superstock; 266 Jeff Foott/Bruce Coleman; 266/7 David Muench; 268 Sal Maimone/Shostal/Superstock; 269l John Egan/Hutchison Library; 269r The Image Bank; 270 Michael Melford/Colorific!; 270/1 Francois Dardelet/The Image Bank; 272 Tony Stone Assoc.; 272/3 Mitchell Funk/The Image Bank; 274 Robert Francis/Robert Harding Picture Library; 274/5 David Hanson/Tony Stone Assoc.; 276 Michael Freeman/Bruce Coleman; 276/7 Zefa Picture Library; 278 John Shaw/Bruce Coleman; 278/9 Robert Perron/Bruce Coleman; 280 Tim Thompson; 280/1 Gene Ahrens/Shostal/Superstock; 282t Sepp Seitz/Susan Griggs Agency; 282b Rene Burri/Magnum Photos; 284 Susan McCartney/Colorific!; 284/5 Charles Thatcher/Tony Stone Assoc.; 286l Larry Dunmire/Photo Network; 286r Erik Aeder/Photo Network; 286/7 Pictor International; 288 Dan McCoy/Rainbow; 288/9 Kevin Forest/The Image Bank; 290 Tom & Michele Grimm/International Stock Photography; 290/1 J. Robert Stottlemyer/International Stock Photography; 292 Stephen Trimble; 292/3 Dallas & John Heaton/Tony Stone Assoc.; 296 Bierwagen/Miller Comstock/Zefa Picture Library; 296/7 Kenneth W. Fink/Ardea; 297 Robert Frerck/Click/Tony Stone Assoc.; 298 Erwin & Peggy Bauer; 298/9 Forest C. Brown/Shostal/Superstock; 300l Kevin Schafer/Peter Arnold; 300r Erwin & Peggy Bauer; 301 Trevor Wood/Stockphotos; 302l F. Stuart Westmorland/Tom Stack & Assoc.; 302r C. Krebs/Stockmarket/Zefa Picture Library; 302/3 Frank S. Balthis; 304/5 D & J Heaton/Colorific!; 306 Erich Hartmann/Magnum Photos; 306/7 Steve Terrill; 308/9 David Muench; 310 McKinney/Shostal/Superstock; 310/1 David Muench; 311 McKinney/Shostal/Superstock; 312 Stephen Krasemann/NHPA; 312/3 Chad Ehlers/Photo Network; 313 Magnum Photos; 314l Harald Sund/The Image Bank; 314r Tim Thompson; 314/5 G. Heilmann/Zefa Picture Library; 316 Larry Dunmire/Photo Network; 316/7 D. Buwalda/ANA/The John Hillelson Agency; 317 David Jesse McChesney/Photo Network

In conjunction with *Explore America*, Avenues, Inc., offers a 12-inch raised relief world globe.

For more information, write to:
Avenues, Inc.,
300 East 42nd Street,
New York, NY 10017